002048544

D1765880

WITHDRAWN

ASSERTING JURISDICTION

INTERNATIONAL AND EUROPEAN LEGAL PERSPECTIVES

The essays in this collection explore the various ways in which a number of key European and International legal institutions attempt to define the boundaries of jurisdictional competence. The principle questions addressed are: (a) Does the relevant institution have a jurisdictional competence adequate to the challenges that it faces? (b) What are the parameters that bear upon the exercise of a particular jurisdictional competence? (c) What are the effects, positive or negative, of extending, restraining or creating a particular jurisdictional competence on those subject to its jurisdiction, other actors and the rule of law itself? Examples of the institutions covered in this book are the Security Council, the European Court of Justice, NATO, the International Court of Justice and the State.

Asserting Jurisdiction

International and European Legal Perspectives

Edited by
Patrick Capps
Malcolm Evans
and
Stratos Konstadinidis

HART PUBLISHING
OXFORD AND PORTLAND, OREGON
2003

Published in North America (US and Canada) by
Hart Publishing
c/o International Specialized Book Services
5804 NE Hassalo Street
Portland, Oregon
97213-3644
USA

© The Editors and contributors jointly 2003

The authors and editors have asserted their right under the Copyright, Designs and
Patents Act 1988, to be identified as the authors of this work.

Hart Publishing is a specialist legal publisher based in Oxford, England. To order further
copies of this book or to request a list of other publications please write to:

Hart Publishing, Salters Boatyard, Folly Bridge, Abingdon Rd, Oxford, OX1 4LB
Telephone: +44 (0)1865 245533 Fax: +44 (0) 1865 794882
email: mail@hartpub.co.uk
WEBSITE: http//:www.hartpub.co.uk

British Library Cataloguing in Publication Data
Data Available

ISBN 1-84113-305-1 (hardback)

Typeset by SNP Best-set Typesetter Ltd., Hong Kong
Printed and bound in Great Britain by
Biddles Ltd, www.biddles.co.uk

Acknowledgements

We would like to acknowledge our grateful thanks to the School of Law at the University of Bristol without whose financial and moral support the EC/International Law Forum—and hence this book—would not have happened. Nor would it have happened without the administrative assistance of Shirley Knights, Pat Hammond and Rachel Nee and the research assistance of Marc McGee. We must note the support of two former colleagues—Phoebe Okowa and Chanaka Wickremasinghe—who were moving spirits behind the Forum. The willing compliance to the editorial process by the contributors to this volume made our lives less burdensome than might reasonably have been expected. His co-editors would like to extend warm thanks to Stratos Konstadinidis. After many years of work at the University of Bristol, he is returning to his native Greece to take up an Associate Professorship at the Democritus University of Thrace. He has been an essential and driving force behind the EU International Law Forum and his presence in the School of Law will be sorely missed.

Patrick Capps   Malcolm Evans   Stratos Konstadinidis
Bristol   *Bristol*   *Bristol*
October 2002   *October 2002*   *October 2002*

Contents

I THEORETICAL APPROACHES TO THE ASSERTION OF JURISDICTION

II   APPROACHES TO THE ASSERTION OF JURISDICTION BY POLITICAL BODIES

III APPROACHES TO THE ASSERTION OF JURISDICTION BY ADJUDICATIVE BODIES

x   *Contents*

List of Contributors

Sir Franklin Berman QC is Visiting Professor of International Law at the University of Oxford and is a Barrister at Essex Court Chambers. He was formerly Legal Adviser to the Foreign & Commonwealth Office.

Alan Boyle is Professor of Public International Law at the University of Edinburgh.

Patrick Capps is Lecturer in Law at the University of Bristol.

Malcolm Evans is Professor of Public International Law at the University of Bristol.

Hazel Fox QC is an Honorary Fellow of Somerville College, University of Oxford and Barrister at 4–5 Grays Inn Square Chambers. She was formerly Director of the British Institute of International and Comparative Law.

Christopher Greenwood CMG, QC is Professor of Public International Law at the London School of Economics and Political Science and is a Barrister at Essex Court Chambers.

Trevor Hartley is Professor of Law at the London School of Economics.

Jonathan Hill is Professor of Law at the University of Bristol.

Stephen Hyett is a Legal Director at the Department of Trade and Industry, UK.

Stratos Konstadinidis is Associate Professor at the Democritus University of Thrace, Greece.

Abdul Koroma is Judge at the International Court of Justice, The Hague.

Dominic McGoldrick is Professor of Public International Law and Director of the International and European Law Unit at the University of Liverpool.

Iain Scobbie is Reader in International Law at the University of Glasgow.

Brenda Sufrin is Reader in Law at the University of Bristol.

John Usher is Salvesen Professor of European Institutions and Honorary Jean Monnet Professor of European Law at the University of Edinburgh.

Colin Warbrick is Professor of Law at the University of Durham.

Stephen Weatherill is Jacques Delors Professor of EC Law, Somerville College, Oxford University.

Abbreviations

ACHR	–	American Court of Human Rights
ACP	–	African, Caribbean and Pacific States
AJIL	–	*American Journal of International Law*
Ann.Dig.	–	Annual Digest and Reports of International Law Cases
ASIL	–	American Society of International Law
BIICL	–	British Institute of International and Comparative Law
Burr.	–	Burrow's King's Bench Reports
BverfGE	–	Entscheidungen des Bundesverfassungsgerichts (Ger.)
BYIL	–	*British Yearbook of International Law*
Cal.W.Int'l L.J.	–	*Californian Western International Law Journal*
CCSBT	–	Convention on the Conservation of Southern Bluefish Tuna
CDE	–	*Cahiers de droit Europeanee*
CEDAW	–	Committee on the Elimination of Discrimination Against Women
CERD	–	Committee on the Elimination of Racial Discrimination
CITES	–	1973 Convention on International Trade in Endangered Species
CFI	–	Court of First Instance
CLJ	–	*Cambridge Law Journal*
CLP	–	*Current Legal Problems*
CMLR	–	Common Market Law Reports
CMLRev	–	*Common Market Law Review*
Comm.	–	Blackstone's Commentaries
CPR	–	Civil Procedure Rules
DAC	–	Departmental Advisory Committee (on the Law of Arbitration)
DSB	–	Dispute Settlement Body
DTI	–	Department of Trade and Industry
ECHR	–	European Convention on Human Rights
ECJ	–	European Court of Justice
ECLR	–	*European Community Law Review*
ECMR	–	European Community Merger Regulation
ECOWAS	–	Economic Community of West African States
ECR	–	European Court Reports
ECSC	–	European Coal and Steel Community
EEA	–	European Economic Area
EEC	–	European Economic Community

EEZ	–	European Economic Zone
EFTA	–	European Free Trade Area
EHRLR	–	*European Human Rights Law Review*
EHRR	–	European Human Rights Reports
EIPR	–	*European Intellectual Property Review*
EJIL	–	*European Journal of International Law*
ELJ	–	*European Law Journal*
ELRev	–	*European Law Review*
EuGRZ	–	*Europasche Grundrechte-Zeitschrift*
FRY	–	Former Republic of Yugoslavia
FTAIA	–	Foreign Trade Antitrust Improvements Act
FTC	–	Federal Trade Commission
GATT	–	General Agreement on Tariffs and Trade
Hag Rec	–	*Recueil des Cours*
Harv ILJ	–	*Harvard International Law Journal*
HKSAR	–	Hong Kong Special Administrative Region
HRC	–	Human Rights Committee
HRLJ	–	*Human Rights Law Journal*
ICC	–	International Criminal Court
ICCPR	–	International Covenant on Civil and Political Rights
ICERD	–	International Committee for the Elimination of Racial Discrimination
ICESR	–	International Committee on Economic, Social and Cultural Rights
ICJ	–	International Court of Justice
ICJ Rev	–	*Review of the International Commission of Jurists*
ICLQ	–	*International and Comparative Law Quarterly*
ICPAC	–	International Competition Policy Advisory Committee
ICSID	–	International Court for the Settlement of International Disputes
ICTR	–	International Criminal Tribunal for Rwanda
ICTY	–	International Criminal Tribunal for the Former Yugoslavia
IHRR	–	International Human Rights Reports
IJMCL	–	*International Journal of Maritime and Commercial Law*
ILC	–	International Law Commission
ILM	–	International Law Materials
ILO	–	International Labour Organisation
ILR	–	International Law Reports
ITLOS	–	International Treaty on the Law of the Sea
JEPP	–	*Journal of Environmental Policy & Planning*
JIFM	–	*Journal of International Financial Markets*
JWT	–	*Journal of World Trade*
KLA	–	Kosovo Liberation Army
KVM	–	Kosovo Verification Mission

LIEI	–	*Legal Issues of European Integration*
LQR	–	*Law Quarterly Review*
MJ	–	*Maastricht Journal of European and Comparative Law*
MLR	–	*Modern Law Review*
NAFTA	–	North American Free Trade Agreement
NATO	–	North Atlantic Treaty Organisation
NJW	–	Neue Juristische Wochenschrift (Ger.)
NSWLR	–	*New South Wales Law Review*
OECD	–	Organisation for Economic Co-operation Development
OJLS	–	*Oxford Journal of Legal Studies*
ONUC	–	Operation des Nations Unies au Congo
OSCE	–	Organisation for Co-operation and Security in Europe
PACT	–	Plurilateral Agreement on Competition and Trade
PCIJ	–	Permanent Court of International Justice
PL	–	*Public Law*
QMV	–	Qualified Majority Voting
RIAA	–	Reports of International Arbitral Awards
RSC	–	Regulations of the Supreme Court
RTS	–	Radio Television Serbia
SACEUR	–	Supreme Allied Commander Europe
SCR	–	Security Council Resolution
SEA	–	Single European Act
SFRY	–	Socialist Federal Republic of Yugoslavia
SIA	–	State Immunity Act
SLT	–	Scots Law Times
TRIPS	–	Trade Related Aspects of Intellectual Property
UKTS	–	United Kingdom Treaty Series
UNLOS	–	United Nations Convention on the Law of the Sea
UNHCR	–	United Nations High Commissioner for Refugees
UNMIK	–	United Nations Interim Administration in Kosovo
UNPROFOR	–	United Nations Protection Force
UNSCR	–	United Nations Security Council Resolution
UNSG	–	United Nations Secretariat General
UNTAET	–	United Nations Transitional Administration in East Timor
VCLT	–	Vienna Convention on the Law of Treaties
WHO	–	World Health Organisation
WIPO	–	World Intellectual Property Organisation
WTO	–	World Trade Organisation
YEL	–	*Yearbook of European Law*
YJIL	–	*Yale Journal of International Law*

Introduction

PATRICK CAPPS, MALCOLM EVANS AND
STRATOS KONSTADINIDIS

1. THE FORUM

For the past seven years, the School of Law at the University of Bristol has hosted round table fora on matters concerning, and connecting, International and EU law. The most recent Forum, in May 2001, considered matters of jurisdiction, focussing on the manner in which issues of international jurisdiction are addressed by a variety of actors, including judicial and institutional bodies. The speakers were drawn from a number of different backgrounds: academics, practitioners and representatives from various governmental and international organisations. No attempt was made to prescribe or circumscribe the way in which individual participants tackled the topic: indeed, all were encouraged to range beyond the confines of their brief in order to encourage a cross-fertilisation of ideas. However, in order to guard against any residual tendencies towards institutional parochialism or opacity, participants were asked to bear in mind three recurring themes. These were:

(A) Does, or should, the relevant institution have a jurisdictional competence adequate to the challenges that it faces?
(B) What are the parameters that bear upon the exercise of a particular jurisdictional competence?
(C) What are the effects, positive or negative, of extending, restraining or creating a particular jurisdictional competence on those subject to its jurisdiction, other actors and the rule of law itself?

2. STRUCTURE

A notable feature of these papers is simply the diversity of approaches which have been adopted by authors. This makes for illuminating comparisons and, indeed, such comparisons constitute a significant purpose of this work. However, with such variegated approaches and potential points of reference, structuring this work has been peculiarly problematic. In the end, the book has been arranged around three broad themes. First, theoretical issues relevant to the assertion of jurisdiction in international and European law are considered in chapters one to three by Berman, Scobbie and Hill. Attention then turns to a variety of actors, which are divided into 'political' and 'adjudicative' categories. This distinction is rather rough and ready. Distinguishing the 'political' from the 'adjudicative' can be problematic and the notion 'political' can be very widely interpreted. Perhaps for the sake of accuracy, we might have termed what are here called 'political' bodies 'non-adjudicative bodies'. But whilst this might be accurate it is neither elegant nor does it reflect the reality that in the international sphere such bodies exercise a decision-making and decision-enforcing role akin to that of so-called 'adjudicative' bodies, whilst adjudicative bodies themselves may lack capacities generally deemed important, if not essential, to that appellation. But some division needs making and so the second broad grouping concerns assertions of jurisdiction by political bodies such as the European Union and the State. Hartley (chapter 4) and Hyett (chapter 5) examine the jurisdictional relationship between these two types of institution and Sufrin (chapter 6) places these two central institutions in the global context of competition law and policy. Warbrick (chapter 7) and Greenwood (chapter 8) examine jurisdictional issues concerning NATO, the United Nations (UN) and the Security Council.

The third broad group looks at approaches to these questions by adjudicative (if not necessarily judicial) bodies. Fox (chapter 9) examines the jurisdictional issues facing domestic courts in relation to each other and also in relation to international tribunals. Judge Koroma examines the International Court of Justice (chapter 10) and McGoldrick (chapter 11) examines the Human Rights Committee. The International Tribunal for the Law of the Sea is examined by Boyle (chapter 12) and the European Court of Justice (ECJ) is examined by Usher and Weatherill (chapters 13 and 14).

There is obviously a good deal of interconnection between these three themes: indeed, it was to be hoped that there would be. And a number of chapters might easily have been located elsewhere in this volume. For example, Hartley uses a Kelsenian-inspired analysis to examine the political institutions of the European Union and their relation to Member States in terms of allocation of jurisdictional competences. This essay could quite as easily fit into either the first or second parts of this book. Much the same could be said of the placing of Greenwood's analysis of the jurisdictional competences of NATO—which involves an examination of recent decisions of the International Court of Justice, International Criminal, Tribunal for the Former Yugoslavia and the European Court of Human Rights—or Warbrick's analysis of the jurisdictional competence of the Security Council, each of which could be placed in the second or third parts of the book. In fact, one of the striking features of the Security Council is that it does have a Janus-faced character as both adjudicator and executor when there is a threat to international peace and security. At this point, the editorial function becomes less a matter of judgment and more of making a (somewhat arbitrary) decision.

Inevitably, there are omissions from this work. We are conscious that some readers will be aware of other omissions besides. In the ideal world, a more comprehensive array of bodies might have been surveyed. Some of the more notable absentees—the European Court of Human Rights and the International Criminal Tribunal for the Former Yugoslavia, for example—are touched upon in the context of other contributions. Nevertheless, it can only be hoped that the reader will indulge the eclectic choice of inclusion, bearing in mind that it is in the nature of things that some aspirations do not translate into inclusions. Above all else, however, it should be stressed that there was never any ambition to be exhaustive. Our hope is that this volume may focus attention, and shed some light upon, the manner in which jurisdiction is approached by a range of key players in and around the international arena and in so doing, to contribute to the wider debate concerning the question of jurisdiction in international, European and domestic law.

3. THE NATURE OF JURISDICTION

In what follows, we say something by way of introduction to the topic of assertion of jurisdiction. Initially, we briefly examine jurisdiction as a legal concept. Then, we move onto outline some important issues concerning the way in which law demarcates jurisdictional competences horizontally between States and vertically between national and international actors.

A. Jurisdiction as a Legal Concept

'Jurisdiction' is a form of legal power or competence.[1] In a Hohfeldian sense, this means that jurisdiction concerns a competence to control and alter the legal relationships of those subject to that competence via the creation and application of

---

[1] We consider the terms 'legal power' and 'competence' coterminous. However, we will normally use the latter (see R Alexy in n 2 below). This is so as to avoid the connotations with 'actual power'. Legal power is normative, whilst actual power is empirical. The main commentaries on the nature of jurisdiction, at least as far as international legal scholarship is concerned, equate an assertion of jurisdiction with the capacity of an institution to control, regulate or assert power, authority or competence over certain legally recognised relationships between various subjects. A few examples will illustrate this definition. Jennings and Watts in the 9th edn of *Oppenheim's International Law* (Longman, London, 1992) state 'State jurisdiction concerns essentially the extent of each state's right to regulate conduct or the consequence of events' (at 456). Brownlie refers to jurisdiction as a 'power' or 'competence'. See I Brownlie, *Principles of Public International Law* (Oxford University Press, Oxford, 1998, 5th edn) at 301. Akehurst, whilst noting that jurisdiction means different 'things' to different writers, acknowledges that jurisdiction equates to powers of a State or that State's Courts (and presumably, international courts). See M Akehurst, 'Jurisdiction in International Law', (1974) 46 *BYIL* 145 at 145. Bowett contends, following the American Law Institute's Restatement of Law in 1965, that jurisdiction refers to 'the capacity of a State under international law to prescribe or to enforce a rule of law'. See D Bowett, 'Jurisdiction: Changing Patterns of Authority over Activities and Resources', (1983) 53 *BYIL* 1 at 1. Higgins says that jurisdictional rules in international law are 'all about allocating competence' to States so that it is clear which States can exercise authority over whom. See R Higgins, 'Allocating Competence: Jurisdiction' in *General Course on Public International Law* (Martinus Nijhoff, Dordrecht, 1993) vol 5, ch IV 89 at 89.

legal norms.[2] So, for example, a legislature can enact a series of rules which will alter the legal relationships of those subject to that competence (eg citizens or companies). Additionally, those States that have consented to the exercise of so-called compulsory jurisdiction of the ICJ can have some of their legal relationships adjudicated upon by the Court since it has a competence to determine the rights and obligations of States which have consented to its jurisdiction. Now, defining the relationship between the concept of a competence and jurisdiction is not quite this simple: we would not say that an individual's competence to alter contractual relations between himself and a co-contractor meant that the individual had 'jurisdiction' over the contract in question. However, it is sufficient for the purposes of this introduction to identify 'jurisdiction' as a *type* of competence and leave these complications for later work.

B. Permissive and Prohibitive Jurisdictional Approaches

Taking this starting point a little further, perhaps the most familiar example of jurisdiction is when a state asserts its jurisdiction over individuals for various criminal or civil acts. The case which, as far as those conversant in public international law are concerned, is the starting point for understanding how jurisdictional competences are allocated between States over individuals is the decision of the Permanent Court of International Justice in 1927 concerning the collision of the French mail steamer, the Lotus, and the Turkish collier, the Boz-Kourt.[3]

The *Lotus Case* introduces a theory of jurisdiction based upon what Brierly describes as a 'highly contentious metaphysical proposition of the extreme positivist school that the law emanates from the free will of sovereign independent States'[4] but which will be referred to here as a permissive system of allocation of jurisdictional powers. To explain this point, we can do no better than reproduce a section of the decision:[5]

---

[2] Hohfeld says '. . . the person (or persons) whose volitional control is paramount may be said to have the (legal) power to affect the particular change of legal relations that is involved in the problem'. See W Hohfeld, 'Some Fundamental Legal Conceptions as applied in Judicial Reasoning' in (1913–1914) 23 *Yale Law Journal* 16 at 49. Alexy contends, clarifying Hohfeld's rather opaque definition of legal powers, that a legal power corresponds to a capacity to create legal norms and alter the position of those subject to these norms. See R Alexy, *A Theory of Constitutional Rights* (Oxford University Press, Oxford, 2002) at 132–38, 149–59. On Hohfeld's approach to the analysis of fundamental legal conceptions see M Kramer, N Simmonds and H Steiner, *A Debate Over Rights* (Oxford University Press, Oxford, 1998) at 7–22, 148–53 and *passim*. We think that Alexy's reformulation of Hohfeld's legal conceptions, and the mapping of these conceptions onto basic deontic modes, is a more satisfactory and defensible account than those accounts which are concerned with stipulative or reportive semantics. See also GH von Wright, 'Deontic Logic' (1951) 60 *Mind* 1. We should also note that to equate jurisdiction with legal powers is probably overly simplistic and actual legal relationships are likely to be a composite of a number of different legal conceptions. See H Steiner in M Kramer (et al), at 242–45.

[3] *France v Turkey (The Case of the S.S. Lotus)* judgment No 9, (1927) PCIJ, Series A, No 10 Hereafter the *Lotus Case*.

[4] JL Brierly, '*The "Lotus" Case*' (1928) 44 *LQR* 154 at 155.

[5] *Ibid* n 3 at 18–19.

International law governs relations between independent States. The rules of law binding upon States therefore emanate from their own free will as expressed in conventions or by usages generally accepted as expressing principles of law and established in order to regulate the relations between these co-existing independent communities or with a view to the achievement of common ends. Restrictions upon the independence of States cannot therefore be presumed. Now, the first and foremost restriction imposed by international law upon a State is that—failing the existence of a permissive rule to the contrary—it may not exercise its power in any form in the territory of another State. In this sense jurisdiction is certainly territorial; it cannot be exercised by a State outside its territory except by virtue of a permissive rule derived from international custom or from a convention.

It does not, however, follow that international law prohibits a State from exercising jurisdiction in its own territory, in respect of any case which relates to acts which have taken place abroad, and in which it cannot rely upon some permissive rule of international law. Such a view would only be tenable if international law contained a general prohibition to States to extend the application of their laws and the jurisdiction of their courts to persons, property and acts outside their territory, and if, as an exception to this general prohibition, it allowed States to do so in certain specific cases. But this is certainly not the case under international law as it stands at present. Far from laying down a general prohibition to the effect that States may not extend the application of their laws and the jurisdiction of their courts to persons, property and acts outside their territory, it leaves them in this respect a wide measure of discretion which is only limited in certain cases by prohibitive rules; as regards other cases, every State remains free to adopt the principles which it regards as best and most suitable.

At least part of this quotation sets up a conception of international legal obligation whereby States are permitted to act as they please, unless there is a rule of international law—which they have, directly or indirectly, consented to—which prohibits such an act. It is obvious, therefore, why Brierly paints this judgment with a positivist brush. Applying this reasoning to the allocation of jurisdictional competences, States can *assert jurisdiction as they choose*, unless they have consented not to. However, this concept of jurisdictional competence—or indeed international law—cannot be squared easily with the statement of the Permanent Court in the quote above which prohibits States from asserting their jurisdiction extra-territorially or, more accurately, within the territory of another state.[6]

This conundrum can be resolved by recognising that one is trading on two ways of understanding the word 'assert'. So, a state can assert—in the sense of *pre-*

---

[6] There is an ambiguity as to whether this means that States can enforce jurisdiction (a) strictly on the territorial principle; (b) on a looser interpretation of the territorial principle so that it can be extended to ships flying the flag of a particular State or (c) in areas where no State has jurisdiction. For example, the decisions in the *Lotus Case* and *United States v Flores* (1933) 289 US 137 at 155 reflect (b). In *Flores*, a murder on board a US ship on the Congo was deemed to have taken place on board US territory. In the more recent case of *United States v Yunis* 681 F.Supp. (D.D.C 1988), 859 F.2d 953 (DC Cir 1988) there is some ambiguity as to whether restrictions on the exercise of jurisdiction extra-territorially fell under the understanding established in (b) or (c).

scribe—jurisdiction over a subject unless there is a rule to the contrary but it cannot assert—in the sense of *enforce*—its jurisdiction outside of the territory under its control.[7] But we are not sure that such a clear distinction has to be made here between prescription and enforcement jurisdiction as they both embody sets of legal rules which will limit a State's attempt to assert jurisdiction. To explain: 'assert' can be understood to mean 'to state a belief forcefully or authoritatively'. This implies that when a state asserts its jurisdiction it is stating that it believes it has the ability to regulate the acts of a particular subject. Presumably, if States are acting within a normative framework which is regulated by rules of international law, then any attempt to assert jurisdiction must accord with rules of international law. The decision in the *Lotus Case* indicates a permissive regime in that a State can assert jurisdiction unless there is an international law to the contrary. In this sense, prescriptive and enforcement jurisdiction establish international legal rules which can render illegal and hence bar certain attempts to assert jurisdiction.

This appears to be quite a simple conceptual framework and useful statement of international law. However, is it correct? For, despite the centrality of the approach developed in the *Lotus Case*, the law relating to the assertion of jurisdiction appears to follow a different—prohibitive—approach whereby States are *prohibited from asserting jurisdiction unless they are permitted to do*. An early example of this approach is found in the *Cutting Case* in 1887.[8] Here Augustus K Cutting, a US national, was arrested and imprisoned by a Mexican court for committing libel against a Mexican citizen. However, the libellous acts were committed in Texas. TF Bayard, the Secretary of State for the United States Government, challenged the right of Mexico to assert jurisdiction and demanded the release of Cutting claiming that '. . . the judicial tribunals of Mexico were not competent under the rules of international law to try a citizen of the United States for an offense committed and consummated in his own country, merely because that person offended happened to be a Mexican.'[9]

Mexico attempted to justify its assertion of jurisdiction on two grounds: first, that the assertion of jurisdiction by Mexico was in accordance with rules of international law and the 'positive legislation of various countries'[10] and secondly that it was for Mexican courts to decide the scope of Mexican legislation. Bayard rejected both of these grounds arguing, initially, that there was little evidence which supported the Mexican claim that their assertion of jurisdiction was con-

---

[7] See n 6 above.

[8] Foreign Relations of the United States (1887–1888) 751–869 and (1888–1889) 1133–1134. See also JB Moore, *Digest of International Law* (Stevens, London, 1906–II) 225–42.

[9] *Ibid* at p 752. This is an expression of the passive personality principle. It should be noted that on appeal Cutting was released. However, the US maintained its complaint against Mexico. This was because although the supreme court of Chihuahua had released Cutting because the plaintiff had withdrawn his complaint, it supported the decision of the lower court concerning the jurisdictional reach of Mexican law.

[10] *Ibid* at 753.

sistent with international law and State practice. Whilst a State can prosecute their own citizens for acts committed extraterritorially, to extend (effectively, to prescribe) its jurisdiction to acts committed by foreigners outside the territory would impair (a) the independence of States and (b) amicable relations between States.[11] Secondly, he argued that '... if a Government could set up its own municipal laws as the final test of its international rights and obligations, then the rules of international law would be but the shadow of a name and would afford no protection either to States or to individuals.'[12] Combining these two arguments, Bayard concluded that there was 'no principle of international law which *justifies* such a pretension'[13] and 'any assertion of it must rest, as an exception to the rule, either upon the general concurrence of nations or upon express conventions'.[14]

Since Cutting was residing in Mexico when arrested, one would think, following the reasoning in the *Lotus Case,* that there would be no problem with Mexico's assertion of jurisdiction according to international law. This is because there was no treaty between the two States which would prohibit Mexico's assertion, and because Mexico's assertion would not infringe the territorial sovereignty of the United States. But in *Cutting* a different approach is revealed: attempts to assert jurisdiction are *prohibited* unless a State is permitted to do so by a positive rule of international law.

The circumstances where States may be justified in asserting jurisdiction were outlined in *The Harvard Research Draft Convention on Jurisdiction with Respect to Crime* published in 1935.[15] This approach, which requires a State to justify a link which is recognised by international law between itself and the subject over which it seeks to assert jurisdiction is adhered to by Mann. He states:[16]

> [the] search for the State or States whose contact with the facts is such as to make the allocation of legislative competence just and reasonable. It is, accordingly, not the

---

[11] See also *Schooner Exchange v McFaddon* (1812) 7 Cranch. 116. See also FA Mann 'The Doctrine of Jurisdiction in International Law' (1964–I) III *Hag Rec* 1 and J Halpern J ' "Exorbitant Jurisdiction" and the Brussels Convention: Towards a Theory of Restraint' in (1983) 9 *Yale Journal of World Public Order* 369.

[12] Above n 10.

[13] Italics added.

[14] *Ibid* at 754.

[15] See Dickinson's Commentary to this research in (1935) 29 *AJIL Supp.* 443 at 445. Here he describes the five heads of jurisdiction: 'the first [territorial] is accepted as of primary importance and of fundamental character. The second [nationality] is universally accepted, through there are striking differences in the extent to which it is used in the different national systems. The third [protective] is claimed by most States, regarded with misgivings by a few, and is generally ranked as the basis of an auxiliary competence. The fourth [universal] is widely though by no means universally accepted as the basis of an auxiliary competence, except for the offence of piracy, with respect to which it is the generally recognized principle of jurisdiction. The fifth, [passive personality] asserted in some form by a considerable number of States and contested by others, is admittedly auxiliary in character and is probably not essential for any State if the ends served are adequately provided for on other principles' (at 445). Note that all of these heads of jurisdiction (except passive personality) are described in the *Report on Extraterritorial Crime and the Cutting Case.* See n 8 at 772.

[16] FA Mann, above at n 11 at 34–35. See J Hill's contribution to this volume (ch 3)on the relationship between this point in public and private international law.

character and scope inherent in national legislation or attributed to it by its authors, but is the legally relevant contact between such legislation and the given set of international facts that decides upon the existence of jurisdiction.

Whatever one's view is on the passive personality principle being part of international law[17] it is clear that the *Cutting Case* and the *Lotus Case* offer *prima facie* and perhaps radically different ways of conceiving the international law on jurisdiction. How do we explain this tension at the heart of jurisdictional theory? One possible view is that the judges in the *Lotus Case* were having an extreme rush of positivistic blood which—whilst bearing a strong passing resemblance—is actually incompatible with the pragmatics of modern international law.[18] Alternatively, it may be that these two approaches are not as incompatible as has been portrayed, and can be reconciled. For example, Halpern suggests that the permissive approach (referred to as the 'classical approach') does not involve a theory of jurisdictional restraint, which has been rectified by subsequent rules requiring a sufficient link between the State and the subject over which jurisdiction is asserted.[19] Finally, it may be that this ambiguity reflects the elasticity or opacity of the concept of jurisdiction in international law.

By highlighting this ambiguity, we hope to have introduced the topic under discussion in this book. Secondly, we hope to have provided a feed into theoretical explorations which form the first part of this book. Finally, we hope to have illustrated our contention that fundamental questions remain unanswered when considering the assertion of jurisdiction by States and hence why this topic is ripe for reinvestigation. However, the international laws concerning the allocation of jurisdictional competences *between* States is not the end of the matter. A further question concerns the vertical distribution of competences between States, international bodies (such as the EU or UN) and sub-national bodies (such as domestic courts and devolved systems of governance) and the rivalries which they engender.

4. THE VERTICAL DISTRIBUTION OF JURISDICTIONAL COMPETENCES BETWEEN NATIONAL AND INTERNATIONAL INSTITUTIONAL BODIES

The issues raised concerning the allocation of jurisdictional competencies between institutions—and the competition for power which has resulted from this—are perhaps most clearly expressed in the contributions to this book which

---

[17]   Indeed, the US appears to have changed its view on this matter in recent years. See A Lowenfeld, 'U.S. Law Enforcement Abroad: The Constitution and International Law' (1989) 83 *AJIL* 880–93 at 884 and 'U.S. Law Enforcement Abroad: The Constitution and International Law Continued' (1990) 84 *AJIL*, 444–93.

[18]   See J Halpern, (n 11 above) at 372 where he states: '[t]he classical model's [ie the permissive approach] logical consistency, it can be argued, was won at the expense of the adaptability and operability in cases of actual conflict. The theory produced results that were neither flexible nor responsive to the realities of state practice.'

[19]   *Ibid.*

look at the development of an international legal system within the European Union. However, these issues, are common to international legal systems in general. In this section, we highlight some of the main themes concerning the allocation of jurisdictional competences between courts, States and international legal institutions, looking at, initially, political institutions, before moving onto adjudicative institutions.

A. Political Institutions

It was stated above that jurisdiction is a form of legal power or competence to control the legal relations of those subject to that power. The development of international institutions—which are, at least from a functionalist point of view, designed to achieve collective goals which cannot be easily achieved by States acting unilaterally or even bilaterally—has led to conflicts over the allocation of jurisdictional competences. States are often prudentially inclined to try to retain their own independence and avoid being subject to the jurisdiction of international organisations.

This point is clear with regard to general public international law. Often no international agreement can be reached over the scope of common goals, and States proceed with policies which produce exorbitant assertions of jurisdiction and subsequent conflict between States. This point is made by Berman with regard to domestic criminal law (chapter 1) and is made by Sufrin with regard to the competition law and policy of the European Union and the United States (chapter 6). If common goals can be settled on, and institutions devised to achieve them, such institutions are often rendered relatively impotent by the prudential interests of States. For example, Warbrick (chapter 8) points out in his contribution to this volume that the Security Council, which is responsible for the maintenance of international peace and security in international relations, has been granted exceptional powers by the international community over Members States of the United Nations. However, it can hardly be denied that, since its inception, it has been emasculated by the *realpolitik* of States acting according to their individual, rather than common, interests. It may be that the reinvigoration of the Security Council, so that it can effectively assert its jurisdiction over States who represent a threat to international peace and security, will *not* be the answer to this basic issue of world order. Indeed, as Greenwood suggests (in chapter 8), the Kosovo crisis led to the expansion of the NATO's competence to engage in collective self-defence to the point where it may now be that NATO is legally justified using military force to resolve matters of regional or even global security, albeit within tightly bound constraints. The emphasis on States, rather than global institutions, as being better equipped to perform certain collective functions is developed by Scobbie (in chapter 2) drawing on the instances where the international institutions have administered territory.

The issue of the jurisdictional competences required in order for an international institution to be effective, and the conflict this causes between it and States is most obviously expressed in the European Community legal system, if only because this system has been able to wrench considerable power from Member States in order to control them, and either directly or indirectly, control the behaviour of individual subjects. Historically, the struggle over jurisdictional competence between the Community and its Member States is almost as old as the Community itself. A few years after the entry into force of the then EEC Treaty the European Court of Justice delivered its ground-breaking judgments in cases such as *Van Gend en Loos*[20] and *Costa v ENEL*[21] leading to the introduction of fundamental principles of constitutional importance for the young but rapidly developing Community.

Whether one considers these decisions inspired or overzealous, the endowment of Community law with special and unique features resting on the doctrines of direct effect and supremacy has had profound implications for the national legal orders and led to an on-going and never-ending battle to circumscribe as precisely and as tightly as possible the boundaries of competence between this new international organisation and Member States.

The most important reference point for this ongoing dispute over competence between the Community and its Member States and the limits of the decision-making powers of the former must be the EC Treaty itself, the 'basic constitutional charter' of the Community as the Court of Justice has audaciously proclaimed it.[22] However, the weight and impact of the Treaty on this issue depend gravely on its own nature. Does the Community constitute a 'new legal order,'[23] a separate legal system as the Court of Justice declared very early on in the life span of the EC? It is on this thorny issue that concerns the tripartite relationship between national, international and EU Law and its reflection on the problem of competence that Hartley's contribution (chapter 4) is illuminating. He argues that the central accumulation of powers on the part of the EU institutions may ultimately rest upon acquiesce on the part of Member States rather than any particular or fundamental shift of power away from the Nation State.

However, to limit the debate on competence in the EU framework to the clash between the Community and its Member States over the question of competence-sharing would be to miss the spill-over effects of that conflict within the internal structure of the Community and its Member States. In the last ten years or so we have witnessed a significant rise in the number of EU inter-institutional clashes over the 'legal base' of Community law measures, on subjects from voting rights to the level of participation of various EU institutions in the decision-making process, which use the rule of law as a justification for manipulating the delicate issue of inter-institutional balance. On the other hand, there has hardly ever been

---

[20] Case 26/62 [1963] ECR 1.
[21] Case 6/64 [1964] ECR 585.
[22] Case 294/83, *Parti Ecologiste 'Les Verts' v European Parliament* [1986] ECR 1339.
[23] See also Opinion 1/91, First EEA Opinion [1991] 6079, at para 12.

any co-ordinated attempt to look at the internal repercussions and consequences within Member States of the powers vested on regional authorities to acquire rights and undertake duties relating to the application and implementation of Community law within national legal orders. In this context, the contribution of Hyett (chapter 5) in this volume is fascinating as he sets out to explore the internal relationship of regional authorities with the central government over the responsibility for implementing Community law measures, using the UK as a paradigm case.

B. Adjudicative Bodies

As has been suggested, one way to comprehend the rationale of international institutions such as the United Nations or the European Union is as an attempt to achieve the common objectives of States which cannot be achieved by those States acting unilaterally. Adjudicative bodies form an important mechanism by which these objectives can be effectively realised. However, once again, issues of jurisdictional competence are raised. In most international disputes, a particular adjudicative body has to consider whether it can assert its jurisdiction over a particular subject in a dispute. Many factors can inhibit this assertion. The most obvious factor is a lack of consent to the jurisdiction of a particular adjudicative body.[24]

The consent of putative subjects does not have much significance with regard to domestic law. It is much more a case of whether a domestic court chooses to exercise jurisdiction over an individual. This is not simply to do with effectiveness. Principles such as comity, substantive and procedural fairness and sufficient connection between the court and the subject will determine whether the former will assert jurisdiction. Berman (chapter 1) looks at this general problem from the point of view of the international laws which regulate States' conduct, Hill's (chapter 2) contribution is a similar examination from the point of view of private international law and one aspect of Sufrin's contribution (chapter 6) examines the

[24] It should not be assumed that consent is the only issue with regard to the jurisdiction of domestic, international and European courts. There are a number of related limitations which will restrict the power of a court to impose its judgment on the legal relations of the disputants. On this issue see Koroma's contribution to this volume at 195–97. Generally, however, the location of the act, or the time at which the act occurred, can limit the jurisdiction of a court. For example, Greenwood (ch 9) considers the recent *Banković Case* in which the European Court of Human Rights considered whether its jurisdiction can be extended beyond the territorial borders of those States which have ratified it (Decision of 12 Dec 2001). In the same contribution, the temporal aspect is considered by reference to the 10 cases brought to the ICJ by the Federal Republic of Yugoslavia against various NATO States for the latter's actions in Kosovo (ICJ judgment of 2 June 1999). The Court, applying the principle of reciprocity, decided in a number of the cases that Yugoslavia's reservation which limited the ICJ's jurisdiction to those events which occurred *after* its declaration to accept the compulsory jurisdiction of Court meant that the Court's jurisdiction was limited to those events which occurred after Yugoslavia's declaration. Similarly, in the *Pinochet Case*, their Lordships limited the jurisdiction of English Courts over acts of torture committed extra-territorially on a temporal basis. See *R v Bow Street Stipendiary Magistrate and others, ex parte Pinochet Ugarte* (No. 3) [1999] 2 All ER 97.

problem from the point of view of the policies which govern competition law. On this theme, Lady Fox's contribution (chapter 9) examines a number of different constraints placed upon domestic courts focusing on the recent transformation of much of the ECHR into English law. Each contribution identifies and suggests some solutions to key problems which face domestic courts.

In public international law, consent is of vital importance. In his contribution to this book, Judge Koroma (chapter 10) identifies the central pillar of the juris-dictional competence of the ICJ to be the consent of States and the question of *Kompetenz-Kompetenz* is also identified as being of particular concern.[25] The capacity of States to enter reservations when granting consent for disputes to be settled via adjudication, and the way this can limit the jurisdictional competence of such adjudicative bodies, is addressed by McGoldrick (chapter 11) in his expo-sition of recent jurisprudence of the Human Rights Committee which purports to ensure compliance to the International Covenant on Civil and Political Rights (1966). The impact that the interpretative approach adopted by a treaty-consti-tuted adjudicative body can have upon the logic and cogency of the underlying treaty and the intentions of its drafters is illustrated in the essay by Boyle on the International Tribunal for the Law of the Sea (chapter 12).

The principle of consent can also be applied to the European Court of Justice. However, it seems that little attention has been paid to the constitutional principle that the Community operates on the basis of the powers conferred upon it by its Member States. Perhaps this obfuscation owes much to the liberal interpretative approach adopted by the ECJ during, at least, the first thirty years of application of Community law, which was hardly characterised by any textual scrupulousness to the provisions of the Treaty when developing its relevant case law. Usher's analysis (chapter 13) urges caution in the acceptance of this assumption of legal activism by the Court. There have been examples of both restrictive[26] and extensive[27] inter-pretations of treaty obligations by the Court but the overall picture emerging from his analysis is hardly that of a Court which at the first available opportunity seeks to break free from the limitations of Treaty provisions and other secondary Com-munity legislation and create a 'government of judges' for Europe.

Yet the widespread impression remains that the ECJ has been more activist in the first thirty years or so of the Community's lifecycle and more restrained in the last fifteen years or so. This impression is developed and explained by Weatherill

---

[25] See 192–93. A seminal defence of the capacity of the ICJ to determine its own jurisdiction is found in Judge Lauterpacht's individual opinion in *Norwegian Loans Case (France v Norway)* (1957) ICJ Reports, at 34–66 which he elaborated on in the *Interhandel Case (Switzerland v United States)* (1959) ICJ Reports at 117–20.

[26] Particularly in relation to private actions for annulment and the use of the reference mechanism for obtaining preliminary rulings which would have circumvented the procedural limitations of annul-ment actions.

[27] For example, to ensure that bodies issuing legally binding Community acts are subject to judi-cial review, to ensure uniform control of the validity of Community measures and to ensure the uniform interpretation within the Community of international agreements entered into by the Community.

in his contribution (chapter 14) on the role and functioning of the Court in shaping the Community's and Member States' competence respectively. In his view, attaching labels in the abstract to the Court, such as 'activism' or 'restraint', makes little sense unless they are tied into the complex and constantly changing institutional and constitutional environment within which the Community and its institutions operate. He identifies three main reasons which may explain or even justify the restrained approach displayed by the Court in the last decade or so in overbuilding the Community's competence at the expense of national competence. First, the introduction in the Single European Act of qualified majority voting which has gradually but steadily replaced the unanimity required previously for almost any Community legislative action. This has resulted, in turn, in Member States being outvoted in Council and, having lost the political debate, in seeking redress before the Court. However, in this circumstance, the Court must therefore be significantly more respectful to the constitutional limits of the Community's competence. Secondly, the constructive dialogue between the ECJ and national courts has become more sensitive to the constitutional implications of its attempts to circumscribe the limits of Community competence. Thirdly, constitutional and pro-integrative advances are now made by legislative initiatives in the form of frequent Treaty revisions, which considerably undermines the ECJ's role as an institution playing an activist role in the development of the Community. Accordingly, the institution which was previously largely responsible for expanding the Community's jurisdiction has now become the institution ready and willing to guarantee and safeguard the jurisdictional competence of States.

In conclusion, whilst it may be fairly clear what jurisdiction means as a legal concept, the ways in which this plays out in international and European law is not so. Initially, some basic conceptual issues concerning matters of jurisdictional competence remain underdeveloped. For instance, it was argued above that the manner in which international law can regulate the power of States to assert jurisdiction over individuals is relatively unclear. Furthermore, the conceptual frameworks within which we try to comprehend the borders between jurisdictional competences of various institutional bodies can yield radically different answers to the basic constitutional issue of which institution does or should have the competence to regulate the legal relationships of a particular set of actors and what is the extent of these jurisdictional powers. It is hoped that the contributions to this volume will help to clarify some of these basic issues and move the debate forward.

I

Theoretical Approaches to the Assertion of Jurisdiction

1

Jurisdiction: The State

SIR FRANKLIN BERMAN

1. THE NATURE OF JURISDICTION

'Jurisdiction' is a protean concept. Its contours are not readily definable and change over time. They change both in terms of what States wish to do (or would like to be able to do) in the exercise of power externally,[1] and in terms of the willingness of the system of international law to recognise their exercise. However, simply by virtue of the fact that 'jurisdiction' in this sense refers to claims by one State to exercise powers which are likely to impinge on the rights or interests of other States, the fundamental presupposition is that all jurisdictional claims require a basis in international law; the mere assertion of a right by one State is not enough from the point of view of international law unless (or, as the case may be, until) it is accepted by others.[2]

Jurisdiction is thus a claim to exercise powers which, by their very nature, have an international aspect. But the nature of these 'powers' should also be recalled, at the very outset. They are powers over *people*, so powers over individuals themselves (including their liberty), over their property, and over their activities. Even if this were not the age of human rights, it surely needs no further demonstration that powers of that kind need a justification. A 'justification' may however be as much a matter of policy or social need as anything else. It is not the same thing as a legal basis, and claims to jurisdiction need a legal basis.

---

[1] That is, outside their physical territory. See pp 5–7 below.

[2] Cf. the famous *dictum* of the ICJ in the *Anglo-Norwegian Fisheries Case*: 'The delimitation of sea areas has always an international aspect; it cannot be dependent merely upon the will of the coastal State as expressed in its municipal law. Although it is true that the act of delimitation is necessarily a unilateral act, because only the coastal State is competent to undertake it, the validity of the delimitation with regard to other States depends upon international law.' See *Fisheries* case (United Kingdom v Norway) (1951) ICJ 116 at 132. This is not of course the viewpoint of the PCIJ in the *Lotus Case* judgment No 9, (1927) PCIJ, Series A, No 10, but as to this see JL Brierly (1928) 44 *LQR* at 155–56; now see also the Separate Opinion of President Guillaume (especially paras 14–16) and the Joint Separate Opinion of Judges Higgins, Koojimans and Buergenthal (especially paras 49–52) in the *Case Concerning the Arrest Warrant of 11 April 2000* (*Democratic Republic of Congo v Belgium*) decided by the ICJ on 14 Feb 2002 (*Yerodia Case*).

Very often, the legal basis is postulated, rather vaguely, to be 'sovereignty': as in phrases like 'jurisdiction is an inherent attribute of sovereignty', or some such. How far does that take us, though? Not very far, for it is more restatement than explication. Once 'sovereignty' is viewed not as a mystical quality but as a useful shorthand expression for the legal rights and competences inherent in statehood, the statement tells the enquirer little more than that a 'sovereign' has 'jurisdiction', but not what jurisdiction it has—not, in other words, what its content is. And inasmuch as 'sovereignty' has about it nowadays a *residual* flavour alongside the *territorial* flavour it has always had, its usefulness in this context is questionable. It seems a peculiarly inappropriate tool to perform a validating function for national jurisdiction as the latter reaches *beyond* the limits of the national territory. The function of 'sovereignty', if any, seems not to be to validate a jurisdictional claim so much as the refusal of others to accept it.[3]

The treatment of jurisdiction as a topic in the standard international law textbooks tends to be traditional and comfortably familiar. The subject is lumped together as a single whole.[4] It can however be useful, for analytical purposes, to divide the subject into two: civil jurisdiction and criminal jurisdiction. The argument for doing so would be that different considerations apply to each case, or at least that individual considerations take on different shades of weight as between claims to exercise jurisdiction of a civil or of a criminal kind. That is largely true, as the following analysis will demonstrate. Nevertheless, the division by civil and criminal may be misleading, if it obscures the common issues that underlie any claim to exercise a non-territorial jurisdiction. What these issues are comes into focus if one bears in mind that jurisdictional claims can comprise any or all of the following: the claim to *prescribe* (relating to behaviour); the claim to *regulate* (by prohibiting activities, or subjecting them to conditional permission); the claim to *enforce* (to compel by physical or economic means); and the claim to *punish* (relating to breaches of prescriptions or regulations.)[5]

This chapter will confine itself, all the same, to the question of criminal jurisdiction. This is a choice of pure convenience. There are several reasons for it. One is that much of the treatment of civil jurisdiction has become rather stale and repetitive; there seems to be little new to say. Another is that criminal jurisdiction has emerged relatively recently as a topic of particular international interest, and is most certainly topical. It therefore raises issues of a kind that are partly new, and where they are not actually new, nevertheless serve to illuminate eternal questions.

---

[3] Though it is possible to argue that 'sovereignty' provides the positive justification for certain types of protective jurisdiction.

[4] Cf for example, I Brownlie, *Principles of Public International Law* (5th edn, Oxford University Press, Oxford, 1998) at 302. Contrast, however, the more developed treatment of the subject in the 9th edn of *Oppenheim's International Law* (Longmans, London, 1992) under the title 'International Protection of Human Rights', especially at 983–98 and *passim*.

[5] Plus possibly one other claim, which will be discussed below at pp 9–10.

2. EXTRA-TERRITORIAL JURISDICTION FOR CRIMINAL ACTS

Criminal jurisdiction is essentially a jurisdiction to prescribe and to punish. The paradigm case is clearly territorial: jurisdiction in respect of *conduct* within the territory, but also over a *person* who is physically present within the territory. There is certainly an established criminal jurisdiction *in absentia*,[6] but that is nevertheless a side-issue of little central relevance[7] in the present particular context.[8] A further unproblematical issue, in any legal sense, is the exercise of jurisdiction by a State over its own nationals in respect of conduct taking place abroad. The justifying idea seems to be connected with notions of allegiance, and thus possesses an antiquity as respectable as (and in some parts of the world perhaps even older than) that of territorial authority. Between them, these two parameters form a figure which, if not entirely rectilinear, nevertheless ties in, in an entirely recognisable way, with what are generally accepted to be the essential qualities for statehood: people, territory, government and independence.[9]

The fact that there is nothing legally problematical in the exercise by a State of criminal jurisdiction over conduct by its nationals abroad does not dispose of the issue of what conduct: what conduct should be criminalised, or prosecuted, even if committed abroad? If the State's legal powers are unquestioned, then it has a free field of choice; and the exercise of that choice will appear more and more as a matter of pure national policy.

The question was examined *au fond* by a Steering Committee set up by the Home Office in 1996, charged 'to examine the current system of jurisdiction, how it evolved, how it works, and its strengths and weaknesses' and then to assess the implications, both technical and more general, of moving to 'a broad policy of taking extra territorial jurisdiction'.[10] The interest in the Steering Committee's conclusions[11] lies in the fact that it settled for an approach that was neither wholly general nor wholly ad hoc. Starting from the premise of increasing domestic pressure, pressure, that is, that the UK's jurisdiction—especially over a wave of new offences[12]—should not be seen to stop at the border, the Committee clearly felt

---

[6] In Civil Law systems.

[7] Notably because the typical *in absentia* jurisdiction is in an important sense provisional; the convicted person has the right, on capture, to re-open the proceedings against him; but see the restrictions on return by way of extradition in these circumstances, now contained in s 6 of the Extradition Act 1989. Compare the debate which led to the exclusion of *in absentia* trials from the processes of the International Criminal Tribunals for the Former Yugoslavia and Rwanda, and then in due course of the International Criminal Court, summarised in RS Lee (ed), *The International Criminal Court. The Making of the Rome Statute* (Kluwer, The Hague, 1999), at 255–61.

[8] Though not necessarily so in other contexts; see the *Yerodia Case*, n 2 above.

[9] See, for example, *Oppenheim's International Law* (9th edn, Longmans, London, 1992), vol 1 at 120–23; the Montevideo Convention on the Rights and Duties of States 1933, Art 1.

[10] For example, in the criminal field, 'Review of Extra-Territorial Jurisdiction: Steering Committee Report', Home Office Communication Unit, July 1996.

[11] Which would seem never to have been adopted formally as Government policy for the future.

[12] The triggering impulse seems to have been the concern that burst forth in the mid-1990s over 'sex tourism', notably by Western men in Thailand.

what it called 'the attractions . . . of providing a consistent and principled approach'. What it plumped for, however, was a hybrid: a list of 'guidelines' against which decisions could in future be taken whether it would be appropriate in given circumstances to take extended jurisdiction[13] in respect either of new offences or of existing offences which had become the subject of new concern.

The criteria proposed were heterogeneous, and lay at different levels. There should, for example, be no general substitution for extradition;[14] and the new jurisdiction should be effective and enforceable. On the substantive level, the criteria would be the seriousness of the offence, the level of its moral repugnance, the vulnerability of victims, the degree of international consensus that concerted action was needed,[15] and the United Kingdom's standing and reputation internationally. Further, on an extremely practical level, the witnesses and evidentiary material should be likely to be available in the United Kingdom, and the costs of trial should be tolerable.

This all appears soundly pragmatic. It does not however, self-evidently, answer the question how many of these factors have to be present in order to justify taking jurisdiction in a particular case.[16] Nor does it offer any solid prospect of consistency—possibly only that future assertions of jurisdiction would still be characterised by ad hoc expediency, but less of it.[17]

We move to the heart of the matter when we go from jurisdiction over own nationals abroad to the claim to punish foreigners for their conduct abroad.[18] The rubric has an uneasy relationship with the currently fashionable concept of 'international crimes', and raises the question whether the two are essentially the same or essentially different. Is the jurisdiction to punish foreigners for extraterritorial conduct just an incident of the standard legal regime governing international crimes? Or, if not, do criteria of the sort enunciated in 1996 for own nationals, apply equally to non-nationals as well? In *In re Piracy Jure Gentium*,[19] the Judicial Committee of the Privy Council was quite clear that the crimes it was dealing with were crimes 'as defined by international law' but that their trial and punishment was remitted to States, in the absence of international means to that effect.[20] But the question remains, 'Which States?' and as to that the Privy Council's

---

[13]   For example, over British citizens and (possibly) permanent residents, and on the basis of double criminality; the Report is explicit on both points.

[14]   '[T]he principle that offences are best prosecuted in the country where they are committed', as the Report puts it. The Report correctly points out that in very many cases States which assert universal criminal jurisdiction over their own nationals are those which are constitutionally precluded from extraditing own nationals.

[15]   This is because offenders might otherwise slip through the net.

[16]   It merely says that, if one or more of the criteria were satisfied, then it would raise a case for consideration ('particularly if the practical enforcement issues did not appear to be insurmountable'). This is an obvious evasion.

[17]   See also n 51 below.

[18]   'Abroad' begs, of course, the question whether within the jurisdiction of another sovereign, or not; the general assumption assumption in this chapter is the former.

[19]   [1934] AC 586.

[20]   Per Viscount Sankey at 589.

reasoning that any State was entitled to prosecute would seem to be, not a posi-tive proposition of law, but rather the residual effect of their conclusion that nationality had *pro tanto* been lost, so that no one State had the right to object to prosecution by any other.[21]

Is the War Crimes Act 1991[22] on broadly the same or on a different footing? From one point of view it could be thought to be an application of the criteria outlined in the Home Office Steering Committee Report[23] on a basis of con-structive nationality;[24] from another it could be seen as an application of a piracy-type jurisdiction to 'violations of the laws and customs of war'.[25]

One is tempted to wonder at this point about possible international law equiv-alent to the old common lawyer's distinction between *mala prohibita* and *mala in se, mala in se* being acts of such moral turpitude that the law recognises them to be criminal simply on that account, whereas *mala prohibita* are acts that become criminal only when declared to be so by the legislator. It is intriguing that what the seventeenth and eighteenth century dispute over *mala prohibita* and *mala in se* revolved around was the suspending and dispensing power of the Crown. There is more than an echo here of the arguments over extra-territorial criminal juris-diction. A present day facsimile might be that the wider proscription entailed by bringing in the conduct of foreigners abroad is inherently justified in the case of *mala in se*; it is only in the case of *mala prohibita* that specific agreement to that effect is required, presumably by treaty.[26]

3. 'INTERNATIONAL CRIMES'

This brings one naturally to the concept of 'international crimes'. The term is now in frequent use, but too loosely, and that is regrettable. Confusion is rampant on

---

[21] '. . . a person guilty of such piracy has placed himself beyond the protection of any State. He is no longer a national, but 'hostis humani generis' and as such he is justiciable by any State anywhere . . .' *ibid.* Cf. JB Moore, *Digest of International Law* (1906), at 953, in a slightly different formulation, 'The pirate is a sea brigand. He has no right to any flag and is justiciable by all.' But now see the Third United Nations Convention on the Law of the Sea, 1982, Art 105, and the comments in the Separate Opinions in the *Yerodia Case*, n 2 above.

[22] This Act opened the way to prosecution in the UK of alleged Nazi war criminals who had subsequently settled here.

[23] See n 10 above.

[24] S 1(2) limits the jurisdiction to persons who had become British citizens or local residents.

[25] S 1(1)(b).

[26] CK Allen commented in 1931, 'Now, we have all been brought up to regard this distinction between *mala in se* and *mala prohibita* as unsound, exploded, and indeed scarcely worthy of serious consideration. We have been taught this for the reason that the seventeenth and eighteenth centuries went much farther than was necessary or defensible in its theories of *mala in se*. Their doctrine was that these wrongs were illegal because they were immoral: because, in other words, they had been for-bidden by a Divine law which no human authority could possibly abrogate or abridge even if it desired to do so.' (CK Allen, *Legal Duties, and other Essays in Jurisprudence* (Clarendon Press, Oxford, 1931) at 238–39). There seems to be a lesson here for international law; cf the cautious formulation by Judges Higgins, Koojimans and Buergenthal (para 73) in the *Yerodia Case*, n 2 above.

at least the following points: whether the term applies generally to any crime of serious international concern (or international ramifications), as opposed to crimes of purely local impact; alternatively, whether the term applies properly to crimes created by international law, and if so whether the concept refers only to crimes under general international law, or applies equally to crimes created by treaty;[27] alternatively, whether the term connotes unlawful actions by States, but for which State agents are individually answerable; and most of all confusion on the connection between whether a crime is a crime 'under' international law and who has jurisdiction to prosecute and punish it. It was this last confusion—or at least the treatment of the two issues as if they were one—that characterised the Hetherington/Chalmers Report which gave rise to the War Crimes Act 1991.[28] Twenty years on, the speeches in *Pinochet Nos 1 & 3* remain littered with the assumption that 'international crime' and 'universal jurisdiction to prosecute and punish' are to all intents and purposes synonymous, and there is hardly a serious discussion of the point to be found.[29]

The focus of the present chapter is this crucial question of jurisdiction. Whereas it used to be thought that there was a two-way division between national jurisdiction and universal jurisdiction, more recent developments have brought home that the division is in fact a three-way one: national/universal/international jurisdiction. By 'national jurisdiction' should be understood crimes in respect of which the range of prosecutable defendants is determined by the given system of national law; 'universal jurisdiction', conversely, connotes crimes which, under international law, can be prosecuted by any State, without regard to the nationality of the accused or the place where the crime is alleged to have been committed.[30] The contrast between the two can be seen in the Genocide Convention,[31] which creates an international crime but subjects it to national jurisdiction, and the Red Cross Conventions,[32] which set up, within a general category of international crimes (subject to national jurisdiction), a special list which is made subject to a strong

---

[27] The primary operation of which is, as a matter of law, between the Parties only; but note the Genocide Convention 1948, in Art I of which the Contracting Parties 'confirm' that genocide 'is' a crime under international law, and add 'which they undertake to prevent and punish', UKTS 58 (1970), Cmnd 4421.

[28] Report of the War Crimes Inquiry, conducted by Sir Thomas Hetherington and William Chalmers, June 1989 (Cm 744).

[29] With the (partial) exception of Lord Slynn of Hadley in *R v Bow Street Metropolitan Magistrate, ex parte Pinochet Ugarte (Pinochet, No 1)* [1998] 4 All ER 897 (Lords Goff of Chieveley and Phillips of Worth Matravers agreeing, in *Pinochet No 3*); contrast Lord Millett, at [2000] 1 AC 268. Cf also the Separate Opinions in the *Yerodia Case*, n 2 above.

[30] Though a further intricacy remains as to whether the concept permits a wholly *in absentia* jurisdiction without any element of connection to the State of prosecution, this being the situation in the *Yerodia Case*, n 2 above.

[31] n 27 above.

[32] The four Geneva Conventions of 1949 on the Protection of War Victims, and Additional Protocol I thereto, of 1977.

form of universal jurisdiction.[33] On the other hand, 'international jurisdiction'—using the term now in a precise sense—refers to the fact that an international criminal tribunal has been created with the power to try the crime in question. The original examples[34] were the creation first of the International Criminal Tribunal for the Former Yugoslavia (ICTY) and then of the International Criminal Tribunal for Rwanda (ICTR), each with its own subject-matter jurisdiction, confined within a geographical and a temporal condition.[35] The issue has now a stronger and more permanent interest with the conclusion of the Statute of the International Criminal Court.[36]

It also becomes plain, on examination, that alongside this three-fold division of jurisdiction by type lies a much more complex pattern of application than might be imagined at first thought. Thus when we have universal jurisdiction it can be either with or without an obligation to prosecute. The 'grave breaches' regime of the Red Cross Conventions is the paradigmatic example of a strong obligation to prosecute as the complement to a rule of universal jurisdiction; whereas the run of treaty crimes, which is such a marked characteristic of the quarter-century just past, show a consistent pattern characterised by a requirement on States Parties to take extended jurisdiction but short of the universal, and matches that by deliberately eschewing a duty to prosecute.[37] In addition, we have on the one hand international jurisdiction (in the strict sense) enforced by primacy over national courts, as in the case of the ICTY and ICTR. But we also have international jurisdiction (in the identical strict sense) linked to national jurisdictions by a rule of 'complementarity'—and indeed severely restricted by it, and established moreover under a treaty regime which consciously does not impose on the Parties an obligation to take extended national jurisdiction over its subject crimes. This is—of course—the regime of the International Criminal Court.[38]

We can, however, move on one step further from there to see that there is one additional aspect to jurisdiction in the specifically criminal context, namely the issue of international cooperation to make national jurisdiction effective. And one

---

[33] The reference is to the 'grave breaches' regime, which places each High Contracting Party 'under the obligation to search for persons alleged to have committed, or to have ordered to be committed, such grave breaches, and [to] bring such persons, regardless of their nationality, before its own courts': Convention I, Art 49; Convention II, Art 50; Convention III, Art 129; Convention IV, Art 146. It has, however, to be said that (all other issues aside) the pattern of implementation by the Parties hardly corresponds to the apparent scope of the obligation. See GH Aldrich in 'Armed Conflict and the New Law', *Effecting Compliance*, (The British Institute of International and Comparative Law, London, 1993) vol. 2 at p 5.

[34] After, that is, the Nuremberg and Tokyo Tribunals at the end of the Second World War.

[35] See Security Council Resolutions 827 (1993) and 955 (1994) and their Annexes.

[36] Adopted and opened for signature in Rome on 17 July 1998. The Statute entered into force on 1 July 2002.

[37] See p 12 below.

[38] But for a carefully argued alternative view (not accepted by the Government, nor in the event by Parliament), that there was some form of duty, or at least advantage, in asserting universal jurisdiction over ICC crimes, see the Parliamentary debates on the War Crimes Bill: eg House of Commons, Standing Committee D, 3 May 2001.

step further still, to note that criminal jurisdiction is apt to raise an additional issue that seldom, if ever, arises in the context of civil jurisdiction, namely the issue of personal immunity. The particularly awkward and intractable nature of the *Pinochet* litigation lay in the way these two supernumerary elements came together.[39] The reference here to extradition illuminates the increasing internationalisation of the fight against crime. This brings in its train a steady development of an extensive network of inter-State cooperation not merely in criminal investigation but also over prosecution. Looked at from a different angle, this cooperation can be seen as action in support of making (an appropriate) national jurisdiction effective. Inevitably, this raises the question of what forms of national criminal jurisdiction (including their extraterritorial reach) are acceptable—and it does so in a context quite different from the standard case of extraterritorial administrative or regulatory jurisdiction. Without an answer to the question of acceptability, States would find themselves committed to supporting any form of foreign criminal jurisdiction, however exorbitant.[40] It has thus become commonplace that the treaty regime established for any given 'treaty crime' contains, alongside its primary substantive provisions, secondary provisions regulating international legal cooperation, including extradition. These secondary provisions serve, at one and the same time, the purpose of making the treaty regime itself effective[41] and the purpose of establishing *by agreement* the operative arrangements for the exercise and acceptance of jurisdiction by individual States Parties.[42] A problem of a similar kind exists, however, in the general extradition context.[43] National legislation governing the extradition process therefore offers an interesting window into how States view the issue of jurisdiction.[44]

---

[39] Had *Pinochet* not originated in an extradition context, it seems hardly likely that the attempt to prosecute would ever have got so far as to reach the point of creating a *cause célèbre* over Head of State immunity. Had it not started, indeed, under the quasi-automatic regime of the European Convention on Extradition, it seems quite possible that an attempted prosecution would not have got on its feet at all. The dispute between Congo and Belgium that led to the *Yerodia Case* before the ICJ contained the same elements, but arose in quite a different manner.

[40] And in spite of recognised and established objections to certain forms of non-criminal jurisdiction. The awkwardness would of course be compounded by the fact that the impact was quite likely to fall on citizens of the second State who would, in the normal course, look to their national State for protection.

[41] For example, by closing down the possibility of refuge or safe haven for terrorist crimes, expressed in the phrase *aut dedere aut judicare*. See the analyses by President Guillaume and Judges Higgins, Koojimans and Buergenthal in their Separate Opinions in the *Yerodia Case*, n 2 above.

[42] Though not always with perfect success, as witness the *Lockerbie* litigation in the International Court of Justice, the central issue in which can be summarized as being the limits (if any) of the treaty acceptance of the possibility of trial before the courts of a State itself implicated in the impugned criminal act.

[43] Which continues to be heavily relied on by governments even in the context of severe criminal activity that has been addressed by treaty, eg terrorism. See also Part 9 of the Statute of the International Criminal Court, especially the limits in Arts 89 and 90 on 'extradition' to the ICC.

[44] The densely-packed regime of s 2 of the Extradition Act 1989 incorporates, as three-way alternatives, either a condition of reciprocity (with UK extraterritorial jurisdiction), or a nationality criterion, or a specified 'treaty crime' basis.

4. RESULTING QUESTIONS

At this point we can isolate the three questions that seem of particular interest. First, is customary international law capable of creating a crime directly triable in a national court? Secondly, are there, in fact, basic differences (and if so, what?) between the exercise of extraterritorial jurisdiction in the civil and the criminal context? Thirdly, are there circumstances in which the question becomes, not: is it legitimate to exercise criminal jurisdiction over conduct abroad? but rather: is it legitimate not to?

These are all large questions, and whether there is a complete answer to each of them is not immediately obvious, in an area which has been subject to so much recent development. Suggested answers can for the moment be provisional only, as it seems highly likely that this phase of development has not yet come to its end. My own suggestions would be along the following lines.

A. Is Customary International Law Capable of Creating a Crime Directly Triable in a National Court?

The first question is open to a myriad of answers, depending on the characteristic features of the particular national legal system in view. Looking at it simply from the point of view of English law, the answer would seem to be no; international law could not create a crime triable directly, without the intervention of Parliament, in an English court. What international law could, however, do is to perform its well-understood validating function, by establishing the legal basis (legal justification) for Parliament to legislate, so far as it purports to exercise control over the conduct of non-nationals abroad. This answer is inevitably tied up with the attitude taken towards the possibility of the creation of new offences under common law. Inasmuch as the reception of customary international law into English law takes place under common law, and inasmuch as the development of new customary international law remains very much the consequence of international behaviour by the Executive, in which neither the Legislature nor the Courts, nor any other branch of the constitution, need have played any part, it would be odd if the Executive could, by means of that kind, acting in concert with other States, amend or modify specifically the *criminal* law, with all the consequences that flow for the liberty of the individual and rights of personal property. There are, besides, powerful reasons of political accountability, regularity and legal certainty for saying that the power to create crimes should now be regarded as reserved exclusively to Parliament, by Statute.[45]

---

[45] In *Pinochet*, the Appellate Committee showed little eagerness to assert such a power—or that at least was the construction placed by Lord Millett on the opinions of his fellow judges: [2000] 1 AC at 276.

That said, it is also plain that international law is capable of creating obligations of various kinds to prosecute and punish offences. It is not clear whether obligations of that kind can be brought into being only when the offence is itself one under international law (including offences created by treaty), though as a practical matter it seems hardly possible[46] to conceive of the establishment of so precise an obligation without express definition of the offence(s) to which it refers. Nor is it clear whether the obligation has to be expressly stipulated under treaty, or whether it is conceivable that a like duty could be recognized as having come into being as an obligation under customary international law. In favour of the exclusively treaty route speaks the fact that treaty provisions on the subject are seldom in absolute terms.[47] The standard terminology[48] in the mis-named *aut dedere aut judicare* Conventions is to '*submit* the case to [the] competent authorities for the purpose of prosecution' (emphasis added). The reasons for the adoption of this circumscribed form of words are ones of principle, not world-weary resignation. The need not to distort the process by which, in any given jurisdiction, the prosecuting authority decides whether or not to bring charges, and whether or not to proceed with them;[49] and the need not to undermine the independence of the prosecutorial function (against executive interference under cover of the assumption of a treaty obligation).[50]

B. Are There Differences in the Exercise of Extra Territorial Jurisdiction in the Civil and Criminal Contexts?

The second question takes us back to the differences between jurisdictional claims in the criminal and civil fields. How great are they? Are they differences of kind, or just of degree?[51] Recent international experience in respect of crimes with an

---

[46] Except perhaps on a limited bilateral basis.

[47] Apparently the sole exception being the Genocide Convention (n 27 above) and the 'grave breaches' regime of the Red Cross Conventions, but see n 33 above for the discrepancy in the latter case between State practice and the ostensible intention.

[48] Including, ironically, in the Convention Against Torture which formed the central core of the *Pinochet* litigation.

[49] The standard clause is invariably backed by a second paragraph requiring the normal standards both for prosecution and for proof to be applied—a clause which is clearly intended to have both an encouraging and a restraining effect.

[50] The excruciatingly cautious observance of this principle by both the British and the Spanish Governments was yet another notable feature of the *Pinochet* litigation, which illustrated also how prosecutorial independence can cut both ways when other international obligations are in play (*in casu* sovereign immunity) for compliance with which the executive bears the responsibility. For the difficulties that can arise for international law at the level of principle as well as practice where actions of the judicial branch are impugned, cf the *Cumaraswamy* (1999) and *LaGrand* (2001) cases before the International Court of Justice.

[51] This part of the discussion is inevitably based on the assumption that a discernible separation exists between criminal and non-criminal. A strange recent hybrid can be found in the Financial Services and Markets Act 2000, which creates a class of 'civil offences' subject to penalties in many respects indistinguishable from those for serious crime, but under a system in which the penalisable conduct is not precisely defined and the sanctioning process falls well short of the recognised requirements for

international aspect has been very extensive. It has brought out the underlying implications far more clearly than ever before. It therefore places us in a better position to assess whether jurisdictional claims in the criminal and non-criminal fields are all much of a muchness, when it comes down to the essentials. I am inclined to the contrary view that there is a cardinal difference, and it lies at a basic level. The difference resides in the fact that the assertion of extra-territorial jurisdiction of a civil kind is virtually by definition in pursuit of the unilateral interests of the asserting State, or of its nationals.[52] This can be seen most clearly in the regulatory or administrative fields, but it is just as evident, on closer examination, in the traditional field of civil litigation, where the essence lies in the extension of a forum State's legal rules, either of substance or at least of process, to a transaction which has connections with more than one jurisdiction.[53] By contrast, almost the entire trend of modern practice in the field of criminal jurisdiction has been concerned with the protection of international interests, or at least common interests,[54] that being the whole idea that animates both the rash of 'treaty-crime' Conventions and the argument over universal jurisdiction, as well as the creation of truly international jurisdictions.

Therein would seem to lie the explanation why so much of the extensive law and practice over extraterritorial jurisdiction in the civil field has to do with rules and guidelines for the avoidance of jurisdictional conflicts, whereas virtually nothing of the same kind exists in the criminal field.[55] One of the paradoxes of current international practice is that, in its drive to deal effectively (or at least comprehensively) with stigmatised abuses, it has deliberately encouraged the greatest multiplicity of national jurisdictions having parallel competence, without creating any rules for regulating priorities between them.[56]

---

a criminal trial; and imposes moreover an extensive jurisdictional reach under a form of 'effects doctrine' (Part VIII Penalties for Market Abuse, ss 118–27 and 132–33). See R Wright, 'Market Abuse and Market Manipulation: The Criminal, Civil and Regulatory Interface', (2001) *JIFM* 19. There is however no evidence to suggest that this enactment, shaped no doubt to meet the particular circumstances of worldwide financial trading, presages any general change in the British Government's traditional attitude to extraterritorial jurisdiction (or to the prosecution of crime).

[52] An example in the opposite direction might be the current growth area in distraint against the misappropriated property of foreign Heads of State, though that is more frequently seen in an immunities rather than a jurisdiction context; see the 2001 Resolution of the Institut de droit international on the Immunities of Heads of State and Government, and the comment by H Fox, (2002) 51 *ICLQ* 119.

[53] Therein would lie the answer to the not unreasonable objection that, for example, the admission of tort claims in the US courts over the Bhopal factory or in the UK courts over Cape Asbestos must be ranked as serving the interests of the foreign plaintiffs.

[54] A converse case would be the deployment by a State of repressive legislation to penalise political opposition carried out peacefully abroad; but cases of that sort are rare, and would in any case depend for their effectiveness on the subsequent presence of the defendant within the physical jurisdiction of the court.

[55] The rules built into the Statutes of the ICTY, ICTR and ICC deal exclusively with the relative priority as between a given national system and the international jurisdiction; there is also practice in the extradition field on priority as between competing requests.

[56] Cf again, the *Lockerbie* dispute (n 42 above).

A further difference between the criminal and non-criminal fields—though too much should not be made of it—is the extent to which, the more 'international' a particular criminal law policy becomes, the more it relies on a network of inter-State cooperation to make it effective. In other words, criminal jurisdiction, including in its extraterritorial exercise, may have an important function to perform *in support of* the effective jurisdiction of other States, or *a fortiori* of international criminal tribunals. The claim to exercise jurisdiction of this kind and for this purpose falls outside the spectrum listed above, and is in reality a claim to a right (not necessarily extraterritorial) to sustain the effectiveness of another jurisdiction—on the basis that the latter jurisdiction is recognised as the one primarily or properly entitled to deal with a matter.

C. Can it be Illegitimate to Refrain from Exercising Criminal Jurisdiction over Criminal Conduct Abroad?

The third question seeks to take us on from the pure entitlement to exercise criminal jurisdiction in respect of conduct abroad, and focus more precisely on a possible requirement under general international law to do so.[57] Attention has already been drawn above to the fact that negotiations over the suppression of particular crimes by treaty have stopped short of an absolute obligation to prosecute.[58] This suggests that a cautious approach is appropriate. The preceding discussion also shows, however, that a sparing exercise of extraterritorial criminal jurisdiction, with careful attention to the factual circumstances of particular cases, and also to the *consequences* of the assumption of jurisdiction,[59] is morally, politically and legally justifiable, and may indeed be a necessary part of international cooperation. The broad conclusion is scepticism over sweeping propositions, and a preference for incremental development, especially based on treaty negotiation.

5. CONCLUSION

Is it possible to draw even a broad conclusion from the discussion above? The material is disparate, and has not so far been the subject of the analytical atten-

---

[57] Two useful recent studies on the subject are those by the International Law Association's Committee on International Human Rights Law and Practice (*Final Report on the Exercise of Universal Jurisdiction in Respect of Gross Human Rights Offences*, London 2000); and by Amnesty International (*Universal Jurisdiction: the Duty of States to Enact and Implement Legislation*, London, Sept 2001, AI Index no IOR 53/002/2001). The latter is particularly notable for its exhaustive analysis of national legislation and State practice across a very wide spectrum.

[58] Let alone to punish, which clearly depends on the adverse verdict of a competent court following a fair trial.

[59] Cf the debate—necessarily speculative—as to whether the assumption or the declining of jurisdiction over *Pinochet* would do more for the development of democratic accountability in Chile. See also the Separate Opinion by Judge Rezek in the *Yerodia Case*, n 2 above.

tion it deserves. However, the rapid development of practice in the area of criminal jurisdiction, both primary and secondary (ie in support of a foreign jurisdiction, including an international tribunal, recognised to be competent and appropriate) has illuminated the underlying questions sufficiently to permit a more sophisticated analysis from an international law point of view. I retain a healthy scepticism over sweeping propositions, notably as to the superior moral virtue of universal jurisdiction, since they tend to blight the achievement of what is often a highly laudable objective by a backlash of resentment at the overweening exercise of foreign sovereignty.[60] If the aim is *effective* and collaborative international action against crime, the preference must continue to be for incremental development, based on treaty negotiation, and in many cases for international jurisdiction or agreed systems of multiple jurisdiction in preference to universal jurisdiction.

[60] See, again, the Judgment and Separate Opinions in the *Yerodia Case*, n 2 above.

2

New Wine in Old Bottles or Old Wine in New Bottles or only Old Wine in Old Bottles?

Reflections on the Assertion of Jurisdiction in Public International Law

IAIN SCOBBIE

Each venture
is a new beginning, a raid on the inarticulate
With shabby equipment always deteriorating
TS Eliot, *East Coker* (1940), Part 5.

1. INTRODUCTION

Addressing 'theoretical' perspectives of the assertion of jurisdiction in public international law is not only a daunting task, but also a difficult one within the material constraints of this chapter. The 'classic' doctrinal expositions of the law relating to jurisdiction are both complex and lengthy.[1] Rather than engage with contested issues they identify and discuss, such as the extent of a State's power to assert extra-territorial jurisdiction—whether prescriptive or enforcement[2]—in an

---

[1] For instance, M Akehurst, 'Jurisdiction in International Law', (1972–1973) 46 *BYIL* 145 at 255; FA Mann, 'The Doctrine of Jurisdiction in International Law', in FA Mann (ed), *Studies in International Law* (Clarendon Press, Oxford, 1973) at 1 and also 'The Doctrine of Jurisdiction Revisited After Twenty Years', in FA Mann (ed), *Further Studies in International Law* (Clarendon Press, Oxford, 1990) at 1.

[2] For example, consider recent United States practice in the extra-territorial assertion of jurisdiction where economic measures are used for political ends—see, for instance, BM Clagett, 'Title III of the Helms-Burton Act is consistent with international law', (1996) 90 *AJIL* 434; 'A Reply to Professor Lowenfeld', (1996) 90 *AJIL* 641; and 'The Controversy over Title III of the Helms-Burton Act: Who is Breaking International Law—the United States, or the States that have made themselves co-conspirators with Cuba in its unlawful confiscations?' (1996–1997) 30 *George Washington J of Int Law and Economics* 271; AV Lowe, 'US extra-territorial jurisdiction: the Helms-Burton and D' Amato Acts', (1997) 46 *ICLQ* 378; AF Lowenfeld, 'Congress and Cuba: the Helms-Burton Act', (1996) 90 *AJIL* 419; A Reinisch, 'Widening the US Embargo against Cuba Extraterritorially', (1996) 7 *EJIL* 545; General Assembly Resolution 53/10 (3 Nov 1998), *Elimination of Coercive Economic Measures as a*

attempt to construct a coherent theory of jurisdiction, it seems better to trim the discussion in the light of the constraints, and consider some examples which might be seen or be interpreted as new ventures in the realm of jurisdiction. The examples chosen might be seen as international reactions and attempts to redress human rights or humanitarian law abuses in a manner that challenges or supplants the jurisdiction of the State. It could further be argued that these examples represent a conflict between moral value and legal doctrine or, perhaps more crudely, a conflict between natural law and positivism. In any event, they provide a foothold into theoretical issues. Under consideration here, principally, is positivism as a distinctive legal theory—as embodied in the nonetheless diverse works of, for instance, John Austin, Hans Kelsen, HLA Hart, and Joseph Raz—rather than the doctrinal approach to international law that insists on express State consent as a prerequisite to the validation of specific substantive rules. The two are not unrelated but, for present purposes, the focus is necessarily on the jurisprudential concept.

To consider the international assertion of jurisdiction, the examples that have been chosen are:

(i)   the international administration of territory, in particular the contemporary examples of Kosovo and East Timor in contrast to the historical example of Danzig;
(ii) international criminality, which splits into the issues of State and individual criminality. The points to be addressed here are:
   (a) whether the ascription of criminal responsibility to a State can (and/or should) concomitantly attach moral blame to its population as a whole; and:
   (b) the possible implications of the complementary jurisdiction of the International Criminal Court on domestic attempts to deal with human rights or humanitarian law violations using truth and reconciliation commissions.

These three substantive examples involve the contemporary elaboration of fragments of past practice that were not fully articulated within the corpus of international legal doctrine. Rather they constituted only sporadic and relatively isolated attempts to deal with these issues. The most obvious historic example of an 'internationalised territory' is Danzig,[3] but international criminality has perhaps an even more diverse history, encompassing matters such as the *Breisach* trial of 1474 through the trials held in Tokyo and Occupied Germany after World War II to the

---

Means of Political and Economic Compulsion, (1999) 38 ILM 759; and also S Smis and K van der Borght, 'The EU–US Compromise on the Helms-Burton and D' Amato Acts', (1999) 93 *AJIL* 227.

[3] See J Crawford, *The Creation of States in International Law* (Clarendon Press, Oxford, 1979) at 160–69; HWA Verzijl, *International Law in Historical Perspective*, (Sijthoff, Leiden, 1969) vol 2 at 500 *et seq*; and R Wilde, 'From Danzig to East Timor and Beyond: the Role of International Territorial Administration', (2001) 95 *AJIL* 583, for an overview of internationalised territories, including the inter-war status of Danzig.

International Criminal Court.[4] The contemporary expression of these issues differ in that they might be seen as more clearly articulated with norms of general international law. They can all be seen as international assertions of jurisdiction that challenge State sovereignty by relying on claims of moral value embedded in and underpinning the prescriptions of international human rights and humanitarian law. Whether they also challenge sovereignty in a way that challenges orthodox positivist theory is an additional matter, but it is clear that these are not simply domestic pretensions concerning the proper exercise and extent of State power. Accordingly, these issues differ fundamentally from, for instance, contested claims by States to regulate economic matters extraterritorially.

Jurisdictional issues have traditionally been inextricably entwined with that of sovereignty—'Sovereignty in the relations between States signifies independence. Independence in regard to a portion of the globe is the right to exercise therein, to the exclusion of any other State, the functions of a State'[5]—and sovereignty is central to classic theories of legal positivism. This is not to say that sovereignty has been without interest to natural law theories, but with positivism the notion of sovereignty displaces that of constraining moral value as the fundamental axiom organising the State in political and legal theory:

> Sovereignty of course is a comparatively modern expression. Bodin . . . claimed to be its inventor. But . . . the notion went back to a tradition of thought which had already borne its fruits in the Middle Ages. Long before the theorists of the State, the theorists of the Church had resorted to the notion of a *potestas legibus soluta* to make good the claim of the medieval Papacy to world domination . . . The importance of the doctrine of sovereignty can hardly be overrated. It was . . . a decisive factor in the making of modern Europe . . . But it also appeared to undermine the very possibility of natural law thinking. Natural law is not properly law if sovereignty is the essential condition of legal experience. It is not possible to conceive a law of nature if command is the essence of the law.[6]

As *Island of Palmas* itself points out, however, sovereignty is not an immutable concept—'Manifestations of territorial sovereignty assume, it is true, different forms, according to conditions of time and place'.[7] This qualification should not

---

[4] On *Breisach* see G Schwarzenberger, *International Law as Applied by International Courts and Tribunals, Vol II: The Law of Armed Conflict* (Stevens, London, 1968) at 462–66. There is a voluminous literature on the principal German trial, the Nuremberg Trial of the Major German War Criminals, but much less on the Tokyo trials and those held by the Allies in Germany. Accordingly, it is perhaps worth noting some recent monographs that examine these latter examples—T Maga, *Judgment at Tokyo: the Japanese War Crimes Trials* (University Press of Kentucky, Lexington, 2001); P Maguire, *Law and War: An American Story* (Columbia University Press, New York, 2001); and BVA Röling and A Cassese, *The Tokyo Trial and Beyond* (Polity Press, Cambridge, 1993).

[5] *Island of Palmas Case (Netherlands v USA)* (1928) 2 RIAA 829 at 838.

[6] AP d'Entrèves, *Natural Law: an Introduction to Legal Philosophy* (2nd edn, Hutchinson, London, 1970) at 67, note omitted and paragraph break suppressed: see ch 5 generally. On Bodin and sovereignty, see—for instance—CJ Friedrich, *The Philosophy of Law in Historical Perspective*, (2nd edn, University of Chicago Press, Chicago, 1963) at 57 *et seq*; and HF Jolowicz, *Lectures on Jurisprudence* (Athlone Press/University of London, London, 1963) at 73–76.

[7] *Island of Palmas case*, n 5 above, at 840.

be surprising as the award also contains the classic statement of the inter-temporal rule.[8] Indeed, the rigid and impermeable notion of sovereignty expressed in *Island of Palmas*—'this principle of the exclusive competence of the State in regard to its own territory'[9]—has itself been supplanted by developments in the international legal order such as the emergence of international organisation and the contemporary human rights regime.[10] As the Appeals Chamber of the International Criminal Tribunal for the Former Yugoslavia has noted, although there was once:

> a period when sovereignty stood as a sacrosanct and unassailable attribute of state-hood, recently this concept has suffered progressive erosion at the hands of the more liberal forces at work in the democratic societies, particularly in the field of human rights.[11]

The recognition of this is simply to restate the initial question—is the primacy of State sovereignty being challenged by international assertions of jurisdiction that rely essentially on claims of moral value? Further, if this is the case, should it be conceded that the positivist account of law which dominated the nineteenth and twentieth centuries has been displaced by some form of value-laden natural law? The issue is structural; whether certain (identifiable) values can exert a pre-eminent effect that overrides established legal prescriptions without further ado. It is not a question of moral values entering into the political process such that existing law is changed, but rather whether these values simply override conflicting substantive law. This would negate the distinction Raz draws between deliberative and executive reasons in deciding what action should be taken:

> only 'executive' reasons, reasons the existence of which can be established without invoking moral arguments, are legal reasons.[12]

If pre-eminent values exist, whose simple invocation is sufficient to displace conflicting or constraining substantive law, then the positivist agenda has been discarded.[13] We would be witnessing the emergence of a legal alchemy able to

---

[8] *Island of Palmas case, ibid,* at 845—'A judicial fact must be appreciated in the light of the law contemporary with it, and not of the law in force at the time such a dispute in regard to it arises or falls to be settled.' For a recent critical exegesis of this doctrine, see R Higgins, 'Some observations on the inter-temporal rule in international law', in J Makarczyk (ed), *Theory of International Law at the Threshold of the 21st Century: Essays in Honour of Krzysztof Skubiszewski* (Kluwer, The Hague, 1996) at 173.

[9] *Island of Palmas case,* n 5 above, at 838.

[10] For a leading recent account, see TM Franck, *The Empowered Self: Law and Society in the Age of Individualism* (Oxford University Press, Oxford, 1999).

[11] *Prosecutor v Duško Tadić:* decision on the defence motion for interlocutory appeal on jurisdiction (2 Oct 1995), (1996) 35 ILM 32 at 50, para 55.

[12] J Raz, *The Concept of a Legal System,* (2nd edn, Clarendon Press, Oxford, 1980), at 213–14: quotation at 214.

[13] I do not wish here to pursue related issues of 'relative normativity'—on this, see P Weil, 'Towards Relative Normativity?' (1983) 77 *AJIL* 413; J Tasioulas, 'In Defence of Relative Normativity: Communitarian Values and the *Nicaragua* case' (1996) 16 *OJLS* 84; and J Beckett, 'Behind Relative Normativity: Rules and Process as Prerequisites of Law' (2001) 12 *EJIL* 627.

transform State behaviour that is unlawful (if not criminal) to that which is lawful (and thus legitimate).

2. THE INTERNATIONAL ADMINISTRATION OF TERRITORY

A clear example of precisely this form of reasoning preceded the 'internationalisation' of Kosovo. On 23 May 2000, the House of Commons Select Committee on Foreign Affairs issued a report examining Operation Allied Force, the NATO bombing campaign undertaken in March 1999 as a response to Serbian repression of Kosovo. This noted:

> The Government has consistently asserted that the military action taken in the Kosovo campaign has been lawful, and that NATO would not have acted outside the principles of international law. The then Minister of State told the Committee that the Government had determined that the action threatened in October 1998 would have been lawful, and the Foreign Secretary was also clear that there was a legal base for the action which began in March 1999. Both Ministers told us that states had the right to use force in the case of 'overwhelming humanitarian necessity where, in the light of all the circumstances, a limited use of force is justifiable as the only way to avert a humanitarian catastrophe.'[14]

After reviewing the provisions of the UN Charter on the use of force, the Select Committee concluded that '*Operation Allied Force* was contrary to the specific terms of what might be termed the basic law of the international community—the United Nations Charter',[15] and also rejected legal reliance on the dogma of humanitarian intervention.[16] The discourse then shifted to another plane:

> Disputes about international law are not ones which this Committee can resolve, but there is a separate question of morality . . . Whether NATO action was lawful is a very different question from whether NATO action was right.[17]

The opinion then expressed was that Operation Allied Force 'if of dubious legality in the current state of international law, was justified on moral grounds'.[18] Although the United Kingdom was only one of the NATO Member States participating in this operation, NATO employed a similar humanitarian argument in its justification.[19]

---

[14] House of Commons Select Committee on Foreign Affairs, Session 1999–2000, *Fourth Report: Kosovo* (HMSO, London, 2000) vol I, para 124: notes omitted. This report is also at: http://www.publications.parliament.uk/pa/cm199900/cmselect/cmfaff/28/2802.htm. The paragraphs under consideration are found under the *International law* hyperlink. The Government's reply to this report may be found at http://files.fco.gov.uk/fac/4aug00.pdf.
[15] *Ibid* para 128.
[16] *Ibid* paras 129–32.
[17] *Ibid* para 137.
[18] *Ibid* para 138.
[19] See, for instance, the 23 March 1999 press statement issued by NATO Secretary General Solana http://www.nato.int/docu/pr/1999/p99-040e.htm and the transcript of the 25 March 1999 NATO press conference http://www.nato.int/kosovo/press/p990325a.htm.

Further, acting under Chapter VII of the Charter, the Security Council authorised the UN Secretary-General to create an international civil administration for
Kosovo, as it was:

> Determined to resolve the grave humanitarian situation in Kosovo, Federal Republic
> of Yugoslavia, and to provide for the safe and free return of all refugees and displaced
> persons to their homes.[20]

Similar humanitarian sentiments were expressed in Security Council Resolution
1264 that noted the Indonesian readiness to accept the presence of a peacekeeping force in East Timor[21] and invited the Secretary-General 'to plan and prepare
for a United Nations transitional administration in East Timor, incorporating a
United Nations peacekeeping operation'.[22] This humanitarian concern was reaffirmed in Security Council Resolution 1272 which recorded that is was '*deeply
concerned* by the grave humanitarian situation arising from violence in East
Timor'[23] and, again acting under Chapter VII of the Charter, established the
United Nations Transitional Administration in East Timor (UNTAET):

> which will be endowed with overall responsibility for the administration of East
> Timor and will be empowered to exercise all legislative and executive authority,
> including the administration of justice.[24]

Security Council Resolution 1244, authorising the establishment of the United
Nations Interim Administration in Kosovo (UNMIK), is less concise in the enu-
meration of the powers conferred on that body but it is clear that these amount
to the full panoply of governance.[25] Although it has been claimed that the political institutions that have been established in both East Timor and Kosovo 'are
based on the idea of good governance, following the principle of democracy,
which is firmly established in Public International Law',[26] nonetheless:

> Even if there are traces of self-determination, particularly in East-Timor, the power
> of final decision remains with the UN-administration in all areas of government.
> There is no effective performance of autonomous government.[27]

---

[20] Security Council Resolution 1244 (10 June 1999), preambular para 4, SC/RES/1244(1999), http://www.un.org/Docs/scres/1999/99sc1244.htm, and also (1999) 38 ILM 14: the authorisation to the Secretary-General is contained in operative para 10 of resolution 1244. See also MJ Matheson, 'United Nations Governance of Post-Conflict Societies' (2001) 95 *AJIL* 76, at 78 *et seq.*

[21] Security Council Resolution 1264 (15 Sept 1999), preambular para 10, SC/RES/1264(1999), http://www.un.org/Docs/scres/1999/99sc1264.htm, and also (2000) 39 ILM 232. See also Matheson, *ibid* at 81 *et seq.*

[22] Security Council Resolution 1264, operative para 11.

[23] Security Council Resolution 1272 (25 Oct 1999), preambular para 10, SC/RES/1272(1999), http://www.un.org/Docs/scres/1999/99sc1272.htm, and also (2000) 39 ILM 240.

[24] Security Council Resolution 1272, operative para 1.

[25] See, in particular, Security Council Resolution 1244, operative paras 10 and 11.

[26] M Ruffert, 'The Administration of Kosovo and East Timor by the Internatioal Community' (2001) 50 *ICLQ* 613, at 624, notes omitted: see 624–26 for an account of the involvement of the local population in the international administration.

[27] Ruffert, *ibid* at 627.

The extent of these powers is underlined by the first regulation issued by the UN administrations in both territories which defined their authority. Both provided that '[a]ll legislative and administrative authority with respect to the [territory], is vested' in the UN administration and exercised by the Special Representative of the Secretary-General (in the case of Kosovo) or the Transitional Administrator (in the case of East Timor).[28] Only the East Timor regulation expressly provided for any—albeit limited—involvement of the local population in the administration from the outset. Section 1.1 of UNTAET regulation 1999/1 stipulated:

> In exercising these functions, the Transitional Administrator shall consult and co-operate closely with representatives of the East Timorese people.

This was initially implemented by UNTAET regulation 1999/2 (2 December 1999) which established a National Consultative Council. Under section 1.2, it was to be:

> the primary mechanism through which the representatives of the people of East Timor shall actively participate in the decision making process during the period of the United Nations Transitional Administration in East Timor, and through which the views, concerns, traditions and interests of the East Timorese people will be represented.

This Council was subsequently replaced by a National Council, established by UNTAET regulation 2000/24 (14 July 2000) with the aim 'of establishing a legislative mechanism that further enhances the participation of the East Timorese people in the decision-making process during the period of the transitional administration in East Timor', although draft regulations endorsed by the Council are subject to approval by the Transitional administrator.[29]

In Kosovo, local participation in the conduct of its affairs was effected primarily by UNMIK regulation 2000/1 which created the Joint Interim Administrative Structure to allow 'representatives of political forces of Kosovo [to] share provisional administrative authority with UNMIK'. Even so, the 'Special Representative of the Secretary-General retains legislative and administrative authority'.[30] Subsequently regulation 2001/9 established a constitutional framework for provisional self-government to develop 'meaningful self-government in Kosovo pending a final settlement, and establishing provisional institutions of self-government in the legislative, executive and judicial fields through the participa-

---

[28] S 1.1 of both UNMIK reg 1999/1 (25 July 1999) reproduced at http://www.un.org/peace/kosovo/pages/regulations/ and UNTAET regulation 1999/1 (27 Nov 1999), http://www.un.org/peace/etimor/untaetR/. The Transitional Administrator of East Timor is also a Special Representative of the Secretary-General: *see Report of the Secretary-General on Transitional Administration in East Timor*, S/2000/53, (26 Jan 2000), http://www.un.org/peace/etimor/docs/0026162e.htm, para 3.

[29] Reg 2000/24, preambular para 4 and s 2.3. Subsequent political developments were enacted in Reg 2001/2 (16 March 2001), *On the Election of a Constituent Assembly to Prepare a Constitution for an Independent and Democratic East Timor*; 2001/28 (19 Sept 2001), *On the Establishment of the Council of Ministers*; and 2002/1 (16 Jan 2002), *On the Election of the First President of an Independent and Democratic East Timor*.

[30] UNMIK Reg 2000/1 (14 Jan 2000), 1.a.

tion of the people of Kosovo in free and fair elections'.[31] Although this aimed at 'the further development of self-government in Kosovo',[32] the power to enact legislation still remained with the Special Representative.[33] Moreover, the action of the self-government institutions 'shall not in any way affect or diminish the ultimate authority of the [Special Representative] for the implementation of [Security Council Resolution] 1244 (1999)[34] which, *inter alia*, reaffirmed 'the commitment of all Member States to the sovereignty and territorial integrity of the Federal Republic of Yugoslavia'.[35]

The international administrations of Kosovo and East Timor by the United Nations[36] constitute the most manifest and extensive contemporary assertions of an international jurisdiction that acts as a substitute for traditional State (or territorial) sovereignty. Both exhibit a curious resonance with Wilsonian ideals of the putative ethnic State. But both surely must raise the question whether any international organisation, even the United Nations, can adequately and effectively exercise jurisdiction over territory.[37] For instance, in both the United Nations has clearly exercised functions that normally pertain to a State, but without practical experience in governance:

> In recent cases where the United Nations has been asked to assume the administration of local government (as in East Timor and Kosovo), available mission staff had no expertise in sectoral service delivery such as road repair, electrical power, water supply, medical care, or educational services.[38]

The scope of these administrations stands in contrast to the arrangements made for Danzig as 'a Free City . . . placed under the protection of the League of Nations'.[39] Both Kosovo and East Timor have been administered by an international official infinitely more powerful than the League High Commissioner for

---

[31]   UNMIK Reg 2001/9 (15 May 2001), introductory para 4. This was supplemented by Reg 2001/19 (13 Sept 2001), *On the Executive Branch of the Provisional Institutions of Self-Government in Kosovo*.

[32]   Reg 2001/9, preambular para 6.

[33]   See Reg 2001/9, s 9.1.45.

[34]   Reg 2001/9, preambular para 10: see also ch 12.

[35]   Security Council Resolution 1244 (1999), preambular para 10.

[36]   See Matheson, 'United Nations Governance', n 20 above at 77; Ruffert, 'The Administration of Kosovo and East Timor', n 26 above at 614–16; and Wilde, 'From Danzig to East Timor', n 3 above, *passim* for the analysis of earlier examples of UN administration of territory.

[37]   Ruffert, *ibid*, recalls that under Art 81 of the UN Charter, the UN itself can act as the administering authority of a trust territory, but it has never exercised this power. East Timor and Kosovo have not formally been placed under the trusteeship system and Kosovo, as a constituent part of Yugoslavia, cannot become a trust territory by virtue of Art 78 of the Charter—see 615, 621–22 and 629. For exegesis of Arts 78 and 81, see JP Cot and A Pellet (eds), *La Charte des Nations Unies: Commentaire Article par Article*, (2nd edn, Economica, Paris, 1991), at 1139–1142 and 1163–1176; and B Simma (ed), *The Charter of the United Nations: A Commentary* (2nd edn, Oxford University Press, Oxford, 2002) at 1117–18 and 1121–22.

[38]   R Wedgwood and HK Jacobson, 'Foreword to Symposium: State Reconstruction after Civil Conflict' (2001) 95 *AJIL* 1 at 2. This practical problem has been acknowledged by the UN—see the *Report of the Panel on United Nations Peace Operations* (the Brahimi report), A/55/305–S/2000/80(21 Aug 2000), http://www.un.org/peace/reports/peace.operations, para 77 and 127 *et seq*.

[39]   Art 102, Treaty of Versailles, http://www.yale.edu/lawweb/avalon/imt/. On the status of Danzig during the inter-war period, see *Danzig and the ILO* (Advisory Opinion), (1930) PCIJ Ser.C, No 18 (II); Crawford, n 3 above at 163–66; Verzijl, n 3, above at 510 *et seq*; MM Lewis, 'The Free City of

Danzig, whose powers were closely circumscribed by Article 103 of the Treaty of Versailles:

> The High Commissioner will . . . be entrusted with the duty of dealing in the first instance with all differences arising between Poland and the Free City of Danzig in regard to this Treaty or any arrangements or agreements made thereunder.

In both Kosovo and East Timor the Secretary General's Special Representative exercises powers more akin to that of a colonial administrator who is ultimately possessed of all legislative and executive authority, albeit that consultative assemblies exist in both territories. In contrast, Danzig had a popularly elected legislature—the Senate—whose actions were constrained by a constitution, guaranteed by the League. The constitutionality of its actions were subject to review by the League Council and, ultimately, by the Permanent Court.[40]

In East Timor and Kosovo, the United Nations has displaced the State and exercises State functions, but it is patently not a State and lacks the attributes of a State. Thorny yet practically important questions arise, such whether the United Nations could exercise diplomatic protection over the inhabitants of these territories should injury occur for which some State is responsible,[41] or even whether

Danzig' (1924) 5 *BYIL* 89; IFD Morrow, 'The International Status of the Free City of Danzig' (1937) 11 *BYIL* 114; and also CM Kimmich, *The Free City: Danzig and German Foreign Policy 1919–1934* (Yale University Press, New Haven, 1968).

Danzig's status as a Free City was, of course, a compromise between the ethnic self-determination of its predominantly German population, and that of Poland which had been guaranteed access to the Baltic Sea in Wilson's Fourteen Points—on this, see E Goldstein, *Winning the Peace: British Diplomatic Strategy, Peace Planning, and the Paris Peace Conference 1916–1920* (Clarendon Press, Oxford, 1991) at 144–46; Kimmich, *ibid* at 3–22; Lewis, *ibid* at 89–90; and Morrow, *ibid* at 115–16 who describes it as 'a compromise that satisfied nobody and subsequently caused innumerable disputes' (at 115).

See also CA Whomersley, 'The International Legal Status of Gdansk, Klaipeda, and the Former East Prussia', (1993) 42 *ICLQ* 99—who points out that Danzig's status as a Free City has not been altered by any subsequent treaty provision, thus Poland's post-WWII incorporation of Danzig apparently rests simply on general acquiescence (926–27). This situation has been challenged by Danzig's purported 'government-in-exile' which applied for UN membership in 1998—see http://www.danzig-freestate.org/unmembership.html.

[40]   The Danzig constitution was placed 'under the guarantee of the League' by Art 103 of the Treaty of Versailles. Although constitutional issues arose in the *Treatment of Polish Nationals and other Persons of Polish Origin or Speech in the Danzig Territory* (Advisory Opinion) (1932) PCIJ Ser. A/B, No 44. The Permanent Court decisively exercised its powers of judicial review in the *Consistency of Certain Danzig Legislative Decrees with the Constitution of the Free City* (Advisory Opinion) (1935) PCIJ Ser.A/B, No 65).

[41]   Draft Art 1 of the ILC draft Articles on diplomatic protection defines diplomatic protection as 'action taken by a State against another State in respect of an injury to the person or property of a national caused by an internationally wrongful act or omission attributable to another state'—See JR Dugard, Special Rapporteur, *First Report on Diplomatic Protection* A/CN.4/506 (7 March 2000) 11. Further, under the definitive Articles dealing with the *Responsibility of States for Internationally Wrongful Acts*, A/CN.4/L.602/Rev.1 (26 July 2001), adopted by the ILC in Aug 2001 and approved by the General Assembly in resolution 56/83, A/RES/56/83 (12 Dec 2001), Art 44. a makes the invocation of the responsibility of a State dependent on satisfaction of the nationality of claims rule. The UN is not a State, nor are the inhabitants of Kosovo and East Timor its nationals—a point reinforced for Kosovars by 1.2 of UNMIK Reg 2000/18 (29 March 2000), *On Travel Documents*, which provides 'The travel document does not confer nationality upon its holder, nor does it affect in any way the holder's nationality'. It is worth noting that Art 104.6 of the Treaty of Versailles made express provision for the diplomatic protection of Danzig citizens by Poland—see Lewis, 'The Free City of Danzig', n 39 above at 94; and Morrow, 'The International Status of the Free City of Danzig', n 39 above at 117.

the United Nations itself could be responsible for delictual actions of its agent, namely the administering authority.[42] Furthermore, on 10 February 2000, the administering authority in East Timor concluded an Exchange of Notes with Australia continuing the terms of the 1989 Timor Gap Treaty[43] during the transitional period preceding East Timor's independence.[44] Although it has been claimed that treaty making power was conferred on UNTAET by operative paragraph 4 of SC resolution 1272, which authorises 'UNTAET to take all necessary measures to fulfil its mandate',[45] this is a clear exercise of a power which international law expressly designates as an attribute of sovereignty and thus, as such, reserved for the State.[46]

The unanswered—and doctrinally neglected—question is the identification of the legal framework that governs these administered territories. The powers exercised by the Secretary General's Special Representative go far beyond those that might legitimately be exercised by a belligerent occupant[47]—for instance, in East Timor, the agreement with Australia that allows the *de novo* exploitation of Timor Gap hydrocarbon resources;[48] and in Kosovo, the whole-scale alteration of the legal system to make it conform to the law in force on 22

---

[42] Art 57 of the ILC's 2001 articles on the *Responsibility of States for Internationally Wrongful Acts* expressly excludes 'any question of the responsibility under international law of an international organisation, or of any State for the conduct of an international organisation' from the ambit of the articles. On organisational responsibility, see I Scobbie, 'International Organisations and International Relations', in RJ Dupuy (ed), *Manuel sur les Organisations Internationales*, (2nd edn, Nijhoff, Dordrecht, 1998) at 831 at 886 *et seq*; the materials cited therein; and also R Higgins, 'The Responsibility of States Members for the Defaults of International Organisations: Continuing the Dialogue', in S Schlemmer-Schulte and K-Y Tung (eds), *Liber Amicorum Ibrahim Fi Shihata* (Kluwer, The Hague, 2001) 441. Ruffert's argument (see n 26 above at 630), based on draft Art 9 of the 1996 ILC draft articles is presumably superceded by Art 57 (2001).

[43] 11 Dec 1989 Australia/Indonesia Treaty on the Zone of Co-operation in an Area between the Indonesian Province of East Timor and Northern Australia, reproduced (1990) 29 ILM 469; and, with a commentary, in JI Charney and LM Alexander (eds), *International Maritime Boundaries* (ASIL/Nijhoff, The Hague, 1993), vol II, at 1245. For a detailed analysis of the provisions of the treaty, see A Bergin, 'the Australian-Indonesian Timor Gap Maritime Boundary Agreement' (1990) 5 *International Journal of Estuarine and Coastal Law* 383; and WT Onorato and MJ Valencia, 'International Cooperation for Petroleum Development: the Timor Gap Treaty' (1990) 5 *ICSID Review* 1.

[44] For details of the treaty between UNTAET and Australia, see G Triggs, 'Legal and Commercial Risks of Investment in the Timor Gap' (2000) 1 *Melbourne JIL* 98 at 99–105.

[45] Triggs, *ibid* 102: *contra* Ruffert, n 26 above at 630.

[46] See Art 77, 1982 UN Law of the Sea Convention and Art 2, 1958 Geneva Continental Shelf Convention. In the *North Sea Continental Shelf* cases, the International Court of Justice ruled that Art 2 expressed custom—see (1969) ICJ Rep, 3 at 38–39, para 63.

[47] On the powers of a beligerent occupant, see E Benvenisti, *The International Law of Occupation* (Princeton UP, Princeton, NJ, 1993); L Oppenheim, *International Law: a Treatise Vol II: Disputes, War and Neutrality*, 7th edn by H Lauterpacht (Longmans, London, 1952) at 430 *et seq*; I Scobbie, 'Natural Resources and Belligerent Occupation: Mutation through Permanent Sovereignty', in S Bowen (ed), *Human Rights, Self-Determination and Political Change in the Occupied Palestinian Territories* (Nijhoff, The Hague, 1997) 221; and G von Glahn, *The Occupation of Enemy Territory: a Commentary on the Law and Practice of Belligerent Occupation* (University of Minnesota Press, Minneapolis, 1957).

[48] See Scobbie, n 47 above at 234 *et seq*.

March 1989.[49] Further, in both, the applicable indigenous law—which is, more-over, subordinate to regulations enacted by the administering authority—shall not be applied unless it complies with the 1948 Universal Declaration of Human Rights; 1966 International Covenant on Civil and Political Rights (plus protocols); 1966 International Covenant on Economic, Social and Cultural Rights; 1965 Convention on the Elimination of Racial Discrimination; 1979 Women's Convention; 1984 Torture Convention; 1989 Children's Convention; and, in the case of Kosovo, the 1950 European Convention on Human Rights (plus protocols).[50] As the *Brahimi report* pointed out:

> These missions' tasks would have been much easier if a common United Nations justice package had allowed them to apply an interim legal code to which mission personnel could have been pre-trained while the final answer to the 'applicable law' question was being worked out . . . [S]ome headway toward dealing with the problem has been made outside the United Nations system, emphasizing the principles, codes and procedures contained in several dozen international conventions and declarations relating to human rights, humanitarian law, and guidelines for police, prosecutors and penal systems.[51]

'*Several dozen*'? Although undoubtedly laudable, by imposing diverse human rights norms, is it simply that, by deciding on the international administration of a territory, the Security Council can arrogate powers to Special Representatives as it sees fit in order that they might effectively act as benign colonial administrators? The motivation for the administration of these territories was the protection of human rights, but was this an instance of moral value imposing itself on the international legal order? Apparently not, because the Security Council, in both cases, established the administrations relying on Chapter VII powers. Accordingly, despite the novelty of this form of international administration, it is not a recognition of the pre-eminence of value. In Raz's terms, the value impetus was confined to the determinative, not the executive, phase of action.

Nevertheless, there remains the imposition upon the territories, albeit indirectly, of international human rights instruments as the pre-eminent standards of validity within their legal systems. Instruments, it should be noted, to all of which not all of the permanent members of the Security Council themselves subscribe. It can easily be argued that the use of these instruments emanates from the desire to protect and advance human rights in the territories, that they simply set standards that give definition to this contemporary manifestation of a 'sacred trust of

[49] This was effected by UNMIK Reg 1999/24 (12 Dec 1999), as amended by Reg 2000/59 (27 Oct 2000). Reg 1999/24 itself amended Reg 1999/1 (25 July 1999) which provided that the applicable law was that in force before 24 March 1999. Under Art 43 of the Hague Regulations, a belligerent occupant 'shall take all the measures in his power to restore, and ensure, as far as possible, public order and safety, while respecting, unless absolutely prevented, the laws in force in the country'. The classic exegesis of this provision is E Schwenk, 'Legislative Power of the Military Occupant under Article 43, Hague Regulations' (1944–1945) 54 *Yale LJ* 393.
[50] See UNTAET Reg 1999/1 (27 Nov 1999) ss 2 and 3; UNMIK Reg 1999/24 s 1 and 2000/59 s 1.
[51] *Brahimi report*, n 38 above para 81: on the issue of the applicable law, see paras 76–83.

civilisation'. Given the claims made for (at least) an emerging right to democratic government, however, one might wonder whether this enterprise can lay claim to only an attenuated notion of legitimacy.[52] Although the populations of East Timor and Kosovo might well agree with these dominant values of administration, they did not choose them. Given the motivation to protect human rights, should any effective democratic control devolving upon the inhabitants be excluded? The consultative assemblies may propose, but the Special Representatives most definitely dispose. Like despots, albeit benevolent, they are not accountable to the indigenous populations.

3. STATE CRIMINALITY

The notion of government accountability—or democratic entitlement from another viewpoint—has, however, a wider compass. In at least some cases, it surely must be implicated in the ascription of criminal responsibility to States if this idea is to have any moral integrity. It is true that draft Article 19 of the *Draft Articles on State Responsibility* adopted by the International Law Commission in 1996, which defined international crimes of State, was excised from the Commission's final 2001 Articles on the *Responsibility of States for Internationally Wrongful Acts*.[53] Despite the deletion of draft Article 19, it is not otiose to discuss the idea of State criminality. If nothing else, the existence of the idea is assuredly not dependent on the continued existence of the draft Article.[54] Moreover, the terms by which the General Assembly endorsed these Articles, without vote, in resolution 56/83[55] leaves their normative status (and content) open. The second preambular paragraph noted:

> that the International Law Commission decided to recommend to the General Assembly that it take note of the draft articles in a resolution and annex the draft

---

[52] The seminal article on this alleged right is TM Franck, 'The Emerging Right to Democratic Governance' (1992) 86 *AJIL* 46: see also his *Empowered Self*, n 10 above ch 10. A useful collection of essays on this issue is GH Fox and BR Roth (eds), *Democratic Governance and International Law* (Cambridge University Press, Cambridge, 2000).

[53] n 41 above. The status of this Article had been placed in abeyance in 1998 by the Commission—see J Crawford, *The International Law Commission's Articles on State Responsibility: Introduction, Text and Commentaries* (Cambridge University Press, Cambridge, 2002) 27.

[54] There is an extensive literature on crimes of States, see for instance, G Abi-Saab, 'The Uses of Article 19' (1999) 10 *EJIL* 339; I Brownlie, *International Law and the Use of Force by States* (Clarendon Press, Oxford, 1963) 150–66, and *System of the Law of Nations. State Responsibility (Part One)* (Clarendon Press, Oxford, 1983) 32–33; G Gaja, 'Should all References to International Crimes Disappear from the ILC Draft Articles on State Responsibility?' (1999) 10 *EJIL* 365; A de Hoogh, *Obligations Erga Omnes and International Crimes* (Kluwer, The Hague, 1996); A Pellet, 'Can a State Commit a Crime? Definitely, Yes!' (1999) 10 *EJIL* 425; S Rosenne, 'State Responsibility and International Crimes: Further Reflections on Article 19 of the Draft Articles on State Responsibility', (1997–1998) 30 *New York University JILP* 145; and J Weiler *et al* (eds), *International Crimes of State* (de Gruyter, Berlin, 1989).

[55] A/RES/56/83 (12 Dec 2001).

articles to the resolution, and that it consider at a later stage, and in the light of the importance of the topic, the possibility of convening an international conference of plenipotentiaries to examine the draft articles with a view to concluding a convention on the topic.[56]

This recommendation was reflected in operative paragraph 3 of resolution 56/83, in which the General Assembly took note of the Articles and commended 'them to the attention of Governments without prejudice to the question of their future adoption or other appropriate action'. 1996 draft Article 19.2 had provided:

> An internationally wrongful act which results from the breach by a State of an international obligation so essential for the protection of fundamental interests of the international community that its breach is recognised as a crime by that community as a whole, constitutes an international crime.[57]

The French observations on this draft Article[58] are enlightening. Inter alia these noted that the draft Article confused two concepts each embedded in the term 'State', namely:

1. the State in terms of the organs of government, whose activities might give rise to the individual criminal responsibility of those involved in the exercise of governmental functions—ie 'all organs which carry out functions of State authorities, whether of a government, of public offices, or even, in certain cases, of a political party, the members or leaders of which may see their criminal responsibility implicated'; and

2. the notion of the State as 'a more abstract legal entity, characterized by a territory, a population and institutions, an entity which is not, in essence, either good or bad, just or unjust, innocent or culpable'. In this connection, France commented that there 'is a great danger that, if an attempt is made to impose sanctions on a State, its population will be punished'.[59]

The first notion encapsulates the notion of individual criminal responsibility employed by the International Military Tribunal at Nuremberg in the *Trial of the Major German War Criminals,* namely that '[c]rimes against international law are committed by men, not by abstract entities'.[60] With the second, France's complaint appears to be that the acceptance of draft Article 19 could too easily mean that the civilian population as a whole, rather than only the officials directly respon-

---

[56] On the Commission's recommendation, see International Law Commission, *Report on the Work of its Fifty-Third Session (23 April–1 June and 2 July–10 August 2001),* A/56/10, 38–41, paras 61–67; and Crawford, n 53 above at 57–61.

[57] Reproduced, with commentary, http://www.law.cam.ac.uk/rcil/ILCSR/Arts.htm.

[58] Observations of France, http://www.law.cam.ac.uk/rcil/ILCSR/France.rtf, s I.2.A, 4–7.

[59] Both definitions, *ibid* at 7 para (h).

[60] *Trial of the Major German War Criminals (In re Goering and others)* (1946) 13 AnnDig 203 at 221. Given the theme of positivism that underlies this paper, for the argument that the International Military Tribunal rejected positivist based defences in this trial, see SL Paulson, 'Classical Legal Positivism at Nuremberg' (1975) 4 *Philosophy and Public Affairs* 132; and also N Koch, 'Classical Legal Positivism at Nuremberg Considered' (1977) 9 *Case Western Reserve JIL* 161.

sible, would bear the brunt of any adverse measures imposed. It is not difficult to envision examples that fit into this mould; the most obvious contemporary being the impact of sanctions upon Iraq, and historically, possibly the effect post-World War One reparations had upon Germany.

The notion, however, of punishing whole populations dates back to classic publicists of international law such as Vitoria:

> *the whole commonwealth may lawfully be punished for the sin its monarch.* If a sovereign wages an unjust war against another prince, the injured party may plunder and pursue all the other rights of war against the sovereign's subjects, even if they are innocent of offence. The reason is that once the sovereign has been duly constituted by the commonwealth, if he permits any injustice in the exercise of his office the blame lies with the commonwealth, since the commonwealth is held responsible for entrusting its power only to a man who will justly exercise any authority or executive power he may be given; in other words, it delegates power at its own risk. In the same way, anyone may lawfully be condemned for the wrongdoings of his appointed agent.[61]

Although hardly a democrat—'the best form of government is monarchy, just as the universe is controlled by a single Lord and Ruler'[62]—Vitoria is clear that moral blame should only devolve upon a population that has chosen, or allows itself to be led, by a prince who acts wrongfully.[63] Despite the claimed dissociation of State criminality from domestic notions of criminality,[64] surely alleging that a State has acted criminally implies a concomitant blame on the part of the population. This can be only a matter of morality not law. There can be no question of specifically ascribing individual criminal responsibility under international law to everyone. An allegation of State criminality, nevertheless, taints more than the culpable organs and officials. The nature of the obligations that must be breached to give rise to State criminality—aggression, genocide, apartheid[65]—must entail at least the complicity of the population, whether in whole or in significant part. At one extreme, there could be the truly popular commission of an 'international crime' where, with or without the instigation of or example set by the authorities, the population itself engages in the forbidden conduct. The obvious example here is genocide—for instance, that in Rwanda or, the example of 'ordinary Germans', if

---

[61] F deVitoria, 'On Civil Power (*De potestate ciuilli*) (1528), Question 1, Article 9', in A Pagden and J Lawrance (eds), *Francisco de Vitoria: Political Writings* (Cambridge University Press, Cambridge, 1991) 1 at 21: editorial footnote omitted.

[62] *Ibid, Question 1, Article 8* at 18–21: quotation at 20.

[63] Walzer argues, along the same lines, that reparations can be seen as collective punishments—see M Walzer, *Just and Unjust Wars* (2nd edn, Basic Books, New York, 1992) at 297: and also S Levinson, 'Responsibility for Crimes of War', in M Cohen *et al* (eds), *War and Moral Responsibility* (Princeton University Press, Princeton, 1974) 104 at 107–11. The prohibitions of taking reprisals against, taking hostage or levying collective punishments upon protected persons, which are closely related within the *corpus* of international humanitarian law, raise considerations which are not germane to the point in issue in the text.

[64] See Abi-Saab at 344–46 and Pellet at 433–34, n 54 above.

[65] Illustrative international crimes of State, such as these, were enumerated in Draft Art 19.3.

one accepts the Goldhagen thesis, 'pursuing German national political goals—in this case the genocidal killing of Jews':

> Germans' antisemitic beliefs about Jews were the central causal agent of the Holocaust. They were the central causal agent not only of Hitler's decision to annihilate European Jewry . . . but also of the perpetrators' willingness to kill and to brutalise Jews.[66]

This would be an ultimate example of Mill's fear of the 'tyranny of the majority'— 'the will of the most numerous or the most active *part* of the people—the majority, or those who succeed in making themselves accepted as the majority . . . "the tyranny of the majority" is now generally included among the evils against which society requires to be on its guard'.[67] As such, this is simply an abuse of popular dominion that (liberal) human rights guarantees are designed to forestall.

At the other end of the scale, where the population is not itself so directly implicated in the commission of the acts giving rise to the criminal responsibility of the State, does blame not presuppose—in contemporary terms—some degree of democratic control over the actions of the authorities? Ascribing moral blame surely postulates a failure to live up to defined standards of behaviour. Consequently, attributing moral blame to a population entails the judgement that a causal connection exists between that failure and the population's actions in terms of its abilities and opportunities to prevent that failure.[68] What would constitute this causal connection—would it be enough that the population acquiesced in the delicts of the government, whether or not that government was unrepresentative and perhaps repressive, or need there be evidence of the population validating or participating in the government's policies? As Walzer comments:

> free action is [not] impossible even in the worst of authoritarian regimes . . . But in democracies there are opportunities for positive response, and we need to ask to what extent these opportunities fix our obligations, when evil deeds are committed in our name . . . Democracy is a way of distributing responsibility (just as monarchy is a way of refusing to distribute it). But that doesn't mean that all adult citizens share equally in the blame we assign . . . Even in a perfect democracy, it cannot be said that every citizen is the author of every state policy, though every one of them can rightly be called to account.[69]

---

[66] DJ Goldhagen, *Hitler's Willing Executioners: Ordinary Germans and the Holocaust* (Little, Brown, London, 1996): quotations at 7 and 9 respectively. It must be emphasised that Goldhagen's thesis is controversial. Finkelstein comments that it 'is not at all a learned inquiry. Replete with gross misrepresentations of the secondary literature and internal contradictions, Goldhagen's book is worthless as scholarship'—NG Finkelstein and RB Birn, *A Nation on Trial: the Goldhagen Thesis and Historical Truth* (Henry Holt, New York, 1998) at 4.

[67] JS Mill, *On Liberty* (1859), ch 1, note omitted, in G Himmelfarb (ed), (Penguin, Harmondsworth, 1974, first published 1859) at 62.

[68] See, for instance, PA French, 'Morally Blaming Whole Populations', in V Held, S Morgenbesser and T Nagel (eds), *Philosophy, Morality, and International Affairs* (Oxford University Press, New York, 1974) at 266.

[69] Walzer, n 63, above at 298–99: paragraph break suppressed.

Regardless of the answer to this conundrum, to invoke the criminal responsibility of a State must entail concurrently blaming the whole population of that State for the activities of its authorities. This can be seen as another attempt at breaking down the carapace of State sovereignty, and thus the notion of governmental accountability—democratic entitlement from another viewpoint—can be relevant to that of State criminality. If people are responsible for electing a government, are they not equally responsible for the policies it pursues?

In any event, although this notion does display a tendency towards value, it has not yet passed though the deliberative stage to executive adoption, being retained in the 2001 Articles on the *Responsibility of States for Internationally Wrongful Acts* in only a diluted form—'the text . . . is still haunted by the ghost of "international crime" '[70]—in Part Two, Chapter III which deals with serious breaches of obligations under peremptory norms of general international law.[71]

4. RESPONSIBILITY, RECONCILIATION AND THE ROME STATUTE

One might wonder, however, whether the notion of the criminal responsibility of States is counterproductive inasmuch as the concomitant blaming of whole populations, as opposed to only those individually responsible for the impugned acts, could hamper reconciliation and the return to 'normal' inter-State relations. A denounced population could, too easily, act like a beleaguered wagon train and pull a protective circle around itself.[72] Further, in connection with international crimes of State, Crawford has commented that:

> A significant development in recent years has been the establishment of an International Criminal Court. Events during the 1990s have shown again the limited results that can flow from the sanctioning of whole populations, and the dilemma of appearing to punish many in order to sanction a few controlling figures. Where humanitarian or other tragedies are produced, or exacerbated, by the criminal conduct of individual leaders (whether or not they are formally in government), responses against the 'State' or its people seem to miss the point. In the majority of cases of large scale criminal conduct, the people of the State concerned are, either directly or collaterally, victims. Mechanisms are now being developed—of which the Rome Statute is but one element—for holding the individuals involved accountable. In this enterprise, State responsibility has a role, but it is ancillary.[73]

---

[70] Japan, *State Responsibility: Comments and Observations Received from Governments*, A/CN.4/515 (19 March 2001), http://www.un.org/law/ilc/sessions/53/english/cn4515e. pdf, 48.

[71] See Crawford, n 54, above at 35 *et seq* and 242 *et seq*: see also the papers of the Florence symposium on this issue, forthcoming in the *European Journal of International Law* (2002).

[72] Compare H Lauterpacht, 'The Legal Aspect', in CAW Manning (ed), *Peaceful Change: an International Problem* (MacMillan, London, 1937) 135 at 152–53.

[73] J Crawford, *Third Report on State Responsibility*, A/CN.4/507/Add.4 (4 Aug 2000), 5–6, para 372: note omitted.

The Rome Statute of the International Criminal Court aims to provide remedial measures—both criminal and compensatory[74]—for violations of 'the most serious crimes of concern to the international community as a whole', and thus contribute to their prevention.[75] Accordingly it undoubtedly displays a clear commitment to the more effective realisation of the values embedded in human rights and humanitarian law norms. Despite this desire to protect values internationally, the Rome Statute is nevertheless firmly rooted in a Statist paradigm in the assertion of its jurisdiction.

The bases upon which the International Criminal Court is competent to exercise jurisdiction over the crimes within its competence are defined in Article 12.2:

> In the case of Article 13, paragraph (a) or (c), the Court may exercise its jurisdiction if one or more of the following States are Parties to this Statute or have accepted the jurisdiction of the Court in accordance with paragraph 3:
> (a) The State on the territory of which the conduct in question occurred or, if the crime was committed on board a vessel or aircraft, the State of registration of that vessel or aircraft;
> (b) The State of which the person accused of the crime is a national.

By making a link of territory or nationality a necessary threshold for the Court's competence in order that it can be seised of jurisdiction over a given case in the first place, the Court relies on the two most traditional and fundamental bases for the assertion of jurisdiction by a State under international law.

Under the Rome Statute, domestic courts have primacy in prosecution due to the principle of complementarity set out in Article 1. Thus the jurisdiction of the International Criminal Court is essentially residual, to be employed only where the relevant State party is unwilling or unable to prosecute an individual accused of an offence falling within the Court's jurisdiction. The situations in which a case is admissible before the Court are set out in Article 17.1 and 2:

> 2. In order to determine unwillingness in a particular case, the Court shall consider, having regard to the principles of due process recognized by international law, whether one or more of the following exist, as applicable:
> (a) The proceedings were or are being undertaken or the national decision was made for the purpose of shielding the person concerned from criminal responsibility for crimes within the jurisdiction of the Court referred to in Article 5;
> (b) There has been an unjustified delay in the proceedings which in the circumstances is inconsistent with an intent to bring the person concerned to justice;

---

[74] On compensation, see Arts 75 and 79 of the Rome Statute concerning compensation and requiring the creation of a Trust Fund 'for the benefit of victims of crimes within the jurisdiction of the Court, and of the families of such victims'. See also K Kittichaisaree, *International Criminal Law* (Oxford University Press, Oxford, 2001) at 323–24; and W Schabas, *An Introduction to the International Criminal Court* (Cambridge University Press, Cambridge, 2001) at 150.

[75] Rome Statute, preambular paras 4, 5 and 9.

(c) The proceedings were not or are not being conducted independently or impartially, and they were or are being conducted in a manner which, in the circumstances, is inconsistent with an intent to bring the person concerned to justice.

3. In order to determine inability in a particular case, the Court shall consider whether, due to a total or substantial collapse or unavailability of its national judicial system, the State is unable to obtain the accused or the necessary evidence and testimony or otherwise unable to carry out its proceedings.

The principal possible difficulty with this provision is its potential impact on non-penal methods of accountability employed to promote reconciliation after civil conflict which grant amnesties to those who have committed crimes falling within the Court's jurisdiction. Different views were expressed on this point during the drafting of the Statute, and subsequently by commentators.[76]

This issue encapsulates a tension that permeates the jurisdictional mechanisms of the Statute—that of deferring to State sovereignty by giving States the primary right to prosecute with the Court acting as a default mechanism, and that of ensuring the vindication of international obligations owed to the international community as a whole. The Statute provides no clear answer to this dilemma, but it has been suggested that a 'sincere' attempt at non-judicial accountability would be respected by the prosecutor, exercising discretion under Article 53.1.c, by concluding that an investigation of the alleged offences 'would not serve the interests of justice'.[77] The corollary is that an insincere or self-serving national process would not be so respected.

There is perhaps some recent international authority in support of this view. On 14 March 2001, in the *Barrios Altos* case (*Chumbipuma Aguirre et al v Peru*), the Inter-American Court of Human Rights was faced with amnesty laws granted to those involved in human rights abuses by Peru. This concerned the summary execution of fifteen people and the wounding of four others that had taken place in the Barrios Altos area of Lima in 1991. A judicial investigation of the crime did not begin until 1995, but was terminated by the amnesty laws. Before the Court, Peru eventually recognised its international responsibility for the violation of its human rights obligations. The Court commented that such amnesty laws were 'manifestly incompatible' with the Inter-American Convention on Human Rights, because they 'lead to the defenselessness of victims and perpetuate impunity'.[78] This test of 'manifest incompatibility' seems to be at least an indication of how the demands of State sovereignty and international entitlements could be balanced.

---

[76] See, for instance, Schabas, n 74, above at 68–69: and MP Scharf, 'Justice v Peace', in SB Sewall and C Kaysen (eds), *The United States and the International Criminal Court: National Security and International Law* (American Academy of Arts and Sciences, New York, 2000) at 179.

[77] For instance, see Schabas, n 74 above at 69.

[78] Summary report available at http://www.asil.org/ilib/ilib0410.htm#02: this is the archived copy of the American Society's electronic bulletin *International Law in Brief* issued on 9 Oct 2001.

Even so, it is not certain that International Criminal Court prosecutors would follow this example. Under Article 13, an investigation into an alleged crime can be initiated at the request of any State part to the Rome Statute, the Security Council, or on the prosecutor's own initiative. Once again, there appears to be room for a potential conflict between the protection of human rights and that of democratic entitlement. If a population employs a truth and reconciliation mechanism in order to secure an internal political settlement, does the international community have the right to disregard this and insist on prosecution—even where the norms in issue, such as an allegation of genocide, are obligations owed to the international community as a whole? If so, this would amount to the arrogation of a pre-emptive right by the international community, derived from a peremptory norm, to ignore a consensual domestic political settlement.

This, however, only illustrates a more general question regarding remedial action taken for the breach of obligations owed to the international community as a whole. Under Article 48.1 of the 2001 Articles on the *Responsibility of States for Internationally Wrongful Acts*, 'Any State other than an injured State is entitled to invoke the responsibility of another State . . . if . . . the obligation breached is owed to the international community as a whole'. By virtue of Article 48.3, this entitlement is made subject not only to the nationality of claims rule and the requirement to exhaust local remedies,[79] but also Article 45, which provides:[80]

> The responsibility of a State may not be invoked if:
> a. the injured State has validly waived the claim;
> b. the injured State is to be considered as having, by reason of its conduct, validly acquiesced in the lapse of the claim.

This poses the question whether an injured State—for instance, a victim of genocide—can block another's entitlement invoke responsibility under Article 48, even where the obligation breached is peremptory and owed to the international community as a whole. There is no clear answer: States have expressed divided views on the matter, with some arguing that the injured State can extinguish another's entitlement to invoke responsibility while others deny this possibility.[81]

This demonstrates an uncertainty at the heart of the normative structure of international law—what are the precise implications of peremptory norms that generate obligations owed to the international community as a whole? If a State elects not to take remedial action in respect of an injury caused to it by a breach of an obligation owed to the international community as a whole, can another State do so—whether by invoking the responsibility of the delinquent State or by requesting the investigation of an alleged offender by the International Criminal

---

[79] For commentary, see Crawford, n 53 above, at 264–65; and I Scobbie, 'The Invocation of Responsibility for the Breach of 'Obligations under Peremptory Norms of General International Law' (2002) 13 *EJIL* 1201.

[80] See Crawford, n 53 above at 266–69 and 280.

[81] See *State Responsibility: Comments and Observations Received from Governments*, A/CN.4/515 (19 March 2001), 67 (Korea), 68 (Netherlands), and 72 (United Kingdom).

Court? In short, can peremptory norms generate derivative obligations—the obligations to prosecute individuals or to seek redress against a delinquent State—which themselves are pre-emptive and set aside inconsistent domestic laws or decisions?

It cannot be denied that more or less transitory—at times even ephemeral—political considerations are reflected in law, but claims of pre-eminent or universal value are themselves political concepts which can influence, if not structure, substantive law. To illustrate this, one need only consider the theological component of some of the early American colonial compacts, such as the *Agreement of the Settlers at Exeter in New Hampshire, 1639*:

> Whereas it hath pleased the Lord to move the Heart of our dread Sovereigns Charles by the Grace of God King & c. to grant Licence and Libertye to sundry of his subjects to plant themselves in the Westerlle parts of America. We his loyal Subjects Brethern of the Church in Exeter situate and lying upon the River Pascataqua with other Inhabitants there, considering with ourselves the holy Will of God and o'er own Necessity that we should not live without wholesomne Lawes and Civil Government among us of which we are altogether destitute; do in the name of Christ and in the sight of God combine ourselves together to erect and set up among us such Government as shall be to our best discerning agreeable to the Will of God professing ourselves Subjects to our Sovereign Lord King Charles according to the Libertyes of our English Colony of Massachusetts, and binding of ourselves solemnly by the Grace and Help of Christ and in His Name and fear to submit ourselves to such Godly and Christian Lawes as are established in the realm of England to our best Knowledge, and to all other such Lawes which shall upon good grounds be made and enacted among us according to God that we may live quietly and peaceably together in all godliness and honesty.[82]

In the *Exeter Agreement*, theological considerations apparently performed legal alchemy; acting as a philosopher's stone transmuting value into law which at least implied a substantive benchmark for legal validity. The question, accordingly, is whether essentially secular human rights and humanitarian values have come to play a similar and as profound a role in the practice of contemporary international affairs?

This has not happened with the examples of the international assertion of jurisdiction considered. The international administration of Kosovo and East Timor was firmly rooted in powers the Security Council claims to possess under Chapter VII. The notion of international crimes of State is currently in legal abeyance, and its consequence of morally blaming populations perhaps too unexamined to be comfortable. The legal entitlement to pre-empt domestic reconciliation settlements, like the broader question of invoking responsibility where the injured State

---

[82] Text reproduced at http://www.yale.edu/lawweb/avalon/states/nh06.htm: see also the *Fundamental Agreement, or Original Constitution of the Colony of New Haven, June 4, 1639* http://www.yale.edu/lawweb/avalon/states/ct01.htm; the Connecticut *Fundamental Orders of 1639* http://www.yale.edu/lawweb/avalon/order.htm; and the 1620 *Mayflower Compact* http://www.law.ou.edu/hist/mayflow.htm.

desires not to do so, remains murky. All currently display an uneasy tension between human rights and democratic entitlement—a disquieting strain between values. Some might see this as a contradiction, but it would be more productive to decide on their relative importance and ranking. Undoubtedly value is important when deliberating about the substantive content of international law but, at least as far as these examples are concerned, value is not pre-emptive. If the implications of peremptory norms are not yet fully determined, can we really expect more diffuse autonomous moral values to override inconsistent law (whether domestic or international)?

3

The Exercise of Jurisdiction in Private International Law

JONATHAN HILL

1. INTRODUCTION

A. A Lack of Jurisdictional Theory in Private International Law?

(a) General Observations

Whereas there is a huge body of theoretical literature surrounding choice of law and related topics (such as characterisation, renvoi and the incidental question), theoretical aspects of international procedure have attracted less attention from commentators. Indeed, in the volume of the *International Encyclopedia of Comparative Law* devoted to private international law, international procedure is excluded from the chapter concerned with fundamental approaches on the ground that 'its principles are seldom analyzed.'[1] One commentator, writing in the 1960s, observed: 'While in all civilised countries much wisdom, inventiveness and energy have been spent in solving choice of law problems, only little attention has been given to questions concerning international procedure.'[2] While this almost certainly overstates the case, it is has to be conceded that the volume of theoretical literature on aspects of private international law seems to be in inverse proportion to its practical importance.[3]

It is not proposed to devote too much energy to ruminating on why this might be the case. Two suggestions may, however, be offered. First, Huber's *De Conflictu Legum Diversarum in Deversis Imperiis*,[4] which provides the origin of much think-

---

[1] G Kegel, *International Encyclopedia of Comparative Law* (Nijhoff, The Hague, 1986), vol III, ch 1 at 4 (s 2).

[2] LI de Winter, 'Excessive Jurisdiction in Private International Law' (1968) 17 *ICLQ* 706.

[3] Compare, for example, the wealth of material referred to by L Collins (ed), *Dicey & Morris on the Conflict of Laws* (13th edn, Sweet & Maxwell, London, 2000) on topics such as characterisation, the incidental question and renvoi (at 33, n 1; 45, n 68; 65, n 1) with the literature on jurisdiction and judgments (at 385, n 1; 467, n 1).

[4] For Huber's text and an English translation see EG Lorenzen, 'Huber's De Conflictu Legum' in *Selected Articles on the Conflict of Laws* (York University Press, New Haven, 1947) 136 at 162–81.

ing in the field of private international law, primarily dealt with choice of law. Although Huber's work touched on the recognition of foreign judgments, it did not consider jurisdictional questions. Secondly, in the nineteenth century, attempts by common law commentators to provide a principled framework for the law of jurisdiction were not very successful. For example, the early editions of *Dicey's Conflict of Laws* distilled the law of jurisdiction into two principles: 'the principle of effectiveness' (according to which courts have jurisdiction over any matter with regard to which they can give an effective judgment and have no juris-diction over any matter with regard to which they cannot give an effective judg-ment[5]) and 'the principle of submission' (according to which courts have jurisdiction over any person who voluntarily submits to their jurisdiction[6]). In relation to the former principle, Dicey said that an effective judgment is one which is capable of enforcement in the country where it was pronounced.[7] It is instantly apparent that the principle of effectiveness is a wholly inadequate starting-point for a theory of jurisdiction. In the first place, a theory of jurisdiction which is based on the enforceability of judgments fails to take into account that many types of judgment (such as a divorce decree or judgment pronouncing that the defen-dant's conduct does not amount to a breach of contract or the commission of a tort) cannot be enforced—for the simple reason that there is nothing to enforce. But, even in relation to proceedings which lead to a judgment which is capable of being enforced, the principle of submission is defective. JHC Morris, on assum-ing the editorship of *Dicey*, was quick to point out the flaws in Dicey's theory: the effectiveness of an *in personam* judgment 'depends not so much on whether the defendant can be served with process in England as on whether he has assets in England out of which the judgment can be satisfied.'[8] Dicey's general principles were in due course jettisoned completely, but no attempt was made to reconsider what were the general principles underlying the jurisdiction of the English courts. This is perhaps not altogether surprising as private international law's shift in emphasis from choice of law to international procedure did not really start in England until the 1970s.[9]

(b) Some Blind Alleys

It is tempting to try to base a general theory of jurisdiction on a single unifying concept. In a sense this is what has happened in the United States, where a system of jurisdictional principles has been created out of the due process clause of the

---

[5] See AB Keith (ed), *Dicey's Conflict of Laws* (5th edn, Sweet & Maxwell, London, 1932) at 30.
[6] *Ibid* at 32.
[7] See JHC Morris (ed) *Dicey on the Conflict of Laws* (7th edn, Stevens, London, 1958) at 18.
[8] *Ibid* at 27.
[9] Part III (Jurisdiction and Foreign Judgments) of the current edition of *Dicey & Morris on the Conflict of Laws* (13th edn, 2000) runs to more than 400 pages, representing about a quarter of the whole work. The equivalent sections of the 5th edition (1932) fill only 120 pages and constitute little more than one tenth.

University of Ulster LIBRARY

Constitution.[10] The Fourteenth Amendment provides simply that no state 'shall … deprive any person of life, liberty, or property, without due process of law.' If the Supreme Court can fashion jurisdictional principles out of the Fourteenth Amendment could European courts create their own principles from the due process provisions of the European Convention on Human Rights (as implemented in England by the Human Rights Act 1998)?

For good or ill, this question must be answered in the negative. The way in which Article 6(1) of the ECHR is drafted does not suggest a parallel with the US Constitution. Although Article 6(1), which gives litigants a 'right to a fair trial', has been interpreted as including a right of access to the courts,[11] the wording of the provision indicates that it is concerned primarily with the way in which legal procedures are operated. There is nothing in the text of Article 6(1) or the jurisprudence of the European Court of Human Rights to suggest that the exercise of jurisdiction on an exorbitant basis can, without more, involve a breach of the right to a fair trial. Although there may be cases where the European Convention has some bearing on how a specific jurisdictional question is resolved,[12] it is not easy to see how an overarching jurisdictional theory can be constructed out of Article 6. As Aitkins J noted in *The Kribi*:

> Article 6 of the ECHR does not deal at all with *where* the right to a 'fair and public hearing before an independent and impartial tribunal established by law' is to be exercised by a litigant. The crucial point is that civil rights must be determined *somewhere* by a hearing and before a tribunal in accordance with the provisions of Article 6.[13]

It has already been noted that Dicey attempted to construct a general theory of jurisdiction—from the principles of effectiveness and submission—and the result has to be regarded as a failure, whether his principles are seen as descriptive or prescriptive. Others have followed Dicey's lead, whether or not consciously, and suggested that jurisdiction rules can be structured around one of a number of abstract concepts. Over the years there have been various suggestions and it is not possible to consider them all in the context of the current discussion. Two examples will suffice.

    (i) In his Hague lectures of 1963[14] Graveson suggested the theory of the 'proper court'—by analogy with doctrine of the proper law of the contract. He recognised that the selection of the proper court 'presupposes the existence of principles by which one may determine whether or not the court

---

[10] See PB Kurland, 'The Supreme Court, the Due Process Clause and the In Personam Jurisdiction of State Courts' (1958) 25 *U Chi LR* 569.

[11] *Golder v UK* (1975) Series A No 18 and 1 EHRR 524; *Airey v Ireland* (1979) Series A No 32 and 2 EHRR 305. See P van Dijk and GJH. van Hoof, *Theory and Practice of the European Convention on Human Rights* (3rd edn, Kluwer, Boston, 1998) at 418–21.

[12] See Lord Bingham in *Lubbe v Cape Plc* [2000] 1 WLR 1545 at 1561.

[13] [2001] 1 Lloyd's Rep 76 at 87. Emphasis in original.

[14] RH Graveson, 'Comparative Aspects of the General Principles of Private International Law' (1963–II) 109 *Hag Rec* 1.

is proper.'[15] In an earlier article entitled 'Philosophical Aspects of the English Conflict of Laws'[16] Graveson had argued that English private international law was based on the principles of 'justice' and 'convenience'. In connection with the notion of the proper court, Graveson repeated that the relevant jurisdiction principles 'must be found in the philosophical foundations of private international law, the framework of justice, necessity and convenience.'[17]

(ii) A more sustained argument is to be found in Lowenfeld's Hague lectures of 1994.[18] Nevertheless, after a close analysis of many aspects of the law of international jurisdiction, Lowenfeld concluded that the principles which unify the whole area are the principles of reasonableness and fairness.

As JHC Morris pointed out in relation to Dicey's approach, the problem with a general theory is either that it risks having to recognise a great number of exceptions and anomalies or that it is so general to be virtually meaningless.[19] An overarching principle which appeals to a general, abstract notion is largely without content unless and until it is fleshed out by sub-principles. Furthermore, while few could argue with the proposition that jurisdiction should be exercised only if it is 'reasonable' or 'fair', whether the exercise of jurisdiction in particular circumstances is 'reasonable' or 'fair' is intrinsically contestable.

B. An Important Lesson of Public International Law

If attempts to formulate a jurisdictional theory from a single abstract concept are too vague to be very helpful, the next question to consider is whether there are any lessons to be learned from public international law. Since States should act in accordance with international law, the exercise of jurisdiction in private law matters (such as in relation to a contractual dispute) ought to be consistent with the principles of public international law. However, the idea that private international law must not be inconsistent with public international law does not take matters very far. According to one school of thought, customary international law does not restrict in any way the exercise of jurisdiction to adjudicate in private law matters. For example, Akehurst has argued that, apart from rules on immunity for foreign States, diplomats and international organisations, 'customary international law imposes no limits on the jurisdiction of municipal courts in civil trials.'[20] This conclusion is based on the observation that States have laid down rules according to which their courts exercise jurisdiction in cases which have little

---

[15] RH Graveson, at 137.
[16] (1962) 78 *LQR* 337.
[17] (1963–II) 109 *Hag Rec* 1 at 137.
[18] See 'International Litigation and the Quest for Reasonableness' (1994–I) 245 *Hag Rec* 9.
[19] JCH Morris (ed), *Dicey on the Conflict of Laws* (7th edn, Stevens, London, 1958) at 27.
[20] M Akehurst, 'Jurisdiction in International Law' (1972–1973) 46 *BYIL* 145 at 177.

or no connection with that State and that this practice seems to have met with acquiescence by other States.

The conclusion that public international law has nothing to say about jurisdiction in private law matters may be questioned from a number of perspectives. First, whether or not State practice elicits diplomatic protest is by no means the only way of testing whether or not rules of customary international law exist. In the sphere of private international law, there is an important relationship between jurisdiction rules, on the one hand, and the recognition and enforcement of foreign judgments, on the other. One way in which disapproval for the exercise of jurisdiction in private law matters is expressed is by a State's refusal to recognise or enforce a foreign judgment that results from the exercise of jurisdiction on an exorbitant basis. Secondly, given that there are undoubtedly international norms concerning the legitimacy or otherwise of a State's exercise of jurisdiction in criminal cases, it would be surprising if customary international law did not also lay down minimum standards in the field of civil jurisdiction. From the point of view of principle, 'there is . . . no great difference between the problems created by the assertion of civil and criminal jurisdiction over aliens.'[21] Of course, it does not necessarily follow that identical principles are applicable in criminal and civil cases; but the suggestion that the exercise of jurisdiction in civil matters, however exorbitant, can never be contrary to customary international law is both implausible and unattractive. It is important to distinguish the fact that a State can legislate howsoever it chooses from the question of whether the exercise of the State's legislative power is legitimate according to international law.[22] Thirdly, as there is a strong link in historical terms between private international law and public international law, it seems inherently unlikely that public international law has no impact in the field of civil jurisdiction. Fourthly, it has rightly been pointed out that 'the presentation of the different facets of jurisdiction in separate compartments can obscure certain essential and logical points.'[23] As regards the power of States to make decisions and rules enforceable within state territory 'there is no major distinction between the types of jurisdiction.'[24] As customary international law regulates the activity of States in terms of their legislative and administrative action, it would be illogical if it did not also lay down standards in the context of judicial activity because a 'judgment, viz. a command conveyed through the courts, is not essentially different from legislative or administrative action.'[25]

The weight of opinion supports the proposition that the existence of the State's right to exercise jurisdiction is determined by public international law (which, accordingly, provides the standard by which municipal rules can be measured) and that public international law regulates the consequences of the wrongful

---

[21] I Brownlie, *Principles of Public International Law* (5th edn, Oxford University Press, Oxford, 1998) at 302. See also at 313.

[22] See FA Mann, 'The Doctrine of Jurisdiction in International Law' (1964–I) 111 *Hag Rec* 1 at 9.

[23] Brownlie, n 21 above at 312.

[24] *Ibid* at 313.

[25] Mann, n 22 above at 73.

exercise of jurisdiction.[26] However, the recognition that the exercise of jurisdiction in private law matters should be consistent with public international law fails to provide much in the way of concrete solutions to practical problems—other than at the most general level. For example, in the context of civil matters, an unqualified acceptance of the territorial principle (according to which a State 'has jurisdiction over persons and things, and over events occurring, within its territory'[27]) would have the effect of legitimating the exercise of jurisdiction in a wide variety of circumstances on the basis of relatively insubstantial connections. Furthermore, in the vast majority of cases, the territorial principle almost inevitably leads to jurisdiction being concurrent rather than exclusive.[28] The essential tasks of the private international lawyer include identifying with greater precision the types of connecting factor which justify the exercise of jurisdiction in particular types of situation and finding appropriate solutions to the problem of parallel and related proceedings.[29] It seems, therefore, almost inevitable that, except at the most superficial level, in the field of jurisdiction, private international law and public international law will pursue different agendas. Any attempt to identify principles with general validity has to rely on extremely flexible standards (such as 'reasonably close contact'[30]), the significance of which may differ substantially according to the context. Nevertheless, it would be wrong to conclude that private international lawyers have nothing to learn from public international law. What public international law reveals is the relevance (or irrelevance) of purely practical considerations.

In a criminal case, the two protagonists are the State and the defendant; the victim, to the extent that he has any role at all, is normally no more than a bit player. In the international context, the essential jurisdictional question in a criminal case is to determine the limits of each State's jurisdiction (ie the division of competence between States), irrespective of the wishes of the defendant. So, in a criminal case, there can be no question of a State having competence simply on the basis of the defendant's consent. Moreover, in the public sphere, the answer to the jurisdictional question necessarily determines the reach of a State's law. If State A exercises criminal jurisdiction over D, D's actions will be judged according to the standards of the law of State A. Accordingly, in the public sphere, questions of practical convenience are, if not wholly irrelevant, of strictly limited significance. If, for example, D, a UK citizen and English resident, commits a crime

---

[26] Mann, n 22 above at 10–11. See also AF Lowenfeld, 'International Litigation and the Quest for Reasonableness' (1994–I) 245 *Hag Rec* 81 at 82; F. Vischer, 'General Course on Public International Law' (1992–I) 232 *Hag Rec* 21 at 203–4.

[27] DW Grieg, *International Law* (Butterworths, London, 1976) at 210. See also Mann, n 22 above at 41.

[28] See Mann, *ibid* at 10; Vischer, n 26 above at 216–8.

[29] For the purposes of the discussion which follows proceedings are 'parallel' if they involve the same parties and the same issues (broadly speaking, situations which, in the context of Council Regulation [E.C.] No 44/2001 (the 'Brussels I Regulation'), fall within the scope of Art 27); proceedings are 'related' if they could give rise to irreconcilable judgments (broadly speaking, situations which, in the context of the Brussels I Regulation, fall within the scope of Art 28).

[30] Mann, n 22 above at 50.

in France, the scope of the French courts' criminal jurisdiction is not affected by the fact that it may be more convenient for criminal proceedings against D to be conducted in England, rather than in France.

However, in the private sphere, the position is rather different for a number of reasons. First, in a civil matter, there are three protagonists (at least), rather than two: the claimant, the defendant and the State whose jurisdiction is invoked. One of the major themes of much of the theoretical writing in the sphere of private international law is the interplay of the State's (public) interests, on the one hand, and the parties' (private) interests, on the other.[31] Secondly, although in recent years private international law has increasingly been dominated by jurisdictional questions, it is important not to lose sight of the fact that the applicable law is not necessarily the law of the forum. It is perfectly possible for a contractual dispute to be litigated in State A and for the court to apply the law of State B. Thirdly, it is generally accepted that, in a wide variety of cases involving civil and commercial matters, parties can—whether by a contractual agreement or by submission—confer jurisdiction on a forum which, in territorial terms, has no connection with the parties or their dispute.[32]

The combined effect of these factors is to produce a climate in which jurisdictional questions in private international law are seen as raising issues of practical convenience (including expense). One might go further and suggest that jurisdictional thinking in private international law has become too dominated by these practical issues,[33] as a consequence of which more fundamental questions about the proper division of competence between States may be overlooked. Private international lawyers need to be reminded that the fact that it would be convenient for litigation to take place in a particular forum should be, without more, irrelevant. Unless the parties have expressly or impliedly chosen the forum in question, the exercise of jurisdiction is not legitimate if the dispute does not have some territorial connection with that forum.

The dangers of placing to much emphasis on the private interests of the parties (in terms of convenience and cost) at the expense of the more fundamental question of the division of competence between States can be illustrated by two examples.

(i) Under the English traditional rules, CPR 6.20(5)(c)[34] allows the court to exercise jurisdiction in cases where the dispute arises out of a contract governed by English law. It is not necessarily the case that the exercise of

---

[31] See, for example, CMV Clarkson and J Hill, *Jaffey on the Conflict of Laws* (2nd edn, Butterworths, London, 2002) at 566–79; JJ Fawcett, 'Trial in England and Abroad: The Underlying Policy Considerations' (1989) 9 *OJLS* 205.

[32] The principle of party autonomy is not, of course, unlimited even in the private sphere. For example, where a dispute relates to the ownership of land in State A, the parties' agreement to refer the dispute to the courts of State B will have no jurisdictional effect. For consideration of the operation of the principle of party autonomy (and its limits) see P Nygh, *Autonomy in International Contracts* (Clarendon Press, Oxford, 1999).

[33] See WLM Reese, 'General Course on Private International Law' (1967–II) 150 *Hag Rec* 1 at 17.

[34] Formerly RSC Order 11, r 1(1)(d)(iii).

jurisdiction by the English court on the basis that the parties' dispute relates to a contract governed by English law is exorbitant; the requirement that England should be the *forum conveniens* means that in certain cases falling within CPR 6.20(5)(c) there is a substantial territorial connection with the forum.[35] Nevertheless, there are numerous examples in the reported cases where the court exercised jurisdiction even though the particular dispute between the parties had no territorial connection with England at all. In such cases, the justification for the exercise of jurisdiction is often the perceived advantages for the parties if questions of English law are determined by an English court.

For example, in *The Magnum*[36] the plaintiff, a Panamanian company, was the charterer of a vessel owned by a Spanish company. The vessel was insured by the defendant, a Spanish insurance company. The defendant also contracted to cover the plaintiff's interest in the vessel, though the policy did not cover war risks, which were covered by another insurer. While in the Arabian Gulf the vessel was in a collision with another ship. Some of the damage was repaired and the plaintiff recovered the costs from the defendant under the insurance policy. There was, however, some unrepaired damage, estimated at $3.8 million. Before these further repairs were carried out the vessel was hit by a shell and became a constructive total loss and the plaintiff's claim in respect of this damage was paid by the other insurer. Nevertheless, the plaintiff sought to recover from the defendant in respect of the unrepaired damage and, having issued proceedings in England, sought leave to serve out of the jurisdiction under what is now CPR 6.20(5)(c)—on the basis of a good arguable case that the contract between the parties was governed by English law. It is clear that, in territorial terms, the dispute had no connection with England and the defendant carried on business wholly in Spain. The English court's jurisdiction to entertain the action stemmed exclusively from the fact that the putative proper law of the contract was English law.[37] Although Staughton J, at first instance, refused leave to serve out, the Court of Appeal, relying heavily on *Coast Lines Ltd v Hudig & Veder Chartering NV*,[38] allowed the plaintiff's appeal and decided that England was the most appropriate forum.

A similar emphasis on practical convenience can be seen in *Spiliada Maritime Corporation v Cansulex Ltd*.[39] The defendant, a Canadian

---

[35] For the argument that what is now CPR 6.20(5)(c) is contrary to public international law, see Mann, n 22 above at 78; FA Mann, 'The Doctrine of Jurisdiction in International Law Revisited After Twenty Years' (1984–III) 186 *Hag Rec* 9 at 70; FA Mann, *Foreign Affairs in English Courts* (Clarendon press, Oxford, 1986) at 142.

[36] [1989] 1 Lloyd's Rep 47.

[37] See Parker LJ at [1989] 1 Lloyd's Rep 47 at 49.

[38] [1972] 2 QB 34. See also the critical discussion of this case (and *Roneleigh Ltd v MII Exports Inc* [1989] 1 WLR 619) by AF Lowenfeld, 'International Litigation and the Quest for Reasonableness' (1994–I) 245 *Hag Rec* 9 at 110–15.

[39] [1987] AC 460.

company, had no connection with England and the case was concerned entirely with events which took place in British Columbia. The main reason for the House of Lords' decision to allow the plaintiff's appeal[40] and rein-state Staughton J's decision to grant leave to serve out of the jurisdiction under what is now CPR 6.20(5)(c) was the so-called *Cambridgeshire* factor (ie the fact that there were parallel English proceedings involving the same factual questions in relation to another ship, but a different plaintiff). However, the *Cambridgeshire* factor had nothing to do with the dispute between the parties as such and the existence of the *Cambridgeshire* litigation did not provide a territorial link between the *Spiliada* litigation and England. Any substantial benefit to the parties to the *Spiliada* litigation would have accrued primarily to the defendant (who was defending the *Cambridgeshire* litigation at the same time), rather than the plaintiff; but the defendant, who challenged English jurisdiction, was more than content to forego that benefit (such as it was). In any event, as the *Cambridgeshire* litigation was compromised,[41] even if the *Spiliada* case is looked at from the point of view of convenience, rather than territoriality, as things turned out, the *Cambridgeshire* factor was of little more than marginal relevance.

(ii) Both the traditional English rules (under CPR 6.20(3) and (3A)[42]) and the Brussels regime[43] (under Article 6) sanction the exercise of jurisdiction over co-defendants and third parties. A simple illustration is provided by the facts of *The Kapetan Georgis*.[44] In Nova Scotia D2 loaded coal onto a ship belonging to C, but chartered to D1. A few days after the cargo was loaded there was an explosion on board the vessel, causing both damage to the ship and loss of life. C started proceedings in England against D1, which did not challenge the court's jurisdiction. D1 then issued a third party notice against D2. On these facts, the joining of D2 by way of third party proceedings was obviously convenient, because it ensured that D1, if found liable to C, could seek contribution from D2 under the Civil Liability (Contribution) Act 1978. Hirst J gave leave for the writ to be served on D2 out of the jurisdiction under what is now CPR 6.20(3A). It is worth noting that the result would have been the same had D2 been a company domiciled in France (rather than Nova Scotia) as the English court would have had jurisdiction over D2 under Article 6(2) of the Brussels Convention.

The practical justification for jurisdiction being extended to co-defendants and third parties rests on the perceived necessity of there being

---

[40] From the Court of Appeal: [1985] 2 Lloyd's Rep 116.
[41] See *Bibby Bulk Carriers Ltd v Cansulex Ltd* [1989] QB 155.
[42] Formerly RSC Order 11, r 1(1)(c).
[43] Council Reg (E.C.) No.44/2001 and the European Conventions on jurisdiction and the recognition and enforcement of judgments in civil and commercial matters (Brussels Convention of 1968 and Lugano Convention of 1988).
[44] [1988] 1 Lloyd's Rep 352.

one forum which can 'speak with respect to the situation as a whole.'[45] However, whether the issue is phrased in terms of territoriality or substantial connection, from the perspective of the proper division of competence between States, the English court's exercise of jurisdiction over D2 is hard to justify—as D2 had no connection with England and D2's actions occurred entirely in Nova Scotia. Although it is doubtful whether the exercise of jurisdiction over D2 in *The Kapetan Georgis* is consistent with principles of public international law, this type extended jurisdiction over co-defendants and third parties seems to have avoided criticism from commentators. This can be seen as supporting the argument that private international lawyers' minds have been too concerned with practical questions—at the expense of more theoretical ones.

Having said that, it may be possible to detect a slight change of direction. The Hague Conference's Preliminary Draft Convention[46] may be regarded as providing a barometer of current thinking in private international law circles. Article 14, which deals with the issue of multiple defendants, contains an important proviso—namely, that jurisdiction over a co-defendant depends on there being 'a substantial connection' between the State exercising jurisdiction 'and the dispute involving that defendant'. Similarly, Article 16, which covers third party claims, contains the same proviso: there must be a substantial connection between the forum and the dispute involving the third party. These provisions are important because, rather than allowing purely practical considerations to dominate, they reflect a determination to find a proper balance between principle and practicality.

2. THE COMPONENTS OF JURISDICTIONAL REGIMES IN PRIVATE INTERNATIONAL LAW

Before the components of a jurisdictional regime are examined, there is a general point which needs to be emphasised: private international law displays a range of jurisdictional approaches, rather than a single jurisdictional approach. This is because jurisdictional questions arise across the whole range of private law categories: contract, tort, bankruptcy and insolvency, arbitration, marriage, adoption and so on. A jurisdiction rule which provides a satisfactory solution to a contract case might be wholly inappropriate in a divorce case. Even if, as a general rule, a civil court should be entitled to exercise jurisdiction if it is a forum with which the dispute has a substantial connection, what constitutes a substantial connec-

---

[45] AT von Mehren and DT Trautmann, 'Jurisdiction to Adjudicate: A Suggested Analysis' (1966) 79 *Harv LR* 1121 at 1153.

[46] Preliminary Draft Convention on Jurisdiction and Foreign Judgments in Civil and Commercial Matters of 30 Oct 1999 (http://www.hcch.net/econventions/draft36e.html). For more recent developments see 'Summary of the Outcome of the Discussion in Commission II of the First part of the Diplomatic Conference': http://www.hcch.net/e/workprog/jdgm.html.

tion in a tort case would not necessarily be a substantial connection in an arbitration case.

A. Bases of Jurisdiction

For the purposes of analysis, rules and principles which confer jurisdiction in private law matters may be placed within three categories: (i) 'consensual' jurisdiction; (ii) 'connected' jurisdiction (which is made up of four strands: exclusive, general, special and protective); (iii) 'universal' jurisdiction. The first two categories may be found in all jurisdictional regimes. The third has yet to make much of an impact in private international law.

(a) 'Consensual' Jurisdiction

According to the submission principle, a court is competent—notwithstanding the fact that neither the events giving rise to the dispute nor the parties have any connection with the forum—if the parties voluntarily submit to the court's jurisdiction. Such a submission may take the form of a voluntary appearance to defend the claim without challenging the court's jurisdiction or a contractual agreement, typically a jurisdiction clause forming part of a wider agreement.

Although the notion of consensual jurisdiction is broadly accepted in civil and commercial matters, there are strict limits to the scope of such a principle. In the first place, there are certain types of dispute which *ratione materiae* are regarded as falling within the exclusive jurisdiction of a particular court[47] or are regarded as non-justiciable and, therefore, not within the jurisdiction of any court.[48] In such cases, a jurisdiction agreement purporting to confer jurisdiction on a particular court will be regarded as ineffective. In addition, there are certain types of commercial relationship in which there is a significant inequality between the parties and there is a danger that the stronger party may unfairly impose a jurisdiction clause to the detriment of the weaker party. The Brussels regime provides that jurisdiction clauses in consumer and employment contracts are effective only in certain limited circumstances (such as if the clause was entered into after the dispute arose or if it gives the weaker party—but not the stronger party—more choice).[49] Furthermore, in family law matters the parties are not generally able, by an agreement, to confer jurisdiction on an unconnected forum or to oust the jurisdiction of a connected forum.[50] For example, parties neither of whom is

---

[47] Brussels I Reg, Art 22; Lugano Convention, Art 16.

[48] *Buttes Gas and Oil Co v Hammer (No. 3)* [1982] AC 888; *Kuwait Airways Corporation v Iraqi Airways Co (Nos 4 and 5)* [2001] 3 WLR 1117 (CA); [2002] 2 WLR 1353 (HL).

[49] Brussels I Reg, Arts 17, 21; Lugano Convention, Arts 15, 17(5). See also Preliminary Draft Convention, Arts 7.3, 8.2.

[50] See, however, *S v S (Matrimonial Proceedings: Appropriate Forum)* [1997] 1 WLR 1200 in which Wilson J granted a stay of English divorce proceedings on the basis that the parties had made a prenuptial agreement which included a jurisdiction clause in favour of the New York courts.

habitually resident in England cannot confer divorce jurisdiction on the English court by agreement.[51]

(b) 'Connected' Jurisdiction

Notwithstanding the importance of consensual jurisdiction in the commercial context, it is the second component—connected jurisdiction—which lies at the heart of the majority of jurisdictional disputes. It is generally accepted that, in the absence of special factors which may render the exercise of jurisdiction inappropriate or illegitimate, a court is entitled to exercise jurisdiction in a case where there is a connection between the forum and the parties and/or the dispute. It should be emphasised that, for the purposes of private international law, the connection should be significant or substantial. If jurisdiction in private law matters could be exercised on the basis of an insubstantial connection, the problem posed by parallel and related proceedings—which is a major one—would be even greater. One of the most effective ways of counteracting the tendency towards parallel and related proceedings (which is fostered by a jurisdictional system based on an open-textured territorial principle) is to define the permitted bases of jurisdiction more restrictively.

(i) Exclusive 'connected' jurisdiction

At present, the principle of exclusivity plays a limited role in private international law. Since one of the seemingly intractable problems of private international law is that posed by parallel and related proceedings, an argument can be made for expanding the range of situations in which jurisdiction can be exercised by only one forum—notwithstanding the fact that the situation has connections with two or more fora.[52] In current practice, exclusive jurisdiction arises in a limited number of cases where the courts of a particular country are thought to be uniquely appropriate—typically, because of an overwhelming factual connection between the forum and the subject-matter of the dispute. Under the Brussels regime, for example, exclusive jurisdiction is reserved for cases which concern: (i) certain proceedings relating to immovable property; (ii) certain proceedings concerning the formation and dissolution of companies and the decisions of their organs; (iii) certain proceedings concerning entries in public registers; (iv) certain proceedings concerning intellectual property right; (v) proceedings concerning the enforcement of judgments.[53] The exclusive jurisdiction provisions of the Brussels regime are mandatory and cannot be departed from either by an agreement purporting to confer jurisdiction on the courts of another country or by the parties' submission to another forum.

---

[51] Council Reg (EC) No 1347/2000 (the Brussels II Reg), Art 2; Domicile and Matrimonial Proceedings Act 1973, s 5.

[52] See Mann, n 22 above, at 50.

[53] Brussels I Reg, Art 22; Lugano Convention, Art 16.

(ii) General and special 'connected' jurisdiction

It seems that the identification of suitable bases of connected jurisdiction is much harder in the commercial sphere than in the public law context. It is not too difficult to see why this might be the case. The typical public law case involves criminal liability arising out of events causing death, personal injury or property damage. In this situation there are, in effect, only two potential bases of jurisdiction which are consistent with the territorial principle: the place of acting (where the wrongdoer committed the criminal act) and the place of harm (where the victim was injured or killed or where the victim's property was damaged). Furthermore, although it is possible for the wrongdoer to perform the wrongful act in one place and for the victim to suffer injury in another, it is much more common for the place of acting and the place of harm to be the same place. Obviously, in the standard case, there can be no doubt that the State in which the crime was committed is entitled to exercise jurisdiction over the wrongdoer. Even in the less usual case, the wrongdoer's criminal act and the victim's injury each constitute a substantial connection with the place in question. For example, where D in State A fires a gun across the border between States A and B and kills V, who is situated in State B, there is a sufficiently strong connection with both State A (the place of acting) and with State B (the place of harm) to justify the exercise of criminal jurisdiction over D by either State. In the analogous civil cases (ie, multiple locality tort cases in which the defendant's wrongful act is committed in one country and the harm is inflicted on the claimant in another country), it is generally accepted that the claimant should be entitled to sue the defendant in either place[54]—at least if it is reasonably foreseeable that the defendant's conduct at the place of acting may cause injury to the claimant in another place.[55]

However, the majority of civil and commercial cases involve contractual disputes, rather than tort cases. In commercial cases, there are many more potentially relevant connecting factors—such as the place (or places) of negotiation, the place (or places) of contracting, the place (or places) of business of the parties, the place (or places) of performance and the law (or laws) applicable to the contract—and the extent to which these connecting factors should be regarded as substantial or insubstantial is controversial. There are two particular reasons for this.

First, the relevance of a connecting factor depends to a considerable extent on the context. Consider, for example, the significance of a natural person's habitual residence. In commercial matters, habitual residence is regarded as a substantial connection.[56] The same is true in the context of child

---

[54] See, for example, Brussels I Reg Art 5(3); Case 21/76 *Handelskwekerij GJ Bier BV v Mines de Potasse d'Alcase SA* [1976] *ECR* 1735.

[55] See Preliminary Draft Convention, Art 10.1(b).

[56] The Brussels regime uses the term 'domicile' (Art 2), but, as far as English law is concerned, its meaning is largely indistinguishable from habitual residence: Civil Jurisdiction and Judgments Act 1985, s 41; Civil Jurisdiction and Judgments Order 2001 (SI 2001/3929), para 9. The Hague Conference's Preliminary Draft Convention employs habitual residence (Art 3.1).

abduction.[57] However, in relation to disputes arising out of arbitration proceedings, the habitual residence of the parties is, more or less, irrelevant.[58]

Secondly, even if it is agreed that, in a specific context, a particular connecting factor is a substantial one, there may be disagreement as to whether it should be regarded as a basis of general or special jurisdiction. A court with general jurisdiction may adjudicate any type of dispute as long as there is a particular connection between the defendant and the forum. By contrast, a court with special jurisdiction may adjudicate only disputes which are related to the particular connecting factor on which jurisdiction is based. The nature of the problem is well illustrated by the 'place of business' connecting factor. No one would argue that a foreign defendant's place of business in England is an insignificant connection with England for private international law purposes. However, opinion is divided as to whether the existence of a place of business should found general jurisdiction over the foreign defendant or whether it should confer jurisdiction only in relation to disputes arising out of the activities of the place of business in question. Under the traditional rules, the English court is entitled to exercise general jurisdiction over a corporate defendant on the basis of service of process at a place of business in England[59] and this approach is supported by some commentators.[60] However, a more modern view—which is reflected both by the Brussels regime[61] and the Hague Conference's Preliminary Draft Convention[62]—treats a place of business as a basis of special jurisdiction only.

(iii) Protective 'connected' jurisdiction

In general, jurisdiction rules in private law matters treat both parties equally. So, if, in a contractual dispute, C can sue D at the place of performance of D's contractual obligation, D can sue C at the place of performance of C's contractual obligation. In civil and commercial matters, the traditional English jurisdiction rules are based on the assumption that the parties are on an equal footing—in terms of bargaining power and economic resources. So, there are no special rules dealing with consumer contracts, individual contracts of employment or other contracts in which there is a structural inequality between the parties. By contrast, at the international level, it is being increasingly recognised that jurisdiction rules which apply to contracts generally may cause injustice or hardship if applied to contractual situations where one party is prima facie weaker

---

[57] See Hague Convention on the Civil Aspects of International Child Abduction (1980), implemented by Child Abduction and Custody Act 1985, Pt I and Sch 1.

[58] Arbitration Act 1996, s 2.

[59] The traditional rules refer to 'any place of business established by the company in Great Britain' (Companies Act 1985, s 695); or 'any place within the jurisdiction where the corporation carries on its activities' or 'any place of business of the company within the jurisdiction' (CPR 6.5(6)).

[60] AF Lowenfeld, 'International Litigation and the Quest for Reasonableness' (1994–I) 245 *Hag Rec* 9 at 87.

[61] Art 5(5).

[62] Art 9, 18.2(e).

than the other. It has already been seen that, under the Brussels regime, there are rules which limit the effectiveness of jurisdiction clauses in consumer and employment contracts.

With a view to protecting the weaker party, the Brussels regime includes specific rules for employment contracts, consumer contracts and in matters relating to insurance.[63] There are similar provisions dealing with consumer and employment contracts in the Hague Conference's Preliminary Draft Convention.[64] The point to note is that this type of protective jurisdiction rule does not dispense with the requirement for a substantial connection between the forum and the parties and/or dispute; that is to say, protective jurisdiction is a variant of connected jurisdiction, rather than an exception to it. Whereas the general rule under the Brussels regime is that a claimant must bring proceedings in the defendant's forum,[65] a consumer can sue the other party to a consumer contract in his own forum.[66] In this example, protective jurisdiction operates by reversing the usual bias in favour of the defendant in a case where the consumer is the claimant (but not, of course, in cases where the consumer is the defendant).

(c) Universal Jurisdiction

In public international law, according to the universality principle, there are certain types of acts which are so unacceptable that a person who commits such acts may have legal proceedings brought against him in any State. The universality principle seems to have been formulated in relation to piracy[67] and, according to contemporary public international law, all States are under an obligation to 'to co-operate to the fullest possible extent in the repression of piracy on the high seas or in any other place outside the jurisdiction of any State.'[68] More recently, it has come to be accepted that some other crimes in international law, such as war crimes and crimes against humanity, are also subject to universal jurisdiction.[69]

Traditionally, the universality principle has not been seen as having any role to play in private international law. However, it is not obvious why the universality principle should not apply to the civil implications of international crimes to the extent that it applies to the crimes themselves. The universality principle is beginning to exert some influence in the field of civil jurisdiction through the Hague Conference's Preliminary Draft Convention. Although the Preliminary Draft Convention seeks to outlaw certain exorbitant bases of jurisdiction, it is proposed that national courts should, in certain circumstances, not be prevented from exercising jurisdiction in relation to the civil consequences of specific crimes under

---

[63] See Ss 3–5 of ch II of the Brussels I Reg.

[64] Art 7–8.

[65] Art 2.

[66] Brussels I Reg Art 16; Lugano Convention, Art 14.

[67] M Sorenson (ed), *Manual of Public International Law* (Macmillan, London, 1968) at 365.

[68] United Nations Convention on the Law of the Sea 1982, Art 100. For the full text of the Convention: (1982) 21 ILM 1288.

[69] MN Shaw, *International Law* (4th edn, Grotius, Cambridge, 1997) at 473.

international law, notwithstanding that the connection between the dispute and the forum is not substantial.[70]

B. Parallel and Related Proceedings

Some of the components already considered will, in a given set of facts, produce the conclusion that only one forum is competent (such as where connected jurisdiction is exclusive or the courts of one country have consensual jurisdiction and the courts of other countries will not exercise connected jurisdiction in defiance of the parties' agreement). However, it is often the case that more than one forum will be able to exercise jurisdiction over a particular dispute (or over related disputes). This is not, in itself, a bad thing. It is not at all uncommon for a situation to have a substantial connection with more than one forum and, in these circumstances, it is not unreasonable to allow the claimant a choice of forum.[71] The problem is caused by the fact that two parties to a dispute may bring similar proceedings in different jurisdictions. For example, in a divorce case, it is quite possible for W, an English resident, to start divorce proceedings in England and H, a French citizen, to start divorce proceedings in France.[72] Similarly, in a dispute arising out of a contract of sale, the buyer may sue the seller for damages in country X and the seller may sue the buyer for the unpaid price in country Y. Alternatively, C may sue D in country X for breach of contract and D may start proceedings against C in country Y with a view to obtaining a declaration of non-liability. In these scenarios, there is a danger that there will be two sets of proceedings dealing with essentially the same issues. This is wasteful of court time, effort and cost. Furthermore, it is possible that, if both actions proceed to judgment, the judgments will conflict with one another. One of the obstacles to the recognition and enforcement of foreign judgments is the fact that the courts of different countries may exercise jurisdiction over the same dispute and render conflicting judgments.

Accordingly, in recent years, much of the effort in the field of jurisdiction in private law matters has been directed towards seeking to find a solution to the problem of parallel and related proceedings. Just as there is legitimate disagree-

---

[70] See Art 18.3. The text offers two variants. The first variant would permit the exercise of jurisdiction under national law only if the claimant is exposed to a risk of a denial of justice because proceedings in another State are not possible or cannot reasonably be required. According to the second variant, a court could exercise civil jurisdiction only if the State has also established criminal jurisdiction over the crime in question. Whether either variant would affect the outcome of a case such as *Al-Adsani v Government of Kuwait* [1996] 2 LRC 333; (*No 2*) [1996] 2 LRC 344 is doubtful, given that Art 1 of the Preliminary Draft Convention states that '[n]othing in the Convention affects the privileges and immunities of sovereign States or of entities of sovereign States, or of international organisations.' See also *Al-Adsani v United Kingdom* (2002) 34 EHRR 273.

[71] It has been argued that it is unhelpful to describe the exercise this type of jurisdictional choice as 'forum-shopping': see J Hill, 'Jurisdiction in Civil and Commercial Matters: Is There a Third Way?' (2001) *CLP* 439 at 459–60.

[72] See, for example, *De Dampierre v De Dampierre* [1988] AC 92.

ment as to whether certain sorts of connection are sufficient to render a forum a connected one, there are also significant differences of opinion as to how best to tackle these problems.

3. TURNING THE COMPONENTS INTO A PRINCIPLED SYSTEM

A jurisdictional theory based on an abstract notion such as 'reasonableness', 'fairness' or 'justice' simply postpones the point at which more concrete principles have to be formulated in order to provide solutions to specific jurisdictional problems. If progress is to be made it cannot be at the abstract or general level; it is at a lower, intermediate level that the work has to be undertaken. The creation of a jurisdictional system requires two fundamental (and interrelated) questions to be addressed. First, there is a question of priorities. For example, is the avoidance of parallel proceedings more important than the upholding of jurisdiction agreements or less important? Is the avoidance of parallel proceedings more or less important than allowing litigation to proceed in the most closely connected forum? Secondly, there is the question of legal technique—which runs throughout this area. Are jurisdictional problems best solved by hard-and-fast rules, by flexible criteria which confer discretion on the courts or by a hybrid system?

Of course, there are no easy answers to these questions. However, it does not follow that one answer is as good as any other. Some progress towards finding the most satisfactory answer can be made by working from a number of principles which underpin this area. These principles suggest how the two fundamental questions might best be answered.

A. Five Principles

(a) Party Autonomy

As a general rule, the law should strive to uphold private agreements that have been freely entered by the parties.

(b) Protecting the Weaker Party

In certain circumstances where the parties to the dispute are not on an equal footing (for instance, in the context of a consumer contract), the jurisdictional balance should be tilted in favour of the weaker party.

(c) The Non-Effect of an Exorbitant Exercise of Jurisdiction

Perhaps the most fundamental principle of any system of jurisdiction should be that where a court exercises jurisdiction on an exorbitant basis (ie where the court cannot claim to have either consensual or connected jurisdiction) that exercise of jurisdiction should not be accorded extraterritorial effect. This means that where a court exercises jurisdiction on an exorbitant basis, those proceedings should not have the effect of preventing parallel proceedings in another court which is prima facie entitled to exercise jurisdiction (whether on a consensual or connected basis). Furthermore, any judgment which ensues from an exorbitant exercise of jurisdiction should not be entitled to recognition and enforcement in other countries.

(d) Even-Handedness and Comity

Although each country can, subject to international law, determine the content of its own system of private international law, it is clear that any system of private international law must have regard to more than simply parochial concerns; it must take into account the broader interests of the international community in the orderly and rational regulation of international jurisdiction. In addition, on the international plane, States should not operate double-standards. So, if the courts of State A rigorously enforce jurisdiction clauses in favour of the courts of State A, they should enforce jurisdiction clauses in favour of the courts of State B no less rigorously.

Until relatively recently the English courts were generally unwilling to relinquish jurisdiction in favour of a foreign forum—even where jurisdiction had been exercised on the basis of an insubstantial connection with England and a foreign forum was obviously more appropriate.[73] But, in recent years, to use Lord Diplock's somewhat self-congratulatory phrase, 'judicial chauvinism has been replaced by judicial comity.'[74] It would be fair to say that the notion of 'judicial comity' has never been clearly defined. Nevertheless, if it is to mean anything, 'judicial comity' should mean more than the English courts no longer engaging in invidious comparisons between England and other countries in terms of the quality of the administration of justice. A commitment to 'judicial comity' should mean that the courts, in the application of jurisdiction rules and principles, act even-handedly, rather than operating double standards.

(e) Predictability

Although it is not necessary for a jurisdictional system to be simple, it is highly desirable that it should be able to provide predictable solutions to standard problems. The English courts' experience with the *Spiliada* doctrine[75] shows that it is very difficult to create a predictable system if discretion plays too central a role.[76]

---

[73] The *locus classicus* is *Maharanee of Baroda v Wildenstein* [1972] 2 QB 283.

[74] Lord Diplock in *The Abidin Daver* [1984] AC 398 at 411.

[75] The parallel doctrines of *forum conveniens* and *forum non conveniens* as laid down by the House of Lords in *Spiliada Maritime Corporation v Cansulex Ltd* [1987] AC 460.

[76] See Hill, n 71 above at 446–54.

B. A Return to the Two Questions of Policy

(a) Legal Technique: Hard-and-Fast Rules versus Discretion

Although questions of legal technique can arise in any area of law, these questions have loomed large in private international law because, as regards jurisdictional issues, the world is divided into two opposed schools of thought. The civilian approach seeks to resolve jurisdictional problems through an integrated frame-work of hard-and-fast rules.[77] The Brussels regime is the most obvious example of the civilian approach: the role of judicial discretion is reduced to a minimum (though not excluded entirely); there is a limited range of narrowly defined bases of jurisdiction, which a claimant is entitled to invoke as of right; if more than one forum can *prima facie* exercise jurisdiction, priority is given to the court first seised.

At the other end of the spectrum is the common law approach, according to which jurisdiction questions can only be properly resolved on a case by case basis. Under the traditional English rules in civil and commercial matters, discretion is at the heart of almost all jurisdiction questions. The traditional rules include a wide range of jurisdictional bases, some of which do not require there to be a sub-stantial connection with England. For example, a claimant can invoke the English court's jurisdiction by serving process on the defendant during the latter's tem-porary presence in England (notwithstanding the fact that the dispute has no connection with England);[78] equally, the court may give permission for service of process out of the jurisdiction on the basis that the claim arises out of a contract made in England.[79] However, the limits of the English court's jurisdiction are fixed by discretion under the *Spiliada* doctrine. In a case where the defendant is served in England, the defendant can apply for a stay on the basis of the doctrine of *forum non conveniens*, according to which the English proceedings will be stayed if the defendant can establish that there is a more appropriate foreign forum; in a case where the claimant wishes to serve process abroad, the claimant must obtain per-mission for such service, which depends *inter alia* upon his satisfying the court that England is clearly the appropriate forum (ie the *forum conveniens*).

The *Spiliada* doctrine is also used to deal with parallel and related proceedings. The existence of parallel or related proceedings abroad is one of the factors to which the court has regard when seeking to determine which forum is the more appropriate. It is, however, clear that the most closely connected forum may cease to be the most appropriate one if parallel proceedings in a less closely connected forum are well advanced at the time when proceedings in the most closely con-nected forum are commenced. As with all jurisdictional issues under the tradi-tional rules, everything depends on the circumstances of the particular case. In a

---

[77] LI de Winter, 'Excessive Jurisdiction in Private International Law' (1968) 17 *ICLQ* 706 at 720.
[78] *Maharanee of Baroda v Wildenstein* [1972] QB 283.
[79] CPR 6.20(5)(a); see *Roneleigh Ltd v MII Exports Inc* [1989] 1 WLR 619.

case involving *lis pendens* governed by the traditional rules, if the English court gives permission to serve out or refuses to grant a stay, the parties will normally be required to fight on two fronts—both in England and abroad. In exceptional cases, however, the English court may, at the behest of the defendant in the foreign proceedings grant an anti-suit injunction—that is, an injunction ordering the claimant in the foreign proceedings not to pursue those proceedings. In this type of case, assuming that the foreign claimant complies with the terms of the injunction, the English court will have had its way—in the sense that there will be only one set of proceedings in England (the forum which in the eyes of the English court is the most appropriate one).

The foregoing discussion indicates that both the Brussels regime and the traditional rules are extreme models, in the sense that that rely essentially on a single technique, either (rather unsophisticated) hard-and-fast rules or discretion. Not surprisingly, each has positive and negative aspects.

The Brussels regime has the advantage of relative simplicity, but the disadvantage of inflexibility. This is seen particularly in the context of *lis pendens*: one of the defects of a rigid 'first come, first served' rule is that it amplifies the effect of exorbitant bases of jurisdiction. If courts exercise jurisdiction only if they are a connected forum (though not necessarily the most closely connected forum), there is a good practical argument, in terms of simplicity, for the application of a rule which gives priority to the court first seised.[80] However, if courts continue to exercise jurisdiction on exorbitant bases, it hardly seems appropriate to give that exercise of jurisdiction the same preclusive effect as an exercise of jurisdiction by a connected forum. If the court first seised is manifestly not an appropriate forum, it seems almost perverse to require a more appropriate forum to decline jurisdiction on the basis that it was the court second seised.

The pluses and minuses of the common law rules are the mirror image of their Brussels regime counterparts. The common law rules are complex and, because their operation depends on the exercise of discretion, they are unpredictable and offer an almost irresistible temptation for protracted (and wasteful) litigation on jurisdictional points. They are, however, flexible and, on balance, more likely to direct litigation to the most appropriate forum than a system of hard-and-fast rules. Nevertheless, it is questionable whether the perceived advantages—in terms of substantive results—are sufficient to offset the uncertainty and unpredictability which are an inherent feature of the traditional rules.[81]

The drafters of the Hague Conference's Preliminary Draft Convention attempted to steer a middle course between the Scylla of a regime based exclusively on hard-and-fast rules and the Charybdis of one which places discretion at the heart of all jurisdictional questions. Although the Preliminary Draft Convention takes the Brussels regime as its starting-point (and the derivation of many of its provisions is instantly apparent to anyone familiar with the Brussels regime),

---

[80] Like Art 27 of the Brussels I Reg.
[81] Hill, n 71 above.

there are a number of significant differences. At this point of the discussion, the important provision of the Preliminary Draft Convention to note is Article 21.6 which grafts a limited doctrine of *forum non conveniens* onto the framework of hard-and-fast rules which set out the permitted bases of jurisdiction and *lis pendens* rules.

(b) Determining Priorities

The second issue is this: when the components of a jurisdictional model come into conflict with each other, which element should prevail? Should a system of jurisdictional principles give primacy to the goal of litigation taking place in an appropriate forum or attach greater importance to the objective of avoiding parallel proceedings? An approach which adopts a rigid *lis pendens* rule treats the avoidance of parallel proceedings which might lead to inconsistent judgments as the primary objective—even if that is at the expense of ensuring that litigation takes place in *an* appropriate forum, let alone the most appropriate forum. The common law approach entails a different way of thinking about the relationship between the various elements that are relevant to jurisdictional questions. The *Spiliada* doctrine focuses all its attention on ensuring that, as far as possible, litigation is conducted in the most appropriate forum. This means that, even if the English court is the first seised, the proceedings may be stayed, thereby requiring the commencement of proceedings in a more appropriate foreign forum (if such proceedings have not already been started). Similarly, if England is not the court first seised, the English court will not be deterred from exercising jurisdiction if it is satisfied that, notwithstanding the parallel proceedings abroad, it is a more appropriate forum. Furthermore, if the claimant in the foreign proceedings is amenable to English jurisdiction, the court may seek to enforce its assessment of its own appropriateness by granting an anti-suit injunction restraining the claimant from pursuing foreign proceedings which are regarded as vexatious or oppressive. However, within the traditional rules there is no formal hierarchy of factors or principles: in every case, all the relevant factors are put into the melting-pot and the result depends on the weight to be attached to these factors in the particular circumstances of the case.

The Preliminary Draft Convention—like the Brussels regime—seeks to establish a clear hierarchy of principles. However, it does not wholeheartedly endorse the values enshrined by the Brussels system. Under the Brussels regime, it is clear that the goal of avoiding parallel proceedings trumps all other considerations—even the objective of litigation being conducted in a connected forum. The Court of Justice has held that what is now Article 27 of the Brussels I Regulation applies regardless of the domicile of the parties and regardless of the basis on which the court first seised exercised jurisdiction.[82] So, if a French court exercises jurisdic-

---

[82] Case C–351/89 *Overseas Union Insurance v New Hampshire Insurance* [1991] ECR I–3317.

tion over a US company on the basis of Article 14 of the French Civil Code (ie that the claimant is a French national), the English court cannot exercise jurisdiction over parallel proceedings commenced by the US company in England, whether or not England is a more closely connected forum and regardless of the fact that the French court may be wholly unconnected. Arguably, the Brussels regime's focus on the avoidance of parallel proceedings—at the expense of advancing other objectives—is a serious weakness.

The Preliminary Draft Convention makes a serious attempt at reconciling the competing goals of a jurisdictional regime. Except in cases involving exclusive and protective connected jurisdiction,[83] the first priority is to ensure the enforcement of jurisdiction agreements—even in cases where the parties have agreed to the jurisdiction of a court which has no connection with the dispute.[84] The chosen court cannot decline jurisdiction on the basis that it is not an appropriate forum[85] and a court which has jurisdiction over a dispute between C and D1 cannot exercise jurisdiction over D2 (however convenient that may be) if that would be in defiance of a jurisdiction agreement (whether between C and D2 or between D1 and D2).[86]

As between avoiding parallel proceedings and directing litigation to a connected forum, the Preliminary Draft Convention gives less weight to the former and more to the latter. There are various strands to note. First, although Article 21 starts with a simple *lis pendens* rule ('first come, first served'), it goes on to provide that the obligation on the court second seised to decline jurisdiction does not arise if the court first seised is an unconnected forum (which exercised jurisdiction on an exorbitant basis). Similarly, the obligation to decline jurisdiction does not arise if, in the proceedings in the court first seised, the claimant is seeking a negative declaration and, in the proceedings in the court second seised, the claimant is seeking some positive relief (such as damages or an injunction).

Secondly, although the drafters favour hard-and-fast rules over flexible criteria, it is acknowledged that hard-and-fast rules cannot provide all the answers; experience shows that, however carefully bases of jurisdiction are circumscribed, a court which is *prima facie* a connected forum may, in particular circumstances, not have a substantial connection with the dispute. It is for this reason that the Preliminary Draft Convention includes a limited doctrine of *forum non conveniens*. Article 21.6 provides that, in exceptional circumstances (and subject to a number of provisos), 'the court may, on application by a party, suspend its proceedings if in that case it is clearly inappropriate for that court to exercise jurisdiction and if a court of another State has jurisdiction and is clearly more appropriate to resolve the dispute.'

---

[83] Art 4.3.
[84] Art 4.
[85] Art 22.1.
[86] Art 14.2; Art 16.2.

4. CONCLUSIONS

Attempts to formulate a general theory of jurisdiction in private international law have failed to provide a structured way of thinking about jurisdictional problems. Unless fleshed out by more detailed sub-principles, theories based on concepts such as 'reasonableness' or 'justice' fail to offer answers to concrete problems. From this point of view the *Spiliada* doctrine, on which the English traditional rules are built, must be regarded as a failure (albeit, possibly a heroic one).

Although, in the field of jurisdiction, there are obvious parallels between public international law and private international law, there are also very significant differences. These differences are largely a consequence of differing agendas. In the context of public international law, attention is directed to setting out minimum standards. So, for the public international lawyer, the principal task is to identify a threshold below which any exercise of jurisdiction would be incompatible with the principles which regulate the relationships between free and independent States. Although the same question is relevant in the field of private international law (though it is sometimes overlooked), the analysis has moved on to focus on another set of questions. It is not enough to ask whether the exercise of jurisdiction in private law matters would be consistent with principles of public international law. In private international law cases (particularly in the commercial context), the simple application of the territorial principle is likely to lead not only to jurisdiction being exercised on insubstantial connections but also to a high incidence of parallel and related proceedings. For the private international lawyer, one of the major tasks has become to define with greater precision the connections which justify the exercise of jurisdiction in private law matters—with the aim of reducing the number of cases in which jurisdiction is concurrent rather than exclusive.

Equally significantly, attention has turned to the identification of principles according to which a court should decline to exercise jurisdiction, notwithstanding the fact that it would, according to general principles of international law, be a competent forum.[87] This is because it has been increasingly recognised that, in private law matters, the formulation of jurisdictional bases should not be an end in itself; one of the purposes of jurisdiction rules is to facilitate the recognition and enforcement of judgments in countries other than the country of origin. A significant obstacle to the free flow of judgments is the fact that, unless sufficient attention is directed to the avoidance of parallel proceedings, there is a danger that two (or more) courts will exercise jurisdiction over the same basic dispute and render irreconcilable judgments.

In private international law, jurisdictional regimes (at least, in civil and commercial matters) contain a number of components of which the most significant are bases of consensual and connected jurisdiction and mechanisms for dealing with parallel and related proceedings. Disagreement—among lawmakers, judges and commentators—centres on three main areas: (i) the formulation of accept-

---

[87] JJ Fawcett, *Declining Jurisdiction in Private International Law* (Clarendon Press, Oxford, 1995).

able bases of general and special connected jurisdiction; (ii) the emphasis to be placed on hard-and-fast rules or more flexible criteria; (iii) which of the components (consensual bases of jurisdiction, connected bases of jurisdiction or mechanisms for dealing with parallel and related proceedings) should be given priority.

The models in England—the traditional rules, on the one hand, and the Brussels regime, on the other—are located at opposite ends of the spectrum, both in terms of legal technique and their scheme of priorities. Each regime has its problems. The Hague Conference's Preliminary Draft Convention presents a slightly different approach—one which mixes hard-and-fast rules with judicial discretion and which establishes a clear hierarchy of priorities. Whether the Hague Conference can turn the Preliminary Draft Convention into an internationally acceptable and workable convention remains to be seen. Unfortunately, the outlook is not very encouraging.[88]

---

[88] AT von Mehren, 'Drafting a Convention on International Jurisdiction and the Effects of Foreign Judgments Acceptable World-Wide: Can the Hague Conference Project Succeed?' (2001) 49 *Am J Comp L* at 191.

II

Approaches to the Assertion of Jurisdiction by Political Bodies

4

National Law, International Law and EU Law—How Do They Relate?[1]

TREVOR C HARTLEY

1. INTRODUCTION

We all know there is national (municipal) law and there is international law. We know the various theories that try to explain their relationship. But where does European Union law fit into the picture? Is it some kind of third force, separate from both? If it is, on what basis does it obtain validity and how does it relate to the other two? These questions may seem entirely theoretical, but an answer to them could be crucial for understanding some of the major constitutional issues concerning the European Union.

The legal system of the European Union was created by a set of treaties, the first being the ECSC Treaty, signed in Paris in 1951 and expired on 24 July 2002. The latest is the Treaty of Nice, signed in 2000 and not yet in force. In between, there have been a whole lot more, including the EC Treaty (originally the EEC Treaty) and the Treaty on European Union (Maastricht Agreement). These treaties are linked together to form a kind of raft, which in turn supports Community legislation (at one time referred to as 'secondary' Community law). The treaties also create the institutions of the Community, including the Community legislature (the Council, sometimes acting jointly with the Parliament) and the European Court. They give the legislature the power to legislate and the court the power to pronounce judgments. The whole Community legal system, therefore, is founded on the treaties; and the treaties derive their validity, as all treaties must, from international law.

That seems to answer very simply and decisively the questions asked above. Community law is not a third force: it is a satellite system, dependent—ultimately—on international law. It might, however, be objected that, though this was true historically, things have changed. Now, it might be argued, the treaties have become 'constitutionalised', and this puts them in a different position. The theory

[1] Parts of this chapter first appeared in the *Law Quarterly Review* ('The Constitutional Foundations of the European Union' (2001) 117 *LQR* 225) and are reproduced here with the kind permission of the Editor.

of constitutionalisation appears to have originated with an article by Stein in 1981.[2] It gained widespread support when the European Court declared in 1986 that the EC Treaty was the 'basic constitutional charter' of the Community.[3] However, though it is now fashionable to use the language of constitutional law when discussing the Community, the proponents of this theory are wary of saying exactly what it means. It sounds good—and that, some would say, is sufficient.

However, the fact of the matter is that there is nothing contradictory in saying that the treaties are the constitution of the Community, and at the same time saying that they are nevertheless *treaties* under international law. Community law can still be a satellite system even if its founding treaties are a constitution: for many years, international lawyers have referred to a treaty establishing an international organisation as the *constitution* of that organisation; in some cases, that is even its official title—for example, the treaty establishing the International Labour Organization (ILO) is officially called the 'Constitution of the International Labour Organization'.[4] It still remains a treaty.

It may, however, be argued that, though this is true in the case of international organisations like the ILO, the European Union is different: it is more than a mere international organisation; it aspires to become a (federal) State. The Community treaties, it might be argued, have changed their nature: they no longer derive their validity from international law. Their constitutionalisation, it might be said, has cut them free from international law and made them self-validating, just as national constitutions are self-validating.[5] This brings us to the theory of the *Grundnorm*, a theory which tries to explain why law is valid.

2. THE THEORY OF THE *GRUNDNORM*

If one takes the legal system of an independent State and asks why one of its rules is valid, one may be referred to another rule. If one asks why that rule is valid, one will ultimately be referred to some legal rule, perhaps the constitution, the validity of which cannot be explained in terms of any other legal rule, but only in terms of non-legal considerations. Thus, if one asks why the British Parliament can pass any law it deems fit, one might be referred to the constitutional principle of Sovereignty of Parliament. But the only explanation for that principle must be some historical fact, such as Parliament's victory in the English Civil War. Put

---

[2] E Stein, 'Lawyers, Judges and the Making of a Transnational Constitution' (1981) 75 *AJIL* 1.

[3] *Parti Ecologiste 'Les Verts' v European Parliament*, Case 294/83 [1986] ECR 1339; [1987] 2 CMLR 343 (para 23 of the judgment).

[4] This treaty was adopted in April 1919 by the Paris/Versailles Peace Conference convened after the First World War. The same usage applies in French: the French name for the treaty is '*Constitution de l'Organisation Internationale du Travail*'.

[5] This appears to be the view of José Luis da Cruz Vilaça: see JL da Cruz Vilaça and N Piçarra, 'Y a-t-il des limites matérielles à la révision des traités instituant les Communautés européennes?' [1993] *CDE* 3 at 9–13. When he wrote the article, Cruz Vilaça was President of the Court of First Instance.

in slightly different terms, the British Constitution—or, as some would prefer, the rule that the British Constitution is valid—is a *Grundnorm* ('foundation rule'),[6] which may be defined as a rule on which all other rules in the system depend, but which does not itself depend for its validity on any other legal rule.[7] The British Constitution does not derive its validity from international law or any other legal system. The same is true of the United States Constitution, the French Constitution or the German Constitution. Each of these constitutions is, or depends on, an independent *Grundnorm*. Could it be said that the same is true of the legal system of the European Union? Could it be said that, though it was originally a satellite system dependent on international law, it has now broken free and established its own *Grundnorm*?

There is no doubt that a *Grundnorm* can change: an old one can cease and a new one can come into existence. In England, this ocurred in 1688. Under the *Grundnorm* as it existed prior to the 'Glorious Revolution', James II was King of England. The Bill of Rights declared that William and Mary were King and Queen. However, under the English Constitution, an Act of Parliament was valid only if it was assented to by the Monarch. James did not assent to the Bill of Rights, nor, if one assumes that he had abdicated, was it assented to by his heir; therefore, in terms of the old *Grundnorm*, it was void; consequently, it could not make William and Mary King and Queen. If one accepts the old *Grundnorm*, every King and Queen since 1688 has been a usurper and every Act of Parliament since 1688 has been a nullity. It is only by positing a change in the *Grundnorm*, that one can escape from this conclusion.[8]

The fact that the *Grundnorm* can change does not, however, mean that such a change can take place at the whim of a few scholars or because some politicians think it would be desirable. A change of *Grundnorm* is, in legal terms, a revolution. It is a denial of legality, a denial of law itself: what is illegal is deemed to be legal. Instead of judging the legality of an act by the law, one changes the concept of legality to justify what was done. Such an extreme course is possible only in extreme circumstances: it is suggested that it must either be the result of overwhelming force or it must meet with overwhelming acceptance. It normally occurs after a successful revolution, *coup d'état*, civil war or military invasion. The new regime will establish a new constitution. If the existing judges remain in office, they will have to decide whether to accept it. If the new regime so clearly has might on its side that all resistance is useless, a judge might feel that rejection of the new *Grundnorm* would result in his removal from office and replacement by a more pliant individual. In such circumstances, he might consider he had no

---

[6] The term '*Grundnorm*' is taken from the writings of Hans Kelsen, but it is used here simply as a convenient expression to denote the idea defined above. Its use is not intended to import all Kelsen's ideas into the present discussion.

[7] In this definition, the term 'rule' is to be understood as including all legal propositions.

[8] See FW Maitland, *The Constitutional History of England* (Cambridge University Press, Cambridge, 1908), at 283–85; TP Taswell-Langmead, *English Constititutional History* (11th edn, Sweet & Maxwell, London, 1960), at 445–59.

option but to comply.[9] Furthermore, if virtually the entire population supports a proposition that requires a change of *Grundnorm*, a judge might feel he ought to accept it.

Since the Community has not staged a *coup d'état*, and the proposed European military force does not yet exist, there can be no question of overwhelming force. It is equally clear that there can be no question of overwhelming acceptance. If the European *Grundnorm* were to change so as to transform the Community treaties into a self-validating constitution, Community law would no longer apply in the Member States because the Member States accepted it: it would apply whether they liked it or not. Their continuing membership of the European Union would no longer depend on their consent: they would be members whether they liked it or not.[10] Moreover, since the European Court has ruled in numerous cases that Community law prevails over Member-State law, the national law of each Member State would apply in that State only to the extent permitted by Community law. Finally, since the European Court considers that it has the final say on the powers of the Community, the area over which the Community has jurisdiction—and hence the area over which the Member States have jurisdiction—would be outside the control of the Member States. If a change in the *Grundnorm* occurred, one could legitimately say that sovereignty had been transferred to the Union.[11] In a very real sense, the Member States would no longer be independent. Would these propositions command overwhelming acceptance by the peoples of Europe? Clearly not. In most, if not all, Member States, they would be overwhelmingly *rejected*.

It is also clear that any idea of a change of *Grundnorm* would be rejected by the courts of the Member States. The highest courts in two Member States—Germany and Denmark—have already done so in express terms. In Germany, the Federal Constitutional Court (*Bundesverfassungsgericht*) ruled in 1993, in *Brunner v European Union Treaty*,[12] that Community law applies in Germany only because

---

[9] See, for example, *The State v Dosso* PLD 1985 SC 553 (Pakistan), a case subsequently held to have been wrongly decided (*Jilani v State of Punjab* PLD 1972 SC 139); *Uganda v Prison Commissioner, ex p. Matovu* [1966] EA 514 (Uganda); *R v Ndhlovu* [1968] (4) SA 515 (Rhodesia, now Zimbabwe). For analysis of the issues raised in these cases see: J Harris, 'When and Why Does the Grundnorm Change?' (1971) *CLJ* 103; J Eekelaar 'Splitting the Grundnorm' (1967) 30 *MLR* 156 and 'Rhodesia: The Abdication of Constitutionalism' (1969) 32 *MLR* 19; T Honoré, 'Reflections on Revolutions' (1967) *Irish Jurist* 268; SA de Smith, 'Constitutional Lawyers in Revolutionary Situations' (1968) 7 *Western Ontario L Rev.* 93; RWM Dias, 'Legal Politics: Norms behind the Grundnorm' (1968) 26 *CLJ* 233; Brookfield, 'The Courts, Kelsen, and the Rhodesian Revolution' (1969) 19 *U of Toronto L J* 326. One way in which the new regime can avoid these problems is to require all the judges to swear allegiance to it: those who refuse can be dismissed and, if they cause trouble, arrested.

[10] The Community treaties contain no provision permitting a Member State to leave the Union.

[11] As long ago as 1964, the European Court said that the Member States have limited their sovereign rights: *Costa v ENEL*, Case 6/64, [1964] ECR 585 at 593.

[12] Decision of 12 Oct 1993, [1994] 1 CMLR 57; (1994) 33 ILM 388; 89 BVerfGE 155; 20 EuGRZ 429; [1993] NJW 3047. For a full discussion and analysis, see U Everling, 'The *Maastricht* Judgment of the German Federal Constitutional Court and its Significance for the Development of the European Union' (1994) 14 *YEL* 1; N Foster, 'The German Constitution and EC Membership' (1994) *PL* 392; M Herdegen, 'Maastricht and the German Constitutional Court: Constitutional Restraints for an 'Ever Closer Union' (1994) 31 *CMLRev.* 233; J Kokott, 'Report on Gemany' in A-M Slaughter, A Stone Sweet and JHH Weiler, *The European Court of Justice and National Courts—Doctrine and Jurisprudence* (Hart, Oxford, 1998), 77; N MacCormick, 'The *Maastricht-Urteil*: Sovereignty Now' (1995) 1 *ELJ* 259.

laws passed by the German Parliament say it does.[13] It also said that Germany has preserved its status as a sovereign State.[14] In Denmark, the Supreme Court held in *Carlsen v Rasmussen*[15] that Community law applies in Denmark only by reason of, and to the extent permitted by, the Danish Constitution:[16] if the Community tried to legislate beyond those limits, the law in question would have no effect in Denmark;[17] the same would apply to judgments of the European Court.[18] The Supreme Court affirmed that, despite EU membership, Denmark remains an independent State.[19] Although the issue does not appear to have been expressly considered by a court in any other Member State, there are a number of judgments that take it for granted that the original *Grundnorm* remains in force.[20] One can conclude, therefore, that the Community treaties remain what they always have been—treaties under international law.

3. A SEPARATE LEGAL SYSTEM?

Is Community law a separate legal system? Some theorists would say that it cannot be: if Community law is dependent on international law, the most it can be is a

---

[13] [1994] 1 CMLR 57 at 91 (para [55]).

[14] *Ibid.*

[15] Danish Supreme Court (*Højesteret*), judgment of 6 April 1998, *Carlsen v Rasmussen* [1999] 3 CMLR 854. For further discussion, see K Høegh, 'The Danish Maastricht Judgment' (1999) 24 *ELRev.* 80.

[16] S 9.2 (paras [10]–[16]) of the judgment.

[17] S 9.6 (paras [32]–[33]) of the judgment.

[18] *Ibid.*

[19] S 9.8 (para [35] of the judgment).

[20] See, for example, the decisions of the French *Conseil Constitutionnel* in *Maastricht I*, Decision 92–308 DC, 9 April 1992, *Recueil* at 55; [1933] 3 CMLR 345 and *Amsterdam*, Decision 97–394 DC, 31 Dec 1997, JORF NO. 2 of 3 Jan 1998; comment by Mouthaan in (1998) 23 *ELRev.* 592. (In *Sarran et Levacher*, *Conseil d'Etat*, 30 Oct 1998, *Revue française de droit administratif*, 1998, n 14, 1081; *L'Actualité juridique, Droit Administratif*, 1998, 1039, the French *Conseil d'Etat* held that international treaties are subordinate to the French Constitution; the case did not, however, concern the EU: see C Richards, 'Sarran et Levacher: Ranking Legal Norms in the French Repubic' (2000 25 *ELRev.* 192.) In *R v Secretary of State, ex parte Factortame (No 2)* [1991] AC 603 at 659, Lord Bridge said that the duty of a United Kingdom court to allow directly applicable Community provisions to override rules of national law follows from the European Communities Act 1972. The Italian Constitutional Court (*Corte Costituzionale*) has held that Community law cannot prevail over the basic principles of the Italian Constitution, a position which seems incompatible with a change of *Grundnorm*: see *Frontini*, *Corte Costituzionale*, Decision No 183 of 27 Dec 1973, [1974] 2 CMLR 372 (para [21] of the judgment); [1974] RDI 154; *Fragd, Corte Costituzionale*, Decision No 168 of 21 April 1989, English translation in A Oppenheimer (ed), *The Relationship between European Community Law and National Law—The Cases* (Cambridge University Press, Cambridge, 1994) at 653; (1990) I *Foro Italiano* 1855. See, further, M Cartabia, 'The Italian Constitutional Court and the Relationship between the Italian Legal System and the European Union', in Slaughter, Stone Sweet and Weiler, n 12 above, 138–139; B De Witte, 'Sovereignty and European Integration: The Weight of European Legal Tradition', *ibid* 277 at pp 288–89. In Greece, the Sixth Chamber of the Council of State held in *Vagias v DI KATSA*, Decision No 2808/1997 of 8 July 1997, that, though Community law prevails over Greek statutes, it is subordinate to the Greek Constitution: see E Maganaris, 'The Principle of Supremacy of Community Law—The Greek Challenge' (1998) 23 *ELRev.* 179. When the matter was reconsidered by a plenary session of the Council of State (29 judges), a majority side-stepped the issue through a dubious interpretation of the relevant provisions of Community law: see E Maganaris, 'The Principle of Supremacy of Community Law in Greece—From Direct Challenge to Non-Applicaton'(1999) 24 *ELRev.* 426.

sub-system of international law. This is because they would define a legal system as all the legal rules dependent on the same *Grundnorm*.[21] Most lawyers, on the other hand, use the term 'legal system' in a more pragmatic way and might regard the law of a dependent territory as a separate legal system, even if it derives its validity from some enactment of the parent State. In this sense, a legal system may be defined as a set of legal rules (broadly defined) that are mutually consistent (non-contradictory) and are normally applied together. Is Community law a separate system in this sense?

If a group of States conclude a treaty in order to create an international organisation with law-making powers, the question whether the law created by that organisation is a separate legal system (in the sense we are considering) must depend on the intention of those States. Since no express statement of intention appears in the Community treaties, the intention of the Member States must be inferred from the terms of the treaties. These have been analysed elsewhere,[22] and it was concluded that, though the Community treaties contain many novel features, there is nothing in them inconsistent with an intention that Community law should be part of international law. Even their most unusual features—the power of the European Court to hear preliminary references from national courts[23] and the direct effect of Community law[24]—would not be inappropriate in an international organisation governed by international law; indeed, most international lawyers would regard them as highly desirable. Consequently, not withstanding the impressive advance displayed by Community law over traditional international-law regimes, the terms of the treaties do not indicate an intention to create a separate legal system.

Despite this, the European Court has taken the position that Community law is separate from international law. In 1963, it stated, somewhat ambiguously, that the Community constitutes a 'new legal order of international law.'[25] A year later, in *Costa v ENEL*[26] it came out more clearly in favour of separation when it said,

---

[21] See J Raz, *The Concept of a Legal System* (2nd edn, Clarendon Press, Oxford, 1980) at 95 *et seq.*

[22] TC Hartley, *Constitutional Problems of the European Union* (Hart, Oxford, 1999) at 128 *et seq.*

[23] At present, there are at least three other international courts with jurisdiction to give preliminary rulings on a reference from a national court: the Benelux Court, the Andean Court of Justice and the EFTA Court, the last having jurisdiction only to give advisory opinions. On the Benelux Court, see Art 6 of the Treaty establishing the Benelux Court, 1965 (in force on 1 Jan 1974); on the Andean Court, see Arts 28–31 of the Treaty creating the Court of Justice of the Cartagena Agreement, 1979, (1979) 18 ILM 1203; on the EFTA Court, see Art 34 of the Agreement between the EFTA States on the establishment of a Surveillance Authority and a Court of Justice, OJ 1994, L 344 (see, further, P Christiansen, 'The EFTA Court' (1997) 22 *ELRev.* 539 at 542–43). These courts were all established after the European Court; however, in 1907 it was suggested that the proposed International Prize Court (which, in the end, was never set up) should have the power to hear appeals from national courts. Other international courts may well come to have some such power in the future. In fact, one author has written, 'From the perspective of public international law, the novelty of the Community's system of references for preliminary ruling lies less in the conception than in the achievement.' See R Plender, 'The European Court as an International Tribunal' (1983) *CLJ* 279 at 284.)

[24] Discussed below.

[25] Case 26/62, [1963] ECR 1 at 12.

[26] Case 6/64, [1964] ECR 585 at 593.

'By contrast with [*sic*] ordinary international treaties, the EEC Treaty has created its own legal system.' More recently, in 1991, it simply said that the Community treaties have established a 'new legal order.'[27] This view has been accepted by the Constitutional Courts of both Germany and Italy.[28] Since this is a quesion of interpreting the Community treaties, the view of the European Court must be decisive: when they concluded the Community treaties, the Member States gave it the power to interpret them[29] and undertook in the EC Treaty not to submit a dispute concerning its interpretation or application to any method of settlement other than those provided for in it.[30] We must conclude, therefore, that Community law constitutes a separate legal system from international law (or, in more theoretical terminology, a separate sub-system).

This has had important consequences for the relationship between Community law and international law. For example, in *Germany v Council* ('*Banana*' *case*),[31] the Court held that a Community regulation could be valid even though its adoption was contrary to the GATT, a treaty binding on both the Community and the Member States. It is hard to imagine that it could have reached this conclusion if it had regarded Community law as part of international law. Interestingly enough, the example usually quoted of the consequence of declaring Community law separate from international law, *Commission v Luxembourg and Belgium*,[32] would probably have been decided the same way under international law.[33]

4. DISSOLVING THE UNION

One of the consequences of the dependent character of Community law is that the Member States—provided they act unanimously—could dissolve the European Union if they wished. The fact that the Community treaties make no provision for this is irrelevant.[34] The existence of the Union depends on the treaties, which in turn depend on international law. Consequently, international law decides whether the treaties can be terminated. Under international law this is possible if all the parties agree: it is not necessary that the treaties should

---

[27] *First EEA Opinion*, Opinion 1/91, [1991] ECR 6079 (para 21).

[28] *Bundesverfassungsgericht, Internationale Handelsgesellschaft* case, 29 May 1974, [1974] 2 CMLR 540 (para 19); *Corte Costituzionale, Frontini* case, 27 Dec 1973, [1973] CMLR 372 (para 12).

[29] See the various provisions conferring jurisdiction on the Court to interpret the treaties, especially Art 234 [177] EC.

[30] Art 292 [219] EC.

[31] Case C-280/93, [1994] ECR I-4973.

[32] Case 90, 91/63, [1964] ECR 625; [1965] CMLR 58.

[33] D Wyatt, 'New Legal Order, or Old?', (1982) *7 ELRev.* 147 at 160.

[34] Art 97 of the ECSC Treaty states that it is concluded for a period of fifty years from its entry into force, a provision which might be regarded as implying that it cannot be terminated before then; the other treaties contain no such provision, which could be regarded as implying that they can be terminated at the will of the parties, or that they can never be terminated, or neither.

themselves make provision for their termination.[35] The position would be the same even if the treaties expressly provided that they could not be terminated. Such a provision cannot be binding.[36] Take the analogy of a provision in a contract that the contract cannot be terminated even if all the parties agree. That cannot prevent the parties from subsequently agreeing to terminate the contract. One cannot believe that the position is different in the case of a treaty. How could international law decree that an international organisation lives on, if all its members want it dissolved? Such a result would be unrealistic and impractical.

5. AMENDING THE TREATIES

If nothing in Community law can prevent the total repeal of the treaties, nothing can prevent their partial repeal; so nothing in Community law can prevent the repeal of any particular provision in the treaties. Moreover, just as a provision in a contract or treaty stating that the parties will not rescind that contract or treaty (in whole or in part) is of no effect, so too is a provision that the parties will not add a particular provision to their contract or treaty. That also cannot be binding on them. It cannot prevent them from subsequently agreeing to add the provision. It follows that the treaties cannot prevent their amendment.[37]

As is well known, the treaties contain procedural rules governing their amendment. Today, these are contained in Article 48 [N] of the Treaty on European Union. This provides that the Council must deliver an opinion (after consulting the European Parliament and, where appropriate, the Commission) in favour of calling a conference of the representatives of the Governments of the Member States. The conference is then convened and must determine unanimously what amendments are to be made. Though not specified by Article 48[N], the amendments take the form of a new treaty amending the existing treaties. However, for the reasons explained above, Article 48 [N] cannot deprive the Member States,

---

[35] To the extent that the Community treaties contain no contrary provision, this follows from Art 54 of the Vienna Convention on the Law of Treaties 1969, which provides that a treaty may be terminated *either* in conformity with the provisions of the treaty *or* by consent of all the parties. If, however, the Community treaties were regarded as containing some provision impliedly preventing their termination, Art 5 of the Vienna Convention would apply. This states that the Convention applies to the constituent treaty of an international organisation 'without prejudice to any rules of the organization.' In such a case, the matter would be outside the scope of the Vienna Convention and would have to be resolved on the basis of customary international law, under which termination by unanimous consent is (it is suggested) possible.

[36] It is assumed that no question arises regarding the rights of third parties.

[37] For the opposite position, see Cruz Vilaça and Piçarra, n 5 above, a position which draws support from a cryptic statement by the European Court in the first *EEA* case, Opinion 1/91, [1991] ECR 6079 (para 72 of the Opinion). However, it is accepted by most authors, including Cruz Vilaça and Piçarra, that this view is tenable only on the assumption that the Community treaties have broken free of international law and become a new *Grundnorm*: see in particular Cruz Vilaça and Piçarra, n 5 above, at 9–13.

acting unanimously, of the power to amend the treaties without complying with its requirements.[38] Those requirements must, therefore, be regarded as not mandatory but merely directory: failure to comply with them is an infringement of Community law,[39] but does not affect the validity of the amendment.[40] This is borne out by the fact that on two occasions in the past the ECSC Treaty has been amended without following the procedure laid down in it.[41] No one has ever questioned the validity of these amendments.

6. DIRECT EFFECT

Direct effect[42] is concerned with the way in which a provision of one legal system is applied in another. It thus involves the transfer of a provision between systems. The way in which this is determined depends on the relationship between the two systems. If one is dependent on the other (in the sense that it derives its validity from it), the question of transfer must be determined by the primary system. It

---

[38] All the arguments are collected and analysed with lucidity and thoughtfulness in M Deliège-Sequaris, 'Révision des traités européens en dehors des procédures prévues' (1980) *CDE* 539. At the time this article was written, the author was a junior lecturer (*assistant*) at the University of Liège. For a rather clumsy attempt by a professor at the same university to refute her conclusions, see JV Louis, 'Quelques considérations sur la révision des traités instituant les Communautes', *ibid* at 553. A more sophisticated case for the view that the procedural requirements in the Treaty are binding on the Member States is to be found in JHH Weiler and Haltern, 'Response: The Autonomy of the Community Legal Order—Through the Looking Glass' (1996) 37 *Harvard Journal of International Law* 411 at 417–23. The authors of this latter article accept that their argument stands up only if one accepts the theory that the Community treaties have broken free of international law and become a new *Grundnorm*. In international law, it is generally agreed that if a treaty lays down special procedures for its amendment, the States party to it may follow those procedures if they wish, but are not bound to do so: see B De Witte, 'Rules of Change in International Law: How Special is the European Community?' (1994) 25 *Neth. Yb. Int. L* 299 at 312 *et seq*. Weiler and Haltern accept this: see their article at 417–18. For the opposite view, see A Pellet, 'Les fondements juridiques internationaux du droit communautaire' (1997) 5 *Collected Courses of the Academy of European Law*, Book 2, 193 at 214–17. Pellet bases his view on Art 5 of the Vienna Convention on the Law of Treaties (explained above at n 35). However, Art 5 merely excludes the application of the Vienna Convention where its terms conflict with the provisions of the constituent treaty of an international organization: it does not give those provisions any greater effect than they would have had apart from the Convention. The matter therefore falls to be determined by customary international law, under which amendment by unanimous consent without any special procedure is always possible.

[39] In theory, proceedings could be brought against the Member States (all of them!) under Art 226 [169] EC.

[40] If the dictum of the European Court in *Defrenne v Sabena*, Case 43/75, [1976] ECR 455 (para 58 of the Judgment) was intended to deny this, it cannot be right.

[41] The first was the Treaty of 27 Oct 1956, which brought about certain amendments consequent on the return of the Saar to Germany, and the second was the Convention on Certain Institutions Common to the European Communities, which was signed at the same time as the EEC and Euratom Treaties: see P Pescatore, *L'ordre juridique des Communautés européennes* (Presses Universitaires de Liège, Liège, 1975) at 62–63.

[42] See text to n 46, below.

can decide whether provisions of the one system can apply in the other and, if they do, in what circumstances this will occur. If, on the other hand, neither system is dependent on the other, each system decides for itself whether provisions of the other can be transferred to it.

This will be clear from two examples. Assume, first, that the United Kingdom decides to give home rule to a territory under its jurisdiction. It sets up a regional assembly with law-making powers and creates a system of courts for that territory. Clearly, United Kingdom law determines whether provisions of United Kingdom law apply in the dependent legal system or whether provisions of the dependent system apply in the United Kingdom system. This is because United Kingdom law is the primary system.

Now contrast the position where each system is independent of the other. Let us take the relationship between English and French law. English law may have one provision dealing with a particular matter—say, the validity of a marriage— and French law may have another. The question whether an English court will apply the French provision with regard to a particular marriage must depend on English law—the English rules of conflict of laws.[43] Whether a French court would apply the French or the English provision to the marriage would, however, depend on French law. The result is that the same marriage might be valid in English eyes and invalid in French eyes. This is unfortunate, but inescapable in view of the relationship between the two legal systems.

These principles also govern the relationship between international law and national law. Since these two systems are independent of each other,[44] the question whether a provision of international law applies in national law must depend on the latter. This is indeed the case. The law of each country decides to what extent international law has effect as part of the legal system of that country.[45]

The important issue for our purposes is the application of a treaty in the domestic law of the States that are parties to it. If a treaty (or a provision in it) applies in the legal system of such a State without that State having to adopt any legislation specifically providing for the application of that treaty, the treaty is said

[43] Some would say that an English court never applies foreign law as such, but merely applies a provision of English law modelled on the foreign provision: see WW Cook, *Logical and Legal Bases of the Conflict of Laws* (Harvard University Press, Cambridge, 1942) at 20–21. It is true that the English court may not apply the foreign provision in precisely the same way as the foreign court would; nevertheless, it is hardly justified to say that the foreign provision is not applied. For further discussion, see JHC Morris, *The Conflict of Laws* (4th edn by D McClean, Sweet & Maxwell, London, 1993) at 446–47.

[44] This may be rejected by theorists who follow the monist view of international law, but it accords with the actual, real-life relationship between the two systems.

[45] See FG Jacobs and S Roberts (eds), *The Effect of Treaties in Domestic Law* (Sweet & Maxwell, London, 1987) at xxiv (introduction by Jacobs, based on studies of individual countries in later parts of the book). For the United States, see the thoughtful analysis by JH Jackson, *ibid*, 141 at 153–55.

to be 'directly effective' or 'directly applicable'.[46] A treaty that is directly effective is automatically part of the legal system of the State in question. If, on the other hand, it is not directly effective, it cannot be applied in the domestic law of the State without the adoption of legislation to make provision for this.

When States sign a treaty, they normally agree to achieve a certain result, but reserve to themselves the right to determine the means by which this will be brought about. If the desired result involves an alteration of their law, their law decides whether this will follow automatically from the treaty (direct effect) or whether legislation will be necessary. In certain States (sometimes called 'monist'), direct effect is possible;[47] in others (sometimes called 'dualist') it is not.[48] In both cases, however, it is by virtue of the law of the State in question that the treaty is applied: in a 'monist' country, it is the rule permitting the direct application of treaties (a rule that may be anything from a judge-made principle to a constitutional provision); in a 'dualist' country, it is the legislation passed to give effect to the particular treaty in question. In this latter case, the legislation may take various forms. At one end of the spectrum, it may simply amend national law to bring it into line with the treaty, possibly without even referring to it.[49] At the other end, it may provide that the treaty (contained in a Schedule to the legislation) will have the force of law in the country concerned.[50] In this last situation, the only real difference between a 'dualist' and a 'monist' country is that in the former there is a separate legislative measure each time a treaty has to be applied in the domestic legal system, while in the latter there is one measure providing for the application of all future treaties.[51]

---

[46] It is not necessary to consider the arguments that raged at one time on a possible distinction between direct effect and direct applicability: the differences, if they exist, are of no consequence for our discussion.

[47] This does not mean that every treaty will be directly effective: the law of the State in question specifies the requirements for direct effect. Frequently, it must be shown that the treaty is self-executing. This concept was explained as long ago as 1829 by the United States Supreme Court in *Foster and Elam v Neilson* 2 Pet. 253 at 314, where it distinguished a treaty provision which 'operates of itself, without the aid of any legislative provision' from a provision in which one of the parties 'engages to perform a particular act'. In the former case, the treaty provision is self-executing; in the latter, it is not.

[48] The distinction between the 'monist' and 'dualist' approaches is actually more complex and far-reaching than this, since it concerns the over-all relationship between international and domestic law: see I Brownlie, *Principles of Public International Law* (5th edn, Oxford University Press, Oxford, 1998) at 31 *et seq*. In adopting these terms, we are not, however, raising these wider questions: we are simply using the terms as handy tags to denote the two approaches set out in the text above. Even if the terms are used in this limited sense, however, the statements in the text are still something of an over-simplification: see FG Jacobs in Jacobs and Roberts, n 45 above, at xxiv–xxvi.

[49] In such a case, there might be some justification in saying that the treaty is not applied as such, but rather that a rule of national law is modelled on the treaty: see n 43 above.

[50] For an example of this latter method, see s 2(1) of the Carriage of Goods by Sea Act 1971, which provides that the Hague-Visby Rules (an international agreement) will have the force of law in the United Kingdom. For a more detailed discussion of the position in the United Kingdom, see R Higgins in Jacobs and Roberts, n 45 above, at 126–29.

[51] Even though the United Kingdom is a 'dualist' country, legislation adopted to give effect to a treaty will, if possible, be interpreted in such a way as to conform to the treaty: *James Buchanan & Co. Ltd v Babco Forwarding and Shipping (UK) Ltd* [1978] AC 141; *Fothergill v Monarch Airlines Ltd* [1981] AC 251; see further, AV Dicey and JHC Morris, *The Conflict of Laws* (13th edn, Sweet & Maxwell, London, 2000) at 9–16. This rule can apply even if the United Kingdom legislation does not refer to the treaty, provided it is shown that the legislation was passed to give effect to it.

Since Member-State law is not dependent on Community law, it follows that Community law cannot apply in the legal systems of the Member States unless Member-State law says so: no rule of Community law can itself bring this about.[52] In Article 249 [189] EC, the Member States agreed that EC (originally, EEC) regulations would be directly applicable in all Member States. This meant that, unlike the position in most treaties, the parties to the EC Treaty agreed not only to achieve a certain result, but also agreed on the means by which this would be brought about (direct effect). In other words, all the Member States undertook to adopt the 'monist' position in this particular case.[53] Though unusual, such a provision is in no any way contrary to international law.[54]

Having undertaken this, the Member States then had to carry it out. In the case of the 'monist' countries, the rule of national law making general provision for direct effect—the rule making that country 'monist'—was sufficient; in the case of 'dualist' countries, on the other hand, a special rule had to be adopted for the purpose. In the United Kingdom, this was section 2(1) of the European Communities Act 1972, which states that all provisions of Community law (including those to be adopted in the future) that under Community law are to be given legal effect without further enactment (direct effect) will be directly effective in the United Kingdom. It is only by virtue of this provision that Community law is directly effective in the United Kingdom. Thus, while the obligation to give direct effect to certain provisions of Community law stems from the treaties, the *carrying out* of that obligation is a matter for national law.

7. SUPREMACY

If a provision of one legal system is applied in another, it may conflict with a provision of the latter. When this occurs, the principles discussed above must determine which provision prevails. Thus, where an international treaty is applied in

---

[52] See, for example, *Brunner v European Union Treaty, Bundesverfassungsgericht,* decision of 12 Oct 1993, [1994] 1 CMLR 57; (1994) 33 ILM 388; 89 BverfGE 155, in which the German Constitutional Court stated that Community law applies in Germany only because the German laws ratifying the Community treaties said that it would (para [55] in the CMLR text).

[53] Art 249 [189] also states that directives are binding as to the result to be achieved but they leave to each Member State the choice of form and methods, thereby making the effect of a directive in the legal systems of Member States dependent on national legislation. Thus, provision was made both for instruments of a 'monist' character and for those of a 'dualist' character, each to be used where appropriate. The novelty of this was not the recognition of these two approaches, but the fact that all the parties to the treaty agreed to adopt the same appproach in any given case. The advantage of this is that each Community measure applies in the same way in every Member State. Unfortunately, the European Court has distorted this scheme by holding that directives can have a limited direct effect: see *Van Duyn v Home Office,* Case 41/74, [1974] ECR 1337. It has also ruled that treaty provisions can be directly effective: *Van Gend en Loos,* Case 26/62, [1963] ECR 1. For further discussion, see TC Hartley, n 22 above, at 24–30.

[54] See JH Jackson in Jacobs and Roberts, n 45 above, at 154; see also R Plender, 'The European Court as an International Tribunal' (1983) *CLJ* 279 at 287–88; cf the Advisory Opinion of the Permanent Court of International Justice in the *Danzig Railway Officials* case (1928) PCIJ Ser. B No 15.

the legal system of one of the parties to it, the question whether the treaty over-rides national law must be determined by the law of that State. In the case of a 'monist' country, the rule providing for the direct effect of treaties may also indicate their position in the legal hierarchy; otherwise, there will usually be a judge-made rule. In the United States, for example, a treaty that is directly effective[55] has the same position in the legal hierarchy as a federal statute: it prevails over earlier federal statutes but is subordinate to later ones.[56] This is a judge-made rule, though it is partly derived from Article VI, section 2, of the United States Constitution.[57] In the Netherlands, on the other hand, the Constitution provides that directly effective treaties prevail over both prior and subsequent legislation.[58]

In the case of a 'dualist' country (such as the United Kingdom), the status of a treaty depends on the instrument by which it was given legal effect. If words from a treaty are incorporated into a statute (either with, or without, a reference to the treaty), they take effect as part of that statute: it is the statute, not the treaty, that is applied. If there is a conflict with another legal provision, the conflict is not between the treaty and the other provision, but between the statute and the other provision. The normal rules determine which prevails. If, on the other hand, the statute says that the treaty has the force of law, it makes sense to say that the treaty itself is being applied. Nevertheless, it is applied only because the statute says so; consequently, the status of the treaty is the same as that of the statute. In both cases, therefore, the position of the treaty in the legal hierarchy depends on that of the legislation by which it was given effect. If this was a statute, it will prevail over earlier statutes, but not over later ones. If it was subordinate legislation, it will have the same status as that legislation.[59] These rules can, however, be changed if the legislation which gave effect to the treaty so provides. The Human Rights Act 1998 is an example: though it gives (limited) effect to the European Convention on Human Rights in the domestic law of the United Kingdom, it provides that the Convention does not prevail over *any* United Kingdom legislation, either subsequent or prior.[60]

These rules do not normally prevent States from carrying out their treaty obligations. Since most treaties merely require the parties to achieve a given result, the status of the treaty in their domestic law does not matter as long as the result

---

[55] Not all international agreements count as 'treaties' in the United States, and not all 'treaties' are directly effective. For the details, see JH Jackson in Jacobs and Roberts, n 45 above, at 142–59.

[56] See JH Jackson, *ibid* 141 at 162. For further details, see *ibid* at 159–64.

[57] Art VI, s 2 reads: 'This Constitution, and the Laws of the United States which shall be made in Pursuance thereof; and all Treaties made, or which shall be made, under the Authority of the United States, shall be the supreme Law of the Land; and the Judges in every State shall be bound thereby, any Thing in the Constitution or Laws of any State to the Contrary notwithstanding.' This establishes that treaties prevail over State legislation, but does not clearly determine their position with regard to federal legislation.

[58] See HG Schermers in Jacobs and Roberts, n 45 above, at 112–14.

[59] The status of subordinate legislation normally depends on that of the statute under which it was adopted.

[60] See ss 3 and 4. This is said to have caused some bemusement in the House of Lords: see KO Ewing, 'The Human Rights Act and Parliamentary Democracy' (1999) 62 *MLR* 79 at 88, n 57.

is achieved. The fact that the treaty could be overridden by later legislation is not a breach of the obligations under it, if this does not in fact occur. If it occurs inadvertently, the matter can be put right as soon as the conflict is evident. For example, the United Kingdom was a party to the European Convention on Human Rights for many years before the Human Rights Act 1998 came into force. Whenever it appeared, perhaps in a judgment of the European Court of Human Rights, that United Kingdom law conflicted with a provision of the Convention, the position was rectified by the amendment of the offending legislation.[61]

The European Court has never expressly rejected these principles, but it has been loath to give express acceptance to them. The first time the question came before it, in *Van Gend en Loos*,[62] the Court took great care to avoid considering it. The case arose when a Dutch tribunal[63] asked the European Court to give a ruling on the direct effect of Article 12 of the EEC Treaty (as it then stood), and it was argued by the Dutch and Belgian Governments that the question whether the Community provision prevailed over a conflicting provision of Dutch law depended on Dutch law, and therefore fell within the exclusive jurisdiction of the Dutch courts. The European Court did not deny this, but said it had not been asked to rule on Dutch law, but merely to interpret the Treaty.[64] When the Belgian Government insisted that no answer the European Court might give could possibly have any bearing on the proceedings before the Dutch tribunal, it replied that it was none of its business why the Dutch tribunal had chosen to ask the questions it had or whether its answer would be relevant to the proceedings before it: all that mattered was that the questions concerned Community law.[65]

There is no provision in the treaties stating that Community law prevails over Member-State law. It could, however, be argued that Article 249 [189] EC, which (as we have seen) provides that regulations are directly applicable, implies that they should be given at least a certain degree of supremacy.[66] The numerous statements by the European Court that directly effective Community law prevails over Member-State law, both prior and subsequent, are based on the proposition that

---

[61]   In this respect, the position will not be greatly changed by the Human Rights Act, though amendments are now more likely to be made as a result of a ruling by a United Kingdom court.

[62]   Case 26/62, [1963] ECR 1; [1963] CMLR 105.

[63]   The *Tariefcommissie*, a tribunal concerned with customs duties.

[64]   [1963] ECR at 10–11.

[65]   *Ibid.* Since the Netherlands is a 'monist' country and the Dutch Constitution provides that treaties prevail over Dutch legislation, the Dutch tribunal would have been willing to give primacy to a provision of the EEC Treaty, provided it was self-executing (see n 47 above). The Dutch Government considered that this was a question for Dutch law to decide. The Dutch tribunal, however, referred it to the European Court, perhaps because it thought that the correct interpretation of the Community provision would assist it in reaching a decision. In these circumstances, it was not unreasonable for the European Court to say that the Dutch tribunal's reasons for making the reference were none of its concern. However, once it had surmounted the jurisdictional hurdle, the European Court went on to consider not only whether the Community provision was self-executing (it held that it was), but also whether the Member States had implicitly agreed to give self-executing treaty provisions direct effect (it held that they had). This last point was not relevant in the case of the Netherlands, but the Court was obviously preparing its position for future battles against 'dualist' States.

[66]   *Costa v ENEL*, Case 6/64, [1963] ECR 585 at 594.

this is what the Member States (implicitly) agreed when they signed the treaties:[67] there is no other source from which such a principle could be derived.

Have the Member States carried out this agreement? Here we have a problem. As we have seen, Community provisions can have effect in Member States only by virtue of Member-State law, and the extent to which they prevail over domestic law also depends on a rule of Member-State law. However, all rules of Member-State law derive their validity from the national constitution: consequently, they cannot be valid if the constitution declares them invalid. Since the rule providing for the supremacy of Community law is itself a rule of Member-State law, its validity too depends on the national constitution. This means that the supremacy of Community law in a country always depends, in the last analysis, on the constitution of that country. If the constitution imposes limits on such supremacy, there is no way those limits can be avoided—unless the constitution itself is amended.

This is most obvious in those countries with written constitutions. In Germany, for example, the Constitutional Court has stated expressly that Community law applies in Germany only because the treaties were approved by the German Parliament. Since the German Parliament is subject to the Constitution, it could not grant the Community any powers that conflicted with the Constitution. Although the Constitution permits Germany to confer powers on an international organization like the Community, those powers must not be open-ended: they have to be defined in advance. This means that the Community cannot be given the power to extend its powers, what the Germans call *Kompetenz-Kompetenz*. The German Constitutional Court has, therefore, ruled that any Community measure that contravenes this principle would be inapplicable in Germany.[68] The Danish Supreme Court has reached a similar conclusion.[69] Section 20 of the Danish Constitution permits the delegation of powers to an international organisation, but this too requires that they be defined in advance. The Supreme Court held, therefore, that if a Community measure went beyond the powers conferred on the Community, the Danish courts would declare it inapplicable in Denmark. In both Germany and Denmark, the national courts would be the ones to decide.

Similar views have been expressed by courts in other Member States (though they have not always been so clearly formulated).[70] So far, however, there has been no case in which a Community provision has actually been held to infringe the constitution of a Member State. If this were to happen, the European Court would presumably declare that the State in question had infringed the treaty.[71] That State

---

[67] *Ibid.*

[68] *Brunner v European Union Treaty, Bundesverfassungsgericht,* Decision of 12 Oct 1993, [1994] 1 CMLR 57 (see further n 12 above).

[69] *Carlsen v Rasmussen,* Danish Supreme Court (*Højesteret*), judgment of 6 April 1998, [1999] 3 CMLR 854 (see further n 15 above).

[70] See n 20 above.

[71] The European Court claims that Community law must always prevail over national constitutions: see, for example, *Simmenthal,* Case 106/77, [1978] ECR 629. For the more lenient rule under international law, see the Vienna Convention on the Law of Treaties, Art 46. In view of its theory that Community law is separate from international law (discussed above), the European Court would almost certainly regard international law as inapplicable in this case.

would then have to amend its constitution, if this were possible.[72] If not, all the Member States would have to work together to find a solution, possibly by amending Community law.

An example of the way in which Community law can be changed to accommodate national constitutional problems is to be found in the series of cases in which the European Court has developed the Community doctrine of fundamental human rights. Once it became clear that the German Constitutional Court would not permit the application of Community law in Germany if it infringed fundamental human rights as defined in the German Constitution, the European Court declared that fundamental human rights, in which it had previously shown little interest,[73] were 'enshrined in the general principles of Community law and protected by the Court.'[74] In later cases, it has said that it will strike down Community measures that are incompatible with fundamental human rights as recognised in the constitutions of the Member States.[75] At the same time, however, it has insisted that the validity of a Community measure or its effect within a Member State cannot be affected by allegations that it is contrary to fundamental human rights as formulated by the constitution of a Member State.[76] These two statements do not seem entirely consistent; nevertheless, the general message is clear: Member States must accept that Community law prevails over their constitutions, while the European Court will ensure that, at least as far as human rights are concerned, any Community provision that conflicts with the constitution of a Member State will be declared invalid. As a result, the German Constitutional Court, which had originally said it would examine Community measures to ensure that they complied with German notions of fundamental human rights (and refuse to permit their application in Germany if they did not),[77] eventually decided to let the European Court perform this task,[78] though it has not resiled from its position that the German Constitution prevails over Community law in Germany.

The United Kingdom's minimalist Constitution is less likely to produce conflicts of this kind; however, there is one situation in which such a clash could occur. This concerns one of the fundamental provisions of the British Constitution, the rule that Parliament cannot limit its future powers. Since there is no way (short

---

[72] Certain provisions of the German Constitution cannot be amended: *Grundgesetz*, Art 79(3); moreover, in both Germany and in other Member States, it might be politically impossible to obtain the necessary majority to amend the Constitution.

[73] *Stork v High Authority*, Case 1/58, [1959] ECR 17 at 26 (rights under *Grundgesetz*, Arts 2 and 12); *Geitling v High Authority*, Cases 36–8, 40/59, [1960] ECR 423 at 438 (rights under *Grundgesetz* Art 14).

[74] *Stauder v Ulm*, Case 29/69, [1969] ECR 419 (para 7 of the judgment).

[75] *Nold v Commission*, Case 4/73, [1974] ECR 491 (para 13 of the judgment).

[76] *Internationale Handelsgesellschaft*, Case 11/70, [1970] ECR 1125 (para 3 of the judgment). Interestingly, this statement is absent from the *Nold* case (*ibid*), but it reappears in later cases: see, for example, *Hauer*, Case 44/79, [1979] ECR 3727 (para 14).

[77] *Internationale Handelsgesellschaft* case, *Bundesverfassungsgericht*, 29 May 1974, [1974] 2 CMLR 540.

[78] *Wünsche Handelsgesellschaft* case, *Bundesverfassungsgericht*, 22 Oct 1986, [1987] 3 CMLR 225.

of a change in the *Grundnorm*) in which this rule can be altered, it is not constitutionally possible for Parliament to disable itself from legislating contrary to
Community law in the future. If the European Court demanded this (as distinct
from demanding that Parliament should not exercise its power), the United
Kingdom could not comply.

When the United Kingdom joined the Community, Parliament gave Community law the maximum degree of supremacy that was constitutionally possible.
This was done in the European Communities Act 1972. Section 2(1) of this provides for the direct effect of Community law, and section 2(4) provides that all
past and future Acts of Parliament must be 'construed and have effect' subject to
section 2(1). This might appear to limit the power of Parliament to pass legislation that conflicts with directly effective Community law, but all it can be regarded
as doing—since this is all Parliament is constitutionally capable of doing—is to
lay down a rule of interpretation to the effect that, since Parliament had no intention when it passed the European Communities Act of legislating contrary to
Community law and, since it did not believe that it would have such an intention
in the future, subsequent Acts of Parliament should be interpreted as not being
intended to apply to the extent that they conflicted with directly effective Community law. Such a rule of interpretation would prevent unintended conflicts.
However, if Parliament made clear that the legislation was intended to apply
notwithstanding any contrary provision of Community law, the courts would
have to give effect to that.

8. CONCLUSIONS

It will be seen that everything in this chapter follows from its initial premise that
the Community treaties are what they appear to be—treaties under international
law. Once this is accepted, it is possible to rebuild the bridge between Community law and international law, a bridge that once existed but was deliberately
destroyed in the early days of the Community by over-zealous judges and lawyers
who believed they were laying the foundations of a new superstate, a United States
of Europe. If this misconception is abandoned, many apparent problems are
revealed as normal and acceptable; moreover, the concepts and solutions of Community law can then be used to develop the legal systems of other international
organisations of a similar kind.[79]

---

[79] For further discussion of some of the issues considered in this chapter, see T Schilling, 'The
Autonomy of the Community Legal Order: An Analysis of Possible Foundations' (1996) 37 *Harvard
International Law Journal* 389; A Pellet; '*Les Fondements Juridiques Internationaux du Droit Commu-
nautaire*' (1997) V(2) *Collected Courses of the Academy of European Law* 193; D Rossa Phelan, *Revolt
or Revolution—The Constitutional Boundaries of the European Community* (Roundhall/Sweet &
Maxwell, Dublin, 1997); O Spiermann, 'The Other Side of the Story: An Unpopular Essay on the
Making of the European Community Legal Order' (1999) 10 *EJIL* 763; TC Hartley, *Constitutional Problems of the European Union* (Hart, Oxford, 1999), chs 7–10 (on sovereignty).

5

The Member States' Competence and Jurisdiction under the EU/EC Treaties

STEPHEN HYETT

1. INTRODUCTION

The issue of Member States' competence and jurisdiction under the EU/EC Treaties raises a large number of issues. This chapter considers two of them. On the one hand membership of the European Union involves a transfer of powers from the Member States to the European Communities.[1] This is the area where issues about Member States' competence have traditionally been considered. On the other hand, in federal States and States where powers are devolved to regional authorities, there is a transfer of competence in respect of certain matters to those regional authorities. Such a Member State therefore faces the situation where power in respect of certain matters is, on the one hand, transferred to the European Community, whilst, on the other hand, power in respect of certain matters, which may or may not include powers transferred to the European Community, rests with regional authorities. However, not only are the Member States concerned with these issues. Third countries, either directly or in the context of international organizations, are affected by them. Where powers have been transferred to the European Community, third countries need to take that into account. Similarly, within the European Union, questions arise as to the extent to which the competence of regional authorities should be recognised within the legal order created by the European Union.

The Treaties establishing the European Community have created a legal structure which is unique within the international legal order. It is a Community

---

[1] There are, at present, three Communities governed by separate Treaties: the European Community, the European Atomic Energy Community and the European Coal and Steel Community. The last ceases to exist on 24 July 2002. For convenience, this chapter deals with the European Community. The position in relation to the European Coal and Steel Community (the ECSC) is different to that in relation to the European Community: see I Macleod, ID Hendry and S Hyett, *The External Relations of the European Communities* (Oxford University Press, Oxford, 1996) ch 23. For an analysis of the position under the Euratom Treaty, see *ibid* at ch 22. One of the issues being considered by the Convention on the Future of the European Union is whether the European Union should have legal personality and, if so, the nature of that personality.

having powers stemming from a limitation by its Member State of their sovereignty and involves a transfer of powers within certain fields from those Member States to the Community. At a comparatively early stage in the development of the European Community, the European Court of Justice ruled that the European Economic Community had the power to enter into international agreements in place of the Member States in certain circumstances.[2] This has a fundamental effect on the Member States, since the consequence is that the Community itself enters into the international commitment instead of the Member States.

The existence and nature of the European Community's competence in the field of external relations is one of the most striking features of Community competence. After all, the power of a State to act internationally is an important attribute of statehood. One of the consequences of the external competence of the European Community is that the power of a Member State to act as an individual State where a matter falls within the competence of the European Community is not exercised directly; instead the Member State acts through the European Community.

In parallel, issues of competence arise within Member States which have a federal structure or where powers are devolved to regional authorities within the Member State. In such States the power to legislate and carry out executive functions of government are exercised by regional authorities in relation to certain matters.

Therefore, an analysis of the competence and jurisdiction of such a Member State of the European Union involves considering the effect of the competence and jurisdiction of the European Community and the powers of the constituent parts of the State, that is the national government and the regional authorities.

These are matters which are important politically. As mentioned above, the power to enter into agreements with other States and to participate as a member in international organizations is an important function of the State. In addition, the State has the responsibility to comply with the international obligations into which it has entered. For example, negotiations may be taking place on a new international convention relating to the environment. Some aspects will be within the competence of the European Community; other aspects will be within the competence of the Member States. In the United Kingdom, as a general rule, environmental matters are within the competence of the devolved administrations so far as Scotland, Wales and Northern Ireland are concerned.

Equally, these are matters of practical relevance to the State, its regional authorities, industries and citizens. For example, the Government wants the design and development of a major technological enterprise to take place in the United Kingdom and the Scottish Executive wants some of this to take place in Scotland. Financial assistance for the particular plant is within the competence of the Scottish Executive. Industrial policy relating to research and development in the industry concerned and support for it is within the competence of central gov-

---

[2] Case 22/70 *Commission v Council* [1971] ECR 263 (henceforth known as the *AETR* Case).

ernment. It is necessary for both central government and the Scottish Executive to comply with the State aid rules in the EC Treaty. It is also necessary to comply with the multilateral rules on subsidies contained in the World Trade Organisation Agreement on Subsidies and Countervailing Measures. This is a matter within the exclusive competence of the European Community. If an action were to be brought by one of the members of the World Trade Organisation in respect of support by the Scottish Executive or the United Kingdom government, the action would be brought against the European Community. This is because subsidies is a subject which falls within the common commercial policy, a matter within the exclusive competence of the European Community.

2. COMPETENCE OF THE EUROPEAN COMMUNITY: JUDICIAL DEVELOPMENT

The original Treaty of Rome appeared to confer limited powers on the European Economic Community, as it was called then, to act externally. There were express powers to enter into agreements in only two areas. Article 113[3] provided for the conclusion of agreements relating to the common commercial policy. Article 238[4] provided for the conclusion of agreements with one or more States or international organisations establishing an association involving reciprocal rights and obligations, common action and special procedures. These became known as Association Agreements. There were also provisions about co-operation with various international organisations.[5]

However, those Treaty provisions did not answer two questions. First, they did not describe the nature of the competence conferred on the Community. In particular, they did not describe what consequences there were for the powers of the Member States. If one considers Article 113,[6] it comes within the Title of the Treaty dealing with the common commercial policy. Article 110 sets out the purpose of the Community's common commercial policy. It provides that the Member States, by establishing a customs union between themselves, aim to contribute to the harmonious development of world trade, the progressive abolition of restrictions on international trade and the lowering of customs barriers. Article 113 provides for the common commercial policy to be based on uniform principles. The Commission is to submit proposals to the Council for implementation of the common commercial policy. Where agreements need to be negotiated, the Commission is to make recommendations to the Council which authorises the Commission to open the necessary negotiations. Article 114 (which has now been repealed) provided for the agreements to be concluded by the Council. However,

---

[3] Now Art 133.
[4] Now Art 310.
[5] Arts 229 to 231 (now Arts 302 to 304).
[6] In this paragraph numbering of Articles before the Treaty of Amsterdam is used.

neither Article 113 nor Article 114 stated whether the Member States should continue to have an independent power to act in areas covered by the common commercial policy. The second question the Treaty provisions did not answer was whether the Community had the power to conclude agreements in areas where an express power had not been conferred. The Treaty was silent on this question as well.

The second question was answered in the *AETR* case.[7] That case concerned the arrangements for negotiating and concluding a revised version of an international agreement covering the work of crews of vehicles engaged in international road transport. The subject matter of the *AETR* fell within the scope of a regulation adopted by the Council, Council Regulation 543/69 on the harmonisation of certain social legislation relating to road transport. The arrangements agreed by the Council were on the footing that the revision of the *AETR* would be negotiated and concluded by the Member States. The Commission brought an action in the European Court of Justice challenging the Council's proceedings on the ground that competence in respect of the *AETR* belonged exclusively to the Community.

The Court held:

17. Each time the Community, with a view to implementing a common policy envisaged by the Treaty, adopts provisions laying down common rules, whatever form these may take, the Member States no longer have the right, acting individually or even collectively, to undertake obligations with third countries which affect those rules . . .

18. As and when such common rules come into being, the Community alone is in a position to assume and carry out contractual obligations towards third countries affecting the whole sphere of application of the Community legal system . . .

19. With regard to the implementation of the provisions of the Treaty the system of internal Community measures may not be separated from that of external relations.

The Community's competence can therefore arise by being expressly conferred in a Treaty article or by implication from a Treaty article.

The Court also dealt with the first question, that is the nature of the competence conferred upon the Community and its effect on the powers of Member States. In the particular circumstances of the *AETR*, the Court held that competence over the subject matter of the Agreement had been transferred completely from the Member States to the Community; the Member States no longer had the right to undertake obligations which would affect those rules. The Court thus recognised that, in this context, the external competence of the Community was exclusive.

---

[7] See n 2 above.

The issue of the nature of the competence conferred by Article 113 was considered in Opinion 1/75.[8] The case concerned the OECD Local Cost Standard. A number of questions were referred to the Court of Justice under Article 228(6)[9] of the Treaty, which enables an opinion to be sought from the Court as to whether an agreement envisaged is compatible with the provisions of the EC Treaty. The Court held that the Treaty provisions concerning the conditions under which agreements on commercial policy must be concluded showed that the exercise of concurrent powers by the Member States and the Community in the matter of the common commercial policy was impossible. The competence of the Community was thus exclusive.

Indeed, the decisions of the Court on external competence are a part of the development of the fundamental concepts of Community law made by the European Court of Justice in the 1960s and 1970s. These concepts are principally those relating to the nature of the Community legal order and, related to this, the supremacy of Community law. In *Costa v ENEL*[10] the Court described the nature of the European Community as follows:

> By creating a Community of unlimited duration, having its own institutions, its own personality, its own legal capacity, and capacity of representation on the international plane, and more particularly, real powers stemming from a limitation of sovereignty or a transfer of powers from the States to the Community, the Member States have limited their sovereign rights, albeit within limited fields, and have thus created a body of law which binds both their nationals and themselves.

In *Costa v ENEL* the Court also developed the concept of the supremacy of Community law. A cardinal feature of Community law is its supremacy over the national law of the Member States. The principle of the supremacy of Community law was clearly established in this case where the Court of Justice rejected the argument that a national court was obliged to apply national legislation adopted later than, and inconsistent with, the EEC Treaty. The Court said:

> [I]n accordance with the principle of the precedence of Community law, the relationship between the provisions of the Treaty and directly applicable measures of the institutions on the one hand and the national law of the Member States on the other is such that those provisions and measures . . . render automatically inapplicable any conflicting provisions of current national law . . . [and] preclude the valid adoption of new national legislative measures to the extent to which they would be incompatible with Community provisions . . . [E]very national court must, in a case within its jurisdiction, apply Community law in its entirety and protect rights which the latter confers on individuals and must accordingly set aside any provision of national law which may conflict with it, whether prior or subsequent to the Community rule.

---

[8] [1975] ECR 1355.
[9] Now Art 300(6).
[10] Case 6/64 *Falminio Costa v ENEL* [1964] ECR 585 at 593–94.

The approach of the Court of Justice in the *AETR* Case is an application of the principle of the supremacy of Community law.

The nature of the legal order created by the EC Treaties is clearly described in the Court of Justice's First EEA Agreement Opinion (Opinion 1/91).[11] The European Economic Area Agreement extended certain provisions of the EC Treaty to the other parties to that Agreement. The Court described the *raison d'être* of the European Community and contrasted it with the purpose of the EEA Agreement. It said:

(16) [As] far as the Community is concerned, the rules on free trade and competition which the [EEA] agreement seeks to extend to the whole territory of the Contracting Parties have developed and form part of the Community legal order, the objectives of which go beyond that of the agreement.

(17) It follows inter alia from Articles 2, 8a and 102a of the EEC Treaty that that Treaty aims to achieve economic integration leading to the establishment of an internal market and economic and monetary union. Article 1 of the Single European Act makes it clear moreover that the objective of all the Community Treaties is to contribute together to making concrete progress towards European unity.

(18) It follows from the foregoing that the provisions of the EEC Treaty on free movement and competition, far from being an end in themselves, are only means for attaining those objectives.

. . .

(20) The EEA is to be established on the basis of an international treaty which, essentially, merely creates rights and obligations as between the contracting parties and provides for no transfer of sovereign rights to the intergovernmental institutions which it sets up.

(21) In contrast, the EEC Treaty, albeit concluded in the form of an international agreement, none the less constitutes the constitutional charter of a Community based on the rule of law. As the Court of Justice has consistently held, the Community Treaties established a new legal order for the benefit of which the States have limited their sovereign rights, in ever wider fields, and the subjects of which comprise not only the Member States but also their nationals. The essential characteristics of the Community legal order which has thus been established are in particular its primacy over the law of the Member States and the direct effect of a whole series of its provisions which are applicable to their nationals and to the Member States themselves.

The extent of the Community's competence in the field of external relations has been determined by a combination of decisions of the Court of Justice, treaty amendment and practice. There have been a number of cases in the Court of Justice on the extent of Community competence where the tendency has been for the Commission to push for an extension of the competence of the Community

---

[11] [1991] ECR 6079.

and to argue that the Community has exclusive competence. One or more of the Member States, and at times the Council, have challenged this.

One of the most important examples of this tension between the Member States and the Commission is Opinion 1/94 on the World Trade Organisation Agreements.[12] For many years there had been considerable discussion on whether Article 113 (now Article 133) applies to trade in services. The outcome of the GATT Uruguay Round was a series of multilateral trade agreements, including a General Agreement on Trade in Services, the GATS, and the Agreement on the Trade Related Aspects of Intellectual Property, the TRIPS Agreement. The Commission maintained that all the agreements giving effect to the Round, including the GATS and the TRIPS Agreements, fell within the common commercial policy and that they should consequently be concluded by the Community alone on the basis of Article 113. This was not accepted by all of the Member States, except Belgium, or, significantly, by the Council. The Court decided that most means of providing services did not fall within the common commercial policy but that one means did, that is the cross frontier supply of services which do not involve any movement of persons. So far as the TRIPS Agreement was concerned, the Court held that the parts of the TRIPS Agreement dealing with intellectual property rights were outside the common commercial policy. Therefore, a number of aspects of the TRIPS Agreement were within the competence of the Member States who should therefore be parties to the Agreement as well as the European Community.

The outcome of the Opinion was that the European Community and the Member States became members of the World Trade Organisation since some matters fell within the exclusive competence of the Community whereas others were within the competence of the Member States. The Court of Justice emphasised the importance of co-operation between the Community and the Member States in the implementation of the World Trade Organisation Agreements.

3. COMMUNITY COMPETENCE: TREATY DEVELOPMENT

Until the Treaty on European Union (the Maastricht Treaty) the developments in the concepts governing internal competence had been largely the result of decisions of the European Court of Justice or the practice of the Member States and the Community institutions.

The Treaty on European Union brought a significant number of areas within the express competence of the Community for the first time. The amendments made by the Treaty on European Union to the Treaty establishing the European Community provided expressly for the Community to have competence in a

---

[12] [1994] ECR I–5267.

number of areas such as public health, culture, education and youth. The Member States sought to define the nature of the Community's competence in these areas including the nature of its external competence. The Member States wished to enable the European Community to act in these areas. But equally they were concerned that the Treaty provisions should recognise that action by the Community would be secondary to action by the Member States. They therefore sought to limit the power of the Community to act internally by stating that action by the Community should supplement or complement action by the Member States. The Community's power to legislate was also limited. In particular it could not adopt measures to harmonise the laws and regulations of the Member States.

So far as external competence was concerned, the provisions conferring power on the Community expressly refer to the powers of the Member States. The relevant provisions[13] provide that the Community and the Member States are to foster co-operation with third countries and the competent international organisations in the relevant sphere. In agreeing these provisions, the Member States, as contracting parities to the Treaty on European Union, expressly set out the extent of the Community's external competence. To the extent that the Community has competence in the relevant sphere, it is shared between the Community and the Member States. The relevant provisions clearly envisage that the Community's policies in these areas are to co-exist with those of the Member States. The Community action is to support that of the Member States, not to replace or supersede what they do.

The Maastricht Treaty established the European Union with its three pillars:

the three Communities, the European Community, the European Coal and Steel Community and the Euratom Community;
the common foreign and security policy; and
co-operation in the fields of justice and home affairs.

Activity in the second and third pillars takes place intergovernmentally, outside the Community Treaties, and according to their own procedures. The legal concepts governing activity in these pillars are therefore different to those applying to activity in the first pillar.

The Member States gave further consideration to the issue of external competence in the Inter-Governmental Conference leading to the Treaty of Amsterdam, in particular the extension of the common commercial policy to trade in services and intellectual property. The result was that the Treaty of Amsterdam added a new paragraph to Article 133. The reason behind the amendment was a concern by the Commission and a number of Member States that the participation by both the Community and the Member States in the implementation of the WTO Agreements would cause problems. A new paragraph was inserted into Article 133. It did not change the law but empowered the Council to do so. It gave the Council

---

[13] Art 149 (formerly Art 126) in respect of education and youth, Art 151 (formerly Art 128) in respect of culture and Art 152 (formerly Art 129) in respect of public health.

power, acting unanimously on a proposal from the Commission and after consulting the European Parliament, to extend Article 133 to international agreements and negotiations on services and intellectual property insofar as they were not covered by the Article.

In the event that power was not exercised. Matters were taken forward in the Treaty of Nice. Article 133 is amended so that the common commercial policy now applies to all aspects of trade in services and to the commercial aspects of intellectual property. However, the amendments expressly provide that certain agreements are subject to unanimity rather than qualified majority voting, the usual voting procedure under Article 133. The amendments also provide that an agreement may not be concluded by the Council under the Article if it includes provisions which would go beyond the Community's internal powers, in particular by leading to the harmonisation of the laws or regulations of the Member States in an area for which the Treaty rules out such harmonisation.

The amendments expressly state that agreements relating to trade in cultural and audio visual services, educational services, and social and human health services are to continue to fall within the shared competence of the Community and the Member States. Such agreements are to be concluded jointly by the Community and the Member States.

Therefore the Member States, as contracting parties to the Treaty establishing the European Community, determined the scope of the extension of Community competence in the field of services and intellectual property. In the period since 1992 the principal developments in external competence have thus been achieved by the Member States themselves in the Treaty provisions they have agreed. This is in contrast to earlier developments which were largely achieved by decisions of the European Court of Justice. However, in relation to matters within the scope of the EC Treaty, those Treaty provisions build on the jurisprudence of the Court and accept the concepts developed by the Court rather than seeking to devise something new. In contrast, in relation to the common foreign and security policy and co-operation in the field of justice and home affairs the Member States have sought to devise new rules and concepts.

4. COMMUNITY COMPETENCE: POSITION OF THIRD COUNTRIES

The two previous sections have looked at the division of competence between the Community and the Members States and the way that the Community institutions, such as the Court of Justice, the Commission and the Council, on the one hand, and the Member States, on the other hand, have viewed it. However, in the context of external competence that division of competence affects other States and international organisations. If the Community or the Member States assert jurisdiction, is it accepted by the other States or international organisations? In many cases it has been accepted, such as in the GATT and now the World Trade Organisation. In some cases on the other hand, other States or international organisations have not permitted the Community to be a party. Often the rules of an international organisation do not permit it.

In the *AETR* case itself, the Court recognised that the other parties to the revision of the *AETR* would have been disconcerted by the substitution, at a late stage in the negotiations, of the Community as sole party in place of the individual Member States. This meant that, although the Member States would continue to take part in the negotiations, they would need to act in the interests of and on behalf of the Community in accordance with the obligation of co-operation under what is now Article 10 of the EC Treaty.

The obligation of cooperation is important in this context. In the case of a number of international organisations, competence is shared between the Member States and the European Community but the rules of the organisation provide that only States may be members. An example is the International Labour Organisation (the ILO). A number of aspects of the work of the ILO were held by the Court of Justice to be within the exclusive competence of the Community. However, only States may be members of the ILO. The Community has only the status of non-voting observer. In its Opinion 2/91[14] the Court stressed the importance of close co-operation between the Community and the Member States in the negotiation and implementation of conventions drawn up within the ILO framework.

That said, the Community is a party to a very large number of international agreements, either alone or with the Member States, and is a member of a large number of international organisations. This testifies to the success of the assertion by the Community of its capacity to enter into international agreements.

In the case of agreements to which both the Member States and the Community are parties, difficulties can arise in determining whether the Community or the Member States have competence for a particular matter. It is often difficult to determine where the Community's competence begins and ends. This has the effect that any attempt to provide a statement of the Community's competence would have to be drawn in ambiguous or vague terms and therefore be of little use in practice. In addition, the boundaries of Community competence change and a statement made at the time of concluding an agreement will become outdated as Community law develops. However, third parties to agreements where both the Community and the Member States are parties have on occasion insisted on a declaration of the respective responsibilities of the Community and its Member States. In these circumstances, the Community and its Member States have made statements, commonly known as declarations of competence, describing the Community's competence. It is usually in general terms, points out that the position is liable to change over time and states that the declaration is without prejudice to the allocation of responsibilities of the Community and the Member States under the Treaties establishing the European Communities.[15]

---

[14] [1993] ECR I–1061.
[15] See, for example, the declaration of competence made in respect of the Climate Change Convention ([1994] OJ L33/11).

Another issue that has concerned third parties to international organisations is the attribution of votes. In some cases, for example several fisheries organisations, the Community entirely replaces the Member States and exercises one vote in its own name, the Member States having no votes. In other cases, when the Community votes on matters within its competence, it exercises the votes of the Member States which are also members of organisation; the Member States cannot then exercise their votes. In a couple of rare cases, the Community and the Member States participate together in the organisation and the Community is accorded a vote in addition to those held and exercised by the Member States.[16]

5. COMPETENCE WITHIN THE UNITED KINGDOM: THE STATUTORY FRAMEWORK

In many of the Member States the power to act in respect of a particular matter is allocated to a specified organ of the State. There is no common model. Some Member States have a federal structure, for example Germany and Belgium. In others, such as Spain and the United Kingdom, powers have been devolved to regions or countries which make up the State in question. This chapter focuses on the position in the United Kingdom.

One of the fundamental principles of the constitution of the United Kingdom is that the supreme constitutional authority is the Crown in Parliament. Under this principle or theory, the tiers of government derive their powers from the Crown in Parliament. Thus, the devolved authorities in Scotland, Northern Ireland and Wales derive their powers, or competence, from Acts of the Westminster Parliament.

The devolution legislation for the countries of Scotland, Northern Ireland and Wales is different, particularly in the case of Wales. The Scotland Act 1998 establishes a Scottish Parliament with the power to enact primary legislation, known as Acts of the Scottish Parliament.[17] There are certain limitations on its power or competence.[18] In particular, the legislation must relate to Scotland, it must not relate to a reserved matter and it must not be incompatible with European Community law or rights derived from the European Convention on Human Rights. Reserved matters are listed in Schedule 5 to the Act and are the matters which are outside the competence of the Scottish Parliament. They include certain matters relating to the constitution, defence, the currency, fiscal, economic and monetary policy, immigration and nationality, intellectual property, postal services, telecommunications and social security. If a matter is not expressly reserved to Westminster, it is devolved to the Scottish Parliament.

---

[16] For examples, see I MacLeod, ID Hendry and S Hyett, *The External Relations of the European Communities*, n 1 above at 174.

[17] S 18.

[18] Set out in s 29.

Also reserved are international relations. The reservation includes relations with territories outside the United Kingdom. It also includes relations with the European Communities (and their institutions) and other international organisations, regulation of international trade and international development assistance and cooperation. However, the reservation does not extend to:

(a) observing and implementing international obligations, obligations under the European Convention on Human Rights, and obligations under European Community law, or

(b) assisting Ministers of the Crown in relation to any matter which falls within this reservation.

The Scotland Act establishes the Scottish Administration. These are Scottish Ministers and they have the power to act in respect of devolved matters. Therefore, if a matter is within the legislative competence of the Scottish Parliament, Scottish Ministers have the power to act. They have the power to make subordinate legislation which would be within the competence of the Scottish Parliament and they have the power to carry out administrative functions which fall within devolved competence.[19]

The Northern Ireland Act 1998 confers power on the Northern Ireland Assembly which, like the Scottish Parliament, has the power to adopt primary legislation, know as Acts.[20]

There is a large degree of overlap between reserved matters under the Scottish Act (and thus outside the legislative competence of the Scottish parliament) and matters which have not been transferred to the Northern Ireland Assembly under the Northern Ireland Act. However, there are a number of important differences. For example, employment relations are reserved matters so far as Scotland is concerned but devolved to Northern Ireland. On the other hand, criminal law is devolved to Scotland but is a reserved matter so far as Northern Ireland is concerned.

The Northern Ireland Act is different to the Scotland Act in that it contains a list of excepted matters which are outside the legislative competence of the Northern Ireland Assembly[21] and a list of reserved matters in respect of which the Assembly may legislate but only with the consent of the United Kingdom Government.[22] The list of excepted matters includes a paragraph dealing with international relations in the same terms as the equivalent reservation in the Scotland Act. As is the case in Scotland, Northern Ireland Ministers have the power to act where a matter is within the competence of the Northern Ireland Assembly.

[19] S 54.
[20] S 5.
[21] Sch 2.
[22] Sch 3.

The Government of Wales Act 1998 does not establish a legislature. It establishes a National Assembly for Wales[23] which has certain powers conferred on it and to which functions can be transferred.[24] It does not, however, have the power to enact primary legislation. When the National Assembly was established a number of power to adopt secondary legislation were transferred to it by an Order in Council. Additional powers could be transferred to it by further Orders in Council. In addition, a number of Acts confer powers directly on the Assembly.[25]

6. OBSERVING AND IMPLEMENTING EC AND INTERNATIONAL OBLIGATIONS

The consequence of the devolution legislation is that competence in respect of many areas where the European Community has competence have been devolved. This applies particularly in the cases of Scotland and Northern Ireland but also to a lesser extent in Wales. All three devolved administrations have competence, for example, in respect of agriculture and fisheries, areas of exclusive Community competence. They all also have competence in respect of the environment, an area of mixed Community and Member States' competence. They all have competence in respect of financial assistance to industry. The powers here are subject to control by the European Community's State aid rules, a matter falling within the exclusive competence of the Community.

The essence of devolution is that the devolved administration has responsibility for determining its own affairs on devolved matters within the scope of its competence. This means that the devolved administrations can have a different policy to that of central government. However, central government will want to ensure that the devolved authorities do not act in a way that is inconsistent with the international commitments of the United Kingdom. Conversely, where a matter is within the competence of a devolved authority, the United Kingdom will look to the devolved administration to implement an international obligation entered into by the United Kingdom. In its turn, a devolved administration is dependent on the United Kingdom government for advancing its interests in international relations in respect of devolved matters, since international relations have not been devolved.

Considering first the issue of ensuring that the devolved authorities comply with the international obligations[26] of the United Kingdom, all three Acts draw a distinction between obligations under the Treaties establishing the European Communities and under the European Convention on Human Rights on the one

---

[23] S 1.
[24] S 21.
[25] For example, the Children's Commissioner for Wales Act 2001.
[26] International obligations are defined as any international *obligation* of the United Kingdom other than obligations to observe and implement Community law or rights under the ECHR: s 126(10) Scotland Act 1998 and s 98(1) of the Northern Ireland Act 1998. See also s 108(6) of the Government of Wales Act 1998.

hand and other international obligations on the other hand. The former are treated as an issue of competence or vires, whereas the latter are enforced by order-making powers. Both the Scotland Act 1998 and the Northern Ireland Act 1998 provide that it is outwith the competence of the Scottish Parliament and the Northern Ireland Assembly respectively to enact a provision which is incompatible with Community law or rights under the European Convention on Human Rights. Thus a provision which is outside the competence of the legislature concerned is ultra vires. The consequence is that control is judicial. The provision in question can be challenged as ultra vires in Court proceedings. Similarly actions of the Scottish Administration, Northern Ireland Ministers and Departments and the National Assembly for Wales which are incompatible with Community law or rights under the European Convention on Human Rights are ultra vires.

In contrast, compliance with other international obligations is secured by giving the Secretary of State, a Minister of the central government, the power to prevent legislation going forward to Royal Assent and to make orders. Thus, in the case of Scotland, the Secretary of State has the power to make an order prohibiting the Presiding Officer of the Scottish Parliament submitting a Bill for Royal Assent.[27] There is an equivalent power in Northern Ireland reflecting the procedure that Bills of the Northern Ireland Assembly are submitted for Royal Assent by the Secretary of State.[28] The powers are exercisable where the Secretary of State has reasonable grounds to believe that the Bill contains a provision which would be incompatible with any international obligations of the United Kingdom.

Similarly, the Secretary of State has power to take action by order in respect of action by the Scottish Executive,[29] Northern Ireland Ministers and Departments[30] and the National Assembly for Wales[31] which he has reasonable grounds to believe could put the United Kingdom in breach of its international obligations. This power extends to requiring action to be taken by a member of the Scottish Executive for the purpose of giving effect to any such obligation; there is a similar power in respect of Northern Ireland Ministers and Departments and the National Assembly for Wales. In contrast, central government does not have a similar power to make an order where a devolved administration acts in breach of Community law. Instead, as stated above, where the devolved administration has acted in a way that is incompatible with Community law, the action is *ultra vires* and could therefore be challenged in the Courts on this basis. Where the devolved administration fails to implement an obligation required by Community law, the Secretary of State continues to be able to exercise the powers in section 2(2) of the European Communities Act 1972. That section enables secondary legislation to be made for the purpose of implementing obligations under Community law.

---

[27]   S 35 of the Scotland Act.
[28]   S 14(5).
[29]   S 58 of the Scotland Act.
[30]   S 26 of the Northern Ireland Act.
[31]   S 108 of the Government of Wales Act.

The reason for the distinction is that rights under the Treaties establishing the European Communities and under the European Convention on Human Rights are directly applicable in the United Kingdom. In respect of the former, this is the result of section 2(1) of the European Communities Act 1972 which provides for the rights to be recognised and available in law. In respect of the latter, the Human Rights Act 1998 has the effect of making the provisions of the Convention which are binding on the United Kingdom, in effect, directly applicable in the United Kingdom by enabling people to claim their rights under the Convention in the courts and tribunals of the United Kingdom.

On the other hand, other international obligations are not directly applicable in the United Kingdom. In many cases they will have been implemented into United Kingdom law and, on that basis, it could be argued that such obligations should be treated in the same way as obligations under the European Convention on Human Rights. However, it was decided that the nature of the obligations under the European Convention on Human Rights were conceptually different to other international obligations and more akin to Community obligations.

It should be noted that a distinction is made in the Acts between obligations under the Treaties establishing the European Communities and obligations derived from the other pillars of the European Union. As has been mentioned above, Community law obligations are regarded as a matter of vires and thus subject to judicial control. Obligations derived from any other pillars of the European Union are treated in the same way as obligations derived from any other international treaty binding on the United Kingdom. They are therefore subject to the order making power of the Secretary of State and the power of the Secretary of State, in the case of Northern Ireland, not to submit a Bill for Royal Assent.

A large number of actions have been brought in the Scottish Courts raising the questions whether a provision of an enactment by the Scottish Parliament or an action of the Scottish Administration was ultra vires. Most raised an issue as to whether the provision or action was consistent with the European Convention on Human Rights. In contrast, no Bill has been prevented from being submitted for Royal Assent nor have any orders been made in respect of any action on the basis that the Bill or action was incompatible with an international obligation.

The preceding paragraphs have referred to the need to provide for compliance by the devolved authorities with the international obligations, including EC obligations, of the United Kingdom. The converse of this is that the implementation of international obligations, including EC obligations, are to be implemented by the devolved authority where they concern matters which are within the competence of the devolved authorities. The reservation, in the case of Scotland, and exception, in the case of Northern Ireland, of international relations specifically state that they do not include the implementation of international obligations, obligations under the ECHR and obligations under Community law. Therefore, the expectation is that the devolved authorities will implement an international obligation or obligation under Community law which falls within its competence.[32]

The Westminster Parliament remains supreme and could enact legislation if the devolved legislatures in Scotland and Northern Ireland fail to do so. However, there is a convention known as the Sewel Convention which provides that the United Kingdom Parliament would not normally legislate with regard to devolved matters except with the agreement of the devolved legislature. Similarly, regulations could be adopted under section 2(2) of the European Communities Act 1972 if the devolved authority failed to implement an obligation under Community law.

The powers referred to in the preceding paragraphs for central government to act to ensure compliance with international obligations, Community law and ECHR obligations are intended to be reserve powers. The national government would want to exercise them only as a last resort. They are the legal mechanism for reconciling that, on the one hand, the devolved authorities are responsible for determining their own affairs in devolved matters and that, on the other hand, the national government is responsible for international relations, including relations with the European Union. However, it is in the interests of neither the central government nor the devolved administrations that conflict should arise between them. There therefore needs to be a mechanism for ensuring co-operation between central government and the devolved administrations. Similarly, the devolved administrations are dependent on the national government to represent their interests in international matters, since international relations are not a devolved matter, but are reserved to Westminster. A devolved administration could not, for example, enter into an agreement with a third country. There therefore needs to be a means for enabling the devolved administrations to have an effective voice in the conduct of international relations and relations with the European Union. Administrative arrangements, known as 'concordats', set out the arrangements which apply between the United Kingdom government and each devolved administration for the handling of international relations and business with the European Union.[33]

The concordats between the UK Government and each of the devolved administrations are not intended to constitute a legally enforceable contract or to create any rights or obligations which are legally enforceable. They are intended to be binding in honour only. Those relating to business with the European Union recognise that relations with the European Union are the responsibility of the UK Government, as the Member State. However, they provide that the devolved administrations are to be as directly and fully involved as possible in decision making on European Union matters which touch on devolved areas. The inten-

---

[32] For example, the legislation to enable the United Kingdom to ratify the Rome Statute of the International Criminal Court is a combination of Westminster legislation, the International Criminal Court Act 2001, and legislation of the Scottish Parliament, the International Criminal Court (Scotland) Act.

[33] See the Memorandum of Understanding and supplementary agreements between the United Kingdom Government and the devolved administrations dated July 2000 published on the Cabinet Office website and as Command Paper 4806.

tion is to secure the development of a United Kingdom line which will reflect the United Kingdom interest as a whole and to which the devolved administrations will adhere. They provide for the provision of information to enable the devolved administrations to participate in the formulation of United Kingdom policy. They provide for Ministers and officials to attend meetings of the Council of Ministers. Those Ministers and officials are to support and advance the single United Kingdom negotiating line and work as part of the United Kingdom team. In appropriate cases Ministers from the devolved administration can speak for the United Kingdom in the Council.

There is also a concordat with each of the devolved administrations dealing with international relations. They set out how the United Kingdom Government and each of the devolved administrations will cooperate with respect to international relations. They recognise the interest the devolved administrations have in international policy making in relation to devolved matters. They require the Foreign and Commonwealth Office, and other United Kingdom Departments leading on particular matters, to provide the devolved administrations with information and advice on international developments which may affect their devolved respon-sibilities. They provide for close cooperation with the objective of promoting the overseas interests of the United Kingdom and all its constituent parts.

7. RELATIONSHIP BETWEEN THE EUROPEAN UNION AND DEVOLVED AUTHORITIES

The Treaty establishing the European Union contains little direct recognition of the interests of authorities below the level of national governments.[34]

So far as the European Community is concerned the competence of regional bodies is not recognized directly. There is some recognition of the interests of regions in that there is a body, the Committee of the Regions, which is consulted on legislative measures to be adopted by the European Community in such areas as the environment, public health, education and vocational training, but it is specifically excluded from a role in international co-operation and more significantly, since these are devolved matters in the United Kingdom, agriculture and fisheries. Furthermore, the Committee of the Regions is not intended as a representative body of the various regional authorities in the European Union.

It is perhaps not surprising that the role of regional bodies, such as the devolved administrations in the United Kingdom, is not recognised by the European Union Treaties. This is because they are treaties between sovereign States and deal with the relations between those States and the supranational institutions they have established under them. That said, the nature of the legal order described by the

---

[34] The Treaty on European Union makes reference to subsidiarity. For example Art 1 provides that the Treaty marks a new stage in the process of creating an ever closer union among the peoples of Europe, in which decisions are taken as closely as possible to the citizen.

European Court of Justice in such cases as *Costa* v *ENEL* gives rights to nationals of Member States. If the legal order created by the EC Treaty is capable of giving rights to nationals, it might have been possible for the Court to have given recognition to divisions of competence, where this exists, in a Member State. However, the result of the case law of the Court is that the European Union Treaties are concerned with relationships between States and the institutions they have established.

The issue was considered in *Région Wallonne v Commission*.[35] The Walloon Region argued before the European Court of Justice that for the purposes of Treaty provisions the term Member State should include public authorities which have taken over the responsibilities of the federal State in respect of the exercise of the powers with which the decision in question was concerned. The argument was rejected by the Court which said:

> ... [I]t is apparent from the general scheme of the treaties that the term 'Member State', for the purposes of the institutional provisions and, in particular, those relating to proceedings before the courts, refers only to government authorities of the Member States of the European Communities and cannot include the governments of regions or autonomous communities, irrespective of the powers they may have. If the contrary were true, it would undermine the institutional balance provided for by the Treaties, which govern the conditions under which the Member States, that is to say, the States party to the Treaties establishing the Communities and the Accession Treaties, participate in the functioning of the Community institutions. It is not possible for the European Communities to comprise a greater number of Member States than the number of States between which they were established.
>
> According to settled case law, although it is for all the authorities of the Member States, whether it be the central authorities of the State or the authorities of a federated State, or other territorial authorities, to ensure observance of the rules of Community law within the sphere of their competence, it is not the task of the Community institutions to rule on the divisions of powers by the institutional rules proper to each Member State, or on the obligations which may be imposed on federal State authorities and the federal State. Thus an action whereby the Commission, under Article 169[36] of the EC Treaty, or a Member State, under Article 170,[37] can seek a ruling from the Court of Justice that another Member State had failed to fulfil one of its obligations can only be brought against the government of the Member State in question, even if the failure to act is the result of the action or omission of the authorities of a federal State, a region or an autonomous community.

The reasoning in the second paragraph is more persuasive than that in the first paragraph, in particular its final sentence. A recognition of the competence of a regional authority would not lead to the European Communities comprising a greater number of States than there are States which established them.

---

[35] Case 95/97 *Région Wallonne v Commission* [1997] ECR I–1787.
[36] Now Art 226.
[37] Now Art 227.

University
of Ulster
LIBRARY

The question has arisen as to whether a regional authority, such as a devolved administration in the United Kingdom, could challenge an act of a Community institution where the act concerned a matter within the competence of the regional authority.

This was one of the issues in *Région Wallonne v Commission*. The question was raised as to whether a regional authority, which has competence in respect of a matter in domestic law, can bring an action in the Court of Justice and, if so, whether it has any privileged status. As mentioned above, the fact that a matter is within the competence of a regional authority does not have the consequence that the authority is to be regarded as the Member State for the purposes of Article 230, since the concept of the Member State, within the meaning of the Treaty provisions concerned with institutions, only applies to the government authorities of the Member States of the European Communities and does not extend to regional governments. However, such an authority is a legal person for the purposes of Article 230.

Article 230 distinguishes between first the Member States, the Council and the Commission which have the right to challenge acts of the Council, the Commission and the European Central Bank in the Court of Justice, secondly the European Parliament, the Court of Auditors and the European Central Bank which have a similar right for the purpose of protecting their prerogatives, and thirdly natural and legal persons who may institute proceedings if the decision is addressed to the person or is of direct and individual concern to him.

The Court has held that a regional authority is a legal person for the purposes of Article 230. However, it must be able to show that the decision is of direct and individual concern. This is not shown by a general interest the regional authority may have in, for example, protecting the level of employment in the geographical region concerned. Reliance by a regional authority on the fact that the application or implementation of a Community measure is capable generally of affecting socio-economic conditions within its territorial jurisdiction is not sufficient to render action brought by that authority admissible.[38]

In the context of the United Kingdom, this means that a devolved administration could, as a matter of European Community law, bring an action in the Court of First Instance if it could show that the decision it sought to challenge was of direct and individual concern to it. Earlier in this chapter the example was given of the Scottish Executive wanting to give financial assistance to a company. If the Commission decided that the financial assistance was incompatible with the common market and should not be granted under the EC State aid rules, the decision, although addressed to the United Kingdom, would be of direct and individual concern to the Scottish Executive. The Scottish Executive could, therefore, as a matter of Community law bring an action before the Court of First Instance. However, relations with the European Union and its institutions are a

---

[38] Case T–238/97 *Cantabria v Commission* OJ [1997] C 318/33. The case concerned a Council Regulation on aid to shipbuilding which contained a provision about a yard in Cantabria.

reserved matter and, therefore, it would be outside the competence of the Scottish Executive, as a matter of United Kingdom law, to bring such an action. An action to challenge the decision would have to be brought by the United Kingdom government.

Is it likely that there will be any change in the way the European Union Treaties recognise, or fail to recognise, the division of powers within Member States? Will there be recognition of the competence of regional authorities in the European Union legal order?

The position of regional authorities was not changed by the Treaty of Nice. Four factors militate against any institutional change in the role of regional authorities in the European Union in the foreseeable future. The first is enlargement of the European Union. Establishing the institutional structure for an enlarged European Union has its own challenges. Secondly, regional authorities in the Member States have different forms; there is no common model which applies in all the Member States. Some Member States have a federal structure but others do not. The diverse powers of regional authorities in the European Union make it difficult to give recognition to them. Thirdly, there is a fear on the part of some Member States of being squeezed between the European Union institutions and regional authorities. Fourthly, the European Union is an international organisation, albeit a unique one, whose contracting parties are nation States.

Significantly, there has been little pressure by regional authorities for change to the Treaties. One area that was considered briefly as part of the Intergovernmental Conference leading to the Treaty of Nice was to amend Article 230 to increase the powers of sub-national authorities to bring actions in the Court of Justice and the Court of First Instance. A proposal was put forward by Belgium to amend Article 230 to enable an entity within a State to bring an action in the Court of Justice in the same way as a Member State can where the entity has a legislative power conferred by the constitution of that State. However, the proposal was not accepted.

Any additional recognition in the European Union Treaties of the role of regional bodies would signify a further development in the status of the Treaties as constitutional documents going beyond agreements between States. The Laeken Declaration on the Future of the European Union does not mention regional bodies. The only recognition is that the Convention established to consider the key issues arising for the European Union's future development (the Convention on the Future of the European Union) has six representatives appointed by the Committee of the Regions as observers: the representatives are not members of the Convention. Despite this, regional bodies, in particular those with legislative competence, are likely to put papers to the Convention.[39] In the

---

[39] A number of authorities with legislative powers have produced reports on their position in the EU. See, for example, the Scottish Parliament Paper 466. See also the reaction of the national Parliament in the House of Commons European Scrutiny Committee Report of 12 June 2002 (HC 152).

meantime, it is for each Member State to establish the mechanism within its legal and constitutional order as to how it involves regional bodies in asserting its competence and that of regional bodies within the European Union.

So far as the position in the United Kingdom is concerned, the devolution settlements have been working well in this area. But there are administrations of similar political complexions in the devolved administrations and at Westminster. The position would be different and there would be greater scope for conflict if there were, for example, a Eurosceptic political party in power in Westminster and more Europhile parties in power in the devolved administrations.

6

Competition Law in a Globalised Marketplace: Beyond Jurisdiction

BRENDA SUFRIN

1. INTRODUCTION

In his seminal 1964[1] article 'The Doctrine of Jurisdiction in International Law', FA Mann introduced the section 'Jurisdiction over Trade Practices' with the remark: 'The State's international right to control restrictive trade practices gives rise to questions which are of so esoteric a character and have been so insufficiently clarified by judicial decisions that an introductory survey of the doctrine of legislative jurisdiction would perhaps do well to refrain from discussing it.' Despite this disclaimer Dr Mann proceeded to give a full analysis of the current state of the case law on international jurisdiction in competition law. That case law was wholly American. In 1964, few countries had had competition laws in place for any significant time and only the US had grappled with the issue of applying them extra-territorially. EC competition law was in it infancy, the first ECJ competition judgment, *de Geus v Robert Bosch*[2] having been delivered but two years previously. Nearly 40 years later the competition law scene has been transformed. EC competition law has grown into a mature system, over 90 countries have competition laws in place or in the process of being established, and the potential problems of conflicting claims of jurisdiction have grown exponentially.

Competition law upholds the policy adopted by a State to maintain and support the workings of the free market. Organising the economy on the basis of competition is an ideological choice. Free markets are believed to lead to the optimal outcomes for society. However, even among States holding to these beliefs, the content of any particular State's law can be different: competition policies can protect competitors rather than customers, take account of issues other than competition matters, exempt certain practices or sectors from their coverage, have different techniques and procedures of enforcement. The objectives of competition law can shift. There are fashions in theory. Even if it is accepted that consumer

[1] FA Mann, *The Doctrine of Jurisdiction in International Law* (1964) 111 *Hag Rec* 1.
[2] Case 13/61 *de Geus v Robert Bosch* [1962] ECR 45: [1962] CMLR 1.

welfare is the objective, the precise means by which this should be achieved may be a matter of dispute. The current orthodoxy is that it is achieved through the pursuit of efficiency, but Porter,[3] for example, now argues that it is achieved through dynamic productivity growth rather than efficiency.

Originally questions of the so-called 'extraterritorial' application of antitrust laws revolved around how far a State (in practice, the US) could apply its laws to foreign companies the consequences of whose behaviour were felt directly within that State. More recently the question has arisen of whether a State's competition laws can be applied to the conduct of foreign companies inside *another* State where that conduct impedes the access of the first State's exporters to markets in the second. Indeed, it can be argued that it is *only* the application of the first State's competition laws to this latter situation which truly involves an extraterritorial element because where a State is trying to prevent anti-competitive conduct in its own territory it is not acting extraterritorially—although this is true of legislative rather than enforcement jurisdiction.[4] In this chapter extraterritoriality will be used for convenience to describe both situations described above, unless the context otherwise requires.

The problem is no longer simply one of some States purporting to assert extraterritorial jurisdiction. It is not merely a question of how far the US (and, the EU amongst others) can enforce their competition laws outside their borders. The process of what is called 'globalisation' presents new challenges to competition laws. 'Globalisation' of the economy, defined by the OECD as 'the geographic dispersion of industrial and service activities and the cross-border networking of companies', describes a world in which many markets are global, multinational enterprise take their decisions in a global context and the impact of corporate transactions and mergers are felt in numerous jurisdictions. Customary international law does not provide adequate solutions to the problems which arise from this phenomenon and the impetus is now towards international cooperation between competition authorities and the establishment of international fora. Furthermore, the liberalisation of international trade and the creation of the WTO, have, it is often asserted, led to private restraints being used to protect national markets in place of the previous government barriers, but at the same time the establishment of a liberalised world trade regime has highlighted the fragmented nature of competition laws.

2. THE EFFECTS DOCTRINE IN US LAW

For the first half-century following the enactment of the original antitrust statute, the Sherman Act of 1890, US courts were reluctant to extend it to cover the conduct

---

[3] Michael E Porter, 'Competition and Antitrust: Towards a Productivity-based Approach to Evaluating Mergers and Joint Ventures' (2001) 46 *Antitrust Bulletin* 919, discussed further by CD Weller, 'Harmonizing Antitrust Worldwide by Evolving to Michael Porters's Dynamic Productivity Growth Analysis' (2001) 46 *Antitrust Bulletin* 879.

[4] See pp 112–14 below.

of companies abroad, In 1909 Justice Oliver Wendell Holmes said in the *American Banana* case[5] that 'the general and almost universal rule is that the character of an act as lawful or unlawful must be determined wholly by the law of the country where the act is done.' By 1945, however, American judges were less shy of applying the antitrust laws to activities which although carried on abroad had an impact within the US. In the *Alcoa* case[6] Judge Learned Hand finally pronounced what has become known as the 'effects doctrine' whereby the Sherman Act applies to agreements concluded outside the US which are intended to affect US imports and to actually affect them. In *Hartford Fire Insurance*[7] the Supreme Court reiterated that jurisdiction could be taken over 'foreign conduct that was meant to produce and did in fact produce some substantial effect in the United States.'[8]

US courts have recognised the controversial nature of claims to extraterritorial jurisdiction and their potential for provoking hostility from other States and used the concept of 'comity' in international law to temper the application of the effects doctrine. Comity is defined as 'the recognition which one nation allows within its territory to the legislative, executive or judicial acts of another nation'.[9] In the leading case of *Timberlane*[10] Judge Choy recognised the effects doctrine as laid down in *Alcoa* but considered that its application had to be balanced against the interests of international comity for 'at some point the interests of the United States are too weak and the foreign harmony incentive for restraint too strong to justify an extraterritorial assertion of jurisdiction'. *Timberlane* did not *deny* jurisdiction to the US courts in the interests of comity, but merely held that it should not be *exercised* where it is outweighed by them.[11] In *Hartford Fire Insurance*[12] Justice Scalia's dissenting view[13] was that comity is an integral part of determining whether the court has jurisdiction in the first place, rather than something to be taken into account when deciding whether to *exercise* jurisdiction. Therefore comity goes to the existence and not to the exercise of jurisdiction.[14] In 1995 the

---

[5] *American Banana Co and United Fruit Co* 213 US 347, 356, 29 S.Ct 511, 512 (1909).

[6] *United States v Aluminum Co of America* 148 F. 2d 416 (2d Cir. 1945); for earlier limitations on the *American Banana* doctrine see *United States v Sisal Sales Corp* 274 US 268, 47 S. Ct 592 (1927).

[7] *Hartford Fire Insurance Co v California* 113 S.Ct 2891 (1993), 509 US 764.

[8] And the Foreign Trade Antitrust Improvements Act 1982 § 6a provides that with respect to foreign commerce other than imports it applies to conduct which has a 'direct, substantial and immediately foreseeable effect' on trade or commerce in the US.

[9] *Hilton v Guyot* [1895] 159 US 113 at 164 employed as the definition of comity in the DOJ/FTC Antitrust Enforcement Guidelines for International Operations, discussed at n 18 below.

[10] *Timberlane Lumber Co v Bank of America*, 549 F.2d 597 (9th Cir 1976).

[11] The criteria laid down in *Timberlane* for making this decision were expanded in *Accord Mannington Mills Inc v Congoleum Corp* 595 F.2d 1287 (3rd Cir 1979). Kingman Brewster called it a 'jurisdictional rule of reason' in *Antitrust and American Business Abroad* (McGraw-Hill, New York 1958). Note that in *Timberlane* itself the Court of Appeals said that as there was no indication of a conflict with the law and policy of the Honduran government, the trial judge could not have dismissed the action on jurisdictional grounds.

[12] *Hartford Fire Insurance Co v California* 113 S.Ct 2891 (1993), 509 US 764.

[13] See also the minority opinion by Judge Adams in *Mannington Mills*, above n 11.

[14] FA Mann, writing in 1984, also disapproved of the 'balancing interests' idea. He considered that if a court has jurisdiction it must exercise it. If, on the other hand, international law says it has no jurisdiction that is the end of the matter. FA Mann, 'The Doctrine of International Jurisdiction Revisited After Twenty Years' (1984) 186 *Hag Rec* 9, the sequel to the celebrated 1964 atricle at n 1 above.

Department of Justice and the Federal Trade Commission issued a set of Antitrust Enforcement Guidelines for International Operations.[15] These explain, inter alia, that the Agencies will take comity into account when deciding to bring action or seek particular remedies. The guidelines list a number of factors which will be taken into consideration: the relative significance to the alleged violation of conduct within the United States, as compared to the conduct abroad; the nationality of the persons involved in or affected by the conduct; the presence or absence of a purpose to affect US consumers, markets, or exporters; the relative significance and foreseeability of the effects of the conduct on the United States as compared to the effects abroad; the existence of reasonable expectations that would be furthered or defeated by the action; the degree of conflict with foreign law or articulated economic policies; the extent to which the enforcement activities of another country with respect to the same persons, including remedies resulting from those activities, may be affected; and the effectiveness of foreign enforcement as compared to US enforcement action.[16] Once the decision to proceed is made, however, this represents a determination by the Executive Branch that the importance of antitrust enforcement outweighs any relevant foreign policy concerns.[17]

Comity also involves the principle of non-interference with the acts of a foreign sovereign. US law recognises (a) foreign sovereign immunity by which the *non-commercial* activities of a foreign government, or its agencies or instrumentalities are immune from the jurisdiction of US courts;[18] (b) the Act of State doctrine, whereby the courts will not sit in judgment on the acts of a government of another State done within its own territory;[19] (c) immunity from antitrust proceedings for those petitioning foreign governments to act in a way which produces anticompetitive outcomes;[20] and (d) the foreign compulsion principle. The last principle is of particular significance. It holds that antitrust laws will not be applied to conduct on the part of private parties in a sovereign state which was 'compelled'

---

[15] *Antitrust   and   Trade   Reg   Rep* (BNA), Special Supplement (6 April 1995); http://www.usdoj.gov/atr/public/guidelines/guidelin.htm, para 3.2.

[16] The Guidelines state, in n 74, that the first six of these factors are based on previous Guidelines and the last two derive from considerations in the US–EC Antitrust Cooperation Agreement which is discussed at pp. 120–22 below.

[17] Guidelines, para 3.2.

[18] Foreign Sovereign Immunities Act 1976, 28 USCA § 1602 *et seq.*

[19] See *Underhill v Hernandez* 168 US 250, 252, 18 S.Ct 83, 84 (1897). In *IAM v OPEC* 649 F.2d 1354 1981 the Ninth Circuit found that a claim against the members of OPEC for price-fixing was barred by the Act of State doctrine: the lower court had found it barred by foreign sovereign immunity. There is some doubt, however, as to whether the acts complained of were non-commercial and also whether the acts were performed on the foreign sovereigns' territories, since the fixed prices were applied elsewhere.

[20] Antitrust Enforcement Guidelines for International Operations, para 3.34. This is by way of extension the immunity from antitrust proceedings accorded to petitions directed at US governmental agencies under what is known as *Noerr-Pennington* doctrine; *Eastern Railroad Presidents Conference v Noerr Motor Freight* 365 US, 127, 81 S.Ct 523 (1961), *United Mine Workers v Pennington* 381 US 657, 85 S.Ct 1585 (1965).

by the foreign sovereign. The problem is what is meant by 'compelled'. The *Hart-ford Fire Insurance* case concerned insurance agreements reached at Lloyds in London whereby re-insurers based in London agreed to boycott certain types of insurance risks in the US. The Supreme Court, by a majority, held that the Sherman Act could be applied to the acts of the British insurers. Justice Souter, delivering the majority opinion, decided that there was no reason to decline juris-diction on comity grounds. This was not a case of foreign sovereign compulsion because although UK law *allowed* the conduct, it did not *compel* it. There was no conflict between British and American policy, and no reason for comity concerns to override the effects doctrine. However, if international comity is only to prevent the US taking jurisdiction in such narrowly drawn conflict situations it will rarely prevail and disregarding another jurisdiction which merely *permits* rather than *compels* conduct is crucially important when applied to merger control, as dis-cussed below.[21] It may be noted that when dealing with internal inconsistencies between federal antitrust law and the laws of US States, it is accepted that immu-nity from the former may sometimes arise as a consequence of the latter, even where the individual or undertaking concerned *could* comply with both.[22]

The position of US law as regards what may be described as 'true' extraterrito-riality—where the foreign acts effect US exports on foreign soil—is embodied in the Foreign Trade Antitrust Improvements Act 1982 (FTAIA).[23] This is worded as an exception,[24] but its effect is that the Sherman Act applies to such acts where the conduct has a 'direct, substantial and reasonably foreseeable effect . . . on trade or export commerce with foreign nations . . .'. The Act does not expressly address the comity issue but it has been said that it would be 'quite bizarre' to conclude therefrom that comity concerns continue to be relevant to cases of imports *into* the US and not to those involving exports.[25] Although the US Agencies consider that they do have jurisdiction over conduct abroad which affects exports,[26] they do not commonly take action against it.[27] The practical enforcement problems in such cases are very great moreover. In the *Fuji* case the US sought to circumvent these and to advance the interests of its exporters not through competition law but through trade law. Kodak alleged that it was unable to penetrate the Japanese market because of anticompetitive activities there, in particular on the part of Fuji's distributors, despite the existence of Japanese anti-monopoly laws. Kodak brought a section 301 Trade Act 1974 petition in the US and the US Trade Rep-resentative referred the Japanese government's conduct in tolerating the anti-

---

[21] See pp 117–19 below.

[22] A Robertson and M Demetriou, '"But that was in Another Country . . .": The Extraterritorial Application of US Antitrust Laws in the US Supreme Court' (1994) 43 *ICLQ* 417 at 421–22.

[23] 15 USC § 6a.

[24] The basic principle of the Act is that the Sherman Act does not apply to the conduct of American exporters in foreign markets.

[25] H Hovenkamp, *Federal Antitrust Policy* (2nd edn, West Publishing Group, St Paul, Minnesota, 1999) at § 21.2b.

[26] Antitrust Enforcement Guidelines for International Operations, para 3.1222.

[27] The first case was *United States v Pilkington* (1994–2) Trade Cases, § 70, 482.

competitive behaviour to the WTO. Access to the WTO dispute resolution procedure is limited to governments. The WTO panel confirmed that only governments are the subjects of WTO obligations and that the WTO rules apply only to government measures, so that private measures could not be reached in this way.[28] This confirmation that the WTO procedures cannot be used to attack anticompetitive conduct which excludes foreign trade may have been one factor which has spurred the US to take a more positive stance towards international competition law cooperation.[29]

3. INTERNATIONAL LAW AND EC LAW

Proponents of the effects doctrine usually justify it in international terms by recourse to the objective territoriality principle which gives a state jurisdiction over acts originating abroad but completed, at least partially, within its own territory. Reliance is placed on the decision of the Permanent Court of International Justice in the *Lotus* case which spoke of States taking jurisdiction in criminal cases 'if one of the constituent elements of the offence, and more especially its effects have taken place there'.[30] It can be argued that a constituent element of the offence has not taken place in a State's territory where the conduct contrary to competition laws takes place outside it but in A-G Mayras's view in *ICI v Commission*,[31] (the first time that the extraterritorial effect of EC competition provisions was before the Court of Justice) the effect of an infringement of cartel law is one of its constituent elements, 'probably even the essential element', and thus the criteria in *Lotus* more than satisfied. A-G Darmon took the same view in *Wood Pulp*[32] and concluded that 'there would appear to be no doubt' that the principle laid down in the *Lotus* 'permits the conclusion to be drawn that consideration of the location of the effects as the basis of a State's jurisdiction is in conformity with the rules of international law'. The ECJ in *Wood Pulp*, however, based its assertion of jurisdiction not on the concept of the effects of the parties' agreement in the Community but on the concept of it having been 'implemented' therein. The Court analysed the infringement of Article 81 as consisting of two elements, the formation of the agreement and its implementation. By doing this it was able to take on board the 'constituent element' issue and it stated simply that the 'Com-

---

[28] *Japan—Measures Affecting Consumer Photographic Film and Paper* WT/DS44/R, 31 March 1998.
[29] See pp 123–26 below.
[30] (1927), PCIJ, Ser. A, no 10 at 23. After a collision on the high seas Turkey instituted criminal proceedings against officers on the French ship when it put into a Turkish port. The PCIJ held that international law did not *prevent* Turkey instituting proceedings: it was not asked whether international law *authorised* it to do so.
[31] Case 48/69 *ICI v Commission (Dyestuffs)* [1972] ECR 619: [1972] CMLR 557. The ECJ justified the taking of jurisdiction by applying the 'single economic entity doctrine' and ascribing the conduct of ICI's Dutch subsidiary to its parent.
[32] Cases 89, 104, 114, 116, 117 and 125–129/85 *A Ahlström Oy v Commission* [1988] ECR 5193: [1988] 4 CMLR 901.

munity's jurisdiction to apply its competition rules to such conduct is covered by the territoriality principle as universally recognized in international law'.

The question of whether the effects doctrine (or, indeed the EC's implementation doctrine) is a doctrine in its own right, is a valid offshoot of the objective territorial principle recognised in the *Lotus* or an illegitimate extension of the principle which infringes the sovereignty of other nations is one of which international lawyers are still divided. The problem for States (including for these purposes the EC) which affect to apply their competition laws extraterritorially on this basis, however, is that merely taking legislative (prescriptive) jurisdiction—whereby, for example, courts pronounce upon the legality of agreements entered into by foreign companies—is not enough. The crucial point is whether a State also has enforcement jurisdiction whereby its authorities can take evidence, conduct investigations, serve proceedings and recover penalties abroad. The distinction between prescriptive jurisdiction and enforcement jurisdiction was recognised by the respective Advocates General in *ICI v Commission* and *Wood Pulp* where both considered that the mere imposition of a pecuniary sanction is a matter of prescriptive jurisdiction and that enforcement jurisdiction is involved only when steps are taken for its recovery, because only then is the State taking coercive measures in the territory of a foreign sovereign.

For some time EC law avoided the issue of whether it too embraced an effects doctrine by employing the single economic entity concept, whereby a parent and subsidiary are considered as one unless the subsidiary exercises real autonomy. On this basis the conduct of ICI's Dutch subsidiary was imputed to the UK parent and the latter brought within the jurisdiction of EC law before the Accession of the UK.[33] Although the single economic entity concept avoids the effects doctrine it does in fact entail the taking of extraterritorial jurisdiction, for the concept is a creature of EC competition laws, not of international law, and it overrides the legal characterisation of the subsidiary as a separate entity in the law of the State of incorporation.[34]

When the ECJ confronted a situation in which the single economic entity doctrine could not be used it deliberately avoided applying an effects doctrine. In the *Wood Pulp* case,[35] the Commission found a number of companies and trade associations with their registered offices outside the Community guilty of infringing Article 81 by a price-fixing cartel. Despite AG Darmon arguing the Commission was entitled to take jurisdiction on the basis of the effects doctrine the ECJ founded jurisdiction on the fact that the pricing agreement was *implemented* inside the Common Market. Such implementation included the direct selling of goods in the Common Market. The use of the 'implementation' rather then 'effects' criteria was deliberate, the ECJ choosing a *sui generis* concept rather than adopting the US one.

---

[33] See *ICI v Commission*, n 31 above.

[34] The single economic entity concept is also applied in US law, see *Copperweld Corp v Independent Tube Corp* 467 US 752, 104 S.Ct 2731.

[35] See n 32 above; J Ferry, 'Towards Completing the Charm. The Wood Pulp judgment' (1989) *EIPR* 19.

4. ENFORCEMENT

Attempts by the US to enforce its antitrust laws abroad have been resisted by other States. A stark example of this was *United States v ICI Ltd*[36] where a US court ordered, on the grounds of infringement of the Sherman Act, the cancellation of agreements between ICI and Du Pont by which Du Pont assigned to ICI certain patents which were to be registered in the UK. ICI was ordered to reassign the patents to Du Pont. ICI, however, had already contracted to licence the patents to British Nylon Spinners. The judge in the New York District Court was aware of the contracts with British Nylon Spinners, and expressly recognized that the UK courts might not give effect to his order. That indeed was the outcome: in *British Nylon Spinners*[37] Danckwerts J granted British Nylon Spinners a decree of specific performance when the company brought an action against ICI to enforce its rights under the contracts. Danckwerts J in effect disregarded the US order, but graciously acknowledged that the US judge had been 'exceedingly moderate and courteous in his references to the possible courses which might be adopted by the English court'[38] and had been 'careful so to limit his judgment that neither his judgment, nor any judgment of mine which the law of England requires me to give, will disturb the comity which the courts of the United States and the courts of England are so anxious and careful to observe.'[39] Danckwerts J declared himself not unwilling to cooperate with the US court but held that he was bound to reach a different result because '[t]he judge was applying an enactment of Congress, which has no application to the United Kingdom.'[40]

British Nylon Spinners was decided at a time when the UK had no legislation prohibiting restrictive agreements—the first Restrictive Trade Practices Act was in 1956[41]—but the attitude of the UK government and courts towards US extra-territorial enforcement of its antitrust laws did not soften even after the UK strengthened its own competition law regime. The UK government's view in 1978, by which time the UK was a member of the EEC which was applying its 'single economic entity doctrine' to catch foreign companies with subsidiaries within its jurisdiction,[42] was summed up by Lord Diplock in *Rio Tinto Zinc Corpn v Westinghouse Electric Corpn.*[43] He said approvingly that Her Majesty's Government regarded 'as an unacceptable invasion of its own sovereignty the use of the United States courts by the United States Government as a means by which it can investigate activities outside the United States of British companies and individuals

---

[36] 105 F Supp 215 (1952).
[37] *British Nylon Spinners Ltd v ICI Ltd* [1955] Ch 37.
[38] *Ibid* at 45.
[39] *Ibid* at 54.
[40] *Ibid* at 45.
[41] Anti-competitive agreements had thitherto been subjected only to the more benign investigatory regime of the Monopolies and Restrictive Practices (Inquiries and Control) Act 1948.
[42] See p 111 above.
[43] [1978] AC 547. The case arose from US efforts to pursue the alleged uranium cartel.

which it claims infringe the antitrust laws of the United States.'[44] The House refused the US court's request for assistance with discovery under the Evidence (Proceedings in Other Jurisdictions) Act 1975. Subsequently the UK passed the Protection of Trading Interests Act 1980 which was ostensibly aimed at 'blocking' the enforcement of any foreign international trade laws, but was in reality directed towards US antitrust laws.[45] First, the Act enables the Secretary of State to direct a person carrying on business in the UK not to comply with the orders of a foreign court or authority affecting international trade which threaten to damage the trading interests of the UK,[46] and not to produce commercial information demanded by the overseas authority which is not within the latter's territorial jurisdiction;[47] secondly, it provides, reinforcing the *Rio Tinto Zinc* judgment, that the UK courts should not make orders to comply with a foreign's court's request for assistance with discovery where the Secretary of State certifies that this 'infringes the jurisdiction of the United Kingdom or is otherwise prejudicial to the sovereignty of the United Kingdom';[48] thirdly the Act requires UK courts not to enforce foreign judgments awarding multiple damages or other judgments designated 'competition judgments' by the Secretary of State;[49] and fourthly, the Act provides, in what is known as the 'claw-back' provision, that British citizens or companies and persons carrying on business in the UK may sue in the UK courts to recover the noncompensatory portion of any damages paid by them following a judgment in foreign court.[50] These last two provisions are aimed at protecting British defendants in US 'treble damages' actions. Private enforcement is a major feature of US antitrust law, and under section 4 of the Clayton Act a successful plaintiff in an action for violation of the antitrust rules is awarded 'three-fold the damages . . . sustained.' These provisions were uncompromisingly and directly aimed at protecting UK companies from the consequences of their actions in the US under US law.

At the time that the Protection of Trading Interests Act was passed it was defended by UK international lawyers while roundly lambasted by American com-

---

[44] *Ibid* at 639.

[45] Other States have also passed 'blocking statutes'. An earlier UK statute, the Shipping Contracts and Commercial Documents Act 1964, in effect blocked the enforcement of foreign orders relating to shipping.

[46] Protection of Trading Interests Act 1980, s 1(1). Three orders have been made under this section: the Protection of Trading Interests (US Re-export Control) Order 1982, SI 1982/885; the Protection of Trading Interests (US Antitrust Measures) Order 1983, SI 1983/900; and the Protection of Trading Interests (US Cuban Assets Control Regulations Order 1992, SI 1992/2449. Two of these did not involve competition law: the first was part of the Siberian pipeline affair and the third concerned US sanctions on trade with Cuba. The second gave rise to the *Laker Airways* litigation in the UK courts which culminated in *British Airways Board v Laker Airways Ltd* [1985] AC 58; see R Whish, *Competition Law* (4th edn, Butterworths, London, 2001) at 408.

[47] *Ibid* s 2.

[48] *Ibid* s 4.

[49] *Ibid* s 5. An order so designating s 81(1A) of the Trade Practices Act 1974 of Australia was made by the Protection of Trading Interests (Australian Trade Practices) Order 1988, SI 1988/569.S.81(1A) to render unenforceable in the UK a provision concerned with the divestiture of assets acquired in contravention of the merger control provisions of the Trade Practices Act.

[50] Protection of Trading Interests Act 1980, s 6.

mentators ('a deplorable measure—a step backward both as a matter of international law and . . . as a matter of English law' wrote Andreas Lowenfield).[51] There was agreement, however, about the inadequacy of traditional formulations of jurisdiction and sovereignty in the field of economic law. AV Lowe admitted the unsuitability of the classical rules on jurisdiction for the regulation of international trade and suggested that the concept of sovereignty needed refinement, so that it could accommodate both notions of the independence of states and of the increasing interdependence of states, without losing its coherence as a legal principle. He considered the comity 'is too uncertain in its origins, its content and its method of application to be relied upon as a self-imposed restraint upon the jurisdictional claims of states.'[52] Lowenfield, on the other hand, considered that the problem of overlapping jurisdictions should be solved not on the basis of sovereignty or power but on the basis of a shared concept of 'reasonableness', using such concepts as due process of law, denial of justice, or substantial lessening of competition.[53] It is interesting to note, however, that despite the increasing transatlantic cooperation in matters of competition law enforcement, the Protection of Trading Interests Act is still in force. The dislike of treble-damages actions, in particular, in the UK, remains as strong as ever.

5. MERGERS

The most acute problem posed by globalisation to national systems of competition laws comes from the multiplicity of multi-jurisdictional mergers. States with systems of merger control use various criteria for deciding which mergers they subject to that regime and which mergers they permit or prohibit.[54] A State which prohibits a merger involving companies incorporated outside its territory is not enforcing its law extraterritorially as such but merely refusing to recognise the merger as creating a legally recognised entity within its own territory. However, the consequences of the merged entity being in such a position in a jurisdiction in which it does business will be enough to stop the merger proceeding, quite apart from the question of fines and penalties.

The EC Merger Regulation establishes a 'one-stop shop' regime whereby concentrations above certain turnover thresholds, described as having a 'Community dimension', are dealt with by the EC Commission and concentrations below those thresholds are left to national authorities. The test which the Commission applies

---

[51] AF Lowenfield, 'Sovereignty, Jurisdiction and Reasonableness: A Reply to AV Lowe' (1981) 75 *AJIL* 629 at 637.

[52] AV Lowe, 'Blocking Extraterritorial Jurisdiction: The British Protection of Trading Interests Act' 1980 (1981) 75 *AJIL* 257, 281. These reservations about comity were, of course, expressed before the Supreme Court judgment in *Hartford Fire Insurance* (see above at p 109).

[53] AF Lowenfield, n 51 above at 637–38.

[54] Although many States have adopted the same or similar criteria.

in permitting or prohibiting a merger is whether or not it 'creates or strengthens a dominant position as a result of which effective competition would be significantly impeded in the common market.'[55] The thresholds in Article 1 (2) are that a) the aggregate world-wide turnover of all the undertakings concerned is more than €5000 million and that b) the aggregate Community-wide turnover of each of at least two of the undertakings concerned is more than €250 million. There is an alternative set of thresholds in Article 1 (3) which are designed to leave the Commission to deal with concentrations of a smaller size which would otherwise be subject to several Member States' systems of merger control. These thresholds start with an aggregate worldwide turnover of €2,500 million and an aggregate turnover of €100 million in each of at least three Member states.[56] The Merger Regulation establishes a 'prior notification' system whereby all mergers having a Community dimension must be notified to the commission before the parties proceed.[57]

Article 1 says nothing expressly about where the undertakings concerned are incorporated, or carry on business, or whether the undertakings must have assets in the Community. Its criteria relate only to a world-wide turnover figure and much smaller Community-wide turnover figures. Article 5, which deals with the calculation of turnover, says that '[t]urnover in the Community or in a Member State, shall comprise products sold and services provided to undertakings or consumers, in the Community or in that Member State as the case may be.'[58] The Court of First Instance confirmed in *Gencor* that Article 1 does not require, in order for a concentration to be regarded as having a Community dimension, that the undertakings in question must be established in the Community or that the production activities covered by the concentration must be carried out within Community territory.[59] It considered that the requirement of 'implementation' within the Community established in *Wood Pulp* was satisfied by the Community turnover criteria in Article 1 and that this turnover could be derived from sales rather than production.[60]

---

[55] EC Merger Regs (ECMR) Reg 4064/89, Art 2(2) and 2(3). The Commission has reviewed the Merger Regulation and has considered whether to change this test to one of 'substantial lessening of competition': see the *Green Paper on the Review of Council Regulation* 4064/89, COM(2001) 745/6 final, 11 Dec 2001; in its Proposal for a Council Regulation on the control of concentrations between undertakings [2003] OJ C 20/4 it proposed to keep the "dominant position" test.

[56] In both Art 1(2) and 1(3) there is a proviso that where each of the undertakings concerned achieves more than two-thirds of its aggregate Community-wide turnover within one and the same Member State there is no Community dimension. This means that the Member State concerned would be left to apply its own national merger control to the transaction.

[57] EC Merger Reg, Art 4(1).

[58] ECMR, Art 5(1), para 2.

[59] Case T–102/96 *Gencor Ltd v Commission* [1999] ECR II–793, [1999] 4 CMLR 971, para 79.

[60] Case T–102/96 *Gencor Ltd v Commission* [1999] ECR II–793, [1999] 4 CMLR 971, para 87. The Court also referred to paragraph 11 of the Regulation's preamble, which refers to a Community dimension existing with regard to concentrations effected by 'undertakings which do not have their principal fields of activities in the Community but which have substantial operations there'. *Ibid* para 84.

Gencor concerned a proposed merger between the platinum and rhodium mining interests in South Africa of Gencor and LPD. Both were companies incorporated in South Africa. Platinum and rhodium are sold throughout the world, mainly in Japan (approximately 50 per cent of world demand), and North American and Western Europe (approximately 20 per cent each).[61] Approximately 70–75 per cent of the world supply of platinum and rhodium comes from South Africa which has 90 per cent of the world reserves. The largest producer, Anglo-American, was also incorporated in South Africa.

All of Gencor's and LPD's production was in South Africa. The proposed merger was notified to the South African authorities, which found that there were no competition problems. The South African government considered that two equally matched competitors would be preferable to the prevailing situation of one dominant firm (Anglo-American).[62] The Commission, however, found the merger to be incompatible with the common market on account of the effect which the creation of the dominant duopoly position would have on *sales* of the metals in the Community.

The Court of First Instance (CFI) said that the jurisdiction assumed by Article 1 of the Regulation was justified under public international law. Such jurisdiction was justified 'when it is foreseeable that a proposed concentration will have an immediate and substantial effect in the Community'. The CFI decided that the prohibited merger would have had such an effect. It then went on to consider whether taking jurisdiction in this case violated a principle of non-interference or violated the principle of proportionality and held that it did not. There is some debate about whether the CFI in *Gencor* did actually apply an effects doctrine in this case.[63] Although the CFI equated the turnover thresholds in Article 1 to the *Wood Pulp* implementation doctrine in determining the Community's jurisdiction, it went on to test the compatibility of this with public international law in 'foreseeable, immediate and substantial effect' terminology redolent of the effects doctrine. However, it is doubtful whether Article 1 does reflect the effects doctrine expressed in these terms.[64] The Community takes jurisdiction under Article 1 if certain turnover thresholds are reached. The level of the threshold is the outcome of political compromise between the Commission and the Member States and reflects the point at which the latter are prepared to surrender control over mergers to the Community authorities rather than the point at which it is genuinely believed that a merger may affect the interests of the Community. As is apparent from *Gencor* itself, it does not necessarily follow from the satisfaction of the thresholds that immediate and substantial effects are foreseeable in the

---

[61] For the exact figures from 1991–1995 see Table 5 in the *Gencor/Lonrho* decision.

[62] Case T–102/96 *Gencor Ltd v Commission* [1999] ECR II–793, [1999] 4 CMLR 971, para 19.

[63] See R Whish, *Competition Law* (4th edn, Butterworths, London, 2001) at 403.

[64] See Y van Gerven and L Hoet, 'Gencor: Some Notes on Transnational Competition Law Issues', (2001) 28 *LIEI* 195.

Community. In *Gencor* the CFI had to decide whether there were such effects by looking at the facts of the case. The Merger Regulation, as noted earlier, embodies a pre-notification system for mergers having a Community dimension. Non-notification is punished with fines.[65] Community law therefore insists upon transactions with a Community dimension being notified to the Commission even though they do not have foreseeable, immediate and substantial effects in the Community—a matter which will be apparent only upon examination. Although the Commission has established a simplified procedure to deal with certain concentrations which do not normally give rise to competition concerns, and can therefore be cleared by a 'short-form' decision, there is no certainty that 'foreign' mergers without substantial and direct effects will fall within the applicable criteria[66] and even if they do there is still a requirement to notify in the first place. The Commission decision in *Samsung*[67] shows that non-notification will be penalised by fines even where there is no suggestion that the transaction raises any competition concerns.

In *Gencor* the CFI went on to consider whether taking jurisdiction over this particular proposed concentration violated the principle of non-interference. This is the principle recognised by US law and considered in *Hartford Fire Insurance*, discussed above.[68] The CFI held that the principle was not violated because there was no conflict between any course of action required by the South African government and that required by the Commission. The South African government had concluded that the merger did not give rise to competition policy concerns and so had permitted it to proceed, but it had not required or compelled it to proceed.

However, the South African government had written a letter to the Commission, five months after the merger was notified under the EC Merger Regulations and five days before the decision prohibiting the merger. The CFI described this letter[69] as having 'first simply expressed a preference having regard to the strategic importance of mineral exploitation in South Africa for intervention in specific cases of collusion when they arose' and as having reached the view that in all the circumstances competition would not be impeded by the concentration. The South African government did not show 'beyond making mere statements of

---

[65] EC Merger Reg, Art 14(1).
[66] Concentrations subject to the procedure are the acquisition of a joint venture within no, or negligible, actual or foreseen activities within the EEA (judged by reference to the joint venture's turnover and the value of the assets transferred); where the parties are not competitors or operating upstream or downstream of one another; or they are competitors or operating upstream or downstream but their market share is below certain thresholds: *Commission Notice on a simplified procedure for treatment of certain concentrations under Council Regulation 4064/89*, OJ [2000] C 218/32.
[67] *Samsung* Case No IV/M.920, OJ [1999] L 225/12, [1998] 4 CMLR 494.
[68] See above at p 109.
[69] *Gencor*, para 104.

principle, in what way the proposed concentration would affect the vital economic and/or commercial interests' of South Africa. In fact the South African letter, while making it clear that the Government was not contesting the policy position of the EU on concentration and collusive practices said:

> ... the South African Government feels that we need to bring to your attention several strategic issues for our country that were not dealt with in the process thus far. The first is that our country has a unique mineral endowment and its exploitation is of central strategic importance to our economy, particularly as regards optimal corporation size and this, strength to maximise such exploitation and beneficitation. Following from this, our large mining corporations offer our country one of its limited opportunities to compete effectively in the global economy. In this light it would be our preferred option to act on actual cases of collusion when they arise and in this regard we would offer our fullest co-operation in investigating and acting upon such practices. Indeed, we would be grateful for assistance from the EU in strengthening our capacity to identify and act upon cases of such collusion. Furthermore, with respect to this specific case ... we feel that in certain situations two equally matched contestants are preferable to the present situation with one dominant mining enterprise in the sector.

It then went on to point out that other countries' platinum reserves could theoretically satisfy world demand for the next twenty years and that the Government was committed to attracting new players on to the mineral resources market.

This letter seems to have been too polite to have any effect on the Commission. It can be read however as an invitation to the Commission to take into account the gulf between the importance to South Africa of a vital industry and the significance of platinum sales in the EU to the latter's economy. It expresses perfectly lucidly that the South African government had allowed the merger to proceed because of the importance of large mining corporations to South African global trade, because it prefers to act against *actual* collusion and because it prefers two equally matched competitors (and by implication does not share the Commission's problem with oligopolistic dominance). This was a different view to that of the Commission but the point about the comparative importance to the two economies of the industry concerned is difficult to ignore.[70] One comes back, however, to the *Hartford Fire* principle—that there is no conflict with a foreign government which has not *compelled* the behaviour. The problem is quite simple—the governments of States with free market economies do not normally require or compel anyone to merge however much they might approve or wish it. They may, however, have systems of merger control which prohibit mergers. Under the interpretation of the non-interference principle expressed in *Hartford Fire* and *Gencor* the jurisdiction which prohibits will always trump the jurisdiction that permits.

The reasons given by the South African Government for not replying to the Commission's enquiries until so late in the merger process ('. . . our lack of specifi-

---

[70] See E Fox, 'The Merger Regulation and its Territorial Reach' [1999] *ECLR* 334.

cally assigned resources in dealing with issues of this nature')[71] is a reminder of the widely different resources States are able to devote to competition law matters. Such a disparity does not, of course, exist between the EC and the jurisdiction which it has most spectacularly come into conflict with in respect of merger control—the US. In *Boeing/McDonnell Douglas*[72] the European Commission came within a whisker of prohibiting a merger between two US producers of commercial jet aircraft which had already been cleared by the relevant American agency, the Federal Trade Commission (FTC). At the last moment Boeing agreed to waive its rights to exclusivity on existing long-term supply contracts, to license patents derived from defence research funding at a reasonable royalty and undertook not to enter further exclusive deals. Notwithstanding the Commission's ultimate clearance of the deal, the Commission's apparent willingness to prevent a merger concerning American companies with implications in the US for the economy, employment and defence policy created great tension. The FTC considered that the deal was not anti-competitive as Boeing already had a high market share and the addition of McDonnell Douglas's share would not be significant. The Commission, on the other hand, looked at Boeing's already dominant position, with its existing exclusive long-term supply and maintenance contracts and the potential from the merger of cross-subsidies which meant that Boeing could benefit from US Government aid given to McDonnell Douglas for military research. Above all, in strengthening Boeing's dominant position it would give it an unfair competitive advantage over Airbus, its only remaining competitor. The Americans, indeed, considered that it was the desire to protect Airbus, jointly owned by British, German, Italian and Spanish firms which drove the Commission's hostility to the deal.

The next time the European Commission was minded to prohibit a merger between two US companies, the *WorldCom/Sprint* case, the matter did not become an issue of opposing jurisdictions, as the US agencies were also prepared to block the deal and it was therefore abandoned. Finally, however, the Commission did prohibit a merger involving two American companies, GE and Honeywell, which had been permitted by the US authorities.

The Commission would, it appears, have been willing to allow the GE/Honeywell merger to proceed if satisfactory undertakings had been given but when it did not receive an acceptable answer to its demands by the date it had to make a decision, it prohibited it outright. The Commission considered that the merger would create dominant positions in the markets for the supply of avionics, non-avionics and corporate jet aircraft and would strengthen GE's existing dominant positions in jet engines for large commercial and regional aircraft.[73]

The Commission's decision in *GE/Honeywell* caused a furore—indeed the well-publicised negotiation and politicking leading up to the decision had already

---

[71] *Gencor*, para 21.
[72] Case Number IV/M.877, [1977] OJ L 336/16.
[73] See *GE/Honeywell—An Insight into the Commission's Investigation and Decision* (2001) Competition Policy Newsletter 5; A Burnside, *GE, Honey I sank the Merger* [2002] *ECLR* 107.

created enormous media interest and diplomatic activity. The US appeared aghast at the temerity of the European Commission and in particular, given the inevitable personalisation of these events, of the Commissioner responsible for competition, Mario Monti. US criticism characterised the decision as being driven by a concern for competitors rather than for competition and the divergence in view between the two jurisdictions was also explained as the US concentrating on short-term benefits to customers in the form of lower prices while the EC worried about long-term effects on competitive structures. Inevitably, questions were raised as to whether the difference between the tests applied—under the US Clayton Act a merger is only blocked if it will lead to a 'substantial lessening of competition', whereas under the EC Merger Regulation the test is the creation or strengthening of a dominant position—was responsible for producing the different results. Even on the day the decision was published, however, Monti played down the differences with the US authorities: 'each authority has to perform its own assessment and the risk of dissenting views, although regrettable, can never be totally excluded. This does not mean that one authority is doing a technical analysis and the other pursuing a political goal, as some might have preferred, but simply that we might interpret facts differently and forecast the effects of an operation in different ways'.[74]

6. EU–US COOPERATION

A picture of two hostile systems of competition law would, however, be misleading. There has been friendly contact and cooperation between the officials of the EC Commission Competition Directorate General (DG Comp, previously DG IV) officials and those of the US Department of Justice Antitrust Division and the Federal Trade Commission from the 1960s onwards, reinforced by their mutual participation in the OECD Committee on competition law and policy.[75] The EC and US authorities now work in close contact with one another. Their co-operation was placed on a more formal footing in 1991 when the US-EEC Competition Laws Agreement was signed.[76] The 1991 Agreement provides for the notification to each other of antitrust enforcement actions by one party which might affect the interests of the other, consultations over notified actions, infor-

---

[74] Commission Press Release, 3 July 2001, IP/01/939.

[75] The OECD 1995 *Recommendation Concerning Cooperation between Member Countries on Restrictive Business Practices Affecting International Trade* which is a revision of earlier documents, provides for cooperation, consultation and notification between members. The 1998 Recommendation on Hard-core Cartels is credited with improving international evidence gathering in cartel cases: see J Klein, *Time for a Global Competition Initiative?* Address at the EC Merger Control 10th Anniversary conference, Brussels, 14 Sept 2000.

[76] For the history of this agreement, see below at p 121. The US has signed similar agreements with Canada (1995), Israel (1999), and Mexico (2000). Two older agreements were entered into with Germany (1976) and Australia (1982). See generally L Fullerton and C Mazard, 'International Antitrust Cooperation Agreements' (2001) 24 *Journal of World Competition* 405.

mation sharing and mutual assistance, and 'positive comity' obligations. Providing for positive comity means that when one party is concerned that anticompetitive conduct in the territory of the other is harming the former's important national interests and believes the conduct to be infringing the latter's laws, the former may request the latter to take action under its own laws against the anticompetitive conduct. These provisions of the 1991 Agreement were elaborated in a second agreement, the 1998 Positive Comity Agreement, which does not cover merger control.

In fact the procedural history of the 1991 agreement is interesting in itself and arguably shows that the relations between EC and US officials can be viewed in terms of what some international lawyers call 'transgovermentalism', a system in which the principal actors in the international order are not unitary States but, inter alia, units of the State which create with their counterparts in other States dense networks of relations through which to address international problems.[77] In 1990 the EC Commission decided that it would be advantageous if arrangements with the US authorities went beyond cooperation under the OECD recommendations and were formalised in a 'legally binding document rather than a non-binding recommendation.[78] Negotiations with the US authorities resulted in the 1991 Agreement, signed in Washington on 23 September 1991 by the Attorney-General and the President of the FTC on behalf of the US government on the one hand and by the Commissioner responsible for competition (Sir Leon Brittan) on behalf of the Commission on the other. The Council of Ministers had no part in the conclusion of the Agreement but the text was sent to the Member States in a letter from the Director-General for Competition two weeks later. During the period of negotiations some Member States did query whether the Commission had the competence to conclude such an agreement but their reservations were ignored. Once the agreement was concluded however, France, supported by the Netherlands and Spain, sought its annulment. The ECJ upheld the challenge and found that the Commission had no competence to enter into international agreements such as this one under Article 300 (then Article 228).[79] Under US law the Agreement was an 'executive agreement' which can be concluded by the President without the approval of Senate (although under international law they have the same effect and status as any other international agreement). The Commission claimed that on the European side the agreement was an international administrative agreement which did not require action by the Council or give rise to any new financial obligations on the part of the Community[80] and

---

[77] See eg AM Slaughter, 'Government Networks: the Heart of the Liberal Democratic Order', in GH Fox and BR Roth (eds), *Democratic Governance and International Law* (Cambridge University Press, 2000).

[78] Commission's Explanatory Note on the Draft Agreement between Government of the United States and the Commission of the European Communities regarding the application of their Competition Laws.

[79] Case C–327/91 *France v Commission, Re the EC–USA Competition Law Cooperation Agreement* [1994] ECR I–3641, [1994] 5 CMLR 517.

[80] *Ibid*, paras 30–31.

which it could therefore negotiate and conclude itself. The ECJ dismissed these arguments and refused to recognise such a category of agreements, holding that under Article 300 only the Council was able to conclude international agreements and that the Commission had exceeded its competence.[81] However, the Members States' problems with the Agreement were with the procedure employed, not with its substance, and it was affirmed by a Decision of the Council and Commission eight months later.[82] The 1998 Positive Comity Agreement was effected by a Decision of the Council from the start.[83]

The 1991 Agreement is considered to have been a great success. Its greatest drawback is the impossibility of exchanging confidential information without the consent of the undertakings concerned where this is not permitted by the party's domestic laws. The EC Commission is prevented from doing this by Article 287 EC and Article 20 of Regulation 17[84] although US law now provides for the possibility of entering into antitrust cooperation agreements under which confidential information can be shared.[85] The US agreement with Australia in 1999 contains such a provision. Where mergers are concerned, however, parties often decide that it is in their interests to allow the authorities to share information, as it results in speedier decisions and reduces the burdens inevitably imposed by having two jurisdictions involved.

The question is, of course, how, with such well-developed co-operation between the US and the EC, an event such as the GE/Honeywell merger could nevertheless occur, and to what extent it shows that conflicts between jurisdictions cannot be avoided however close the ties between them. One reason why *GE/Honeywell* attracted such attention, apart from the sheer size and significance of the deal which the Commission aborted, was the implications for the globalised economy. For if the US and the EC cannot agree on competition matters, what chance is there for harmony with and between states whose state of economic and political development differs far more sharply? Positive Comity, for example, has been described as 'assuming that two or more different countries will recognise and wish to pursue a common interest in enforcing antitrust law'[86] such as co-operation to root out common evils such as international cartels, but the difficulty is that this presupposes that different countries recognise the same phenomenon as an evil. After all, OPEC, the greatest cartel of all, is an organisation of sovereign states.[87]

The basic reason that the US and EC authorities came to a different conclusion in *GE/Honeywell* was that they took a different view of what is called 'conglomerate effects', particularly 'mixed bundling', and of the possibility of market fore-

---

[81] See AJ Riley, 'Nailing the Jellyfish: The Illegality of the EC/US Government Competition Agreement' (1992) 13 *ECLR* 101.
[82] Decision of the Council and Commission, 10 April [1995] OJ L 95/1 and L 131/38.
[83] [1998] OJ L 173/26.
[84] Reg 17 of 1962 OJ Spec Ed (1959–1962) Spec Ed 187.
[85] The International Antitrust Enforcement Assistance Act, 15 USC 6201–6212 (1994).
[86] E Fox, 'Toward World Antitrust and Market Access' (1997) 91 *AJIL* 1.
[87] As the US courts recognised in *IAM v OPEC* 649 F.2d 1354 1981.

closure through vertical integration.[88] These are not issues of principle but matters of economic judgment. Merger control is based on predictions of what will happen on the post-merger market. Competition authorities base their predictions on economic evidence, but different authorities looking at the same evidence can come, and do come, to different conclusions. As Commissioner Monti said in the Press Release quoted above,[89] the risk of dissenting views can never be excluded. To what extent in *GE/Honeywell* the divergence resulted from divergent tests and competition objectives is a matter of intense debate but both Monti and his senior officials were quick to reassure the US authorities in the aftermath of the case that they really were *ad idem* about the goals of competition policy.[90] Monti talked of the 'convergence' between US and EC policy and that theme was taken up by the senior American officials. It seems, however, that when the Americans speak of convergence they mean the adoption by the EC of American approaches. The then Assistant US Attorney General, Antitrust Division, described recent developments in EC law, which have placed a greater emphasis on economic analysis and consumer welfare, as being similar to the 'revolution' in antitrust thinking in the US which changed the application of American law in the 1970s and 1980s. The EC is applauded for successfully playing catch-up.[91] The Deputy Assistant Attorney General identified five key issues, however, where there is divergence In US and EC policies: efficiencies in merger review, fidelity rebates by dominant firms, predatory pricing, the essential facilities doctrine, and monopoly leveraging.[92] On fidelity rebates and the application of the essential facilities doctrine to intellectual property rights he accepted that there is some debate about the correct approach, but on the others he left no doubt that the US has got it right. The 'transatlantic dialogue' is not expected to result in shifts in US policy.

7. INTERNATIONAL INITIATIVES[93]

For some time EC has advocated more ambitious remedies for the competition problems thrown up by the increasing internationalisation of trade. This has no

---

[88] *GE/Honeywell—An Insight into the Commission's Investigation and Decision* (2001) Competition Policy Newsletter 5; M Pflanz and C Caffara, 'The Economics of GE/Honeywell' (2002) 23 *ECLR* 115.

[89] See p 120 above.

[90] For example, M Monti, *Antitrust in the US and Europe: a History of Convergence*, General Counsel Roundtable, American Bar Association, Washington DC, 14 Nov 2001; A Schaub, *Antitrust Law Enforcement—A Shared Transatlantic Vision*, Bi-Annual Conference of the Council for the United States and Italy, New York, 25 Jan 2002.

[91] CA James, *Antitrust in the Early 21st Century: Core Values and Convergence*, speech at the Program on Antitrust Policy in the 21st Century Sponsored by the Directorate General for Competition at the European Commission and the US Mission to the European Union, Brussels, Belgium, 15 May, 2002.

[92] WJ Kolasky, *North Atlantic Competition Policy: Converging Toward What?* Speech at the BIICL Second Annual International and Comparative Law Conference, London, 17 May 2002.

[93] See generally AS Grewlich, 'Globalisation and Conflict in Competition Law' (2001) 24 *Journal of World Competition* 367; AD Mitchell, 'Broadening the Vision of Trade Liberalisation' (2001) 24 *Journal of World Competition* 343.

doubt stemmed from the EC's own highly successful experience in integrating markets and in producing a supranational competition regime for 15 different States. From the mid-1990s. onwards the EU has favored dealing with international competition issues under the auspices of the WTO.[94] This culminated in the EU proposing at the WTO Ministerial Conference at Singapore in 1996 that a working group on trade and competition be set up. This was agreed and resulted in the setting up of the WTO Working Group on the Interaction between Trade and Competition Policy to study the issues 'relating to the interaction between trade and competition policy, including anti-competitive practices, in order to identify any areas that may merit further consideration in the WTO framework.'[95] The EU continued to press through this forum for the creation of a multilateral framework of competition rules within the WTO, and was rewarded when the Declaration adopted by the 4th WTO Ministerial Conference at Doha in November 2001 contained three paragraphs on competition policy.[96] The Declaration recognised the case for a multilateral framework to enhance the contribution of competition policy to international trade and development, and said that the parties agreed that negotiations on trade and competition should take place after the 5th Ministerial conference in 2003. Until then the Working Group would work on formulating certain core principles on: transparency, non-discrimination and procedural fairness; hard-core cartels; modalities of voluntary cooperation; and supporting the development of competition institutions in developing countries. The EU Commission is delighted that a multilateral agreement is finally 'on the agenda.'[97]

This commitment in the Doha Declaration was only possible because previously sceptical countries had become persuaded of the advantages of a multilateral agreement. These included India and Hong Kong, but above all the US. Until recently the US favoured bilateral arrangements, such as those with the EU, and working towards substantive convergence with other jurisdictions, rather than multilateral agreements. Joel Klein, the Assistant Attorney General in the Antitrust Division of the US Department of Justice in the Clinton Administration, and, as such, the chief US antitrust official, was one of the leading sceptics about a competition law agreement within the WTO. His objections were that the substantive differences in States' competition policies would make the negotiations too difficult and the results undesirable; that if the outcome was the adoption of minimum standards of competition rules this might entail a 'race to the bottom'; that it would be inappropriate to establish a dispute settlement procedure to review the individual decision of States' competition authorities; and that a settlement pro-

---

[94] EU Commission, *Competition Policy in the New Trade Order—Strengthening International Cooperation and Rules*, Report of the Committee of Experts, Brussels, 1995, the outcome of the deliberations of the Committee set up by the then Competition Commissioner, Karel Van Miert. The Report proposed a "Plurilateral Agreement on Competition and Trade (PACT) which would have the status of a "Plurilateral Trade Agreement" within Annex 4 of the WTO Agreement.

[95] WTO, Singapore Ministerial Declaration 1996, para 20.

[96] WTO Doha Ministerial Declaration 2001, paras 23–25.

[97] See DG Comp's *Competition Policy Newsletter* (2002) No 1, 27 (Y Devellennes and G Kiriazis).

cedure which was limited to a review of a State's failure to adopt or enforce a national competition law or to cooperate with another State's authorities would only create tensions.[98] Moreover, it has been argued that at a time when US antitrust law has 'shrunk back', under the influence of Chicago school thinking, to a role which is limited to the promotion of efficiency and only prohibiting conduct which lowers output and raises prices to consumers, the US antitrust community is loathe to become involved in international ventures with parties that might see a wider role for antitrust.[99] In 1997 Klein and the US Attorney General, Janet Reno, set up an International Competition Policy Advisory Committee (ICPAC) which reported in February 2000.[100] This report came down firmly against a binding set of competition rules enforced by a supranational authority: efforts at developing a harmonised and comprehensive set of multilateral competition rules administered by a supranational agency were not only unrealistic but also unwise.[101]

However, the Advisory Committee also recognised that relying solely on domestic competition law regimes and extraterritorial enforcement alone was not adequate. It advocated a middle way, saying that the US should continue with its vigorous expansion of bilateral cooperation agreements and positive comity provisions, but should also continue to develop its broader multilateral engagement. This in particular should involve efforts to develop a more broadly international perspective toward competition policy, with the goal of reducing parochial actions by governments and firms; foster greater soft harmonisation of competition policy systems; develop improved ways of resolving conflicts; develop a greater appreciation for the negative spillovers from domestic firm or governmental actions; and develop a degree of consensus among nations on what constitutes best practices in competition policy and its enforcement.

The Committee proposed a 'Global Competition Initiative', a new venue where the scope for collaborations among interested governments and international organisations could be explored and government officials, NGOs and private firms could consult about competition law and policy. In September 2000 Joel Klein spoke very positively in Brussels[102] about the desirability of an international forum along the lines recommended by ICPAC, oriented towards solving practical enforcement-related problems, and involving cooperation with and technical assistance for new antitrust agencies, although he remained opposed to a competition authority within the WTO. This led to the launching in October 2001 of

---

[98] J Klein, 'Working Paper VI 4—Competition Policy objectives' in CD Ehlermann and L Laudati (eds) *European Competition Annual 1997: Objectives of Competition Policy* (Hart Publishing, Oxford, 1998) at 259.

[99] See eg E Fox, 'Towards World Antitrust and Market Access' (1997) 91 *AJIL* 1 at 10.

[100] US Department of Justice: *International Competition Policy Advisory Committee to the Attorney General and Assistant Attorney General for Antitrust*, Final Report, 2000, Washington, available at http://www.usdoj.gov/atr/icpac/finalreport.htm.

[101] *Ibid* ch 5.

[102] J Klein, *Time for a Global Competition Initiative?* Address at the EC Merger Control 10th Anniversary Conference, Brussels, 14 Sept 2000.

the International Competition Network (ICN) by officials from a number of States' competition authorities.[103] According to the Memorandum on its website,[104] the ICN is a project-oriented, consensus-based, informal network of antitrust agencies from developed and developing countries that will address antitrust enforcement and policy issues of common interest and formulate proposals for procedural and substantive convergence through a results-oriented agenda and structure.[105] The Assistant Attorney General under the new Bush administration, Charles A James, had no more enthusiasm than his predecessor for the idea of a global competition agency—'[n]o one seriously believes that the world is ready for a global antitrust code enforced by a global antitrust agency, nor has there been nearly enough convergence to justify the imposition of dispute settlement-based antitrust disciplines in trade agreements, in the WTO or elsewhere'[106]—but the US support for the Doha declaration shows that it is now ready at least to discuss some form of multilateral agreement for cooperation within the WTO.

8. CONCLUSION

The international community has accepted that the time has passed when the only issue to be resolved was how far States could take extra territorial jurisdiction. That issue will not, however, become redundant in the foreseeable future although it should, though cooperation and harmonisation, become more manageable. As the then US Assistant Attorney General said, the question is *should* a particular authority act, and *how*, not whether it can.[107] The real challenge for competition law in the international setting is whether it can truly deliver to developing and less developed countries the benefits which it is claimed to bring to the developed world. National (and EC) competition laws are supposed to enhance consumer welfare by maintaining open competitive markets. The doubts will arise, however, if the result of international co-operation in competition law is merely to allow multinational companies and producers from the rich economies of the developed world untrammelled access to markets elsewhere.

---

[103] Including Australia, Canada, the EU, France, Germany, Israel, Italy, Japan, Korea, Mexico, South Africa, the UK, the US and Zambia.

[104] http://www.internationalcompetitionnetwork.org

[105] A Schaub (then Director-General DG Comp) *Co-operation in competition policy enforcement between the EU and the US and new concepts evolving at the World Trade Organisation and the International Competition Network*, Mentor Group–Brussels, Belgium, 4 April 2002.

[106] CA James, speech at the Program on Antitrust Policy in the 21st Century Sponsored by the Directorate General for Competition at the European Commission and the US Mission to the European Union Brussels, Belgium, 15 May 2002.

[107] *Ibid.*

7

The Jurisdiction of the Security Council: Original Intention and New World Order(s)

COLIN WARBRICK

1. INTRODUCTION

I have used the word 'jurisdiction' in the title to fit in with the overall pattern of
the chapters but it is not the best word to use about international organisations.
'Competence' strikes me as a better one because we are concerned with some form
of limited legal authority, limited in its legal origin, not in the foundational way
in which the various jurisdictions of States are limited, one against another.[1] In
the case of the Security Council its competence derives wholly from the United
Nations Charter. The competence of an organ can be examined from a variety of
perspectives. Three of which should be kept in mind: one is the 'authoritative'
competence of the Security Council—what are the legal effects of the decisions it
takes; another is its 'procedural competence'—what is required for the lawful exercise of its authoritative competence, such as voting majorities and participation
of certain States; and the final one is 'substantive competence'—what is the
subject-matter which falls within the decision-taking capacity of the Security
Council and it is this where the problems and debate arise. The questions are
related. The Council, which is an organ of limited membership within the UN,
has the exceptional power as part of its authoritative competence to reach decisions which are binding on the whole of the membership of the UN and which
take priority over their other international obligations.[2] The substantive competence of the Council includes the power to require States to take various kinds of
measures against another State, including authorising the use of force, for the
preservation or restoration of international peace and security, certain factual
conditions being present.[3] So, we have an exceptional authoritative competence
on substantive matters of the greatest significance for international relations. This

---

[1] See C Warbrick, 'The Principle of Sovereign Equality' in AV Lowe and C Warbrick (eds), *The
United Nations and the Principles of International Law* (Routledge, London, 1994), 204.
[2] UN Charter, Arts 25, 27(3), 103.
[3] Arts 39–42. This note is not going to be concerned with the powers of the Council under
Chapters VI and VIII of the Charter.

remarkable state of affairs has a further feature, that the five permanent members of the Security Council have a power of veto over Council decision-making, a power which they may use to prevent the adoption of a resolution of which they disapprove, even one directed against the activities of a permanent member itself.[4] The adoption of such a radical scheme was possible only because of the circumstances at the end of the Second World War, when, for a short moment, statesmen understood themselves to be at a time of transition, in particular, when the dangers of uncontrolled recourse to armed conflict were graphically apparent.[5] Even so, they remained *states*men—the UN was not conceived of as a world government, it was not, as the International Court was soon to say, a 'super-State'.[6] It was an international organisation with a wide substantive competence but a limited authoritative competence in its plenary organ, the General Assembly.[7] Even in that narrower area of substantive competence of the Council, the old dispensation of international relations was not far below the surface: the United Nations was not given any military forces of its own and it could obtain them only by agreement with the member States under Article 43 of the Charter, a provision which, as is well known, has never been used. The transitional moment of 1945 did not last long and the original intention, a kind of international social contract, that in return for the surrender by States of their right to use force and, on the condition of entrenched power for the permanent members, the Security Council would provide an effective collective guarantee of security for the members of the UN, was never delivered on in the terms in which it was envisaged.[8] In the changed political circumstances of the post-war world, the UN developed other mechanisms for the delivery of this promise but the programme of the Council itself remained the same. As Judge Fitzmaurice said in the *Namibia Advisory Opinion*:

> It was to keep the peace, not to change the world order that the Security Council was set up.[9]

This chapter looks at one part of the Council's recent activities to see if that mission statement remains good and, if it does not, how the various competencies of the Council have developed.

---

[4] See B Simma (ed), *The Charter of the United Nations: A Commentary* (Oxford University Press, Oxford, 1994), 463–67.

[5] R Russell, *A History of the United Nations Charter: the Role of the United States, 1940–1945* (Brookings Institute, Washington D.C., 1958) at 713–41; L Goodrich, *The United Nations Charter* (Columbia University Press, New York, 1960), chs II and III.

[6] *Reparations for Injuries Suffered in the Service of the United Nations* (1949) ICJ Rep. 174 at 179.

[7] With some narrow but not unimportant exceptions, the authoritative competence of the General Assembly is restricted to the power to make recommendations, UN Charter, Arts 10, 11(2).

[8] J Dedring, 'The Security Council', in P Taylor and AJR Groom (eds), *The United Nations in the New Millennium: the Principal Organs* (Continuum, New York 2000), 61 at 62–69.

[9] *Legal Consequences for States of the Continued Presence of South Africa in Namibia (South West Africa) notwithstanding Security Council resolution 276* (1971) ICJ Rep 3 at para 115.

2. THE POWERS OF INTERNATIONAL ORGANISATIONS

It is one thing to say that the competence of an international organisation is to be found in its basic treaty. It is another to identify what the competence of the organisation is. There are several factors which account for this. Many treaties couch the objectives of the organisation in very wide terms, often in a grand pre-ambular statement. While not always so grandly expressed, the powers of individual organs are also written in wide terms. International organisations are intended to last and their founding instruments have a 'quasi-constitutional' character to them. Those charged with their interpretation are likely to find ways of adapting the treaties to the changed circumstances, political, economic, technical, which confront the organisation. The primary responsibility, both in the sense of first in time and in the sense of practical responsibility, for the interpretation of the treaties of international organisations lies with the organs themselves. It is a job which they must do if they are to do any job at all. Only rarely will the decision of the organ be subject to review elsewhere but, in any case, international courts, primarily the ICJ, have taken a flexible approach to the interpretation of the constitutions of international organisations, relying on concepts of implied and inherent powers to overcome gaps in the provisions of the treaty itself and to give effect to the practice of the organisation in interpreting its own constitution.[10] These developments have never been beyond controversy because they run contrary to the orthodoxies of treaty interpretation—that the text is an agreement between States, which should be interpreted narrowly to respect their sovereign rights and in the light of their understandings at the time the agreement was reached.[11] The development of an international constitution through interpretation and practice raises an extra dimension—most of them have provisions for their formal amendment, provisions often requiring more substantial majorities than are required for decision-making in the organs of the organisation.[12] Giving majorities, either by the exercise of the primary interpretation power or by the capacity to establish the practice of the organisation, the chance to 'create' organisation competence runs at odds with the amendment process designed to protect States against the uncovenanted alteration of their obligations.[13]

There is no question that the Charter is read differently now than it would have been in 1945.[14] It is not necessary to go through the catalogue of 'changes' but

---

[10] *Reparations for Injuries*, n 7 above at 180. Generally, E Lauterpacht, 'The Development of the Law of International Organisations by the Decisions of International Tribunals' (1976–IV) 152 *Hag Rec* 377.

[11] I Brownlie, '*The Principles of Public International Law* (5th edn, Oxford University Press, Oxford, 1998) at 633–34.

[12] UN Charter, Art 109.

[13] E Zoller, 'The 'Corporate Will' of the United Nations and the Rights of the Minority' (1987) 81 *AJIL* 610.

[14] B Kingsbury and A Roberts United Nations: Divided World: The UN's Role in International Relations (2nd edn, Clarendon Press, Oxford, 1993).

enough to notice that, where there has been controversy, the resolution of the issue of competence has frequently been in favour of the Organisation. The most important case of this is the acceptance by the ICJ in the *Expenses Advisory Opinion*[15] of the legality of peace-keeping operations, whether established by the General Assembly or the Security Council, based on a reading of the Charter which relied on the implied powers of the Organisation to take action for the effective implementation of its purposes.[16] The advisory opinion did not, of itself, resolve the dispute about financing of peace-keeping operations but its ultimate resolution has cast no doubt on the powers of the Security Council to establish peace-keeping operations, even in the absence of specific authority in the Charter.[17] The settlement of the dispute with which the *Expenses Advisory Opinion* concerned was on ambiguous terms but further practice has reinforced the Court's judgment about Security Council competence.[18] However, reliance on subsequent practice must be undertaken with caution. The leading judicial authority is the ICJ's opinion in the *Namibia Advisory Opinion*.[19] The question arose about the binding effect of a Security Council resolution (Resolution 284) in the face of an abstention by a permanent member. Article 27(3) of the Charter reads in part:

> Decisions of the Security Council . . . shall be made by an affirmative vote of nine members, including the concurring votes of the permanent members . . .

The ICJ upheld the validity and the binding effect of resolution 284 but the terms on which it did so bear emphasising. The proceedings of the Council, 'extending over a long period supply abundant evidence' that the Council and the permanent members have 'consistently and uniformly' interpreted the practice of abstention by a permanent member as not being a bar to the adoption of resolutions and that this practice had been 'generally accepted by the Members of the United Nations' such that it 'evidences a general practice of the organisation.'[20] Of course, in a matter as confined as voting practice, the establishment of the general practice, its consistency and uniformity, was relatively easy and there had been sufficient opportunities for this identified practice to develop. This was, after all, a matter of authoritative competence. In more diffuse circumstances, especially innovative claims of substantive competence, satisfying the strict tests set here will be much more difficult but, protected, as the Council will usually be, from authoritative review, the prospects for it developing new lines of substantive competence over time are there, perhaps the main consideration being endorsement of or acquiescence in the practice by the generality of the membership outside the Council.

---

[15] *Certain Expenses of the United Nations (Art 17, paragraph 2 of the Charter)* (1962) ICJ Rep 151.
[16] *Ibid* at 167.
[17] Simma, *The Charter of the United Nations,* n 5 above at 590–91.
[18] *UN Bluebook on Peacekeeping.*
[19] n 9 above.
[20] n 9 above at para 22.

3. THE COLD WAR PERIOD AND THE COUNCIL

I do not want to do more than draw attention to the obvious point that the political divisions between the permanent members had serious consequences for the operation of the Charter scheme by the Security Council. The absence of Article 43 agreements meant that Article 42 could not operate in the manner intended, so that the prospects for the coercive use of force by the UN appeared to be ruled out. However, the development of peace-keeping by the Council in those rare interludes of consensus did contain the germs of ideas which were to be relied on in greater measure after 1989. I refer to two, both much contested at the time. The first was the claim of ONUC to use force for the implementation of its mandate in the Congo insofar as it affected the rebel authorities in Katanga Province and their foreign mercenary supporters.[21] While it subsequently became a mark of a peace-keeping force that its power to use force was restricted to personal self-defence,[22] there was here the suggestion that the Council could go further and invest a force with a wider authority, the right to use force to carry out its mandate (whether or not that might affect its designation, then the only one available, as 'peace-keeping'). The other, and it turned out of greater moment, was the authorisation to the United Kingdom to use its naval force to enforce the 'Beira Blockade' as part of the measures taken with respect to the situation in Rhodesia.[23] The authorisation to use force had effect on the States of the flag of any ship which the British Navy intercepted. While the British authorities could not be obliged to provide the warships, other States were obliged to submit to the inspections, not, it seems to me, as a result of the decision to impose the sanctions under Article 41 but because of the binding effect of a decision under Article 42, but there other views. The important point for the present is that a device had been found which went some way to filling the gap left by the absence of Article 43 agreements. It was not the UN which used the force but an able and willing State. The Security Council authorisation was a necessary condition for the lawfulness of the exercise of the force thus volunteered. The challenge to Council competence was not made on the basis of the authorisation to the UK but on the more fundamental ground that the situation in Rhodesia did not constitute a threat to international peace and security and thus action to deal with could not be justified as falling within Chapter VII.[24] In general, though, the feature of criticism of the Council in this period was that it was not using the powers that it had rather than that it was acting beyond its authority.

---

[21] G Abi-Saab, *The United Nations Operations in the Congo, 1960–1964* (Oxford University Press, Oxford, 1978).

[22] Simma, n 4 above at 589.

[23] Security Council Resolution 221, para 5: 'Calls upon the Government of the United Kingdom to prevent . . . by the use of armed force if necessary breaches of the Beira Blockade.'

[24] M McDougal and W Reisman, 'Rhodesia and the United Nations: the Lawfulness of International Concern' (1968) 62 *AJIL* 1 at 5–13 (examining and rejecting the criticism).

4. NEW WORLD ORDER

International lawyers were, perhaps for as long as a nano-second, gratified by President George Bush's invocation of the new world order which was to succeed the Cold War, a world order which would be conducted according to the rule of international law.[25] The foremost item in the catalogue of law would be the Charter and, at least from one angle, there had (almost) been a return to the original Charter model in the response of to the invasion of Kuwait by Iraq in 1990. The Council condemned the invasion (though it stopped short of characterising it as an act of aggression);[26] it established a stringent sanctions regime against Iraq and authorised the use of force by the 'Coalition' to enforce it;[27] and it authorised the use of 'all necessary measures' both for the removal of Iraqi forces from Kuwait and 'for the maintenance of peace and security in the region'.[28] There were some academic criticisms of items in the Council's activities, notably whether or not there was a power to move to the use of force under Article 42 before economic measures under Article 41 had proved not to be effective.[29] There remains, in my view, an uncertainty about whether the force actually used was force by way of collective self-defence or force authorised by Resolution 678. The ambiguity arises because the Coalition's action stopped at a stage when it could have been justified as self-defence, that is to say, when the invading force had been expelled from Kuwaiti territory and the government of Kuwait restored to power there. *If* the force were authorised under Chapter VII, then there arose certain questions about the nature and limits of the power of the Council to authorise States (or international organisations) to use force.[30] This was, of course, coercive force. It looked like the force which the Security Council could have taken under the original scheme of the Charter but could the Council legally authorise someone else to exercise that power?

The fact that the question was raised at all was an indication of a trend which developed almost immediately the new political circumstances in the world allowed the Council to take more action than it had done in the Cold War period. Questions began to be asked about its competence to do so.[31] One needs to distinguish the political issue from the legal one here. Even where there is no doubt about the substantive competence of the Council to act, that competence is in the nature of a legal power. The political question is whether or not that power should

---

[25]   C Greenwood, 'New World Order or Old? The Invasion of Kuwait and the Rule of Law' (1992) 55 *MLR* 153.

[26]   Security Council Resolution 660, para 1.

[27]   Security Council Resolution 665, para l: 'such measures commensurate to the specific circumstances as may be necessary . . .'

[28]   Security Council Resolution 678, para 2.

[29]   B Weston, 'Security Council Resolution 678 and Persian Gulf Decision-Making: Precarious Legitimacy' (1991) 85 *AJIL* 516.

[30]   ND White, *Keeping the Peace* (2nd ed Manchester University Press, Manchester, 1997) at 123–25.

[31]   JE Alvarez, 'Judging the Security Council' (1996) 90 *AJIL* 1 (with a comprehensive review of the debates).

be exercised in these circumstances—the decision not being wholly one about desirability but one which takes into account the material force available to the Council and the financial consequences for the Organisation. The legal questions come in series:

1. Is there a threat to or breach of the peace or act of aggression?
2. If there is, does the action the Council proposes to take fall within its powers under Article 41 or Article 42?
3. If it is, is it necessary for the maintenance or restoration of international peace and security?

Although these are legal questions and capable of legal determination, in practice, they are first political questions for the Council itself determining its own jurisdiction. Through the 1990s, the Council showed an increasing willingness to characterise situations as threatening international peace. The step from inter-State conflict to the consequences of internal wars had already been taken in the Rhodesian case. The Council found that the situation in Somalia in 1993[32] and Haiti in 1994[33] constituted threats to international peace. Even more ambitiously, the Council characterised Libya's failure, inter alia, to renounce terrorism and to comply with (the non-binding) Resolution 731 requiring the surrender of terror-ist suspects[34] as threats to the peace. The Council takes an increasingly broad view of both the kind of situation which constitutes a threat to international peace and the proximity of the situation to a breach of the peace.[35] Although States have from time to time differed from the Council majority about this kind of decision, there has as yet been no opportunity for judicial consideration of any particular determination.[36] Even were one to arise, the combined effects of a claim of non-justiciability of the question and the claim that a practice had arisen which allowed a very wide nature of threat to fall within Article 39 makes it unlikely that the ICJ would fail to endorse a determination of the Council. There are one or two instances where the Council has claimed to be acting under Chapter VII but where it has not made a specific finding that any situation constituted a threat to inter-national peace and security.[37] In these cases, the resolutions went on to impose obligations on States to introduce sanctions against trade with an identified territory. Here, there is a question about the procedural competence of the Council—may the resolution have binding effect for States in the absence of a specific Article 39 determination? One can imagine circumstances in which the question could be tested and a crucial issue in answering it would be the extent

[32] Security Council Resolution 733.
[33] Security Council Resolution 940.
[34] Security Council Resolution 748.
[35] B Conforti, *The Law and Practice of the United Nations* (2nd rev., edn, Kluwer, The Hague, 2000) at 171–79 (with some criticism of the practice).
[36] See Pt 5 below.
[37] Most notably, Security Council Resolution 1160 (on Kosovo); also Resolution 1220 (Sierra Leone).

to which a practice had grown up within the Council and which had been accepted by the Members of the UN of regarding such resolutions as binding.

One related practice would seem to have passed the threshold and become part of the way the Council does its work. Once it has said that it is acting under Chapter VII, the Council no longer specifies the precise provision under which action is being taken. This is relevant to the second and third questions set out above—where is the Charter authority for the action proposed by the resolution and can a case be made that the action is necessary for the maintenance or restoration of international peace and security? At the first level, one must distinguish the question of whether the action lies within the competence of the Council at all and, if it does, whether it should be embarked upon in this situation. It is the first of these which is of present concern. Much of the activity of the Council has been in the field of what once was called peace-keeping but which, after Secretary-General Boutros Boutros Galli's papers, *An Agenda for Peace*[38] and, especially its Supplement,[39] must now be broken down into a series of categories— preventative operations, peace-keeping in the orthodox senses of observing or helping to implement peace-agreements reached between the protagonists, peace- building—the process of bringing about a settlement (which might then be the subject of a peace-keeping operation)—and peace-enforcement—the active and, if necessary, forcible implementation of the conditions for peace-building and of any settlement which emerges, missions which may run in parallel with other operations.[40] The big difference between An *Agenda for Peace* and its *Supplement* was the recognition that the UN itself was unlikely ever to be provided with the armed force necessary to carry out forcible action, meaning the gamut of peace- enforcement.[41] Instead, it would rely on what have become to be known as 'coali- tions of the able and willing', States, groups of States or international organisations with the capacity to bring and use their own force to implement a mandate given by the Council. Military action may be the principal element in the UN pro- gramme, as it was in the Gulf War, where the object was to remove the Iraqi forces from Kuwait,[42] or it might be a small element in support of what is essentially a more tradition peace-keeping mission, such as the NATO air support for the safe areas in Bosnia.[43] Resort to parallel peace-building/peace-enforcement operations in Bosnia[44] and in Kosovo[45] and in East Timor[46] have involved the creation of UN operations with ambitious mandates to administer territory and work to the implementation of elaborate peace agreements.

---

[38] *An Agenda for Peace*, A/47/227 (1992).

[39] *Supplement to An Agenda for Peace*, A/50/60 (1995).

[40] For instance, the United Nations Mission in Kosovo (UNMIK), a UN force, and K-FOR, a Security Council authorised force, Security Council Resolution 1244, paras 5 and 11, 7 and 9.

[41] *Supplement*, n 39 above at paras 77–80.

[42] Security Council Resolution 678—' "those States aiding Kuwait" (the Coalition)—authorised to use "all necessary means".'

[43] Security Council Resolution 836, paras 5, 9–11.

[44] Security Council Resolution 1031.

[45] n 40 above.

[46] Security Council Resolution 1272.

A quite different kind of initiative by the Council was the decision to establish the International Criminal Tribunal for the Former Yugoslavia,[47] followed by the resolution to do the same for Rwanda.[48] The particularity of these innovations in terms of the competence of the Council is that the Tribunals clearly cannot be regarded as exercising any authority delegated by the Council of its own powers to act. The Council can create peace-keeping bodies; it could, subject to the existence of Article 43 arrangements, institute UN enforcement forces; but it could not be a court.

It was possible to see the initial response of the Security Council to Iraq's invasion of Kuwait as a modified version of the original scheme of the Charter because the situation—the armed intervention of one State into another—was the typical case against which the Charter was directed. As events with respect to Iraq progressed and as the nature of other circumstance brought to the Council's attention in the early 1990's rapidly demonstrated, the Gulf War was an untypical example of a situation which threatened international security. Instead, the Council was called upon to confront situations which were predominantly internal—civil wars, like those in Bosnia and in Angola, and complete breakdowns of governmental authority, as was the case in Somalia. Where peace-keeping forces in their various guises had been deployed in the Cold War era, there had generally been some 'peace to keep', an agreement between the contending parties, including consent to the deployment of the UN force, which neither involved itself nor became involved in any serious conflicts. In the 1990s, all this changed. The challenge to the Council was to find ways of controlling, reducing and eliminating threats to international security emerging from within a single State, where the parties by no means accepted the authority of the UN. In fashioning the responses, there were sometimes differences between the Members of the Council about what action was desirable and feasible, but there was little serious division about the competence of the Council to take or to authorise action which was thought to be required and possible.

We are faced with three kinds of substantive competence question as a result of these developments. They are:

1. Are there any limits to the power to set the mandate of a UN force which the Council delegates authority to act?
2. Are there any limits to the power of the Security Council to authorise the use of force by States or international organisations?
3. What is the basis for the Council establishing bodies to exercise powers which the Council itself does not have?

First, may the Council set up UN forces to administer territory (I use this as being the widest form of mandate adopted by the Council)? The mandates and powers of such bodies are so much greater than those given to traditional peace-

[47] Security Council Resolution 827.
[48] Security Council Resolution 955.

keeping forces that there is a case for saying that they are different in kind, so that the authority in the Council, confirmed by the *Expenses Advisory Opinion*, does not necessarily go so far.[49] The resolutions to establish these missions have enjoyed wide support in the Council[50] and, where there has been some reservation, it has not been on the basis that the Council lacked the substantive competence to do what was proposed.[51] For instance, China's abstention on the resolution to set up UNMIK in Kosovo was grounded on the lack of condemnation of the illegality of the NATO bombing campaign, rather than any doubts about the *vires* of the decision, which, it said, was taken in the discharge of the Council's primary responsibility for the maintenance of international peace and security.[52]

The series of resolutions go a considerable way to demonstrating that the members of the Council regard the conferring of these very broad, quasi-governmental powers on a UN body as falling within the Council's competence. For the civilian components of them alone, it probably would not be necessary to rely on Chapter VII. It is the force element which requires the precise justification which comes from Chapter VII. However, a different aspect of substantive competence then arises, the second question set out above. It has been usual to say that the Council 'delegates' its authority to the 'able and willing' actors to use force for the mandate laid down by the Council. 'Delegation' is a legal notion and one which does not allow for the unlimited conferring of power by one person on another. Most obviously, of course, the delegator may not confer on the delegatee a power which the former does not itself possess. The UN has the power to use coercive force under Article 42. Does the concept of delegation impose any restrictions on its power to permit other persons to exercise this power? That it does has been contended for Dr Sarooshi in an elaborate argument which identifies the essence of the power of delegation.[53] The concern here is that the delegator, the Council, will lose control of the operations which it has authorised, either because the political and military command structures are resistant to effective external accountability or because the mandate granted to the State or international organisation becomes inappropriate over time for the UN's purposes, though not for the States taking action, and yet the Council finds it difficult to retrieve the authority it had granted. Dr Sarooshi says that there are three conditions for the lawful delegation of Chapter VII powers:

(a) the objective for which the delegation is made (the mandate) must be clearly specified;

---

[49] For a description of some of this activity, see M Ruffert, 'The Administration of Kosovo and East Timor by the International Community' (2001) 50 *ICLQ* 613.

[50] The authority of the Council 'cannot be doubted'. See M Matheson, 'United Nations Governance of Post Conflict Societies' (2001) 95 *AJIL* 76 at 85.

[51] For instance, Resolution 1272 on East Timor was approved unanimously.

[52] Press Release, SC/6686, 10 June 1999, p 11.

[53] D Sarooshi, *The United Nations and the Development of Collective Security: The Delegation by the UN Security Council of its Chapter VII Powers* (Oxford University Press, Oxford, 1999), chs 4 and 5.

(b) there is a duty in the Council to exercise (effective) supervision over the way the delegated powers are used;

(c) the Council must impose on the delegatee an obligation to report to the Council on the way in which the power is being used.[54]

The second two points, which clearly are related, touch both the ends (the execution of the mandate), which also involves a *vires* question about the limits of the mandate, and the means (the way in which the mandate is being implemented). The development of practice during the 1990s showed some convergence with Dr Sarooshi's criteria in the form which the resolutions took. There is no other instance of the practically untrammelled authority to use force allowed to the Coalition in Resolution 678.[55] Time unlimited mandates are increasingly rare. There is generally a regular system of reporting to the Council through the Secretary-General, whose reports, both as the to setting up of the missions and about their implementation have become an increasingly important source of information about UN operations. What hardly ever seems to be an issue is the general substantive competence of the Council to use the device of delegation to compensate for the absence of a force component in its own armoury of measures. The recent elaborate debates in the Council[56] and the Brahimi Report on Peace-keeping[57] are not concerned with matters of competence but on issues of effectiveness whenever the institution is resorted to by the Council. Having adopted a slightly different methodology to Dr Sarooshi's, Dr Blokker reaches the conclusion that the members of the UN have accepted the 'authorisation' model, subject to limitations designed to maintain accountability to Security Council of the participating States or international organisations, such as are compatible with the need of those States or organisations to have sufficient operational control over the activities of their forces.[58] Both Dr Sarooshi and Dr Blokker take the view that the delegation/authorisation mechanism is a constitutional development, the necessity for which is brought about by the absence of Article 43 agreements, endorsed by the practice of the Council and the acceptance of the member States.

There are those who voice doubts about some of these developments. Dr Gazzini has suggested that there is a need for greater operational control than the Council normally reserves to itself if the delegation/authorisation is to be lawful.[59] He points to the 'dual key' arrangements under Resolution 836, in which NATO was authorised to use air force to protect the UN designated safe areas in Bosnia but for which authorisation from the UN was required in each case.[60] The cir-

---

[54] *Ibid* at 155.

[55] J Lobel and M Ratner, 'Bypassing the Security Council: Ambiguous Authorisations to Use Force, Cease-Fires and the Iraqi Inspection Regime' (1999) 93 *AJIL* 124, especially at 148–52.

[56] Security Council Resolution 1327, Annex 2.

[57] UN Doc A/55/305, S/2000/809.

[58] N Blokker, 'Is the Authorisation Authorised? Powers and Practice of the UN Security Council to Authorise the Use of Force by 'Coalitions of the Able and Willing'' (2000) 11 *EJIL* 541 at 560–67.

[59] T Gazzini, 'NATO Coercive Military Activities in the Yugoslav Crisis (1992–1999)' (2001) 12 *EJIL* 391.

[60] *Ibid* at 398–99.

cumstances in Bosnia, particularly the presence of UNPROFOR personnel on the ground, might have explained this cautious approach to the actual use of force. It was, however, an unhappy arrangement, notably in the failure to provide protection for Sbrenicia.[61] The danger is an obvious one, that too great an insistence on participation in operational matters, whether political or military, may lead to inefficiency in the deployment of force, a matter of increasing importance as the capacity of the opponent increases. Striking the balance between appropriate UN control and operational effectiveness of authorised State or international organisation military force focuses on the division between delegation and authorisation. If we take the maximum arguments about what lawful delegation requires, it would be argued that the Council could not permit a State to use force under less control than it would be if exercised by the Council itself. Even if States were prepared to supply force on these conditions, practical considerations militate against this kind of arrangement. 'Authorisation' does not have the same legal essence as delegation, at least in the practice of the UN. Its parameters develop in practice. The practice of the Council, as Dr Blokker indicates, is moving in favour of specific, time-limited mandates, combined with wide operational autonomy to the States or organisation supplying the force. It might be premature to say that this practice has attained the intensity and uniformity or the degree of endorsement by the wider Membership required by the ICJ's test in *Expenses Advisory Opinion* but the appearance is that the need for fighting efficiency is prevailing over the strict requirements of the Charter.[62]

The change of language between Dr Sarooshi's 'delegation' and Dr Blokker's 'authorisation' is otherwise of little consequence in the particular circumstances which they are considering. There are, though, differences between the terms which may have consequences for the substantive competence of the Council. To repeat the fundamental proposition of delegation, the delegator can delegate only powers which it has. The same is not true of necessarily true of authorisation. A licensing authority has the power to authorise qualified persons to undertake certain activit:es, say, to run a casino. It is not required that the licensor have the power itself to operate gambling establishments: indeed, to the contrary, for such an involvement might be a disqualification from the fair exercise of the authorising power. As I have indicated, in practical terms, it does not seem to make much difference how we classify the exercise of Council authority with respect to the use of force. It is a relevant consideration, though, where the Council purports to set up a body to do something which it (the Council) may not do. This is the third matter set out earlier. The establishment of the *ad hoc* international criminal tribunals is such a case. The Council has no power to be a court itself. It is the case

---

[61] Report of the Secretary-General on the Fall of Srbrenicia, UN Doc A/54/549 at www.un.org/peace/srbrenicia.pdf.

[62] T Eitel, 'The UN Security Council and its Future Contribution in the Field of International Law' (2000) 4 *Max Planck Yearbook of United Nations Law* at 53, 58, 61, underlining the role of precedent in Security Council practice and the furtherance of what he calls' Council Law', all the more important because of its wide and binding effect.

that the ICJ has said that the General Assembly can create courts[63] and, so long as certain other factors are taken into account, there is no reason why the same should not be true of the Council, subject to relating the decision to the exercise of the Council's function of maintaining international peace and security. A possible difficulty arises because of the wording of Article 29 of the Charter. It says,

> The Security Council may establish such subsidiary organs as it deems necessary for the performance of its functions.

Since the adjudication of criminal charges is not (and could not be) a 'function' of the Council, there appears to be an internal *vires* hurdle to be jumped if the setting up of the tribunals is to be justified. One way might be to take a particular view of 'functions' and argue that among the 'functions' of the Council is the maintenance and restoration of international peace and security and that the Council may establish courts where it deems it necessary to do so for the discharge of that responsibility. Dr Sarooshi takes a different approach. Article 7(2) allows that:

> Such subsidiary organs as may be found necessary may be established in accordance with the present Charter.

He finds here a third head of competence for the Council: it may set up subsidiary bodies under Article 29 to discharge its own functions; it may delegate its functions to willing States and international organisations; and it may establish subsidiary organs to do jobs which it (the Council) may not do but which the Council finds necessary in order to carry out its tasks.[64]

Dr Sarooshi's approach would provide the first step towards establishing substantive competence to establish a criminal court. However, there have been reservations about the actual exercise of this power. Some States have argued that an international criminal jurisdiction may only be established by treaty, the argument being that the jurisdiction of the international court is derivative from the national jurisdiction of States, part of their inherent capacities which can be yielded only by treaty.[65] A rather different point was made by the defence in the *Tadic* case, where it was argued that the very notion of subsidiariness to the Security Council rendered the independence of any court so established illusory.[66] The Appellate Chamber in *Tadic* acknowledged the point but took the view that the intention of the Council was the crucial element. It intended to set up a court;

---

[63] *Effect of Awards of Compensation made by the United Nations Administrative Tribunal* (1954) ICJ Rep 47.

[64] D Sarooshi, 'The Legal Framework Governing United Nations Subsidiary Organs' (1996) 67 *BYIL* 413 at 425–28.

[65] See observations of Brazil, S/PV 3271, 25 May 1993 (Yugoslavia Tribunal) and S/PV 3453, 8 Nov 1994 (Rwanda Tribunal). Brazil voted for both resolutions, citing the 'unique' and 'special' circumstances, perhaps an attempt to diminish any reliance on a 'practice of the organ' argument for the future.

[66] *Prosecutor v Tadic*, Case No IT–94–1–AR72, A.Ch., Decision on Defence Motion for Interlocutory Appeal on Jurisdiction, paras 38–39.

the court was to conduct itself independently of any interference by the Council and was able to do so.[67] Of course, there were factors which clouded the position: the Security Council could always order the termination of the Tribunals; the judges' terms were relatively short; and the financing of the Tribunals was an annual matter in the hands of the General Assembly. Whether or not the Appellate Chamber had the jurisdiction to consider the lawfulness of its own creation (which I doubt) and, even if it had, whether or not it was wise to exercise it are issues of some controversy.[68] The Appellate Chamber did uphold the Council's competence, specifically, it said, under Article 41 to create a criminal court. The Tribunals have done their best to demonstrate that they *are* courts. Although the finalisation of the Statute of the International Criminal Court has changed the position somewhat, the Council has not retreated entirely from the field, as its attempts to establish a hybrid criminal jurisdiction to deal with crimes committed in Sierra Leone shows. Nonetheless, the desire to set an international criminal court free of Security Council influence was one of the strongest factors motivating those who sought the creation of what is now the International Criminal Court by treaty and the relationship between that Court and the Security Council was one of the most highly contested issues in the drafting process.[69]

5. ACCOUNTABILITY

We find a constant expansion of the Security Council's substantive competence, a matter of great importance because it is combined with the authoritative competence of the Council. States become bound to comply with Council decisions over an increasingly wide field, in some cases, like the criminal courts, quite beyond any anticipation. The power of the Council is all the more significant because of its small membership and because of the preferred position of the permanent members. It is not surprising, then, that there have been calls for greater accountability of the Council for the ways in which it exercises its formidable authority. Much of this activity is a claim for greater political control, most particularly through the reform of the Council. I do not propose to examine this matter, except to note that by no means all of the proposals are concerned with making Council action more difficult to achieve—those who wish the abolition of or control over the veto power are clearly looking for more, not less, Council action.

---

[67] *Prosecutor v Tadic* Case No IT–94–1–T, T.Ch.II, Decision on the Prosecutor's Motion Requesting Protective Measures for Victims and Witnesses, para 30.

[68] M Shahabuddeen, 'The Competence of a Tribunal to Deny its own Existence', in Sienho Yee and Wang Tieya (eds), *International Law in the Post-Cold War World: Essays in Memory of Li Haopei* (Routledge, London, 2000) at 473.

[69] L Yee, 'The ICC and the Security Council' in R Lee (ed), *The International Criminal Court: the Making of the Rome Statute* (Kluwer, The Hague, 2000) at 143.

Legal control over the Security Council is likely to be piecemeal and adventitious. There is no institutionalised system of judicial review in the Charter, so routine, legal control of the use of the Council's powers is not available.[70] Nonetheless, it is accepted that the Council is not a legal Alsatia.[71] *If* jurisdiction in a tribunal exists and *if* the lawfulness of a Council decision is essential to its decision, the tribunal is not precluded from determining the question. The powers of the Council are wholly derived from the Charter and they may be limited by the operation of other rules of international law. There is nothing about these questions, still less a particular rule of law, which makes them unamenable to judicial appreciation. However, there are various factors which might make a court reluctant to impose to intrusive a regime of legal control on the Council. The Charter clearly confers on the Council a wide discretion in matters of international peace and security. The position of the permanent members, none of whom must have been opposed in order that a decision could have been reached at all, requires careful respect because of their responsibilities under the Charter. Some questions, like the determination of the existence of a threat to the peace, are close to non-justiciable, both on grounds of lack of legal standards and because of the sensitivity of the matters of evidence. This position is no different in any principled way from the limits of judicial review of governmental action in domestic law. Other questions, including those of authoritative competence have already been shown to be susceptible to judicial determination. The same is true about substantive competence, as the *Expenses Advisory Opinion* demonstrates. This latter opinion, in particular, shows the importance of the arguments raised by Dr Sarooshi and Dr Blokker. It cannot be precluded that questions of substantive competence will fall to be determined by a court. In this respect, the *Lockerbie* cases add an extra dimension to what has gone before.[72] Previous cases before the ICJ have been by way of its advisory jurisdiction and, as the machinations to resolve the dispute which continued after the *Expenses Advisory Opinion* showed, they are precisely advisory. If the Court were to accept Libya's argument about the unlawfulness of the Council resolutions directed against it, the Court would not have the power to quash them, as a national administrative court might, but it would, presumably, have to decide upon the obligations of the States involved without regard to the decisions of the Security Council.

It is usual to think of putative legal control of the Security Council in terms of the jurisdiction of the International Court of Justice. The growing range of international tribunals means that this is too narrow a view. If the lawfulness of a Secu-

---

[70] D Akande, 'The International Court of Justice and the Security Council: Is there room for Judicial Control of the Political Organs of the United Nations?' (1997) 46 *ICLQ* 309.

[71] I Brownlie, 'The Decisions of Political Organs of the United Nations and the Rule of Law' in R MacDonald (ed), *Essays in Honour of Wang Tieya* (Martinus Nijhoff, Dordrecht, 1994) at 91, 93–95. Brownlie makes a point which it is not possible for me to take on in this chapter, that general international law imposes limitations on the exercise of the Security Council's powers, even where its internal, substantive competence is established.

[72] *Questions of Interpretation and Application of the 1971 Montreal Convention arising from the Aerial Incident at Lockerbie (Libya v UK) (Preliminary Objections)* (1998) ICJ Rep 1, para 50.

rity Council resolution might arise incidentally in litigation before the ICJ, then so it might in cases before other courts, such as it did, albeit unhappily, in *Tadic* before the Yugoslavia Tribunal and (the same question) before the Rwanda Tribunal.[73] Of course, the same possibilities arise for the ITLOS or the WTO Panels, *mutatis mutandis.* Although it will usually be the case that human rights questions will arise with respect to the powers and conduct of any court the Security Council has created,[74] it cannot be completely ruled out that questions about the legality of Security Council resolutions could come before human rights courts, for instance, the compatibility of a Council order that one State transfer a defendant to another State for trial with the applicant's fair trial rights. Because the decisions of the Council increasingly call for States to take action against individuals, whether it be surrendering them to the ad hoc tribunals or by punishing them for breaches of sanctions regimes, it can be anticipated that the lawfulness of Security Council action will be challenged in national tribunals. Although the matter did not ultimately fall for decision, the question of the legality of the establishment of the Rwanda Tribunal was raised by a defendant facing surrender to Arusha in proceedings in England.[75]

6. CONCLUSION

For all that the Security Council has been able to sustain its claims for an increasingly wide substantive competence, there has been something of a tendency for some States to seek to act without the Council's involvement. Military action against Iraq after the cease-fire by the United States and United Kingdom (and originally France) and the NATO bombing campaign against Yugoslavia with respect to the situation in Kosovo are the prominent examples, where there was no claim, however contestable, that the right were based on self-defence.[76] The powers of States to use force outside the very wide parameters of Security Council competence remain to be determined but, even if sustained to any significant degree, there still is a necessary role for the Council. While unilateral recourse to force might make practical, if not legal, sense, the recourse to compulsory, non-forcible measures will seldom be effective if not supported by a binding Council-resolution,[77] nor may institutions like the criminal tribunals be established nor missions like the peace-building operations in Kosovo be readily undertaken

---

[73] *Prosecutor v Kangabashi* No ICTR–96–15–T, T.Ch.II, paras 17–29.

[74] *Naletilic v Croatia*, ECtHR No 51891/99 (inadmissible).

[75] Muvunyi, see http://news.bbc.co.uk/hi/english/world/africa/newsid_632000/632682.stm and *ibid* newsid_999000/999902.stm.

[76] S Chesterman, 'Passing the Baton: the Development of the Security Council's Enforcement Powers from Kuwait to Kosovo' in Yee and Tieya (eds), n 68 above, 148.

[77] For a recent example, see Security Council Resolution 1373, which calls upon all members to take action against terrorist activity, particularly the financing of terrorist groups, while the use of force against Afghanistan was justified under the right of self-defence, the *quintessence* of a unilateral right.

without the binding and plenary effect of Council resolutions. Which brings us back to the starting point—the Council has evolved through a process of constitutional development but has it changed so much that Judge Fitzmaurice's characterisation of it simply as a peace preserving and restoring body no longer holds? Does it have a role play in creating a world order? I stay with Boutros-Boutros Galli, that the UN is an organisation of States, able to act within its powers only with the support of its Members.

This, as much as any legal consideration, is the decisive factor governing the effective, substantive competence of the Council but it is possible to analyse the developments since 1989 in other ways. One alternative is argued for powerfully by Professor Gowlland-Debbas.[78] She identifies an inchoate but real 'international community', a developing rather than accomplished concept from the legal point of view. The values of the international community can be identified but the institutional structure for protecting them is skeletal. However, Professor Gowlland-Debbas identifies the increasing participation by the Security Council in the promotion of international community values as a significant step to repairing this deficiency.[79] She extracts from the practice, not an *ad hoc* and incremental modification of the original peace-maintaining role of the Council, but a process in which the Council identifies situations incompatible with the core values of the international community, including violations of international law, and fashions responses designed to preserve or restore the enjoyment on these values. It is a claim to a nascent form of international governance and it acknowledges that the exercise of this broad power demands regimes of accountability, both legal and political, so that the Council is constrained to act in the interests of the international community and not merely those of its dominant members.[80] I dare say that Judge Fitzmaurice would raise an eyebrow at such suggestions.

---

[78] V Gowlland-Debbas, 'The Functions of the United Nations Security Council in the International Legal System' in M Byers (ed), *The Role of Law in International Politics: Essays in International Relations and International Law* (Oxford University Press, Oxford, 2000), 269.

[79] *Ibid* at 285.

[80] *Ibid* at 310.

8

Jurisdiction, NATO and the Kosovo Conflict

CHRISTOPHER GREENWOOD

1. INTRODUCTION

While the 1999 military intervention by the North Atlantic Treaty Organisation (NATO) in Kosovo might appear to have little to do with the concept of jurisdiction discussed in most of the chapters in the present volume, it nevertheless raises important questions of jurisdiction (or competence) in a wider sense. Military action by the world's most powerful military alliance was undertaken against a State (which was not a member) for the express purpose of ending human rights abuses and reversing the effects of 'ethnic cleansing'. Although the action was taken against the background of a series of United Nations Security Council Resolutions on Kosovo and culminated in the Security Council granting a mandate to a NATO-led force (KFOR) to enter Kosovo, NATO commenced its military action without any authorization from the Security Council. The action thus raises the question whether NATO was competent to take the action it did. That question cannot be answered simply by reference to the provisions of the North Atlantic Treaty; it requires examination of the place and role of NATO within international law as a whole.

In addition, the NATO action led to proceedings in two international courts—the International Court of Justice and the European Court of Human Rights—and an inquiry in a third—the International Criminal Tribunal for the Former Yugoslavia. These proceedings highlighted the question to what extent NATO, its Member States and the members of their governments and forces were subject to the jurisdiction of other international bodies in relation to the Kosovo campaign. In the *Cases Concerning Legality of Use of Force* brought by the Federal Republic of Yugoslavia (the FRY) during the NATO campaign against ten of the NATO Member States, the International Court of Justice had to determine whether there was a prima facie basis for its jurisdiction over those States.[1] In *Banković v Belgium*

---

[1] Proceedings were brought against Belgium, Canada, France, Germany, Italy, the Netherlands, Portugal, Spain, the United Kingdom and the United States of America. The Orders of the Court refusing the FRY's request for provisional measures of protection and ordering the removal of the cases against Spain and the United States of America from the Court's list are each reported under

and Others, the European Court of Human Rights examined whether the inhabitants of Belgrade could be considered to have been within the jurisdiction of any
or all of the NATO States during the air campaign.[2] Finally, the Office of the Prosecutor of the International Criminal Tribunal for the Former Yugoslavia conducted a preliminary inquiry into whether there were grounds for considering
charges against individuals on the NATO side in relation to the Kosovo conflict.[3]
The approaches to jurisdiction taken by the two courts and the Office of the Prosecutor in these proceedings are also considered in this chapter.

Accordingly, Part 2 of this chapter will review the factual background. Part 3
will briefly describe the legal status of NATO. Part 4 will consider whether NATO
was entitled to act as it did over Kosovo. Parts 5 and 6 will examine the International Court and European Court cases respectively, while Part 7 will consider the
report compiled for the Prosecutor of the International Criminal Tribunal. Part
8 will briefly state some conclusions. Space does not permit investigation of the
legality of the conduct of the NATO campaign (a matter which this writer has
considered elsewhere).[4]

2. FACTUAL BACKGROUND

It is not the purpose of this chapter to give a history of the Kosovo crisis[5] but a
few salient features of the events prior to the NATO campaign require brief
mention. In 1989, Kosovo, a province of the Republic of Serbia (itself at that time
one of the six republics of the Socialist Federal Republic of Yugoslavia (SFRY)),
lost most of the autonomy which it had previously possessed. For the next ten
years its government was largely directed from Belgrade. Approximately eighty
percent of the two million inhabitants of Kosovo at this time were ethnic Albanians. While the Serbs were, therefore, a minority within the Kosovo population,
Kosovo had an important part in Serb history and culture and contained some of
the most important churches and monasteries of the Serbian Orthodox Church.
Kosovo remained largely peaceful throughout the conflicts of 1991–1995 which
marked the collapse of the SFRY and the creation of the FRY by Serbia and
Montenegro. While there were warnings to the FRY about excessive use of force

the title *Case Concerning Legality of Use of Force*, (1999) ICJ Rep 124 (Belgium), 259 (Canada), 363
(France), 422 (Germany), 481 (Italy), 542 (The Netherlands), 656 (Portugal), 761 (Spain), 826 (United
Kingdom) and 961 (United States of America).

[2] (2002) 11 Butterworths Human Rights Cases 435.
[3] *Final Report to the Prosecutor by the Committee established to review the NATO Bombing Campaign
against the Federal Republic of Yugoslavia*, (2000) 39 ILM 257.
[4] See C Greenwood, 'The Application of International Humanitarian Law and the Law of Neutrality in the Kosovo Campaign' (2001) 31 *Israel Year Book of Human Rights* 109.
[5] On that subject, see the *Kosovo* Report, published by the Independent International Commission
on Kosovo (Oxford, 2000); M Glenny, *The Balkans 1804–1999: Nationalism, War and the Great Powers*
(Granta, London, 2000); *Waging Modern War: Bosnia, Kosovo, and the Future of Combat* (2001) (by
the then NATO Supreme Allied Commander in Europe) and M Ignatieff, *Virtual War: Kosovo and
Beyond* (Chatto & Windus, London, 2000).

in Kosovo during this period,[6] the status of Kosovo as part of Serbia (and thus of the FRY) was not questioned by the outside world and the Dayton Peace Agreement, which ended the conflict in Bosnia-Herzegovina in 1995,[7] did not deal with Kosovo.

The 1990s, however, saw the growth of a separatist movement amongst the Albanian majority in Kosovo. As part of that movement, Albanians increasingly boycotted official institutions in Kosovo and established their own unofficial bodies in parallel. By 1998 there had also emerged a paramilitary separatist movement, the 'Kosovo Liberation Army' (KLA or UCK) which embarked on a campaign of violence against the Serbian and FRY authorities and those co-operating with them. Terrorist activity by the KLA and increasingly repressive action by the FRY led the Security Council to adopt, on 31 March 1998, the first of a series of Resolutions on Kosovo.

Resolution 1160 (1998) (adopted by fourteen votes to none, with China abstaining) condemned:

> the use of excessive force by Serbian police forces against civilians and peaceful demonstrators in Kosovo, as well as all acts of terrorism by the Kosovo Liberation Army or any other group or individual and all external support for terrorist activity in Kosovo, including finance, arms and training.

While affirming 'the commitment of all Member States to the sovereignty and territorial integrity of the Federal Republic of Yugoslavia', the Resolution called for a substantially greater degree of autonomy and self-administration for Kosovo. During the next few mouths, however, the United Nations Secretary-General reported that violence in Kosovo intensified and warned that, if the FRY Government persisted with its policies, it could 'transform what is currently a humanitarian crisis into a humanitarian catastrophe'.[8] A further report by the Secretary-General in September 1998 commented that there had been 'a sharp escalation of military operations in Kosovo, as a result of an offensive launched by the Serb forces'.[9]

On 23 September 1998 the Security Council adopted Resolution 1199 (1998) (again by fourteen votes to none with China abstaining). Like Resolution 1160 (1998), it was adopted under Chapter VII and the decisions which it contained were legally binding. The Security Council stated that it was

> [g]ravely concerned at the recent intense fighting in Kosovo and in particular the excessive and indiscriminate use of force by Serbian security forces and the Yugoslav army which have resulted in numerous civilian casualties and, according to the estimate of the Secretary-General, the displacement of over 230,000 persons from their homes . . .

---

[6] See the Memorandum by the United Kingdom Foreign and Commonwealth Office, House of Commons Paper (1999–2000) 28–II, 1, at para 13.
[7] (1996) ILM 75.
[8] UN Doc S/1998/834 at para 11.
[9] UN Doc S/1998/834 Add 1.

and

> [d]eeply concerned by the rapid deterioration in the humanitarian situation through-
> out Kosovo, alarmed at the impending humanitarian catastrophe as described in
> the report of the Secretary-General, and emphasising the need to prevent this from
> happening.

The Council required, *inter alia*, that both sides establish a ceasefire and that the
FRY cease all action by the security forces affecting the civilian population, order
the withdrawal of security used for civilian repression and make rapid progress,
to a clear timetable, in the dialogue with the Kosovo Albanian community called
for in Resolution 1160 (1998), with the aim of agreeing confidence-building measures and finding a political solution to the problems of Kosovo.[10]

NATO had been involved from an early stage in this process. When it became
clear that the FRY was not taking the steps required by Resolution 1199, NATO's
governing body, the North Atlantic Council, issued activation orders for air strikes
against the FRY to commence four days later unless the FRY complied with the
requirements of Resolution 1199. The air strikes did not take place, because of a
package of agreements which included an undertaking by the FRY to withdraw
some of its forces from Kosovo, agreement between the FRY and the OSCE for
the deployment to Kosovo of the Kosovo Verification Mission (KVM), an
unarmed civilian mission from the Organization for Co-operation and Security
in Europe (OSCE)[11] and an agreement between NATO and the FRY for aerial
verification by NATO.[12] The conclusion of these two agreements was welcomed
by the Security Council in Resolution 1203 (1998), which referred to 'the continuing grave humanitarian situation throughout Kosovo and the impending humanitarian catastrophe' and emphasised 'the need to prevent this from happening.'

On 15 January 1999 the KVM reported that FRY soldiers and Serbian special
police had been responsible for a massacre at the village of Racak in Kosovo, in
which 45 Albanian civilians were killed.[13] The FRY refused to allow the Prosecutor of the International Criminal Tribunal for the Former Yugoslavia, Judge Louise
Arbour, access to Kosovo to investigate the massacre, even though Resolution 1203
(1998) required it to do so.

These developments led to what became known as the Rambouillet/Paris talks
between the FRY/Serbian authorities and the Kosovo Albanian parties under the
auspices of the international 'Contact Group' (France, Germany, Italy, the Russian
Federation, the United Kingdom and the United States of America).[14] The Contact

---

[10]   SC Res 1199 (1998) at para 4.

[11]   UN Doc S/1998/978.

[12]   UN Doc S/1998/991.

[13]   The report was noted and the action of the FRY and authorities condemned in a Security Council
Presidential Statement on 19 Jan 1999; UN Doc S/PRST/1999/2.

[14]   See M Weller, 'The Rambouillet Conference on Kosovo' (1999) 75 *International Affairs* 211. For
documents relating to the talks, see M Weller (ed), *The Crisis in Kosovo: 1989–1999, from the Dissolution of Yugoslavia to Rambouillet and the Outbreak of Hostilities* (Documents & Analysis Publishing,
Cambridge, 1999) Vol I at 392 *et seq.*

Group put forward proposals for an agreement which would provide for a cease-fire, a peace settlement in Kosovo involving a large measure of autonomy, and the presence of an international military force to guarantee that settlement.[15] The first round of these talks appeared to produce a broad measure of agreement on a package which was known as 'the Rambouillet Accords'.[16] The text of the Accords was endorsed by the Contact Group on 23 February 1999. The FRY/Serbian delegation wrote to the negotiators on that day in broadly favourable terms. When the talks reconvened on 15 March 1999, however, the FRY/Serbian delegation sought radical changes to the Accords.[17] At the same time, FRY armoured forces advanced into the Podujevo region of Kosovo and the numbers of refugees and displaced increased. The negotiators from the European Union, the Russian Federation and the United States of America responded that 'the unanimous view of the Contact Group' was that only technical adjustments could be made at that stage.[18] On 19 March 1999 the co-chairmen of the conference (France and the United Kingdom) announced that the attitude of the FRY/Serbian delegation meant that there was no purpose in continuing with the talks.

On 22 March 1999, the NATO Secretary-General, Dr Javier Solana, announced that he had given authority for air strikes to begin. In his Statement, Dr Solana stated that:

> We are taking action following the Federal Republic of Yugoslavia Government's refusal of the International Community's demands:
> Acceptance of the interim political settlement which has been negotiated at Rambouillet;
> Full observance of limits on the Serb Army and Special Police Forces agreed on 25 October 1998;
> Ending of excessive and disproportionate use of force in Kosovo . . .
> This military action is intended to support the political aims of the international community.[19]

The NATO air campaign commenced on 24 March 1999 and lasted until 10 June 1999. On 26 March 1999 the Russian Federation, together with Belarus and India who were not members of the Security Council, proposed that the Council adopt a Resolution which would have characterised the NATO resort to force as 'a flagrant violation of the United Nations Charter, in particular Articles 2(4), 24 and 53' and determined that the NATO action constituted a threat to international peace and security.[20] The draft Resolution was defeated by twelve votes (Argentina, Bahrain, Brazil, Canada, France, Gabon, Gambia, Malaysia, Netherlands, Slovenia, United Kingdom and United States of America) to three (China, Russia and Namibia).

---

[15] The decision to hold the talks was welcomed by the Security Council, UN Doc S/PRST/1999/5.
[16] The text of the Accords is published in UN Doc S/1999/648.
[17] See Weller, *The Crisis in Kosovo*, n 14 above at 480 *et seq.*
[18] *Ibid* at 490.
[19] NATO Press Release (1999) 040; www.nato.int/docu/pr/1999/p99-040e.htm.
[20] UN Doc S/1998/328.

At the beginning of June 1999, the FRY Government effectively capitulated and agreed to an international military presence in, and the withdrawal of FRY forces from, Kosovo. On 10 June 1999 the Security Council, by fourteen votes to none with China abstaining, adopted Resolution 1244 (1999).[21] The adoption of this Resolution followed the acceptance by the FRY of principles for a settlement drawn up by the Group of Eight countries (the G8: Canada, France, Germany, Italy, Japan, the Russian Federation, the United Kingdom and the United States of America) in May 1999 and the principles drawn up the European Union envoy, Mr Ahtisaari, and the Russian envoy, Mr Chernomyrdin,[22] and marked the end of the conflict. The Resolution welcomed the G8 principles and effectively adopted them. In paragraph 3 of the Resolution, the Security Council demanded:

> that the Federal Republic of Yugoslavia put an immediate and verifiable end to violence and repression in Kosovo, and begin and complete verifiable phased withdrawal from Kosovo of all military, police and paramilitary forces according to a rapid timetable.

The Resolution also created a United Nations civil administration (UNMIK) and authorised the deployment to Kosovo of an international military force, described as an 'international security presence' (KFOR).

3. THE NORTH ATLANTIC TREATY ORGANISATION

NATO was created by the Washington Treaty on 4 April 1949[23] and thus celebrated its fiftieth anniversary during the Kosovo campaign. It was created as a collective self-defence pact in the context of the Cold War and the heart of the Washington Treaty is Article 5, which provides that:

> The Parties agree that an armed attack against one or more of them in Europe or North America shall be considered an attack against them all and consequently they agree that, if such an armed attack occurs, each of them, in exercise of the right of individual or collective self-defence recognized by Article 51 of the Charter of the United Nations, will assist the Party or Parties attacked by taking forthwith, individually and in concert with the other Parties, such action as it deems necessary, including the use of armed force, to restore and maintain the security of the North Atlantic area.
>
> Any such armed attack and all measures taken as a result thereof shall immediately be reported to the Security Council. Such measures shall be terminated when the Security Council has taken the measures necessary to restore and maintain international peace and security.

---

[21] The Council had also adopted Res 1239 (1999) on 14 May 1999. Resolution 1239 expressed the grave concern of the Council with the humanitarian aspects of the Kosovo crisis, especially the plight of refugees and displaced persons.

[22] These principles are attached as Annexes 1 and 2 (respectively) to SC Res 244 (1999).

[23] 34 UNTS 243.

In addition, Article 7 provided that:

> This Treaty does not effect, and shall not be interpreted as affecting, in any way the rights and obligations under the Charter of the Parties which are members of the United Nations, or the primary responsibility of the Security Council for the maintenance of international peace and security.

In the decade after the end of the Cold War, membership of NATO increased to the point where there were nineteen members—all of them members of the United Nations—by the time of the Kosovo campaign.[24] In addition, NATO had begun to take on tasks outside the original role of collective self-defence, including, for example, providing air power (under authorization from the Security Council) in support of UNPROFOR in Bosnia and Herzegovina in 1994–1995, the first time that NATO forces had been used in combat. As well as being a collective self-defence alliance, NATO came to be seen by many as a regional arrangement within the meaning of Article 53 of the United Nations Charter and, as such, empowered to engage in enforcement action if authorized to do so by the United Nations Security Council.

The governing body of NATO is the North Atlantic Council, which is composed of representatives of all nineteen member States. The Council acts by consensus. The senior political official, the Secretary-General, and the senior military commander, the Supreme Allied Commander in Europe (SACEUR) are answerable to the Council. It was the Council which took the decision to authorize military action against the FRY over Kosovo, although the timing of the action was a matter decided by the Secretary-General (at the time, Dr Javier Solana of Spain). Once the campaign had started, the conduct of that campaign was largely a matter for the SACEUR (the US General Wesley Clark) and his staff, in co-ordination with the Secretary-Greneral. The bombing missions themselves were carried out by air force units from a wide range of member States, although the US forces made by far the largest contribution.

4. THE LEGALITY OF THE NATO ACTION

Was NATO's use of force in this case lawful?[25] While the Washington Treaty is important in considering the first question, it cannot be decisive. All of the NATO member States are bound by the United Nations Charter, Article 2(4) of which provides that:

---

[24] Belgium, Canada, the Czech Republic, Denmark, France, Germany, Greece, Hungary, Iceland, Italy, Luxembourg, the Netherlands, Norway, Poland, Portugal, Spain, Turkey, the United Kingdom and the United States of America.

[25] For discussion of this question, see the evidence by Professors I Brownlie, C Chinkin, V Lowe and C Greenwood to the House of Commons Foreign Affairs Committee, reproduced in (2000) 49 *ICLQ* 876; B Simma, 'NATO, the United Nations and the Use of Force' (1999) 10 *EJIL* 1; A Cassese, 'Ex Injuria Jus non Oritur' (1999) 10 *EJIL* 23; A Cassese, 'A Follow-Up: Forcible Humanitarian Countermeasures and Opinio Necessitas,' (1999) 10 *EJIL* 791; and C Greenwood, 'Humanitarian Intervention: the Case of Kosovo' (1999) *Finnish YBIL* 141.

> All Members shall refrain in their international relations from the threat or use of force against the territorial integrity or political independence of any State, or in any other manner inconsistent with the purposes of the United Nations.

For the resort to force over Kosovo to have been lawful, therefore, it had to comply with this provision. Article 2(4), however, does not stand alone. The Charter expressly recognises two situations in which resort to force is lawful—individual or collective self-defence (the right to which is preserved by Article 51 of the Charter) and enforcement action taken by, or under the authority of, the United Nations Security Council. In addition, the provisions of the Charter have to be read as a living instrument construed against the background of the practice of the parties to the Charter and evolving customary international law.

There can be no doubt that the Kosovo campaign was not an instance of collective self-defence of the kind envisaged in Article 5 of the Washington Treaty, There had been no armed attack by the FRY against any of the NATO member States. Indeed, since Kosovo was not a separate State but a part of the FRY, the use of force there by the FRY (though excessive and unlawful) did not amount to an armed attack for the purposes of Article 51 of the Charter.

Nor was this a case of enforcement action. NATO has no independent power to take enforcement action. In common with other regional arrangements and *ad hoc* groups of States ('coalitions of the willing'), NATO is empowered to take enforcement action to restore international peace and security only if authorised to do so by the United Nations Security Council.[26] The three Security Council Resolutions on Kosovo adopted before 24 March 1999 established that the situation in Kosovo was a threat to international peace and security and that there was an impending humanitarian catastrophe[27] but they did not authorize military action. Resolution 1244 (1999), adopted after the cessation of the fighting, did authorize NATO deployment into Kosovo and thus, in a sense, endorsed the effects of the air campaign. It would, however, be reading too much into that Resolution to see it as retrospectively authorizing the campaign itself.

But if NATO is not 'self-authorizing' as an international policeman, nothing in the United Nations Charter or the Washington Treaty precludes it from using force on the basis of a right which its member States possess independent of any mandate from the United Nations Security Council. Indeed, that is exactly what it was established to do, for in using force by way of collective self-defence as envisaged in Article 5 of the Washington Treaty, NATO would be exercising collectively a power which each of its member States possess individually under customary international law and Article 51 of the United Nations Charter.[28]

The question therefore becomes whether the Member States of NATO had the power to take military action for the purpose of putting an end to the violations human rights and ethnic cleansing in Kosovo. In essence, do States have a right

---

[26] See Art 53 of the United Nations Charter.
[27] See Pt 2 above.
[28] See the decision of the International Court in the *Case Concerning Military and Paramilitary Activities in and against Nicaragua* (1986) ICJ Rep, 14. (1986) 76 ILR.

of humanitarian intervention and, if so, were the circumstances in Kosovo in 1999 such as to bring that right into play?

It is plain that this was the basis on which the United Kingdom justified the NATO action. As early as October 1998, the Foreign and Commonwealth Office had circulated among NATO governments a note in the following terms:

> Security Council authorization to use force for humanitarian purposes is now widely accepted (Bosnia and Somalia provide firm legal precedents). A UNSCR would give a clear legal base for NATO action, as well as being politically desirable.

> But force can also be justified on the grounds of overwhelming humanitarian necessity without a UNSCR. The following are the criteria which need to be applied:

> (a) that there is convincing evidence, generally accepted by the international community as a whole, of extreme humanitarian distress on a large scale, requiring immediate and urgent relief;
> (b) that it is objectively cleat that there is no practicable alternative to the use of force if lives are to be saved;
> (c) that the proposed use of force is necessary and proportionate to the aim (the relief of humanitarian need) and is strictly limited in time and scope to this aim—ie it is the minimum necessary to achieve that end. It would also be necessary at the appropriate stage to assess the targets against this criterion.

> There is convincing evidence of an impending humanitarian catastrophe (SCR 1199 and the UN Secretary General's (UNSG) and UNHCR's reports). We judge on the evidence of FRY handing of Kosovo throughout this year that a humanitarian catastrophe cannot be averted unless Milosevic is dissuaded from further repressive acts, and that only the proposed threat of force will achieve this objective. The United Kingdom's view is therefore that, as matters now stand and if action through the Security Council is not possible, military intervention by NATO is lawful on grounds of overwhelming humanitarian necessity.[29]

Once the NATO action started, the United Kingdom Permanent Representative to the United Nations told the Security Council that

> The action being taken is legal. It is justified as an exceptional measure to prevent an overwhelming humanitarian catastrophe. Under present circumstances in Kosovo, there is convincing evidence that such a catastrophe is imminent. Renewed acts of repression by the authorities of the Federal Republic of Yugoslavia would cause further loss of civilian life and would lead to displacement of the civilian population on a large scale and in hostile conditions.

> Every means short of force has been tried to avert this situation. In these circumstances, and as an exceptional measure on grounds of overwhelming humanitarian necessity, military intervention is legally justifiable. The force now proposed is directed exclusively to averting a humanitarian catastrophe, and is the minimum judged necessary for that purpose.[30]

---

[29] Quoted in A Roberts, 'NATO's 'Humanitarian War' over Kosovo' (1999) 41 *Survival* 102 at 106.
[30] S/PV 3988 at 12; 24 March 1999.

Similar statements were made by a number of other NATO States.[31]

That does not, of course, mean that those governments are right in their view of international law. Whether there is a right of armed humanitarian intervention has long been the subject of controversy. It has been argued that, because the United Nations Charter contains a prohibition of the use of force and no express exception for humanitarian intervention, there can be no question of international law recognising a right of humanitarian intervention.[32] That is, however, to take too rigid a view of international law. In particular, it overlooks both the underlying principles on which the United Nations Charter is based and the development of customary international law, particularly during the last decade or so. It is important to remember that international law in general and the United Nations Charter in particular do not rest exclusively on the principles of non-intervention and respect for the sovereignty of the State. The values on which the international legal system rests also include respect for human rights and 'the dignity and worth of the human person.'[33] Upholding those rights is one of the purposes of the United Nations and of international law. It is not, therefore, a case of a single, dominant principle of the non-use of force, but rather a case of two different, but equally important, principles of international law each of which has to be considered. While nobody would suggest that intervention in the sense in which that term is used here is justified whenever a State violates human rights, international law does not require that respect for the sovereignty and integrity of a State must in all cases be given priority over the protection of human rights and human life, no matter how serious the violations of those rights perpetrated by that State.

The evolution of international law in this regard was emphasised by the Representative of the Netherlands in his speech in the Security Council on 10 June 1999 when he said that:

> We sincerely hope that the few delegations which have maintained that the North Atlantic Treaty Organisation (NATO) air strikes against the Federal Republic of Yugoslavia were a violation of the United Nations Charter will one day begin to realise that the Charter is not the only source of international law.
>
> The Charter, to be sure, is much more specific on respect for sovereignty than on respect for human rights, but since the day it was drafted the world has witnessed a gradual shift in that balance, making respect for human rights more mandatory and respect for sovereignty less absolute. Today, we regard it as a generally accepted rule of international law that no sovereign State has the right to terrorize its own citizens. Only if that shift is a reality can we explain how on 26 March the Russian-Chinese draft Resolution branding the NATO air strikes a violation of the Charter could be so decisively rejected by 12 votes to 3.[34]

---

[31] See, for example, the statements made in the same meeting of the Security Council by the Representatives of the United States of America (pp 4–5), Canada (p 6), the Netherlands (p 8) and the statement by Belgium before the International Court of Justice, CR 99/15.

[32] See, eg M Littmann, *Kosovo: Law and Diplomacy* (Centre for Policy Studies, London, 1999).

[33] Preamble to the United Nations Charter.

[34] UN Doc S/PV.4011 at 12.

Moreover, international law is not confined to treaty texts. It includes customary international law. That law is not static but develops through a process of State practice, of actions and the reaction to those actions. Since 1945, that process has seen a growing importance attached to the preservation of human rights. Where the threat to human rights has been of an extreme character, States have been prepared to assert a right of humanitarian intervention as a matter of last resort.

It is true that, until quite recently, the body of State practice which could be invoked in support of a right of humanitarian intervention was not great.[35] Nineteenth century interventions are scarcely a useful guide in the era of the Charter and, in any event, were at best equivocal instances of humanitarian intervention in any case. The three instances usually invoked by supporters of humanitarian intervention in the period 1945–1990 are also an uncertain guide. India's intervention in East Bengal in 1971,[36] Tanzania's overthrow of the Amin Government in Uganda in 1979[37] and Vietnam's use of force against the Pol Pot regime in Cambodia in the same year all raised the question of humanitarian intervention and certainly contributed something to the evolution of the law on this subject. Although, in each case, the intervening State and its supporters rested their case primarily upon the right of self-defence, the extent of their conduct be justified without reliance on some broader principle.

Two instances of State practice since the end of the Cold War are still more important. First, in the summer of 1990, the Economic Community of West African States (ECOWAS) intervened in Liberia in an attempt to put a stop to appalling violations of human rights occurring in the civil war there. The objectives of the ECOWAS operation, as set out in a declaration issued by the ECOEAS Heads of State and Government on 9 August 1990,[38] which emphasised that the peace-keeping force was going to Liberia

... first and foremost to stop the senseless killing of innocent civilian nationals and foreigners, and to help the Liberian people to restore their democratic institutions. ECOWAS intervention is in no way designed save one part or punish another.

It is unclear whether the government of President Doe, which by then controlled very little of Liberia, consented to the deployment of the ECOWAS force. If it did, then the initial deployment could be seen as peace-keeping by consent, undertaken by a regional organization, although the main rebel group in Liberia was opposed to the deployment. In September 1990, however, Doe was killed by one of the rebel groups. An interim government was then established largely at the

[35] For an excellent review of the State practice, see SD Murphy, *Humanitarian Intervention: The United Nations as an Evolving World Order* (Philadelphia, University of Philadelphia Press, 1996). Murphy's latest writings suggest that he considers the law may have evolved beyond what he thought at the time of writing his book, cf. his 'The Intervention in Kosovo: A Law-Shaping Incident?' (2000) 94 *Proceedings of the American Society of International Law* 302.

[36] TM Franck and NS Rodley, 'After Bangladesh: The Law of Humanitarian Intervention by Military Force' (1973) 67 *AJIL* 275.

[37] SK Chatterjee, 'Some Legal Problem of Support Role in International Law: Tanzania and Uganda' (1981) 30 *ICLQ* 755.

[38] UN Doc S/21485.

instigation of ECOWAS. Despite the protests of Doe's vice-president, who claimed that under Liberia's constitution he automatically assumed the functions of President on Doe's death, this government was headed by Dr Amos Sawyer, a figure from outside the Doe regime who owed his position to ECOWAS. Moreover, during 1991 and 1992 it became clear that the interim government was being actively opposed by the largest rebel group, headed by Charles Taylor. It seems, therefore, that the legal basis for the ECOWAS intervention cannot rest on the consent of the original Liberian Government, as that government soon ceased to exist and was replaced by the interim regime created by ECOWWS. As a regional arrangement, ECOWAS can take enforcement action only with the consent of the United Nations Security Council,[39] something which was not formally given in the summer of 1990. The intervention seems, therefore to involve the assertion a right of humanitarian intervention.

International reaction to the intervention was generally supportive of ECOWAS, although there was criticism from some members of that organisation of an operation which involved intervention in the affairs of a State. In January 1991 and again in May 1992 the President of the Security Council issued a Statement to the effect that the members of the Security Council commended the ECOWAS effort 'to promote peace and normalcy in Liberia.'[40] During 1992, however, ECOWAS requested assistance from the Security Council, a request endorsed by the Foreign Minister of the interim government in Liberia, and on 19 November 1992 the Council unanimously adopted Resolution 788 (1992). That Resolution formally determined that 'the deterioration of the situation in Liberia constitutes a threat to international peace and security, particularly in West Africa as a whole' and condemned the attacks on ECOWAS by Taylor's forces. The Council then went on to impose a mandatory arms embargo under Chapter VII of the Charter, prohibiting all deliveries of weapons and military equipment to Liberia, other than for the sole use of the ECOWAS forces.

The second case was that of Iraq. Following Iraq's defeat in the Kuwait conflict, there were risings against Saddam Hussein in the Kurdish north of the country and in the predominantly Shiite south of Iraq. By the end of March 1991 it was clear that those risings had been defeated and that the Iraqi armed forces were engaged in a particularly brutal campaign of suppression, which was being conducted without any regard for the requirements of common Article 3 of the Geneva Conventions of 1949 (on armed conflicts within a State) or the human rights agreements to which Iraq was party, such as the International Covenant on Civil and Political Rights (1966). Hundreds of thousands of Kurds and Shiites fled their homes. The plight of the Kurdish refugees attracted particular attention. Many of them were stranded in the mountains near the border with Turkey in appalling winter conditions. Turkey closed its border after thousands of refugees had crossed over from Iraq and on at least one occasion Turkish troops crossed into Iraq in an attempt to force refugees away from the border.

[39] United Nations Charter, Art 53.
[40] UN Docs S/22133 and S/23886.

The Security Council's response was to adopt Resolution 688 (1991). In paragraph 1 of that Resolution, the Council condemned

> ... the repression of the Iraqi civilian population in many parts of Iraq, including most recently in Kurdish populated areas, the consequences of which threaten international peace and security.

While it was the situation in the Kurdish north which was uppermost in everyone's minds at the time, the wording of this paragraph makes clear that the Resolution was equally applicable to the repression of the Shiites in the south. Resolution 688 went on to demand that Iraq, 'as a contribution to removing the threat to international peace and security in the region,' immediately cease this repression. The Council insisted that Iraq allow 'immediate access by international humanitarian organizations to all those in need of assistance in all parts of Iraq.' The Resolution also appealed to all Member States to contribute to the relief effort.

Resolution 688 broke new ground in the degree to which it involved the Security Council in taking a stand against a State's ill-treatment of its own people. It was described by the United Kingdom Foreign Secretary, the Rt Hon Douglas Hurd, as having 'pushed forward the boundaries of international action.'[41] Nevertheless, although some of its language is reminiscent of Chapter VII, it did not make a formal determination that there was a threat to international peace and security but merely described the situation in Iraq as having created such a threat. Above all, Resolution 688 contained no express provision regarding the enforcement of the Resolution either by the United Nations or by individual Member States.

Nevertheless, the United Kingdom, the United States and a number of other countries deployed air and ground forces to northern Iraq as part of a policy of creating 'safe havens' for the Kurdish refugees. Iraq was told not to use military aircraft and helicopters in the Kurdish areas and was eventually forced to withdraw its ground forces from a large tract of territory in the north.

So far as the legal basis for the intervention is concerned, it was repeatedly said that the measures taken were consistent with Resolution 688 (1991). That Resolution was undoubtedly an important part of the background to the intervention. Its recognition that the situation in Iraq threatened international peace and security made clear that the western States were not intervening in a purely domestic matter, since the situation had already been 'internationalized'. Moreover, the humanitarian objectives of the intervention were the same as those of the Resolution. Nevertheless, Resolution 688 could not, on its own, furnish a legal basis for the intervention. It contained no equivalent of the authorisation given to the coalition States in Resolution 678 (990) to use 'all necessary means' to end Iraq's occupation of Kuwait. Nor was the operation undertaken with the consent

---

[41] Speech given at the Lord Mayor's Banquet on 10 April 1991. Transcript provided by the Foreign and Commonwealth Office.

of the Iraqi Government. Although Iraq did not resist and complied with the demand that it remove its forces from the main Kurdish areas, it repeatedly protested against what it described as an infringement of its sovereignty.[42]

It is difficult, therefore, to resist the conclusion that the intervening States were in practice asserting a right of humanitarian intervention of some kind. That conclusion is reinforced by statements made in August 1992 when a new 'no fly' zone was imposed in southern Iraq. This new measure was taken after a report from Dr van der Stoel, the United Nations Special Rapporteur, had painted a bleak picture of human rights violations in the Shiite areas. The United Kingdom, the United States and France responded by issuing a demand that Iraq cease all military flights south of the 32nd parallel and announced that they would enforce this ban by flying patrols of their own over southern Iraq. When the Foreign Secretary was asked in a radio interview about the legality of this action, given that there was no specific authorisation for it in any Security Council Resolution, he replied:

> But we operate under international law. Not every action that a British Government or an American Government or a French Government takes has to be underwritten by a specific provision in a UN Resolution provided we comply with international law. International law recognizes extreme humanitarian need . . . We are on strong legal as well as humanitarian ground in setting up this 'no fly' zone.[43]

The actions in Iraq received widespread international support. Moreover, with the exception of Iraq, very few States challenged the assertion of a right of humanitarian intervention in this case or attacked the underlying claim that a right of intervention existed in an extreme humanitarian case. The Iraq and Liberia cases thus contain a substantial body of State practice in support of the existence of a right of intervention in an extreme case of humanitarian need.

That practice is reinforced by the reaction to the Kosovo intervention. Neither the Security Council nor the General Assembly condemned the action and the Russian proposal to do so was defeated in the Council by twelve votes to three, the majority including seven States which had no connection with those taking the action. Moreover, the adoption of Resolution 1244 (1999), even though it does not amount to retrospective authorization of the NATO action, is difficult to reconcile with the view that NATO had committed an egregious violation of a fundamental rule of international law.

Against that, it has to be admitted that there is reluctance amongst many governments, particularly amongst the non-aligned, to accept the principle of humanitarian intervention.[44] Nevertheless, it is the practice of States in respect of

---

[42] Cf R Jennings and A Watts, *Oppenheim's International Law* (9th edn, Longmans, London, 1992), vol I at 443, n 18, which suggests that intervention might be justified in 'a compelling emergency, where the transgression upon a state's territory is demonstrably outweighed by overwhelming and immediate considerations of humanity and has the general support of the international community.'

[43] (1992) 63 *BYIL* 824.

[44] See United Nations Press Release GA/SPD/164 (18 Oct 1999).

concrete situations in which that principle is at stake, rather than in abstract statements, which speaks loudest. In my opinion, there is enough of the former practice to support the existence of a right of humanitarian intervention in extreme cases (the limits of which are considered below).

In my opinion, modern customary international law recognises a right of military intervention on humanitarian grounds by States, or by an organisation like NATO. It does, however, treat the right of humanitarian intervention as a matter of last resort and confines it to extreme cases. The cases in which that right has been exercised suggest the following conditions:

(a) that there exists—or there is an immediate threat of—the most serious humanitarian emergency involving large scale loss of life;
(b) military intervention is necessary, in that it is the only practicable means by which that loss of life can be ended or prevented; and
(c) the Security Council is unable to take such action, for example because of the exercise or threatened exercise of the veto.

Moreover, as with self-defence, the action taken must be proportionate to the end to be achieved and must comply with the requirements of the law of armed conflict in respect of matters such as targeting. These are objective criteria and, in determining whether they are met in any individual case, the existence of authoritative and impartial acceptance of the existence of an emergency and the need for military action is obviously of great importance. It is therefore necessary to consider whether they were met in Kosovo.

With regard to the first condition, there is no doubt that there was a humanitarian emergency in which large-scale loss of life was threatened. While some of the worst atrocities in Kosovo occurred immediately after the start of the NATO campaign, it is evident that these were the product of a campaign by the Yugoslav forces which had been planned before the intervention of NATO. Moreover, the existence of a grave humanitarian crisis in Kosovo had been objectively verified well before the intervention. As was demonstrated in Part II, above, as early as 23 September 1998 the United Nations Security Council expressed alarm at what it described as 'the impending humanitarian catastrophe'. The Council also referred to the 'extensive civilian casualties' and the displacement of 230,000 people from their homes as a result of the fighting.[45] It repeated these expressions of concern in October 1998[46] and in the Presidential Statement in January 1999 condemning the massacre of civilians at the village of Racak.[47] The Council also determined that the situation in Kosovo amounted to a threat to international peace and security.

Those determinations were not made on the basis of material submitted only by the NATO States. The scale of the humanitarian crisis before the NATO inter-

---

[45] SC Res 1199 (1998).
[46] SC Res 1203 (1998).
[47] UN Doc S/PRST/1999/2.

vention was demonstrated in a briefing given to the Security Council by the United Nations High Commissioner for Refugees, who explained that by 23 March 1999 UNHCR was providing assistance to 490,000 refugees and displaced persons from Kosovo (a quarter of the population of the province).[48] The OSCE Report, based upon the eye-witness accounts of the 2,000 KVM monitors in Kosovo also testified to the existence of a humanitarian catastrophe by 24 March 1999.[49] In these circumstances, there was well documented evidence that the requirement of a grave humanitarian emergency was met and an objective determination by the Security Council that that was so. It is also relevant that the actions of the FRY were in clear breach of its obligations under binding decisions of the Security Council.

The second requirement—that military action offered the only practicable option for dealing with that emergency—involves a more complex judgement. Nevertheless, the NATO intervention occurred only after the repeated violations by the FRY of its obligations under the Security Council Resolutions and its undertakings to withdraw forces from Kosovo, the failure to secure an agreement at Rambouillet and Paris and the withdrawal of the OSCE verification mission in the face of an offensive by the FRY forces which was itself in violation of international law. The reaction of the majority of the non-NATO States on the Security Council to the commencement of the NATO military action suggests that they considered that this requirement too was satisfied.[50] The defeat of the Russian draft Resolution by the large margin of twelve votes to three was particularly significant in this respect.

The third requirement, that the Security Council was unable to take the necessary action, is again a difficult matter of judgement. Nevertheless, once it is accepted that military action was necessary, the implacable opposition of the Russian Federation and China to the military action which did occur, in the face of clear majority support in the Council, and the Chinese veto of the renewal of the mandate for Macedonia strongly suggest that the Council could not have taken a decision to authorise military action.[51]

Finally, it is necessary to consider whether the use of force by NATO met the requirement of proportionality recognised by, for example, the United Kingdom in its 1998 memorandum to the NATO members. As a matter of general principle, the use of force for humanitarian purposes muse be limited to what is necessary and proportionate to achieving the humanitarian goals of the operation, in this case halting the violations in Kosovo and reversing the effects of the ethnic cleansing there so that the refugees and displaced could return home in safety.

---

[48] Briefing by Mrs Ogata to the Security Council, 5 May 1999 (the text can be found at: www.unhcr.ch/refworld/unhcr/hcspeech/990505.htm).

[49] OSCE, *Kosovo/Kosova: As Seen, As Told: an analysis of the human rights findings of the OSCE Kosovo Verification Commission October 1998 to June 1999* (1999).

[50] See, in particular, the views expressed in the debate on 24 March 1999 (UN Doc S/PV.3988) by Bahrain (at 7), Malaysia (at 9–10), and Slovenia (at 19).

[51] That was the view expressed by Malaysia (S/PV.3988 at 10; S/PV.3989 at 9) and evidently accepted by the majority which voted against the Russian draft Resolution.

This principle, together with the rules of international humanitarian law applicable to the conduct of all international armed conflicts,[52] necessarily restricts the range of what may lawfully be attacked. They do not, however, mean that NATO action should have been confined to Kosovo itself. Targets many miles from Kosovo were capable of making an effective contribution to FRY military action. It was legitimate to attack such targets so long as the principles set out above were respected.

The hard truth which has to be faced is that the use of force cannot be a half-hearted matter. Faced with a major humanitarian catastrophe in Kosovo, neither NATO nor anyone else had ground troops available in the region which could be deployed in sufficient numbers and with sufficient speed to force an entry into Kosovo against what would almost certainly have been powerful opposition from the Yugoslav Government forces. The result was that the only realistic option was the use of air power, at least initially. Moreover, the capacity of air power to stop the ethnic cleansing in Kosovo in its tracks was extremely limited. The only hope lay in seeking to coerce the Milošević Government into stopping its actions in Kosovo by inflicting a heavy price on its military infrastructure across the entire country.

5. PROCEEDINGS BEFORE THE INTERNATIONAL COURT OF JUSTICE

The NATO air campaign was the subject of proceedings instituted by the FRY before the International Court of Justice against ten of the NATO States while the campaign was in progress.[53] The FRY maintained both that the NATO resort to force was a violation of the principles of *jus ad bellum* enshrined in the United Nations Charter and that the conduct of the campaign violated obligations contained in a wide variety of treaties ranging from the Geneva Conventions to the Convention on Navigation on the River Danube. In each case the FRY sought provisional measures against the respondent State in the form of an order that the respondent State should immediately cease military action against the FRY pending the hearing of the merits.

In order to obtain provisional measures, however, an applicant must demonstrate the existence of a prima facie basis for jurisdiction on the merits. The jurisdiction of the Court extends only to States, so that NATO itself could not be a respondent. The FRY therefore attempted to establish that the Court had jurisdiction—at least prima facie—over the ten respondent States. The Court held, by large majorities, that the FRY had failed to satisfy this threshold requirement.

---

[52] As explained in Part 1, above, these principles are not the subject of the present article.

[53] See the *Cases Concerning the Legality of the Use of Force*, n 1 above. At the time of writing, the cases against the respondents other than Spain and the United States of America were still before the Court. The eight remaining respondents have all objected to the jurisdiction of the Court and the admissibility of the applications. The writer acted as counsel for the United Kingdom in these proceedings; the present chapter represents his personal views.

The result is scarcely surprising. None of the treaties which were the basis for the FRY's substantive claim contain provisions conferring jurisdiction on the International Court and the two bases for jurisdiction advanced by the FRY[54]—Article IX of the Genocide Convention, 1948, (which was invoked against all the respondents) and Article 36(2) of the Statute of the Court, the so-called 'Optional Clause' (which was invoked against six out of the ten)—were rightly rejected by the Court.

Even assuming that the FRY was a party to the Genocide Convention, a position which it has subsequently repudiated, Article IX manifestly offered no basis for jurisdiction against Spain and the United States of America, both of which had entered reservations rejecting the application of that provision when they became party to the Convention. Moreover, Article IX confers jurisdiction only with regard to a dispute 'relating to the interpretation, application or fulfilment' of the Genocide Convention. Not surprisingly, the Court held that

> the essential characteristic [of genocide] is the intended destruction of a 'national, ethnical, racial or religious group' (*Application of the Convention on the Prevention and Punishment of Genocide, Provisional Measures Order of 13 September 1993*, [1993] ICJ Reports, 345 at para 42); . . . the threat or use of force against a State cannot in itself constitute an act of genocide within the meaning of Article II of the Genocide Convention; and . . . in the opinion of the Court, it does not appear at the present stage of the proceedings that the bombings which form the subject of the Yugoslav Application 'indeed entail the element of intent, towards a group as such, required by [Article II]' (*Legality of the Threat or Use of Nuclear Weapons, Advisory Opinion*, [1996] (I) ICJ Reports, 240 at para 26).[55]

In effect, the FRY was seeking to use Article IX of the Genocide Convention as a device to establish jurisdiction over complaints relating to quite different agreements. The FRY's interpretation of the Genocide Convention would have entailed watering down the crime of genocide to the point that it became synonymous with virtually any violation of the laws of war.

The other provision relied on by the FRY—Article 36(2) of the Statute of the Court—could afford jurisdiction only in the event that both the FRY and the respondent State in question had each made a valid declaration accepting the Court's jurisdiction under that provision and the dispute fell within the scope of both declarations. The FRY had purported to make a declaration under Article 36(2) on 25 April 1999 (a month after the commencement of the NATO campaign and three days before the FRY filed its applications against the respondent States). It then sought to rely upon that declaration as a basis for jurisdiction in

---

[54] In the case against Belgium, the FRY also attempted at a late stage to rely upon a bilateral treaty. The Court held that this treaty had been invoked too late in the proceedings (para 44 of the Judgment).

[55] Judgment in the case against Belgium, para 40.

the proceedings against those respondent States which had extant declarations under Article 36(2) (Belgium, Canada, the Netherlands, Portugal, Spain and the United Kingdom).

In view of the dispute regarding the status of the FRY, the question immediately arose whether the FRY declaration was valid. If, as the Security Council and the General Assembly had decided, the respondent States claimed and the FRY has now accepted, the FRY was not at the relevant time a member of the United Nations, then it was not a party to the Statute of the Court and could not have made a valid declaration under Article 36(2) of that Statute. The Court, however, understandably chose not to decide that question in provisional measures proceedings when there were other, more obvious, reasons for holding that there was no basis for jurisdiction. In the cases against Spain and the United Kingdom, Article 36(2) of the Statute could not have provided a basis for jurisdiction, because those two States had accepted the jurisdiction of the Court only as between themselves and another State which had made a similar declaration not less than one year earlier. The FRY's declaration, even if valid, plainly did not fulfil that requirement. In the cases against Belgium, Canada, the Netherlands and Portugal, the Court held that the FRY declaration was insufficient to establish jurisdiction because of the FRY's own reservations. The FRY declaration accepted the jurisdiction of the Court as between the FRY and other States with Article 36(2) declarations 'in all disputes arising or which may arise after the signature of the present declaration [ie after 25 April 1999], with regard to the situations or facts subsequent to this signature.'[56] The Court held that the dispute which the FRY wished to bring before the Court had arisen before 25 April 1999. That was clear from the terms of the FRY applications, which referred primarily to events before that date, and from the debates in the Security Council on 24 and 26 March 1999 in which the legality of the NATO action was the subject of extensive discussion. The Court rejected the suggestion that the air campaign could be sliced up like salami so that each air raid gave rise to a fresh dispute. The decision is not a technical one. The temporal reservation in the FRY's declaration was carefully drafted to ensure that no proceedings could be brought against the FRY in respect of the abuses in Kosovo which had led to the NATO campaign. It was entirely in accordance with precedent and principle that the FRY was not allowed, in the words of the old saying, 'to have its cake and eat it'.

At the time of writing, eight of the ten cases remain on the Court's List. If they proceed, the Court will have to consider a number of jurisdictional issues, including whether it has jurisdiction over individual members of NATO in respect of actions undertaken by NATO itself, an argument briefly canvassed by Belgium in the provisional measures proceedings.

---

[56] The full text of the FRY declaration is quoted at para 23 of the Judgment in the case against Belgium.

6. THE PROCEEDINGS IN THE EUROPEAN COURT OF HUMAN RIGHTS

On 23 April 1999, during the air campaign, NATO forces attacked the building in Belgrade which housed the studios of Radio Television Serbia (RTS). This attack led to proceedings in the European Court of Human Rights by relatives of some of the sixteen people killed in the attack and one of the persons who was wounded. They claimed that the attack involved violations of the right to life, under Article 2 of the European Convention on Human Rights, and the right to freedom of expression, under Article 10. The respondents were the seventeen NATO States which were also parties to the European Convention on Human Rights (ie all of NATO except for Canada and the United States of America). The applicants maintained—on the basis of a representation about the decision-making process of NATO which was contested by the respondents—that each respondent State was individually responsible for the attack, irrespective of whether its forces had been involved in the particular operation.

On 19 December 2001, the Grand Chamber (composed of seventeen judges) unanimously decided that the application was not admissible. The Grand Chamber found that the application was inadmissible on the substantive ground that the Convention did not apply. The scope of application of the European Convention is determined by Article 1, which provides that:

> The High Contracting Parties shall secure to everyone within their jurisdiction the rights and freedoms defined in Section 1 of this Convention.

This provision makes clear that the Convention does not apply to every act for which a State Party is responsible. Before the question of responsibility is even reached, there is a threshold requirement that the alleged victim must be within the jurisdiction of that State. Moreover, it is the alleged victim, not the agent who commits the alleged violation, who must be within the jurisdiction of the respondent State. As the Court pointed out 'the Convention was not designed to be applied throughout the world, even in respect of the conduct of the contracting States.'[57] Since the Court held that those killed and injured in the RTS building in Belgrade had not been within the jurisdiction of any of the respondents at the time of the attack on the building, the Convention did not apply to that attack. There was, therefore, no question of any of the respondent States having violated the Convention, even if they were responsible for the attack.

It is important to be clear what the Grand Chamber did and did not decide. It did not decide that the European Convention is not applicable in wartime. There is good authority for the proposition that human rights treaties do not cease to

---

[57] Judgment at para 80. The Court contrasted Art 1 of the European Convention with the position under common Art 1 of the Geneva Conventions, 1949, which requires each State 'to respect and ensure respect for the provisions of the present Convention in all circumstances'.

apply in time of armed conflict.[58] The *Banković* decision, however, is not about *when* the Convention applies but *to whom*. The Court's insistence that Article 1 means what it says and that the action of a State in bombing targets in the territory of an adversary does not suffice to bring those affected by the bombing within the jurisdiction of that State does not challenge the proposition that the Convention is applicable in time of war or armed conflict. What it does decide is that, whether in time of war or in time of peace, the Convention applies to the conduct of a State only if the person complaining of that conduct was within the jurisdiction of that State at the relevant time. That will normally include all persons on the territory of the State and may also include persons subject to its control outside its territory, such as the population of occupied territory (a matter considered below). It will not, however, include persons who are outside the territory and the control of the State, even when they are affected by its actions.

The question decided by the Court in *Banković* is also quite distinct from the question whether, in matters directly related to an armed conflict, the standards of behaviour required by hunan rights treaties are modified or overridden by the standards contained in international humanitarian law. It is noticeable that, in its *Nuclear Weapons* Opinion, the International Court considered that, in order to decide whether a taking of life in armed conflict was 'arbitrary' and thus contrary to the right to life provisions in Article 6 of the International Covenant on Civil and Political rights (the counterpart of the provision on which the *Banković* applicants relied), reference had to be made to international humanitarian law, as the *lex specialis*. In effect, it was the standard set by international humanitarian law which governed.

In the case of the European Convention on Human Rights, Article 15 permits a party to derogate from certain provisions of the Convention 'in time of war or other public emergency threatening the life of the nation . . . to the extent strictly required by the exigencies of the situation, provided that such measures are not inconsistent with its other obligations under international law.' Article 15(2) prohibits derogation from Article 2 'except in respect of deaths resulting from lawful acts of war.' No derogation had been made in respect of the Kosovo conflict. Accordingly, the applicants argued that, even if the attack on the RTS building had been lawful under international humanitarian law, the deprivation of life would still have been contrary to Article 2 of the European Convention (none of the exceptions in which easily fits the taking of life in combat). As an alternative, they argued that, if Article 2 had to be read in the light of international humanitarian law, the attack on the RTS building was contrary to that law. The grounds on which the case was decided meant that the Court in *Banković* did not have to reach these issues.

---

[58] See, in particular, the Advisory Opinion of the International Court of Justice on *Legality of the Threat or Use of Nuclear Weapons*, (1996) ICJ Reports 226; (1996) 110 ILR 163, at paras 24–25. Art 15 of the European Convention does, however, permit States to derogate from certain provisions of the Convention in time of war or national emergency.

The Court's interpretation of Article 1 was firmly grounded in the principles of interpretation set out in Articles 31 and 32 of the Vienna Convention on the Law of Treaties, 1969, whose provisions the Court has long accepted as applicable to the interpretation of the European Convention.[59] The application of those principles required the Court to ascertain the 'ordinary meaning to be given to the phrase "within their jurisdiction" in its context and in the light of the object and purpose of the Convention.'[60] It also required the Court to take account of any relevant rules of international law applicable to the parties to the Convention.[61] The Court held that Article 1 of the Convention must be considered to reflect the essentially territorial nature of the concept of jurisdiction in public international law.[62] Only in exceptional cases were persons within the territory of one State considered to be within the jurisdiction of another State. This conclusion was entirely understandable, indeed inevitable, given the language and purpose of Article 1, which imposes upon States a positive obligation to '*secure* to everyone within their jurisdiction the rights and freedoms' in the Convention.

The Court found that this interpretation was consistent with the subsequent practice of the parties to the Convention, none of which had ever made a derogation under Article 15 of the Convention in respect of military operations outside its territory, as it might have been expected to do had it considered that the Convention applied to such operations. In addition, the Court held that its reading of Article 1 was confirmed by the *travaux préparatoires* (which showed that the phrase 'persons within their jurisdiction' had been adopted in place of 'all persons residing within their territories', because of concern to ensure that the Convention was applied to persons who could not be considered as residents but were nevertheless present in the territory of a State).[63]

In passing, it may be observed that the meticulous care which the Court showed in ensuring that it took full account of other relevant rules of international law in establishing the meaning of the term 'jurisdiction' in Article 1—which included the citation of a long list of juristic writings on international law and other materials from outside the specialist literature of human rights—is a welcome recognition on its part that international human rights law and agreements are themselves part of international law as a whole.[64] The Court did not succumb to what Sir Robert Jennings has described as 'the tendency of particular tribunals to regard themselves as different, as separate little empires which must as far as pos-

---

[59] See *Golder v United Kingdom* (1975) 56 ILR 200 at para 29; *Johnston v Ireland* (1987) 9 EHRR 203 at para 51; *Loizidou v Turkey (Preliminary Objections)* (1995) 20 EHRR 99 at para 73.

[60] Judgment at para 56; Vienna Convention, Art 31(1).

[61] Judgment at para 57, citing Vienna Convention, Art 31(3)(c).

[62] Judgment at paras 59–61.

[63] Judgment, paras 62–65.

[64] The Court has recently relied on this principle in its three decisions on sovereign immunity and the Convention, *Al-Adsani v United Kingdom* (2002) 34 EHRR 273; *Fogarty v United Kingdom* (2002) 34 EHRR 302 and *McElhinney v Ireland* (2002) 34 EHRR 322.

sible be augmented.'[65] In addition, while it repeated its customary insistence that the Convention was a 'living instrument', to be interpreted in accordance with contemporary notions of human rights, the Court's reference to the *travaux préparatoires* shows that, when it is the scope of the Convention as opposed to the standards set by individual provisions, the intentions of the drafters remain relevant.

The Court had no hesitation in concluding that the applicants had failed to demonstrate that the *Banković* case was one of the exceptional ones in which the jurisdiction of a State extended to persons outside its territory. In fact, the applicants' arguments largely ignored the concept of jurisdiction and sought to hold the respondents liable on the basis of the effects of their acts. The Court rejected the notion that 'jurisdiction' could be equated with 'effect'. It was right to do so; to have held that the persons in the RTS building were within the jurisdiction of one of the respondent States—and the applicants were, of course, arguing that they were simultaneously within the jurisdiction of *all* seventeen respondents— would have deprived Article 1 of the Convention of all substance.

The *Banković* decision does not involve a retreat by the Court from its previous decisions. There is, of course, no doctrine of *stare decisis* in the jurisprudence of the European Court and, even if there were, the Grand Chamber in *Banković* would have been free to depart from earlier decisions of the seven judge Chambers at the very least. In fact, however, the *Banković* decision involves no departure from established case law. As the Court held,

> . . . the case law of the Court demonstrates that its recognition of the exercise of extraterritorial jurisdiction by a contracting State is exceptional: it has done so when the respondent State, through the effective control of the relevant territory and its inhabitants abroad as a consequence of military occupation or through the consent, invitation or acquiescence of the government of that territory, exercises all or some of the public powers normally to be exercised by that government.[66]

The Court was clear that the line of decisions which held that, since the Turkish intervention in 1974, persons in Northern Cyprus have come within the jurisdiction of Turkey for the purposes of Article 1,[67] was distinguishable. The Court attached considerable weight to the fact that both Cyprus and Turkey were already parties to the Convention in 1974, so that the persons concerned were entitled to the benefits of the Convention before the Turkish military intervention.[68] That consideration was not applicable in *Banković*, because the FRY was not party to the Convention. Moreover, the respondents did not exercise effective control— certainly in the sense in which that term was used by the Court in the *Cyprus* cases—over any part of the FRY.

---

[65] Sir Robert Jennings, 'The Proliferation of Adjudicatory Bodies' in *ASIL* Bulletin, *Educational Resources on International Law*, No 9, Nov 1995, p 2 at p 6.

[66] Judgment at para 71.

[67] *Loizidou v Turkey*, n 59 above.

[68] Judgment at para 80.

Similarly, the Court had no difficulty in distinguishing the decision in *Soering v United Kingdom*,[69] in which the Court had held that the United Kingdom would violate the Convention if it extradited Soering to the United States of America in circumstances where there was a real risk that he would be sentenced to death. In that case, Soering, who was in a United Kingdom prison, was clearly within the jurisdiction of the United Kingdom at the relevant time.

The decision in *Xhavara v Albania and Italy*[70] that the passengers on board an Albanian merchant ship intercepted on the high seas by an Italian warship were within the jurisdiction of Italy was based on the existence of an agreement between the two countries for inspections of this kind and involved a classical example of a 'pooling' of jurisdiction in respect of shipping. *Issa v Turkey*[71] decides almost nothing of relevance because the Chamber which decided that the case was admissible was not confronted with any argument about Article 1.

Finally, it is important in dispel the illusion that the decision in *Banković* is somehow a setback for international human rights or the rule of law in international society. Tempting as it may be to some to argue that human rights treaties should always be interpreted in the most expansive way, so as to extend the reach of human rights law, it cannot be right to ignore a provision as fundamental as Article 1 of the European Convention and to convert the Convention from one which requires the parties to secure a network of rights to a defined group of people into one which imposes liability for certain actions wherever committed. The rule of law requires respect for the integrity of treaties and a recognition of the fact that international tribunals are not free to make up the law as they go along.

Nor is it at all correct to suggest—as did the applicants in Banković—that to hold the European Convention inapplicable would leave the NATO States free to behave as they pleased outside their own territories. Both in Kosovo and elsewhere, those States are subject—in the conduct of their military operations—to the requirements of international humanitarian law. In contrast to the provisions of the European Convention, the principles of international humanitarian law constitute a detailed body of law specifically designed for application in armed conflict. Moreover, in the Kosovo conflict, the members of the NATO armed forces were subject to the jurisdiction of the International Criminal Tribunal for the Former Yugoslavia and could be brought to trial if they violated international humanitarian law.

7. THE INTERNATIONAL CRIMINAL TRIBUNAL FOR THE FORMER YUGOSLAVIA

It is to the Tribunal that it is now necessary to turn. International humanitarian law has long expressly provided for its enforcement through criminal proceedings against individuals. Nevertheless, while the grave breaches machinery established

---

[69] (1989) 11 EHRR 439.
[70] 11 Jan 2001, unreported.
[71] 30 May 2000, unreported.

by the Geneva Conventions and Additional Protocol I[72] requires States to take action in cases of grave breaches and to bring offenders to justice irrespective of nationality, proceedings of this kind have in fact been almost unknown. In the case of Kosovo, however, there was already in existence an international tribunal able to exercise criminal jurisdiction. The International Criminal Tribunal for the Former Yugoslavia (ICTY), which was established by United Nations Security Council Resolution 827 (1993), had 'the power to prosecute persons responsible for serious violations of international humanitarian law committed in the territory of the former Yugoslavia since 1991.'[73] Although drawn up with the conflicts in Bosnia-Herzegovina and Croatia in the early 1990s in mind, the Statute was not limited to those conflicts and was clearly applicable to events in Kosovo (as the Security Council recognized in Resolutions 1160 and 1199 (1998)).

The attacks by the FRY armed forces and police on the majority community in Kosovo led to the indictment, on 22 May 1999, by the ICTY Prosecutor of the then FRY President, Slobodan Milošević, and a number of other prominent political and military figures on charges of war crimes and crimes against humanity.[74] While this indictment was dismissed as a political gesture by Mr Milošević at the time, the new government of the FRY surrendered him to the custody of the Tribunal in 2001. At the time of writing, Mr Milošević is in custody and being tried on these, and other charges.

The Prosecutor also considered that the ICTY had jurisdiction over any serious violations of humanitarian law which might have occurred in the NATO air campaign. Although her stance in this regard attracted some criticism in political circles, it was plainly correct. The ICTY's jurisdiction under Article 1 of its Statute is confined to the territory of the former Yugoslavia but it is not limited to offences committed there by Yugoslavs and clearly extends to offences by NATO personnel. The Prosecutor established a committee to inquire into various allegations that NATO forces had violated international humanitarian law and to advise whether there was 'a sufficient basis to proceed with an investigation into some or all of the allegations or into other incidents related to the NATO bombing.'[75] The committee concluded that no investigation should be commenced.[76] The Prosecutor accepted that recommendation and told the Security Council that

> there is no basis for opening an investigation into any of those allegations or into other incidents related to the NATO bombing. Although some mistakes were made by NATO, I am very satisfied that there was no deliberate targeting of civilians or of unlawful military targets by NATO during the bombing campaign.[77]

[72] First Geneva Convention, Art 49; Second Geneva Convention, Art 50; Third Geneva Convention, Art 129; Fourth Geneva Convention, Art 146; Additional Protocol I, Art 85.

[73] Statute of the Tribunal, Art 1.

[74] The indictment is published on the ICTY website, http://www.un.org/icty/indictment/english/mil-ii990524e.htm. On 24 May 1999, Judge Hunt confirmed the indictment, Case no IT–99–37–I.

[75] *Final Report to the Prosecutor by the Committee established to review the NATO Bombing Campaign against the Federal Republic of Yugoslavia* (2000) 39 ILM 1257 at para 3.

[76] *Ibid* at para 91.

[77] United Nations Security Council 4150th Meeting; S/PV.4150, p 3, col 1.

The committee's report and the conclusions drawn by the Prosecutor have attracted much criticism. Most of that criticism has come from those who wanted to see charges brought against Members of the NATO armed forces and who accused the committee of adopting too lenient a stance in its appraisal of the NATO actions.[78] More surprisingly, however, others have criticised the committee for subjecting decisions taken in the heat of the moment and sometimes in conditions of considerable danger to too close and detached a scrutiny. Both criticisms are misconceived. The report suggests neither undue leniency nor an excessive dose of hindsight. While scrutiny of military decisions with a view to prosecution is never a comfortable experience for those who might be the subject of charges, it is what the Geneva Conventions and Additional Protocol I envisage and what has been applied to non-NATO defendants by the ICTY for several years. What the report shows is that armed forces today cannot expect to be immune from the kind of legal scrutiny—seeking to apply rules which have long been binding on all States—which has become commonplace in other walks of life. It also shows that a body like the committee established by the Prosecutor of the ICTY is capable of applying those rules in a fair and sensible manner.

8. CONCLUSIONS

The above analysis suggests that the resort to force by NATO in Kosovo was within the powers of that organisation as a matter of international law. Although NATO has no express provision in its constitution for taking action on humanitarian grounds, the parties to that treaty have interpreted it as extending beyond the collective action in self-defence for which it was originally intended. That is something they are entitled to do, so long, of course, as the action which NATO actually takes is not contrary to general international law. Provided that NATO does no more than exercise collectively rights which its members possess under general international law, no such contravention will occur.

In the case of Kosovo, NATO exercised the right of humanitarian intervention which States possess under customary international law when it resorted to force. Its subsequent participation in KFOR involved the exercise of powers conferred by the Security Council in Resolution 1244 (1999).

The various proceedings considered in Parts 5 to 7 of this chapter demonstrate the extent of scrutiny to which NATO was subject. Although none of the three tribunals which considered the matter has jurisdiction over NATO as such, the exercise of jurisdiction over member States or individual officials or airmen would clearly involve an indirect exercise of jurisdiction over NATO itself. That

---

[78] See, eg P Benvenuti, 'The ICTY Prosecutor and the Review of the NATO Bombing Campaign against the Federal Republic of Yugoslavia' (2001) 12 *EJIL* 503.

jurisdiction was exercised by the European Court of Human Rights and the Prosecutor of the International Criminal Tribunal although both rejected the complaints before them. The decisions of the International Court of Justice so far suggest that there is no jurisdiction over the respondent members of NATO at the behest of the FRY.

III

Approaches to the Assertion of Jurisdiction by Adjudicative Bodies

9

Approaches of Domestic Courts to the Assertion of International Jurisdiction

HAZEL FOX

1. INTRODUCTION

This chapter is concerned with domestic courts and their stance in the assertion of international jurisdiction. It seeks to examine the way in which the private litigant's remedies in domestic courts are affected by those courts' response, both positive and negative, to international requirements relating to jurisdiction. Such a discussion, however, must first be prefaced by some reminder of the characteristics of domestic courts, and, in particular, the characteristics which distinguish them from the international tribunals and procedures addressed by the other contributors. In chapter 10, Judge Koroma stresses how the political support for the International Court of Justice depends on strict adherence to the consent of States for its jurisdiction, and, in chapter 2, Iain Scobbie examined the authority of UN administrations in East Timor and Yugoslavia as dependent on the mandate of the Security Council. The basis and source of domestic courts' authority and hence capacity to assert jurisdiction is very different.

Speaking in very general terms, courts in any recognized State demonstrate common features. First they pre-date, often by centuries if not even millennia, the international procedures to which they are being compared; the social and cultural context of such courts differs from modern international tribunals. Secondly, the source of their authority, though historically developed out of a feudal lord's court, customary courts, or merchant courts, derives from the central authority in control of the country, initially a central authority based on personal rule but today on legislation enacted by a democratically elected body representative of the population of the country. It should be stressed that this is the source of authority which provides domestic courts with democratic legitimacy. The signatory Governments to the European Convention on Human Rights in reaffirming their belief in the preamble in 'the fundamental freedoms which are the foundations of peace and justice' declared that they were 'best maintained on the one hand by an effective political democracy and on the other by a common understanding and observance of the human rights upon which they depend.' This maintenance of an effective political democracy, which the governments set at the forefront of the human rights agenda, is often overlooked—yet without the structure of effective political democracy the conferment of human rights is worthless. Domestic courts constitute an important element in that structure, and the substation of legal order which these courts provide is often taken for granted by such international procedures as deal in the self same subject matter. The purpose of domestic criminal courts is to maintain peace and good order and the purpose of domestic civil courts is to resolve the disputes of those coming within their jurisdiction according to law and justice, as largely shaped to reflect and meet domestic interests and needs.

The consequence of these characteristics is that domestic courts primarily direct their attention to internal affairs, to exercising an internal competence. In so far as they take account of foreign affairs, they adopt an attitude of 'do as you would be done by', expressed as comity and respect for the similar internal competence of the domestic courts of other States. The traditional response of domestic courts to the demands and constraints of international law is well described by the Court of Appeal in its recent attempt to rationalise the doctrines of non-justiciability and act of state when it calls for a 'balanced answer to the conflicting needs of private rights, sovereign immunities, and international relations.'[1]

2. INTERNATIONAL LAW AND DOMESTIC LAW

Before going further, it is necessary to qualify somewhat what are described as 'domestic courts'. This chapter is confined to English courts, and even with that limitation it may well seem over-generalised. In relation to English courts, it is currently necessary to qualify one of the characteristics described above, which is the content of the law which the courts apply. The traditional constraints in English law on the reception of international law are well known: no alteration of legal rights without incorporation of treaties by legislation,[2] the exclusion of customary international law which is contrary to statute[3] and the changes which have brought about their relaxation. The primacy of EC law over domestic law and its direct effect conferring rights on individuals within the domestic system have accustomed English courts to admit a large body of external law into English law. The enactment of the Human Rights Act 1998 has conferred a supervisory role on English courts over primary legislation and they do so by applying standards set by a treaty and interpreted by a court external to the domestic system. International law today pervades English law and English courts treat international law

---

[1] See *Kuwait Airways v Iraq Airways No 2* [2002] EWCA Civ 284.
[2] *R v Secretary of State for Home Dept, ex parte Brind* [1991] 1 AC 696.
[3] See *Triquet v Bath* [1764] 3 Burr 1478, and more recently *Trendtex Trading Corporation v Central Bank of Nigeria* [1977] 1 QB 529.

as an objective system of principles and rules, not open to a range of permissible interpretations by the domestic courts of different countries.[4]

3. INTERNATIONAL LAW AND THE JURISDICTION OF DOMESTIC COURTS

We now turn to the constraints and demands imposed on the private litigant's day in court by the restriction or enlargement, by international law, of the domestic court's jurisdiction. These restrictions and enlargements will be considered in relation to the person of the defendant and the subject-matter of the claim and each of these as they relate to acts and persons within or outside the territory of the UK. But first it is necessary to examine a constraint which every litigant has to face on coming to the court; has the court jurisdiction to hear the case?

Jurisdiction is the foundation of a domestic court's operation, yet there is no single accepted basis for its exercise, nor does international law offer much guidance. Article 14 of the French Civil Code bases jurisdiction on the nationality of the claimant regardless of the lack of any connection of the defendant with the forum territory. Another basis of jurisdiction, generally now treated as exorbitant, is the presence of property of the defendant on the territory of the state—the 'toothbrush left in the hotel room'—which enables the court to assume jurisdiction.[5] Common law courts adopt a territorial approach based on physical presence within the forum state's territory. These different bases of jurisdiction give rise to conflicts between courts in the assertion of jurisdiction. A further complication arises from the use of discretion in the exercise of jurisdiction whatever its basis. Civil courts exercise a defined competence without any discretionary power; an approach which is reflected in the rules relating to domestic courts' jurisdiction set out in the Brussels I Regulation[6] which provides a general rule that proceedings are to be brought in the court of the country of the defendant's domicile. This system of defined competences has the merit of certainty but results in rigidity and highly technical outcomes.[7] In England, jurisdiction is founded on the presence of the defendant within its territorial boundaries, on submission and, in addition, in certain specified (but widely drawn) circumstances on a discretion to permit service of process on a defendant outside the territorial jurisdiction. This extraterritorial extension of civil jurisdiction is set out in Civil Procedure Rules,

---

[4] For example, in rejecting a construction of the Geneva Convention on the Status of Refugees 1951 as relating to persecution by the state but not to persecution by non-state actors the House of Lords stressed that the convention set one objective rule which all countries were under obligation to apply. *Re v Secretary of State for the Home Department, Ex parte Adan* [2001] 1 All ER 593.

[5] Interestingly the US Foreign Sovereign Immunities Act 1976 abolishes this *jurisdictio ad fundandum* against a ship or other property of a state as a basis of exercise of jurisdiction; s 1010 (1). In Scotland, however, this basis of jurisdiction is still used. See for example, *Forth Tugs Ltd v Wilmington Trust Co* [1987] 3 SLT 153; 107 ILR 641.

[6] EC 41/2001.

[7] *Re Harrods (Buenos Aires) Ltd (No 2)* [1992] 1 Ch 72; [1991] 4 All ER 334.

rule 6.20.[8] The jurisdictional provisions which it sets out and which are relevant for our purposes are: (a) the defendant's domicile; (b) the defendant as a 'necessary or proper party' to English proceedings; (c) a contract concluded or breached within the English jurisdiction or governed by English law; (d) in tort, damage sustained or an act causing such damage committed in England; and, (e) property located in England.

Unlike the defined competences of civil courts, common law courts present a jungle of separate and independent broadly based jurisdictions all over the world with potential excesses curbed by the exercise of discretion which these courts are recognised as possessing. The discretion of the court is manifested through a number of devices—enforcement of jurisdictional clauses, *lis alibi pendens, forum non conveniens* and anti-suit injunctions.

The exercise, through these devices, of such discretionary power may result in the assertion or denial of jurisdiction over a case containing a foreign element, but English courts confine their reasons to the facts of the case and, unlike US courts, are wary of shaping their decisions by reference to wider policy issues or the need for cooperation in the sharing of jurisdiction with other countries' courts. In general English courts will be unwilling to exercise jurisdiction unless there is a sufficient English interest or connection. In the words of Lord Goff of Chieveley:

> In a world which consists of independent jurisdictions, interference, even indirect interference, by the courts of one jurisdiction with the exercise of jurisdiction of a foreign court cannot in my opinion be justified by the fact that a third jurisdiction is affected but is powerless to intervene. The basic principle is that only the courts of an interested jurisdiction can act in the matter; and if they are powerless to do so, that will not of itself be enough to justify the courts of another jurisdiction to act in their place.[9]

Thus, in this case the court declined to exercise jurisdiction over a British national to aid the Indian courts enforce their exclusive jurisdiction over a third jurisdiction, the court of the State of Texas in the United States. It was 'no part of the function of the English court to act as an international policeman' (in the words of Stephen Kentridge QC, the successful advocate in the case).

In determining the sufficiency of the interest to justify an exercise of jurisdiction, however, English courts demonstrate flexibility and an alertness to changing moral standards in business. In *Lubbe v Cape plc,*[10] the House of Lords refused an application for a stay on grounds of *forum non convenien,* and allowed proceedings to continue in England in respect of a group action against the parent company incorporated in England on behalf of some 3000 persons, nationals of

---

[8] Previously found in Order 11, rule 1 of the Rules of the Supreme Court.

[9] *Airbus Industrie GIE v Patel and others* [1988] 2 All ER 257, per Lord Goff of Chieveley at 270–1.

[10] [2000] 4 All ER 289. Peter Muchlinski, 'Corporations in International Litigation: Problems of Jurisdiction and the United Kingdom Asbestos Cases' (2001) 50 *ICLQ* 1.

South Africa, who suffered personal injuries while working in an asbestos factory in South Africa operated by a subsidiary of the British company. The responsibility of the parent English company for ensuring observance of proper standards of health and safety by its overseas subsidiaries was held to be a sufficient interest for the English court to retain jurisdiction.

It is interesting to compare the approach of the English courts with that taken by the US Supreme Court in the *Union Carbide* case arising from the Bhopal disaster, the facts of which were somewhat similar. It was claimed that a US incorporated parent company had negligently failed to ensure that its overseas subsidiary based in India observed adequate standards of health and safety in respect of its workforce. The court declined jurisdiction because of the 'floodgates' argument in that it would overload the workload of the US courts to permit proceedings relating to foreign disasters to be brought before them and it ruled that India should deal with industrial disasters occurring within Indian territory.[11] In *Lubbe v Cape plc* the House of Lords dismissed public interest arguments such as matters concerning its own convenience or workload, the issue of forum shopping or an unwillingness to relieve less well equipped courts in other countries of their litigation burden. It stated that its examination was limited to the 'interests of private parties and the ends of justice . . . questions of judicial *amour propre* and political interest or responsibility have no part to play.'[12]

4. INTERNATIONAL STANDARDS WITHIN DOMESTIC LAW

The cases considered in the previous section illustrate both the *unwillingness* of English courts to exercise their jurisdiction where there was no interest in the subject matter of the claim from a substantive point of view, and their *willingness* to exercise jurisdiction where damage abroad may have been caused by a failure to maintain proper standards when conducting business from the UK. These are cases relating to and challenging the direct assertion of international jurisdiction by domestic courts over a case involving a foreign element. However, indirectly, a domestic court's increasing acceptance of international standards as prevailing over internal law standards also constitutes, by stealth, an extension of the domestic court's jurisdiction over subject-matter formerly treated as a purely international matter. There are many treaties incorporated into English law—such as the Geneva Convention on the Status of Refugees (1951)—where the Court applies international criteria and standards. But of more significance for our purposes is the European Convention on Human Rights and the line of ECHR decisions relating to violations of Article 6 (1) in conjunction with Article 13 where a rule of English law removing a range of civil claims or conferring immunities on a large

---

[11] *Union Carbide Corp Gas Plant Disaster at Bhopal, India in Dec 1984*, 634 F Supp 842 (DC NY 1986).
[12] *Lubbe v Cape plc*, n 10 above, per Lord Bingham of Cornhill at 282.

group or category of persons has been treated as a denial of a fair hearing or effective remedy.[13] Taken to extremes, this line of cases offers the litigant in his day in the English court an opportunity to reexamine the whole of English substantive law, and even more extraordinarily, the whole of the domestic law of other countries if the plea of a state immunity were set aside as contrary to Article 6(1), as was sought by applicants in three recent cases before the court in Strasbourg.

The idea that Article 6(1) can be used to challenge the removal of entire categories of civil claims from consideration by a court was first raised in the *Golder* case[14] in the context of the exclusion of prisoners from communicating with their solicitors. In *Osman*,[15] the Commission applied Article 6(1) to defeat a blanket police immunity which the House of Lords in *Hill*[16] had considered reasonable to ensure the operational efficiency and effectiveness of the police.[17]

Following this, there was apprehension that a similar approach might be taken with regard to social services with the effect that failures in child care would, in disregard of the provided statutory procedure, be actionable in proceedings in negligence. If so applied, and taken to extremes, such rulings could lay open the whole of English substantive law to reformulation and revision. Further, as will be seen below, such applications afford an opportunity to challenge the immunity *ratione personae* which domestic law grants to the state and members of a diplomatic mission. Thus, disguised as a procedural right to a fair trial, a human rights provision was invading domestic law so as to enlarge the domestic court's jurisdiction over persons which failed to satisfy the domestic laws' conditions of entitlement to sue. However, in the most recent case relating to the statutory obligations of local authorities to safeguard the welfare of children,[18] the European Court of Human Rights, itself, has shown caution. It found that the neglect of the social services to take protective measures in respect of

---

[13]   Art 6.1 reads: 'In the determination of his civil rights and obligations or of any criminal charge against him, everyone is entitled to a fair and public hearing within a reasonable time by an independent and impartial tribunal established by law. Judgment shall be pronounced publicly but the press and public may be excluded from all or part of the trial in the interests of morals, public order or national security in a democratic society, where the interests of juveniles or the protection of the private life of the parties so require, or to the extent strictly necessary in the opinion of the court in special circumstances where publicity would prejudice the interests of justice.'

Art 13 reads: 'Everyone whose rights and freedoms as set forth in this Convention are violated shall have an effective remedy before a national authority notwithstanding that the violation has been committed by persons acting in an official capacity.'

[14]   *Golder v UK*, Series A no 18 (1975) 1 EHRR 524.

[15]   *Osman v UK*, (2000) 29 EHRR 245.

[16]   *Hill v Chief Constable of West Yorkshire* [1988] 2 All ER 238.

[17]   The Court however, decided the issue on proportionality holding the bar to be a disproportionate restriction on the applicant's right of access since it provided a watertight defence to the police preventing any enquiry into competing public-interests considerations, such as the failure to protect the life of a child.

[18]   *Z and Other v United Kingdom* (2002) 34 EHRR 3. Allegations of lack of care of four children under the age of nine were brought to the notice of the Bedfordshire social services but despite visits by care officers the local authority failed over a period of four and a half years to remove the children or to take other steps to bring to an end their mistreatment with the consequence that all the children sustained severe psychiatric damage.

mistreatment of children over a period of four and a half years constituted a violation of Article 3, as a failure to provide the children with adequate protection against inhuman and degrading treatment. However, the inability of the victims to sue in negligence 'flowed not from an immunity but from the applicable principles governing the substantive right of action in domestic law,'[19] therefore it was not for the court to rule on the appropriate content of domestic law. Nonetheless, the Court held there was a 'gap' in domestic law, giving rise to an issue under Article 13, rather than Article 6, in that where failure was alleged by the authorities to protect people from the acts of others, a mechanism for determination of liability and award of compensation was required to be made available to the victims.

5. ASSERTIONS OF JURISDICTION WHEN A FOREIGN STATE IS PARTY TO ENGLISH PROCEEDINGS

This clearly illustrates the manner in which domestic litigation against private individuals is increasingly determined by reference to standards set by international law. A further question concerns how international law affects the assertion of jurisdiction by the English court in respect of a foreign state when it is made a party to proceedings. Whilst there is no bar to a foreign State initiating or consenting to proceedings in an English court, English law applies the customary international law rule derived from equality of states and confers immunity from criminal and civil proceedings when a foreign state is made a party to proceedings; it also extends such immunity to the person of serving members of a foreign diplomatic mission in England and widens it to cover, save with three stated exceptions, their private acts as well as acts performed in the course of their official functions. In the words of Lord Millett:

> It is not a self-imposed restriction on the jurisdiction of its courts which the United Kingdom has chosen to adopt. It is a limitation imposed from without upon the sovereignty of the United Kingdom itself.[20]

In three recent decisions, the European Court of Human Rights has confirmed that 'sovereign immunity is a concept of international law, developed out of the principle *par in parem non habet imperium*, by virtue of which one State shall not be subject to the jurisdiction of another State.'[21]

Responding to evidence derived from State practice of other countries the UK rather belatedly accepted that customary international law limited its restriction on the institution of domestic proceedings against states to activities in exercise of sovereign or governmental authority, *jure imperii*. In consequence the State Immunity Act 1978 (SIA) lists a number of exceptions to the immunity from civil

---

[19] *Ibid* at para 100.
[20] *Holland v Lampen-Wolfe* [2000] 1 WLR 827; [2000] 3 All ER 833 at 847–8.
[21] *Al-Adsani v UK* (2002) 34 EHRR 11 at para 54; *Fogarty v UK*, (2002) 34 EHRR 12; *McElhinney v Ireland and UK*, (2002) 34 EHRR 13.

proceedings, chief among them being commercial transactions entered into by the state and personal injury claims committed by act or omission of the state within UK territory. One restrictively drafted exception, section 4, permits claims to be brought against a state in respect of a contract of employment where the contract was made or to be performed wholly or in part in the UK. The section is not applicable to nationals of the employing State or third state nationals and is not applicable to employment of members of a diplomatic mission (SIA s 16 (1) (a)). In the *Fogarty* case, these provisions were the subject of a complaint against the United States by an Irish national who alleged sex discrimination in respect of a job application for a post within the US Embassy in London. The English indus-trial tribunal applied s 16 (1) (a) of the State Immunity Act 1978 and refused to exercise jurisdiction over a dispute relating to the internal administration of a diplomatic mission. With no remedy available in the domestic court the applicant took her case to Strasbourg, asserting: (a) that the case concerned discrimination in a job application, not a contract of employment; (b) that she was not seeking a court order for employment by the USA but pecuniary damages, and; (c) that in any event the immunity as provided in the SIA was excessive since neither inter-national law nor the practice of the UK in its own embassies abroad supported absolute immunity with regard to employment claims by employees of diplomatic missions. The UK government replied that its courts in refusing jurisdiction were responding to a constraint of international law which gave exclusive jurisdiction over the internal organisation of a State to that States' courts and its internal law.

On one view, the applicant's claim can be seen as establishing 'a gap', a failure under either Article 6(1) or 13 of the Convention on the part of the UK author-ities to provide an effective remedy by way of compensation for discrimination in job appointment; on another, international law confers exclusive jurisdiction on the employing state in the appointment of its public officials. Once again, the evo-lution of the case law of the European Court of Human Rights complicates the argument. The Court has been hesitant to construe appointment, conditions of service and reinstatement of civil servants as constituting a 'civil right' to entitle a fair hearing before a court under Article 6(1), although recently it has proposed the adoption of 'a functional criterion based on the nature of the employee's duties and responsibilities'[22] and ruled that Article 6 should apply to all public employ-ees, other than those who 'wield a portion of the State's sovereign power.'[23]

In the *Fogarty* case the European Court of Human Rights side-stepped this par-ticular issue. It ruled, without deciding whether the applicant's case came within the category of an employment dispute involving public servants, that the grant of immunity by the English court to the defendant State was a proportionate limi-tation of the right of access in respect of alleged discrimination in the recruit-ment process for service in a diplomatic mission. It took the view that the rule in section 16(1)(a) of the State Immunity Act 1978 which extended immunity to all

---

[22]   *Pellegrin v France*, (2001) 31 EHRR 26 at para 64.
[23]   *Ibid* at para 67.

staff of the diplomatic mission, and not merely its senior members, had not been shown to 'fall outside any currently accepted international law standards.'[24] Interestingly, in their concurring opinion Judges Caflisch, Costa and Vaji stressed the non-justiciable nature of the acts complained of. They said:

> It is inconceivable that a State, when appointing those who will represent it abroad—including clerical staff,—would have to submit to the standards set by the laws and procedures of another State, in particular those of their host country.[25]

6. ASSERTIONS OF JURISDICTION WHERE THE SUBJECT MATTER RELATES TO INTERNATIONAL RELATIONS

The restriction on jurisdiction which English law recognises in relation to the person of a foreign state is also observed as to the subject-matter of the claim. When we come to consider the domestic court's exercise of jurisdiction over acts committed outside its jurisdiction English law at present applies similar constraints to those observed when a foreign state is a party to the proceedings. In litigation between private parties English law regards international law as imposing certain constraints on the adjudication of affairs relating to another state or between foreign States. Lord Wilberforce in *Buttes Gas and Oil Co v Hammer (No 3)*[26] declared a general principle of judicial restraint or abstention, that the courts will not adjudicate upon the transactions of foreign sovereign States because with 'no judicial or manageable standards by which to judge the issues . . . the court would be in a judicial no man's land.'[27]

Recently in *Kuwait Airways Corp v Iraqi Airways Co (No 2)*,[28] the court had to consider this doctrine of non-justiciability in relation to the validity of legislation enacted by Iraq after the invasion of Kuwait expropriating the assets of the Kuwait airline. The Court of Appeal concluded that justiciability has to be addressed as a threshold issue but the constraint it imposes upon the court's jurisdiction is restricted to the public acts *jure imperii* of a state. Consequently it was open to the court to continue its investigation, apply the act of state doctrine[29] and to adjudicate private law rights. The Iraqi legislation came within the public policy exception. The legislation so clearly contravened UN Security Council resolutions which were binding on the UK and clearly established principles of international law that it was considered contrary to public policy for the English court to give

---

[24] *Fogarty*, n 21 above at para 37.
[25] *Ibid* at O–I, para 1.
[26] [1982] AC 888.
[27] *Ibid* at 938.
[28] 24 April 1998 Mance J and see n 1 above.
[29] The English court will in general recognise the validity of acts of another state such as legislation with effect within its own territory subject to an exception for public policy: *Luther v Sagor* [1921] 3 KB 532; *In re Claim by of Helbert Wagg & Co Ltd* [1956] 1 Ch 323; *Oppenheimer v Cattermole* [1976] AC 249.

effect to Iraq's exercise of sovereign authority within its own territory. The House of Lords confirmed the lower court's refusal to recognise or enforce the Iraqi legislation but did so on the basis of a public policy exception to both act of state and non-justiciability without reference to the need for any distinction between public and private acts.[30]

There are elements in this last decision which resemble the arguments deployed in *Fogarty* where the immunity accorded to the internal administration of a foreign state is not solely an immunity of the defendant *ratione personae* but by reason of the subject matter *ratione materiae*. The English doctrines both of immunity and of non-justiciability seem to be approximating to the civil court's distinction between competence *ratione personae* and *ratione materiae*. Philippe Cahier explains the difference between the notion of the 'immunite de jurisdiction', which paralyses the sanction of the law as against the person who enjoys that immunity, and the notion of 'irrecevabilite', which prevents the court from adjudicating a matter pertaining to another legal order.[31] This distinction seems apposite where a foreign State is sued in England in respect of acts committed outside the UK. In *Al-Adsani v Government of Kuwait* the English Court of Appeal accepted a plea of immunity as barring adjudication of a claim of torture in contravention of Article 3 of the ECHR, alleged to have been committed by Kuwaiti officials in a prison in Kuwait.[32] The UK State Immunity Act applies a more rigorous jurisdictional connection with the UK for personal injuries claims brought against a state than the Civil Procedure Rules do for claims brought against private individuals; it only removes immunity for personal injury claims where they were caused by an act or omission *in the UK*[33] and Al-Adsani could not bring himself within the exception. In any event, as with the US Supreme Court decision in *Saudi Arabia v Nelson,*[34] the UK maintains that the management of a foreign State's prison is to be categorised as an activity in exercise of sovereign authority—in effect the wielding of a portion of a State's sovereign power.

Wielding a portion of the State's sovereign power is not, however, a total justification in international law for a denial of jurisdiction by a domestic court. Whilst the restrictive doctrine of State immunity accommodates itself within a distinction drawn between private and public[35] acts of the State, it does not readily fit a

---

[30] *Kuwait Airways Corp v Iraqi Airways Co (No. 2)* [2002] UKHL 19, 16 May 2002. For the CA decision see [2001] 2 Comm 557 CA and n 1 above.

[31] P Cahier, *Droit diplomatique centomporaine* (2nd edn, E Droz, Geneva, 1964) at 233.

[32] 107 ILR 536.

[33] See SIA Art 5.

[34] 125 L Ed 2d 47 (Sup Ct 1993), 100 ILR 544.

[35] The European Commission of Human Rights has held that the raising of the plea of State immunity before the Irish court, where the applicant had decided to sue does not bring him within the jurisdiction of the UK for the purposes of application of the Convention; *McElhinney v Ireland and UK,* (2000) 29 EHRR CD 214; in the particular case the applicant has not exhausted local remedies within the UK. The plea of State immunity in the Irish court was also upheld, 12–5, by the European Court of Human Rights on the ground that despite state practice relating to an exception for personal injuries incurred within the forum State, the Irish court had not fallen 'outside currently accepted international standards' in affording immunity for the act complained of, the acts of a soldier on foreign territory 'a core area of state sovereignty', *McElhinney* (judgement), n 21 above at para 38.

classification of acts which international law itself identifies as violations of fundamental human rights. The applicant, Al-Adsani, took the UK before the European Court of Human Rights for violation of Articles 3, 6 and 13 because of the English Court's refusal to allow proceeding to be brought against Kuwait. He alleged that the violation of the torture prohibition in Article 3 trumped in international law the immunity *ratione materiae* for acts *jure imperii*, which is otherwise afforded to a State.[36]

In arguing this, Al-Adsani relied on the House of Lords' decision in *Pinochet No.3*[37] which it was claimed introduced a new exception to State immunity where the commission of international crimes violating human rights was at issue. However, an analogy to the restrictive doctrine of immunity and its distinction between private and public acts does not provide a way forward since it does not explain how immunity is withdrawn, as *Pinochet No 3* suggests it is, in respect of the commission of an international crime in the course of official functions and for the purposes of the State. A technical way out may be to declare an irrebuttable presumption of international law that all such acts of participation in an international crime are to be construed as private acts, but this exposes serving heads of State or government when on an official visit or business abroad to the risk of arrest and prosecution.

The International Court of Justice in the *Arrest Warrant* case has now made plain that immunity of heads of state and of a Minister for Foreign Affairs prevails whilst they remain in office over any criminal proceedings in respect of participation in war crimes or crimes against humanity.[38] The position as to the immunity from criminal proceedings of such persons when out of office in respect of such offences, even if committed in the course of official duties, remains uncertain. *Pinochet No 3* would remove immunity, the majority in the International Court of Justice would retain it. These conflicting decisions pose a dilemma for future courts: is the tenure of office to be treated as the true ground of immunity from both criminal and civil jurisdiction of an alleged perpetrator of international crime in the State's name? Or is a distinction to be made between immunity from civil and criminal jurisdiction with acts, even amounting to international crimes committed whilst in office, being treated as acts of the state itself for which immunity from civil jurisdiction still applies?

The three recent decisions in the European Court of Human Rights referred to previously have provided some support for the drawing of such a distinction between immunity for criminal liability of officials and civil liability of the State. The European Court of Human Rights rejected Al-Adsani's claim and found no violation of the torture prohibition in Article 3, there being no act of torture alleged to have been committed within the jurisdiction of the UK and no causal

---

[36] *Al-Adsani v UK*, (2002) 29 EHRR CD 99.

[37] *R v Bow Street Metropolitan Stipendiary Magistrates and others, ex parte Pinochet Ugarte (No 3)* [2000] AC 147.

[38] *Arrest Warrant of 11 April 2000 (Democratic Republic of Congo v Belgium)*, decided by the ICJ on 14 Feb 2002.

connection of the UK with the alleged torture in a prison in Kuwait. But the Court accepted that a claim for damages for personal injuries sustained from torture abroad constituted a civil right in English law sufficient to entitle the applicant to access to a court for civil trial pursuant to Article 6(1). Nonetheless it held such access was not absolute and that 'the grant of sovereign immunity to a State in civil proceedings pursues the legitimate aim of complying with international law to promote comity and good relations between States through the respect of another State's sovereignty.'[39] Further it held the limitation of state immunity on the right of access to a court to be proportionate and that a State continued to enjoy immunity from civil suit in the courts of another State for acts of torture, despite the growing recognition of the special character of the prohibition of torture as a peremptory norm. Such a norm might override immunity relating to criminal liability for acts committed within a State's jurisdiction, as in *Pinochet*, so as to render a former head of State criminally liable for torture committed on the orders of the State. But the Court declared itself unable to discern from international instruments, judicial authorities or the 1999 ILC Report discussing the denial of immunity for certain human rights violations, any change to the rule of immunity of a state from civil suit.[40]

Time is needed to digest the full significance of the Strasbourg Court's decision and the dissent of eight judges for the future development of the law of state immunity as well as its contribution to the understanding of the concept of a *jus cogens* norm and the scope of *erga omnes* obligations. The Court was clearly very aware of the rapid changes taking place and the difficulty of determining the validity of municipal law by reference to ill defined customary international law.

7. CONCLUSION

As stated at the beginning of this chapter, one purpose of national courts is to maintain peace and good order. State immunity is one technique to advance that purpose. The events of 11 September which brought to the fore what had largely been forgotten in recent decades, namely the prime responsibility of the State to protect the physical security of its citizens, may produce a new recognition of the value of State immunity.

It is as well to remind ourselves, as Vaughan Lowe, the Chichele Professor of International Law at the University of Oxford noted in his recent inaugural lecture, much of the moral force of modern international law proceeds from extra-legal perceptions of right and wrong, leaving the lawyers belatedly trying to fit their legal doctrines to an international jurisdiction which in the popular mind is already morally justified.[41]

---

[39]   *Al-Adsani UK (judgment)*, n 21 above at para 54.

[40]   *Ibid* at paras 55–61.

[41]   As with attempts to justify in international law NATO's action in Kosovo. See *Banković* Case: *Banković and Others v Belgium and 16 Other Contracting States*, Application No 52207/99 (12 Dec 2001).

Whilst I have provided material to give some idea of the ebb and flow of the jurisdictional tide as it seeps into the English court, I would like to end with a query concerning a *State's* day in the International Court of Justice. Should we not begin to think whether the time has come for some similar jurisdictional tide to flow into the International Court of Justice? If it is legitimate to read into customary international law's designation of an act as an international crime an implication that it may be enforced in a national court without the consent of the interested State, then why is it not equally legitimate to read a similar implication so as to give jurisdiction without consent to the International Court to determine whether a State is responsible for violation of fundamental human rights? Again, if a State by operation of state immunity is accorded exclusive jurisdiction to provide a remedy for human rights violations, should that 'exhaustion of local remedies' permit compulsory resort to the International Court where no diplomatic settlement or municipal law remedy in the wrongdoer State's court is forthcoming?

In support of the national courts of third States assuming jurisdiction over another State's violations of human rights, it is often argued that, where the consent of States is absent and deprives the ICJ of consensual jurisdiction, and a defaulting state gives no remedy within its own courts, the domestic court of another State should, as the sole source of remedy, extend its jurisdiction over violation of fundamental human rights committed by other States and their officials. But if it remains true that compliance still rests on consent of States, whether for observance of an ICJ judgment or enforcement of a domestic court's decision, would it not be far better for the international tribunal itself to take jurisdiction? The extension of the domestic jurisdiction of one State over another State without the latter's consent can look dangerously like some form of hegemony or neo-imperialism. Surely the right course is for the International Court of Justice to assert its jurisdiction.

10

Assertion of Jurisdiction by the International Court of Justice

JUDGE ABDUL G KOROMA

The question of asserting or ascertaining jurisdiction is, for any adjudicative body, an obligatory procedure prior to the settlement of disputes on the merits. From the international adjudicator's standpoint, it is an operation that must be undertaken with humility and with an awareness of the dangers of overreaching.

The International Court of Justice, building on the jurisprudential heritage of its predecessor, the Permanent Court of International Justice, has attempted to follow a principled approach to asserting jurisdiction that is respectful of that mindset. I believe that the Court's experience in that regard is meaningful and could provide useful guidelines to other tribunals or bodies whose experience is relatively more limited. Of course, I do not contend that the Court's way of examining whether a case falls within its jurisdiction is always perfectly suited for other international abjudicative bodies. I maintain nonetheless that the Court's practice constitutes an interesting and highly relevant comparative basis.

Before I delve into the marrow of this topic and come to grips with the ICJ's method of jurisdictional assertion, I would like to make two points of a terminological nature. First, the notion of jurisdiction is highly intertwined with the concept of competence, to a point where the terms are often used interchangeably, as is the case in the Statute of the ICJ itself. Literature on this subject treats one notion as the particular application of the other in a given case. Thus, jurisdiction relates to the Court's capacity to decide a concrete case with final and binding force, while competence adds to jurisdiction the notion of propriety.[1]

Secondly, I would like to call attention to another distinction, this one between jurisdiction and seisin, which deals with the formal requirements linked to the institution of proceedings. The validity of the seisin of the Court is assessed on the basis of the Rules of Court and of its Statute and does not per se require the prior ascertaining of jurisdiction. In other words, strictly speaking, the Court

---

[1] S Rosenne, *The Law and Practice of the International Court, 1920–1996* (Martinus-Nijhoff, The Hague, 1997) vol II at 536; G Fitzmaurice, *The Law and Procedure of the International Court of Justice* (Grotius, Cambridge, 1986) vol I at 109–10.

could be properly seised in a case that it has no jurisdiction to hear and adjudicate upon. In the obverse situation—where the Court has jurisdiction but was not properly seised—the Court generally will not pay heed to a defect in the procedural act that can be remedied by the applicant State, as was decided in the *Mavrommatis* case and often followed since.[2]

1. BASIC PRINCIPLES

A. Jurisdiction Is Derivative of State Consent and Corollary Principles

Given the consensual nature of international law, no general obligation requiring that a dispute be submitted to an international tribunal exists. The prescription for the pacific settlement of disputes can also be satisfied by way of inquiry, negotiations, mediation and conciliation—as is provided under Article 33 of the UN Charter—so that adjudication is by no means mandatory under general international law. The Court cannot therefore assume that it has jurisdiction; it is bound to first undertake the examination of the issue in order to come to a positive conclusion in this respect.

There are four ways for the Court to be granted jurisdiction over contentious disputes, as provided under paragraphs 1 and 2 of Article 36 of the Statute of the ICJ. First, States can grant the Court jurisdiction over a specific dispute by way of a special agreement (*compromis*); secondly, the Court may be granted jurisdiction to settle disputes that relate to the performance of obligations arising out of a specific treaty; also, in the case of general treaties or conventions—which may be bilateral, regional (eg the Pact of Bogotá) or universal (eg the General Act for the Pacific Settlement of Disputes revised in 1948 by the General Assembly of the United Nations)—'judicial settlement' by the Court is added to other means of settlement. In such cases, the granted jurisdiction is not limited to the settlement of disputes relating to the performance of obligations arising out of a specific treaty. They may apply to legal disputes relating to a variety of treaties as well as to customary international law disputes. They are a form of *conventional* compulsory jurisdiction to be distinguished from the compulsory jurisdiction under Article 36, paragraph 2, of the Statute; thirdly, States can make a declaration of acceptance of the compulsory jurisdiction of the Court in legal disputes pertaining to international law, its respect and the reparation of its violation—the so-called compulsory jurisdiction under Article 36, paragraph 2, of the Statute (the optional clause system). No matter which of these ways is at issue, the Court's jurisdiction depends upon State consent. The means of conferring jurisdiction on

---

[2] See for instance *Mavrommatis Palestine Concessions, Judgment No 2*, (1924) PCIJ. Series A, No 2, and *Case Concerning Military and Paramilitary Activities in and against Nicaragua (Nicaragua v United States of America), Jurisdiction and Admissibility*, (1984) ICJ Rep 392 at 404.

the Court just noted all fit within one of the following two categories: *ante hoc* and *ad hoc* acceptance of the Court's jurisdiction. To these, one must add the possibility of *post hoc* acceptance of jurisdiction by a respondent State following the filing of an application against it, better known as the doctrine of *forum prorogatum*. In this respect, it is important to distinguish the concept of consent from the notion of willingness, especially when consent is given *ante hoc*.

The seminal role of consent to jurisdiction was assessed in the *Factory at Chorzów* case, where the Permanent Court of International Justice linked the process of asserting jurisdiction to ascertaining the intention of the Parties to confer jurisdiction upon it.[3] This approach has been reasserted many times since and still constitutes today the cornerstone of the Court's approach to asserting jurisdiction. It also explains many aspects of the careful and strict approach of the Court to asserting jurisdiction.

Many principles derive from the consensual nature of the Court's jurisdiction. For instance, reservations to optional clause declarations are not to be interpreted restrictively, and the *contra proferentem* rule does not apply in such instances.[4] Also, the search for the correct assertion of the parties' intention with respect to their Article 36, paragraph 2, declaration and reservations accompanying it is not confined to textual analysis but is also informed by the context in which the declaration and/or the reservation was made.[5] Fourthly, it means that the Court cannot invite a third State to participate in proceedings in order that all the States whose rights might be affected by the Court's decision be heard, as in the *Certain Phosphate Lands in Nauru* case.[6]

Also, the more State consent is tailored to a particular dispute, as is the case in special agreements, the easier it is for the Court to read a genuine intent by States to confer upon it jurisdiction to settle the dispute. A more general expression of consent, in an optional clause for instance, will require a more careful approach in order to ensure that the consent is not construed more broadly than it was intended to be. Both methods of interpretation are aimed at the very same objective, that is, conforming to the parties' intention.

In other words, despite the fact that the desire to read jurisdiction broadly— in a teleological manner, as some Judges have already asserted[7]—is often well-intended and aims to give the Court a greater part in the pacific settlement of conflict, the Court confines itself to a more modest role by relying on stricter views of State consent. When the sensitivity of the disputes submitted to the Court is considered, together with the importance of such disputes for the parties, the latter approach appears to be the path of wisdom and ensures more likely respect for the authority of the Court's decisions.

---

[3] *Factory at Chorzów, Order of 21 November* (1927) PCIJ, Series A, No 12.

[4] *Fisheries Jurisdiction (Spain v Canada)*, (1998) ICJ Rep 432 at 452–453, paras 43–44 and 454, para 50.

[5] *Ibid* at 454, para 49.

[6] (*Nauru v Australia*), (1992) Judgment of 26th June.

[7] See the opinions of Judges Alvarez and Read in the *Anglo-Iranian Oil Co, Preliminary Objection, Judgment, ICJ Reports* (1952) ICJ Rep 93 at 132 and 145; also S Rosenne, n 1 above at 570.

B. The *Compétence de la Compétence*

After this first glance at the general philosophy behind the rules dealing with the recognition or conferral of jurisdiction by States, I will say a few words on the Court's authority over disputes concerning the existence of jurisdiction. The relevant principle is provided for in paragraph 6 of Article 36 of the Statute: 'In the event of a dispute as to whether the Court has jurisdiction, the matter shall be settled by the decision of the Court.' Of course, this attribute is far from being limited to the ICJ. Indeed, both the Permanent Court of International Justice and the ICJ recognised—in the *Peace Treaties*[8] and *Nottebohm*[9] cases—that the *compétence de la compétence* is a general feature of all international tribunals.

Generally speaking, the power of an institution to determine its own competence is a feature of significant importance as, in a certain way, it endows that institution with the capacity to develop its own capacity and to fix for itself the limits of its capacity. It is a precious gift, but a dangerous one, as can easily be imagined. Indeed, it would be vain to deny that a tribunal takes a certain interest in its jurisdiction and that such interest—albeit of a clearly different nature and intensity than the parties' interest in a case—coupled with the power of decision, can appear troublesome at first glance.

I do not believe however that this intellectual discomfort should be sustained very long. In practice, the Court's *compétence de la compétence* has never been perceived as an absolute power but rather as a form of competence. This bears two consequences. First, the impact of the Court's capacity to rule on its competence is severely limited by the prescriptions of the consensual nature of its jurisdiction. Indeed, the Court never seises disputes *proprio motu* but always has a passive attitude in terms of the disputes that come before it. In other words, the interpretive power of the Court and its authority on competence is counterbalanced by the States' discretion in formulating an acceptance of jurisdiction. The interplay of State autonomy and Court authority on jurisdictional matters works as a check-and-balance device, although this is so only to a limited extent. In theory, the Court could even act *proprio motu* on jurisdiction despite the parties' agreement, a possibility alluded to by Fitzmaurice in his treatise on *The Law and Procedure of the International Court of Justice*[10] as well as by Lord McNair in his opinion in the *Anglo-Iranian Oil Co.*[11] case. However, such action has never been undertaken by the Court. In practice, the Court will be deferential to the parties' agreement on jurisdiction, relegating the *proprio motu* power to the realm of the rhetorical.

---

[8] *Interpretation of Peace Treaties with Bulgaria, Hungary and Romania, First Phase, Advisory Opinion,* (1950) ICJ Rep 65 at 74.
[9] *Nottebohm (Liechtenstein v Guatemala)* (1955) ICJ Rep 4.
[10] n 1, above.
[11] (1952) ICJ Rep 93.

Secondly, the Court's jurisdictional powers are restricted by the development of a principled approach to jurisdictional assertion, an approach marked by a philosophy—maybe not of containment—but at least of committing no over-reach. For the Court's authority does not take root in any compliance mechanism that can constrain State behaviour. It rather remains highly dependent on the compliance pull generated by the legitimacy of its decisions. Thus, the Court's interest in the expansion of its jurisdiction is offset by its own interest to remain an authoritative institution.

2. PRECONDITIONS FOR JUSTICIABILITY

Now, assuming the proper seisin of the Court, how is the International Court of Justice to assert its jurisdiction in a given instance? What are the material elements that the Court will look at in the determination of the existence of a jurisdictional basis to adjudicate?

Article 38, paragraph 1, of the Statute of the ICJ provides that the function of the Court is 'to decide in accordance with international law such disputes as are submitted to it'. In the *Nuclear Tests* cases, the Court labelled the existence of a dispute 'the primary condition for the Court to exercise its judicial function'.[12]

The next question that naturally flows therefrom is how to define a dispute. The Court's jurisprudence is quite consistent on this issue in referring to the Permanent Court's decision in the *Mavrommatis* (Preliminary Objection) case, where it was stated that 'a dispute is a disagreement on a point of law or fact, a conflict of legal views or of interests between two persons'.[13] When the dispute arises between parties to a convention concerning obligations arising therefrom, there will be a dispute where there persists: 'a situation in which the two sides hold clearly opposite views concerning the question of the performance or non-performance of certain treaty obligations.'[14]

The determination of the existence of a dispute lends to an objective examination of the claims of the parties. The mere assertions by the parties as to the existence or non-existence of a dispute are not regarded as conclusive.

Where the Court's jurisdiction is invoked on the basis of what is known as the optional clause system, under Article 36, paragraph 2, of the Statute of the Court, the Court is also often asked to decline to exercise jurisdiction on the basis that a dispute is not legal in character, as required by the Article. For instance, in the *Corfu Channel* and in the *Military and Paramilitary Activities in and against Nicaragua* (Merits) cases, the Court disregarded claims that the political implica-

---

[12] Rosenne, n 1 above at 518, n 3.
[13] Rosenne, n 1 above at 519.
[14] See n 8 above.

tions of the disputes rendered them non-legal and thus should prevent the Court from exercising jurisdiction.[15]

3. ASSERTION OF JURISDICTION IN ITS VARIOUS COMPONENTS

The aim of the Court's jurisdictional exercise was aptly phrased by Fitzmaurice in his treatise on the ICJ:

> The heart of the question almost always is, not whether *a* consent has been given, but *what* it is that has been consented to—or, more particularly, what and how much is covered by the consent given.[16]

The assertion of jurisdiction consists of a single enterprise, but it deals with the many facets of jurisdiction. Traditionally, three dimensions to jurisdiction are identified: *ratione materiae, ratione personae* and *ratione temporis*. Before I consider these three elements, I would like to underscore that there are two levels at which the exercise of jurisdictional assertion can take place, depending on the type of procedure taking place. A summary assertion of jurisdiction will be undertaken by the Court when it is requested to indicate provisional measures in order to ensure the preservation of the rights of the parties, in accordance with Article 41 of the Statute and Article 61 of its Rules. In such cases, the Court examines whether it has *prima facie* jurisdiction. By doing so, the Court does not make a provisional finding as to the existence of jurisdiction to hear the case on the merits, but it rather acknowledges the existence of a priori jurisdiction to indicate interim measures. This has two consequences. First, it implies that our Court could in the first instance issue interim measures and conclude, at a later stage, that it has no jurisdiction on the merits of the case, as it did in the *Anglo-Iranian Oil Co.* case.[17] Second, interim measures cannot survive absent jurisdiction, so that an eventual finding of the absence of jurisdiction entails that the said measures will be rescinded.

The second and more common level of examination, which precedes the consideration of the case on its merits, is a full assertion of jurisdiction. Under such a procedure, the Court goes beyond a *prima facie* appreciation and comes to grips with the merits and cogency of the arguments establishing or denying its competence. In the *Fisheries Jurisdiction (Spain v Canada)* case, the Court explicitly established its complete authority on the issue of jurisdiction, stating that it is a question of law. On that basis, the Court asserted the fundamental rule of the absence of any burden of proof in jurisdictional matters.[18]

[15] *Corfu Channel (United Kingdom v Albania)* (1947) ICJ Rep and *Military and Paramilitary Activities in and against Nicaragua* (Nicaragua v United States), Merits (1986) ICJ Rep.

[16] Fitzmaurice, n 1 above vol II at 513.

[17] (1951) ICJ Rep. It is worth pointing out that such an award of interim measures is legally binding on the parties even if ultimately the Court does not have jurisdiction. See the decision of the ICJ in the *LaGrand case (Germany v United States of America)* (2001) Judgment of 27 June.

[18] *Fisheries Jurisdiction (Spain v Canada), Jurisdiction of the Court, Judgment,* note 4 above at 450, para 38.

A. Jurisdiction *Ratione Materiae*

The first facet of jurisdiction is the material element, which deals with the subject-matter or the nature of the dispute. But this should not be confused with the definition of the subject-matter of the dispute which belongs first of all to the Applicant without prejudice to the power of the Court to interpret the subject-matter of the dispute. This is usually not a problem in instances where a case was brought before the Court by way of special agreement or under a treaty provision with respect to a dispute dealing with the interpretation or application of the treaty. Of course, it means nothing to the admissibility and merits of the claims made, but that is a totally different story.

When jurisdiction allegedly rests on a declaration made under the optional clause system, assessing whether a dispute falls within the scope of a declaration and is not excluded by a reservation thereto becomes important. The Court recently insisted in the *Fisheries Jurisdiction (Spain v Canada)*[19] case on the importance of distinguishing the dispute itself from the arguments used to sustain submissions pertaining to the dispute. In other words, when the Court examines whether the subject-matter falls within the scope of the declaration, it considers the subject-matter of the dispute and not the subject-matter of the claims strictly speaking.

Of course, the qualification of the dispute for the purposes of determining whether it rests within the scope of the Court's jurisdiction is not undertaken with regard to the legality of the acts in which the dispute originates. Equally, the legality of matters exempted from jurisdiction under the optional clause does not govern the interpretation of reservations. Legality of State conduct is dealt with at the merits stage only.

B. Jurisdiction Ratione Personae

Requirements pertaining to the *ratione personae* jurisdiction of the Court are stated under Article 35 of the Statute of the Court. As is provided in Article 35, the International Court of Justice is open to State parties to its Statute. While all Members of the United Nations are *ipso facto* parties to the Statute, States not Members of the United Nations may also become parties to the Statute under Article 93, paragraph 2, of the UN Charter. The conditions for becoming a party to the Statute were originally set in General Assembly resolution 91 (I) and are the following: (1) a general acceptance of the provisions of the Statute; (2) acceptance of all the obligations of a Member of the United Nations under Article 94 of the Charter; and (3) an undertaking to contribute in an equitable manner to the expenses of the Court to be determined by the General Assembly. Liechtenstein, in the *Nottebohm* case, Switzerland, in the *Interhandel* case, and Nauru, in the

---

[19] note 4 above.

Certain Phosphate Lands in Nauru (*Nauru v Australia*) all acted as parties before the Court under Article 93, paragraph 2, of the UN Charter.

Article 35, paragraph 2, of the Statute also provides for the possibility that the Court be open to States not party to the Statute under the conditions set up by the Security Council, which were laid down in its resolution 9 (1946). In order to fall into that category, a State has to deposit a declaration accepting the jurisdiction of the Court, in accordance with the UN Charter, the Statute of the Court and its Rules, to undertake to comply in good faith with the decisions of the Court and to accept all the obligations of a Member of the UN.

Also, it is worth noting that the Court, referring to the PCIJ's decision in the *S.S. 'Wimbledon'* case, considered in its Order of 8 April 1993 in the *Application of the Convention on the Prevention and Punishment of the Crime of Genocide* case, 'that proceedings may validly be instituted by a State against a State which is a party to . . . a special provision in a treaty in force, but is not party to the Statute, and independently of the conditions laid down by the Security Council in its resolution 9 of 1946.'[20]

C. Jurisdiction Ratione Temporis

The *ratione temporis* aspect of jurisdiction calls into play the timing of the occurrence of a dispute. In this respect, unless there is a limitation as to the timing of the dispute or of the acts causing it, it appears that the Court will read acceptances of jurisdiction as potentially retroactive. This was the case, for instance, in the *Application of the Convention on the Prevention and Punishment of the Crime of Genocide* (Preliminary Objections).[21] Of course, when jurisdiction derives from a treaty, the potential retroactivity of the Court's jurisdiction is distinct from the retroactivity of the obligations arising out of the treaty itself.

Where the dispute originates in a continuous act that took place over a certain length of time and where the jurisdiction granted to the Court takes effect as of a given moment during the occurrence of the acts, the Court has to examine whether the series of acts is severable into many disputes or whether it should instead be considered as a single ongoing continuous dispute. Such was the analytical framework employed by our Court in the cases opposing the Federal Republic of Yugoslavia and the ten NATO States.[22]

D. Mutuality and Reciprocity

The question of mutuality and reciprocity arises in the context of acceptance of the Court's jurisdiction in a treaty or in Article 36, paragraph 2, declarations.

---

[20] *Application of the Convention on the Prevention and Punishment of the Crime of Genocide, Order of 8 April 1993* (1993) ICJ Rep 3 at 14, para 19.

[21] *Judgment*, (1996) ICJ Rep 595 at 617, para 34.

[22] *Legality of Use of Force* (*Yugoslavia v Belgium*) (1999) ICJ Rep Order 124 and following 9 cases.

When both parties have expressed their consent to the Court's jurisdiction in a single or in identical documents, the mutuality and reciprocity are easily established. When this is not the case, the Court has to ensure that the dispute falls in a field covered by the acceptances of all the parties. Problems may be caused by reservations to a treaty or to a declaration or by different drafting of those instruments. When such is the case, the Court has first to determine which acceptance is the more limited in scope and then to undertake the examination of whether the dispute is covered in that acceptance. This is the approach that was followed, for instance, in the *Anglo-Iranian Oil Co.* case.[23]

4. THE ADVISORY JURISDICTION OF THE ICJ

The focus so far has been on how the Court asserts jurisdiction in contentious cases. However, the advisory jurisdiction of the Court—provided for under Article 96 of the UN Charter—remains very important, and the opinions rendered thereunder definitely contribute to the clarification of international law in certain fields. But as contentious jurisdiction is more in tune with the topic, I will limit myself to stating some of the principles guiding the Court's approach with respect to requests for advisory opinions.

Two categories of organs can request advisory opinions. First, the main political organs of the United Nations, the General Assembly and the Security Council, can request an opinion on *any* legal question. Secondly, other organs of the UN and specialized agencies can put legal questions to the Court, provided that those questions arise within the scope of their activities. Thus, the assertion of advisory jurisdiction, rather than being concerned with the notion of consent, aims at assessing whether the subject-matter of a question falls within the scope of the activities of the requesting body. Defining the scope of activities of a UN organ will be undertaken on the basis of the constitutive instrument of the relevant organ, as well as on its practice.

The former President of the International Court of Justice, Judge Gilbert Guillaume, in a recent speech to the General Assembly, alluded to the opportunity of allowing an international tribunal to request through the General Assembly an advisory opinion from our Court on a question of general international law raised in a case before such tribunal. In the context of the proliferation of international tribunals, the coming into being of such a procedure could significantly boost the importance of the advisory jurisdiction of our Court, in addition to promoting an embryonic international judicial architecture.

Two final points on our Court's assertion of advisory jurisdiction. First, the Court will not review the motives of the organ or of the member States in their request for an advisory opinion. This point was central to our Court's Opinions

---

[23] (1952) ICJ Rep 93.

on the *Legality of the Use by a State of Nuclear Weapons in Armed Conflict*[24] and on the *Legality of the Threat or Use of Nuclear Weapons.*[25] Secondly, the existence of jurisdiction does not create an obligation for a tribunal to exercise it. There is thus an additional criterion of propriety that the Court will consider in deciding whether or not to deliver an advisory opinion.

5. CONCLUSION

In conclusion, I will revert to a theme introduced earlier on, that of judicial restraint or humility. The Court's task of stating the law and of settling disputes in a peaceful way is undeniably an important one. Its role, no matter how well intended and nobly conceived, remains limited by the various constituent elements of international society, of which State consent and the willingness to abide by the rules of the international community form the core. In asserting its jurisdiction, an international tribunal must pay heed to such factors and itself abide by those rules, for it cannot effectively assume its role by working in a way that jeopardizes its legitimacy. That is what asserting jurisdiction ultimately rests on: a quest for legitimacy, usually found in a more or less distant expression of State consent.

[24] (1996) ICJ Rep 66.
[25] (1996) ICJ Rep 226.

11

Approaches to the Assertion of International Jurisdiction: The Human Rights Committee

DOMINIC McGOLDRICK*

1. INTRODUCTION

That the editors of this book chose the Human Rights Committee (HRC) as one of the exemplars of the 'assertion of international jurisdiction' by an 'adjudicative body' is significant. Rightly or wrongly, the HRC is perceived as the *primus inter partes* of the international human rights treaty organs.[1] Its jurisprudence, practices and procedures have often provided the models for the other organs.[2] Part of the higher profile of the HRC is undoubtedly due to greater degree of focus, visibility and publicity that the right of individual petition under the First Optional Protocol (OP1) has brought.[3] The decisions and views of the HRC are widely reported and reproduced.[4]

A postmodern deconstructionist would also see significance in the placement of the HRC in between the International Court of Justice on one side[5] and international and national arbitration on the other.[6] That posits the Human Rights Committee as a 'quasi-judicial' body. This sits happily with how some members of the committee and academic commentators have described it.[7] That it is not a

*I am grateful to Fiona Beveridge, Steve Wheatley, Helen Stalford and Catrin Le Magareusse for their comments on a draft of this essay. All responsibility remains with the author.

[1] A Byrnes, 'The "Other" Human Rights Treaty Body: The Work of the Committee on the Elimination of Discrimination Against Women' (1989) 14 *YJIL*; P Alston and J Crawford (eds) *The Future of UN Human Rights Treaty Monitoring* (Cambridge University Press, Cambridge, 2000).

[2] The institution of regular meetings of the chairpersons of the treaty organs since 1984 has been one of the factors in the sharing of best practice and procedure.

[3] See PR Ghandhi, *The Human Rights Committee and the Right of Individual Communication* (Ashgate, Aldershot, 1998). Other treaty organs to which there is a right of individual petition, such as ICERD, have attracted few communications. Some treaty organs that have not had a right of petition have sought one, eg the Committee on Economic, Social and Cultural Rights (ICESCR), the Committee on the Elimination of Discrimination Against Women (CEDAW).

[4] For example, in the *International Law Reports* (Cambridge University Press, Cambridge) they are reported on a par with decisions of the European Court of Human Rights.

[5] See the essay by A Koroma in this collection (ch 10).

[6] See the essay by H Fox in this collection (ch 9).

[7] See D McGoldrick, *The Human Rights Committee* (Oxford Clarendon Press, Oxford, 1991, 1994) at para 2.20.

'judicial' body,[8] and it is not a 'court', may be relevant when its approach to the assertion of international jurisdiction is considered.[9] The title of this book is also doubtless carefully chosen—it is concerned with the '*assertion of*', rather than the exercise of, '*international jurisdiction*'. The approach in this essay assumes that it is accepted that (i) the various bodies, organs and entities are all engaged in the *exercise* of international jurisdiction and (ii) that much of what they do is viewed as normal, orthodox and unproblematic. They simply could not function without exercising international jurisdiction. This is certainly the case in relation to the steady expansion of international human rights institutions and procedures of both charter based bodies and treaty organs since 1945.[10] The once central issue of 'domestic jurisdiction' is largely peripheral, though it may, in part, have been reconceptualised into other doctrines and debates such as the margin of appreciation, cultural relativism, and public-private divide.[11]

My assumption, therefore, is that we are really concerned with the '*assertion of*' international jurisdiction that is not viewed as normal, orthodox and unproblematic. More specifically, the concern is with those occasions when the HRC is perceived to be pushing the boundaries of its jurisdiction in the sense of its competence and powers. Given that the HRC is essentially concerned with holding 'States' 'accountable' for 'compliance' with the 'standards' in the International Covenant on Civil and Political Rights (ICCPR)[12] and that the HRC is the sole body with this function, the tension will be between the competence and powers of the HRC and those of the States Parties to the Covenant, that is, the jurisdiction which they assert on the basis of their State sovereignty.[13] Part 2 of this chapter briefly outlines the role and functions of the HRC. Part 3 highlights some important assertions of jurisdiction that have been received as normal, orthodox and unproblematic. Part 4 considers the HRC's assertion of international jurisdiction that achieved the greatest notoriety, namely its approach to reservations. Part 5 considers the HRC's assertion of a principle of automatic succession to human rights treaty obligations. Part 6 puts the issues concerning the 'assertion of international jurisdiction' in the broader context of the evolving international 'legal order'.

---

[8] In *Wellington District Legal Services Committee v Tangiora* [1998] 1 NZLR 129, the New Court of Appeal held that the HRC was not 'an administrative authority or judicial authority' within the meaning of the Legal Services Act 1991.

[9] See the reference to the significance of a 'judicial' body in the observations of the UK on the HRC's General Comment on reservations, considered in Pt 4, below.

[10] See D McGoldrick, 'Human Rights and Non-Intervention', in V Lowe and C Warbrick (eds) *The Declaration of Principles of International Law Concerning Friendly Relations Between States—Resolution 2625* (Routledge, London, 1993) at 85–119.

[11] See AA An-Ha'im (ed), *Human Rights in Cross Cultural Perspectives—A Quest for Consensus* (University of Pennsylvania Press, Philadelphia, 1992); H Charlesworth and C Chinkin, *The Boundaries of International Law* (Manchester University Press/Juris, Manchester, 2000).

[12] I leave aside the contested meaning of each of these terms.

[13] Interesting questions would be raised by the accession of the EC or the EU to international human rights instruments in that neither of those bodies possesses original jurisdiction in the sense that states do.

2. THE ROLE AND FUNCTIONS OF THE HUMAN RIGHTS COMMITTEE

THe HRC is composed of 18 members, elected by the states parties to the ICCPR to serve as independent experts.[14] Generally, the ICCPR's provisions on institutional architecture are brief and the HRC has room for manoeuvre via creative interpretation. The HRC has three principal functions. First, there is a reporting procedure. Within this, reservations have been discussed and examined as a matter of course. Comments are made and conclusions drawn on their validity. States are encouraged to withdraw them. Under Article 40(4) the HRC can transmit 'such general comments as it may consider appropriate' to the States parties. The HRC specifically addressed the issue of reservations in its General Comment 24: 'Issues relating to reservations made upon ratification or accession to the Covenant or the Optional Protocols thereto, or in relation to declarations under Article 41 of the Covenant.'[15] Secondly, there is an individual petitions system under the (First) Optional Protocol (OP1). A number of reservations and interpretative declarations have been considered under this procedure.[16] Thirdly, there is an inter-state complaint system under Article 41, which has never been used, but which does include a reference to reciprocity.[17] The HRC has occasionally adopted statements on human rights issues or as contributions to world conferences. Meetings of States Parties to the ICCPR have had no substantive role in the monitoring systems of the Covenant. The annual report of the HRC is considered by the Third Committee of the General Assembly (GA). States have used that opportunity to comment on the jurisprudence and the practices of the HRC.

3. ASSERTIONS OF JURISDICTION THAT HAVE BEEN RECEIVED AS NORMAL, ORTHODOX AND UNPROBLEMATIC

What is notable is that States have generally not reacted adversely to the jurisprudence of the HRC even when it has been bold and striking. A number of examples can be given.

---

[14] See Art ICCPR 28–39; I Boerefijn, *The Reporting Procedure Under The Covenant on Civil and Political Rights* (Hart, Oxford, 1999) ch 2; McGoldrick, *The Human Rights Committee*, n 7 above ch 2.

[15] A/50/40, Annex V.

[16] On the purposes of the HRC as an adjudicatory body see H Steiner, 'Individual Claims In A World of Massive Violations: What Role For The Human Rights Committee?' in Alston and Crawford (eds), *The Future of UN Human Rights Treaty Monitoring*, n 1 above at 15–53. Steiner does not challenge the legality of what the HRC does. He only suggests it would be better if it sought to play a different role.

[17] In the light of the discussion of the US position on reservations in Pt 4 below, it is interesting to note that the US has made the declaration accepting the HRC's jurisdiction under the Art 41 inter-State complaints procedure.

A. The scope of Article 26

First, the interpretation of Article 26 ICCPR as an 'autonomous' equality and non-discrimination guarantee. This position was originally taken in a series of views under OP1 concerning the Netherlands and encapsulated in General Comment 18 on 'non-discrimination' adopted in 1989.[18] The Netherlands disagreed and considered denouncing the Covenant and re-ratifying with a reservation to Article 26.[19] Having taken a dynamic and purposive interpretation of Article 26, the HRC has then proceeded to be cautious in applying it. In most cases, it has found no violation of Article 26. However, there have been some important findings of violations in relation to social security benefits and education financing.[20] Germany subsequently made a reservation to OP1 concerning Article 26, even though it had made no reservation to Article 26 itself. The HRC's response to the reservation, as expressed in the Concluding Observation's on Germany's report, was rather tepid to say the least.[21] Nonetheless, the HRC's view on Article 26 may have made States, including the UK, more reluctant to accept OP1.[22] However, given that the number of states parties to OP1 has surpassed 104, it is difficult to argue for a significant dissuasive effect. Rather it is defensible to say that the decision on the autonomous status of Article 26 has been accepted and become part of human rights orthodoxy. In the development of Protocol 12 to the ECHR on non-discrimination, the position under Article 26 ICCPR was often recited as 'the' international legal position to which the ECHR should be brought into line.[23] The UK has no plans to ratify Protocol 12.[24]

B. Concluding Observations

Until 1992 there were no country-specific observations by the HRC as a whole at the end of the reporting process on States' compliance with the Covenant. Since

[18] A/45/40, Annex VIA.

[19] The Dutch government received advice from Professor Kooijmans that denunciation was not legally permissible.

[20] See *Waldman v Canada*, Communication No 694/1996, CCPR/C/67/D/694/1996, 5 Nov 1999. See generally D McGoldrick, *The Law of the International Covenant on Civil and Political Rights* (forthcoming, 2004).

[21] 'The Committee regrets that Germany has made a reservation excluding the competence of the Committee under the Optional Protocol with regard to violation of rights as protected by Art 26 of the Covenant', CCPR/C/79/Add 73, Concluding Observations of the HRC on Germany at para 14.

[22] On the UK's practice in relation to reservations see D McGoldrick and N Parker, 'The United Kingdom Perspective on the International Covenant on Civil and Political Rights' in D Harris and S Joseph (eds), *The International Covenant on Civil and Political Rights: Its Impact on UK Law* (Oxford University Press, Oxford, 1995) at 69–90. Ratification of OP1 remains under review.

[23] See Explanatory Report on Protocol 12 (Council of Europe, 2000); G Moon, 'The Draft Discrimination Protocol to the European Convention on Human Rights: A Progress Report' (2000) *EHRLR* 49.

[24] See A Lester, 'Equality and United Kingdom Law: Past, Present and Future' (2001) *PL* 77.

1992 there have been such observations. This significant change in practice by the HRC did not elicit adverse responses from states parties and has been imitated by the other treaty organs.[25]

C. Reporting in Exceptional Situations

The development of special requests for reports in emergency situations only began in 1991 as a response to events in the Former Yugoslavia.[26] The Federal Republic of Yugoslavia submitted a report, which was its overdue third periodic report. The HRC regarded this as being in response to its request.[27] The precedent of special reports was extended to Peru, Serbia, Croatia and Bosnia (for the last two cases it was in their respective interests to be seen to be acting as states and complying with requests from international human rights bodies), Burundi, Angola, Rwanda, Nigeria, and Hong Kong. The new practice did not elicit objections from the states concerned, although not all of them submitted the reports requested, for example, Angola and Rwanda.

D. Follow-Up to Views under OP1

This practice has been developed since 1990.[28] Again, there were no adverse responses from States. Like many other developments, it was effectively treated as an internal matter.

4. ASSERTION OF INTERNATIONAL JURISDICTION—THE APPROACH TO RESERVATIONS

A. Autointerpretation

In the current debates over jurisdiction in relation to reservations, there are echoes of the earlier auto-interpretation debate.[29] The extreme version of that approach is that only states can interpret the scope of their own obligations, including any

---

[25] See I Boerefijn, *The Covenant on Civil and Political Rights*, n 14 above at 292–4 and ch XV.

[26] A/47/40, Annex VIIA; Boerefijn, *ibid* n 14 above, ch XIII.

[27] CCPR/SR at 1144–1147.

[28] See I Boerefijn, 'Follow-up of Views of the United Nations Treaty Bodies', in T Barkhuysen, ML van Emmerik and P van Kempen (eds), *The Execution of Strasbourg Human Rights Decisions in the National Legal Order* (Nijhoff, Dordrecht, 1999), 101; A De Zayas, 'The follow-up Procedure of the UN Human Rights Committee' (1991) 47 *Rev ICJ* 28–35.

[29] See JS Watson, 'Autointerpretation, Competence and Continuing Validity of Article 2(7) of the Charter' (1977) 71 *AJIL* 60. For contemporary debate in a different context see OQ Swaak-Goldman, 'Who Defines Members' Security Interests in the WTO?' (1996) 9 *Leiden JIL*, 361; B Stern, 'Can the US Set Rules for the World?' (1997) 31 *JWT* 5.

reservations. The logical problem with this is that states are effectively under no legal obligation unless they say they are. This is quite simply inconsistent with the notion of a legal obligation. A legal obligation must have some degree of objective content and existence before it can be described as such. When the issue of self-determining reservations has been raised before the ICJ there was no ruling from the court itself, but there were powerful individual opinions which considered them to be illegal, though they differed as to the consequences to be drawn.[30]

B. The Problem

Reservations to treaties in general, and to human rights treaties in particular, are not new phenomenon.[31] In 1951, the ICJ gave its advisory opinion concerning *Reservations to the Convention on the Prevention and Punishment of the Crime of Genocide* in response to a request from the General Assembly.[32] That opinion supported a much more liberal approach to the reservations on the basis that it permitted a much greater degree of participation by States.[33] The International Law Commission in its work of the law of treaties took up this approach. It was reflected in the provisions of the Vienna Convention of the Law of Treaties of 1969 (VCLT).[34] Essentially, in relation to reservations, the VCLT focuses on substance and not form (see Article 2(1)(d)) and provides for a permissive regime.[35] Unless expressly excluded by the treaty or in the case of treaties of a specified nature,[36] States can make reservations unless they are contrary to the object and purpose of the treaty (Article 19). The VCLT also makes complex and flexible provision for dealing with the effects of a reservation by one state on the states parties to the treaty (Articles 20–21).[37] The system of acceptance by default after 12 months means that there is a disposition towards the acceptance of reservations.

[30] See *Case of Certain Norwegian Loans*, (1957) ICJ Rep 9; *Interhandel Case*, (1959) ICJ Rep 6, analysed by J Crawford, 'The Legal Effect of Automatic Reservations to the Jurisdiction of the ICJ' (1979) 50 *BYIL* 63.

[31] See RY Jennings and A Watts (eds), *Oppenheim's International Law* (9th edn., Longman, London, 1992) at 1240–48; P-H Imbert, 'Reservations to Human Rights Conventions' (1981) 3 *Human Rights Review* 28–60; PR Ghandi, 'The HRC: Developments in Its Jurisprudence, Practice and Procedures' (2000) 40(3) *Indian JIL* 405; D Shelton, 'State Practice on Reservations to Human Rights Treaties' (1983) *Canadian Y. Human Rights* 205; M Coccia, 'Reservations to Multilateral Treaties on Human Rights' (1985) 15 *Cal. West I.L.J.* 1.

[32] (1951) ICJ Rep 15.

[33] There was a powerful joint dissent by Judges Guerrero, McNair, Read and Hsu Mo who supported the unanimity rule, *ibid* at 31.

[34] (1969) 8 ILM 679.

[35] See F Horn, *Reservations and Interpretative Declarations to Multilateral Treaties* (Asser Instituut, The Hague, 1988).

[36] Namely, where the application of the treaty in its entirety is an essential condition of the consent of each state to be bound or where the treaty is the constituent treaty of an international organisation.

[37] See C Redgwell, 'Universality or Integrity? Some Reflections on Reservations to General Multilateral Treaties' (1993) 64 *BYIL* 245, and the literature cited there; 'The Law of Reservations in Respect of Multilateral Conventions' in JP Gardner (ed) *Human Rights As General Norms and a State's Right to Opt-Out—Reservations and Objections to Human Rights Conventions* (BIICL, London, 1997) 3.

The VCLT approaches reservations in two stages. The first concerns the validity of the treaty. The second concerns the legal effect of a valid reservation. It is important to keep them separate. The complexity and inter-relation of the provisions in the VCLT makes them difficult to interpret.[38] Moreover, state practice in making reservations and in objecting to reservations presents a confused and inconsistent picture.[39] Lijnzaad has commented that, 'It would appear that States rarely understand their role as a State Party as implying an active stewardship of the treaty, which may include objecting to incompatible reservations . . . A number of states do take an active approach but this seems to be restricted to a regionally limited number of states.'[40] Most States simply do not respond. In the limited number of cases when States have objected, three categories have emerged. States have (i) objected to reservations on the basis that they are incompatible with the object and purpose and stipulated that this precluded treaty relations between the reserving and objecting state; (ii) objected to reservations as incompatible but stipulated that this did not preclude treaty relations between the reserving and objecting states. The effect of the objections on the relevant provisions of the treaty are not stated;[41] and, (iii) objected to the reservation for various reasons but not indicated the legal effect of the objection.

The validity of a reservation is governed by the criteria in the VCLT and in the default situation this is object and purpose test. In general, at the stage of legal effect, acceptance or objection to valid reservations is a policy decision for states and is not conditioned by the criteria of validity. This is, a State can object to a reservation even if it is compatible with the object and purpose of a treaty. It is submitted, however, that acceptance of an invalid reservation is precluded by the structure of the VCLT. Thus, a state cannot purport to accept a reservation which is incompatible with the object and purpose of the treaty and thereby seek to cure the legal invalidity of the reservation. Therefore, the only issues for States faced with an invalid reservation are concerned with its legal effect. There are three possibilities. Either (i) the reservation can be treated as severable, leaving the state bound by the treaty including the provision it had purported to make a reservation to, or (ii) the provisions to which the reservation are attached are severable or(iii) the reservation cannot be severed and this nullifies the consent to the whole of the treaty.

---

[38] See D Bowett, 'Reservations to Non-Restricted Multilateral Treaties' (1976–77) 48 *BYIL* 67; JK Gamble, 'Reservations to Multilateral Treaties: A Macroscopic View' (1980) 74 *AJIL* 372–94.

[39] See R Barrata, 'Should Invalid Reservations to Human Rights Treaties Be Disregarded?' (2000) 11 *EJIL* 413; Committee of Ministers of the Council of Europe, 'Invalid Reservations to International Treaties: Model Response Clauses to Reservations' (1999) 20 *HRLJ* 278. For the text of reservations to the ICCPR and objections to them see http://www.unhchr.

[40] L Lijnzaad, *Reservations to UN Human Rights Treaties: Ratify and Ruin?* (Nijhoff, Dordrecht, 1985) at 409.

[41] This was the case with the objections of some of the European states to reservations by the US to the ICCPR.

The analysis above accords with the majority view,[42] but it is not unopposed.[43] Two schools of thought have emerged, styled by Pellet as 'opposability' and 'permissibility':

> The advocates of opposability considered that the only criterion for the validity of a reservation was that of the objections of other States, while those of permissibility took the view that a reservation contrary to the object and purpose of the treaty was null and void in itself, irrespective of the reactions of the other contracting States.[44]

The VCLT sought to provide a single set of general rules which were capable of governing all types of treaties. Its provisions were designed with the vision of multilateral treaties of wide membership via the creation of a diverse a web of bilateral obligations between different States. The system aims for wider participation in multilateral treaties and in doing so, it accepts that reservations have an important function in securing this objective. Reservations are not necessarily objectionable in principle and do not necessarily reflect bad faith or an unwillingness to accept international human rights obligations.[45] The HRC accepted this:

> The possibility of entering reservations may encourage States which consider that they have difficulties in guaranteeing all the rights in the Covenant none the less to accept the generality of obligations in that instrument. Reservations may serve a useful function to enable States to adapt specific elements in their laws to the inherent rights of each person as articulated in the Covenant.[46]

The principle of reciprocity is deeply rooted in the VCLT regime, for example, in the opposability of a reservation by a non-reserving state against a reserving state.[47] This is important because the central argument of the HRC is that this notion of reciprocity is inconsistent with the nature of human rights treaties:[48]

---

[42] For support for this view see G Gaja, 'Unruly Treaty Reservations' in *Le Droit International A l'heure de sa codification. Etudes en l'honneur de Roberto Ago* vol I (Guifre, Milan, 1987) at 307–30; LDM Nelson, 'Declarations, Statements and "Disguised Reservations" with respect to the Convention on the Law of the Sea' (2001) 50 *ICLQ* 767 at 783–4 and the literature cited there.

[43] For the contrary view see JM Ruda, 'Reservations to Treaties', (1975-III) 146 *Hag Rec* 97; the question was raised by A Pellet in his 'First Report on the Law and Practice Relating to Reservations to Treaties' A/CN.4/470 (1995) at para 124.

[44] ILC Report A/52/10, (1997), n 186.

[45] See G Hand, 'Policy Aspects of Reservations and Objections to Human Rights Conventions' in Gardner, *Human Rights as General Norms*, n 37 above 117; J McBride, 'Reservations and the Capacity of States to Implement Human Rights Treaties' *ibid* 120.

[46] GC 24 at para 4.

[47] See Arts 20–23 VCLT.

[48] In the *Reservations* case the ICJ also recognised this point, 'In such a Convention the Contracting states do not have any interests of their own; they merely have, one and all, a common interest, namely, the accomplishment of those high purposes which are the *raison d'être* of the Convention. Consequently, in a Convention of this type one cannot speak of individual advantages or disadvantages of states, or of the maintenance of a perfect contractual balance between rights or duties', n 32 above at 12. The European Court of Human Rights has similarly rejected the notion of reciprocity in ECHR context except where explicitly stated by ECHR, see Pt 4 K below for comparative perspectives.

... it is the Vienna Convention on the Law of Treaties that provides the definition of reservations and also the application of the object and purpose test in the absence of other specific provisions. But the Committee believes that its provisions on the role of State objections in relation to reservations are inappropriate to address the problem of reservations to human rights treaties. Such treaties, and the Covenant specifically, are not a web of inter-State exchanges of mutual obligations. They concern the endowment of individuals with rights. The principle of inter-State reciprocity has no place, save perhaps in the limited context of reservations to declarations on the Committee's competence under Article 41. And because the operation of the classic rules on reservations is so inadequate for the Covenant, States have often not seen any legal interest in or need to object to reservations. The absence of protest by States cannot imply that a reservation is either compatible or incompatible with the object and purpose of the Covenant. Objections have been occasional, made by some States but not others, and on grounds not always specified; when an objection is made, it often does not specify a legal consequence, or sometimes even indicates that the objecting party none the less does not regard the Covenant as not in effect as between the parties concerned. In short, the pattern is so unclear that it is not safe to assume that a non-objecting State thinks that a particular reservation is acceptable. In the view of the Committee, because of the special characteristics of the Covenant as a human rights treaty, it is open to question what effect objections have between States *inter se*. However, an objection to a reservation made by States may provide some guidance to the Committee in its interpretation as to its compatibility with the object and purpose of the Covenant.[49]

The VCLT provides a residual regime and it is open to states to make specific provision for reservations, including in international human rights instruments. Thus, Article 20(2) ICERD provides that:

A reservation incompatible with the object and purpose of this convention shall not be permitted, nor shall a reservation the effect of which would inhibit the operation of any of the bodies established by the Convention be allowed. A reservation shall be considered incompatible or inhibitive if at least two-thirds of the States Parties to the Convention object to it.

Where such express provision is made the monitoring body may defer to this system. The CERD took the view that any decision it made on the acceptability of a reservation would have no legal effect.[50] However, the reality has been that there have been few objections to reservations and there has never even been a likelihood that the two-thirds requirement would be met. The Committee on the Elimination of Discrimination Against Women (CEDAW) expressly states that it does not permit reservations which are incompatible with the object and purpose of the treaty.[51] CEDAW has previously taken the view that it was incompetent to express a view as to the compatibility of reservations.[52]

[49] GC 24 at para 17. See Y Tyagi, 'The Conflict on Law and Policy on Reservations to Human Rights Treaties', (2001) 72 *BYIL* 181.

[50] A/33/18 at p 35. This reflected advice it received from the UN office of Legal Affairs, *UN Juridical Yearbook* (1976) at 216–18. Individual members of CERD have expressed disagreement with this view.

[51] Art 28. So does the UN Convertion on the Rights of the Child (1989), Art 51(2).

[52] A/42/38 at para 112. See text to n 108 below. The Committee on the Rights of the Child has also been cautious and stressed the dialogue nature of its work.

C. The ICCPR, OP1 and Reservations

Neither the ICCPR nor OP1 prohibit reservations nor mentions any type of permitted reservation. Article 2(1) OP2 (which deals with the death penalty) excludes
reservations with one exception, namely, a reservation made at the time of ratification or accession that provides for the application of the death penalty in time
of war pursuant to a conviction for a most serious crime of a military nature committed during wartime. Reservations were extensively discussed during the drafting of the ICCPR and, to a lesser extent, OP1, but no agreement could be reached,
despite a GA direction that there should be provisions on reservations. The
Human Rights Committee recognised that it would be difficult to apply the object
and purpose test. It is accepted that the absence of a prohibition on reservations
does not mean that any reservation is permitted:

> The matter of reservations under the Covenant and the first Optional Protocol is
> governed by international law. Article 19 (3) of the Vienna Convention on the Law
> of Treaties provides relevant guidance. [n2: Although the Vienna Convention on the
> Law of Treaties was concluded in 1969 and entered into force in 1980—ie after the
> entry into force of the Covenant—its terms reflect the general international law on
> this matter as had already been affirmed by the International Court of Justice in *The
> Reservations to the Genocide Convention* Case of 1951.] It stipulates that where a reser-
> vation is not prohibited by the treaty or falls within the specified permitted categories,
> a State may make a reservation provided it is not incompatible with the object and
> purpose of the treaty. Even though, unlike some other human rights treaties, the
> Covenant does not incorporate a specific reference to the object and purpose test,
> *that test governs the matter of interpretation and acceptability of reservations.*[53]

It is helpful to put the relevant legal periods in chronological order. The issue of
reservations was considered intermittently during the drafting of the ICCPR and
OP1, that is, from 1948 until its adoption in 1966. Both the ICCPR and OP1
entered into force in 1976. The ICJ opinion in the *Reservations* Case was issued
in 1951. The VCLT was adopted in 1969, with significant changes in drafting
between 1966 and 1969. It entered into force in 1980. As a treaty, the VCLT
expressly States that it does not have retrospective application, but much of
the VCLT is recognised as stating customary international law.[54] As the number
of States Parties to the human rights treaties, and to the ICCPR in particular,
expanded, the phenomena of extensive numbers of reservations emerged.[55] There
have been a significant number of reservations to the ICCPR and a number of
reservations to OP1.[56] There has been one reservation to OP2. Only a small

---

[53] GC24 at para 6 (emphasis added).
[54] Art 4, VCLT.
[55] See Gardner, *Human Rights as General Norms*, n 37 above.
[56] See the website in n 39 above; M Schmidt, 'Reservations to United Nations Human Rights
Treaties—the Case of the Two Covenants', in Gardner, n 37 above at 20; Lijnzaad, *Reservations to UN
Human Rights Treaties*, n 40 above at 185–297.

number of reservations to the ICCPR have been withdrawn. The title of one academic commentary, *Reservations to UN Human Rights Treaties: Ratify and Ruin?*[57] clearly expressed the issue. The argument put was that the integrity of the human rights treaty monitoring system was being systematically undermined.[58] In 1994 the chairpersons of the various treaty bodies recommended that the treaty bodies state the position clearly when faced with incompatible reservations.[59] The United States had ratified the ICCPR in 1992 with three reservations, five understandings and two declarations. These were widely discussed and had attracted objections from eleven European States. The first report of the US on its implementation of the ICCPR was scheduled for 1995 so the issues were very much on the HRC's agenda.

D. The HRC's General Comment on Reservations

The HRC's specific response to the phenomena was General Comment 24 on *Issues relating to reservations made upon ratification or accession to the Covenant or the Optional Protocols thereto, or in relation to declarations under Article 41 of the Covenant*, adopted in November 1994.[60] The GC drew specific responses from the US,[61] the UK[62] and France.[63] The GC stated the context as follows:

> As of 1 November 1994, 46 of the 127 States parties to the International Covenant on Civil and Political Rights had, between them, entered 150 reservations of varying significance to their acceptance of the obligations of the Covenant. Some of these reservations exclude the duty to provide and guarantee particular rights in the Covenant. Others are couched in more general terms, often directed to ensuring the continued paramountcy of certain domestic legal provisions. Still others are directed at the competence of the Committee. The number of reservations, their content and their scope may undermine the effective implementation of the Covenant and tend to weaken respect for the obligations of States parties. It is important for States parties to know exactly what obligations they, and other States parties, have in fact undertaken.[64]

---

[57] See n 40 above.

[58] See R Higgins, 'The United Nations: Some Questions of Integrity' (1989) 52 *MLR* 1. Higgins was then a member of the HRC and is considered by some to have been the driving force behind GC 24. The Vienna Declaration and Programme of Action (1993) urged states to avoid reservations as much as possible and to limit the scope of those deemed necessary, UNDoc A/CONF.157/24, Pt I, para 26 Pt II, para 5. The question of competence was not addressed.

[59] UNDoc A/49/537 (1994).

[60] A/50/40, Annex V; C Redgwell, 'Reservations to Treaties and Human Rights Committee General Comment No 24 (52)', (1997) 46 *ICLQ* 390.

[61] US Observations on GC 24, A/50/40, Annex VI; (1995) 16 *HRLJ* 422; 3 *IHRR* 265.

[62] UK Observations on GC 24, A/50/40, Annex VI; (1995) 16 *HRLJ* 424; 3 *IHRR* 261.

[63] French Observations on GC 24, A/51/40, Annex VI; 4 *IHRR* 6.

[64] GC 24 at para 1. By the end of 2000, 55 of the 147 States parties had made reservations.

The GC continued by stating that

> ... the Committee, in the performance of its duties under either Article 40 of the Covenant or under the Optional Protocols, must know whether a State is bound by a particular obligation or to what extent. This will require a determination as to whether a unilateral statement is a reservation or an interpretative declaration and a determination of its acceptability and effects.

> For these reasons the Committee has deemed it useful to address in a General Comment the issues of international law and human rights policy that arise. The General Comment identifies the principles of international law that apply to the making of reservations and by reference to which their acceptability is to be tested and their purport to be interpreted. It addresses the role of States Parties in relation to the reservations of others. It further addresses the role of the Committee itself in relation to reservations. And it makes certain recommendations to present States Parties for a reviewing of reservations and to those States that are not yet parties about legal and human rights policy considerations to be borne in mind should they consider ratifying or acceding with particular reservations.

Paragraph 3 of the GC recalled the orthodox view of international law that it is the substance, and not the form, which is relevant to identifying a reservation:

> It is not always easy to distinguish a reservation from a declaration as to a State's understanding of the interpretation of a provision, or from a statement of policy. Regard will be had to the intention of the State, rather than the form of the instrument. If a statement, irrespective of its name or title, purports to exclude or modify the legal effect of a treaty in its application to the State, it constitutes a reservation. [n 1: Article 2 (1) (d), Vienna Convention on the Law of Treaties 1969.] Conversely, if a so-called reservation merely offers a State's understanding of a provision but does not exclude or modify that provision in its application to that State, it is, in reality, not a reservation.[65]

This approach has been refected in the HRC's jurisprudence. For example, France's 'Declaration' on Article 27 has been interpreted as a reservation to Article 27.[66]

Although the HRC accepted that reservations could serve a useful function in enabling States to adapt specific elements in their laws to the inherent rights of each person as articulated in the Covenant, it was 'desirable in principle that States accept the full range of obligations, because the human rights norms are the legal expression of the essential rights that every person is entitled to as a human being.'[67]

As noted above, the GC then asserted that it is the VCLT's test of compatibility with the object and purpose of the treaty that governs the matter of interpretation and acceptability of reservations. It then proceeded to give more detailed guidance on the 'object and purpose' of the ICCPR and how the test

---

[65] See generally D McRae, 'The Legal Effect of Interpretative Declarations' (1978) 49 *BYIL* 155.
[66] See *T.K. v France*, and *M.K. v France*, A/45/40, 118 and 127 and separate opinions of Ndiaye and Higgins.
[67] GC 24 at para 4.

should be applied to reservations to specific rights and to various categories of reservations.

> 7. In an instrument which articulates very many civil and political rights, each of the many Articles, and indeed their interplay, secures the objectives of the Covenant. The object and purpose of the Covenant is to create legally binding standards for human rights by defining certain civil and political rights and placing them in a framework of obligations which are legally binding for those States which ratify; and to provide an efficacious supervisory machinery for the obligations undertaken.[68]

It is not always easy to clearly identify the object and purpose of a multilateral treaty and so this statement of the object and purpose of the ICCPR is of crucial importance in approaching the issue of reservations. The reference to 'efficacious supervisory machinery' is also significant and is considered below.[69]

> 8. Reservations that offend peremptory norms would not be compatible with the object and purpose of the Covenant. Although treaties that are mere exchanges of obligations between States allow them to reserve *inter se* application of rules of general international law, it is otherwise in human rights treaties, which are for the benefit of persons within their jurisdiction. Accordingly, provisions in the Covenant that represent customary international law (and a fortiori when they have the character of peremptory norms) may not be the subject of reservations. Accordingly, a State may not reserve the right to engage in slavery, to torture, to subject persons to cruel, inhuman or degrading treatment or punishment, to arbitrarily deprive persons of their lives, to arbitrarily arrest and detain persons, to deny freedom of thought, conscience and religion, to presume a person guilty unless he proves his innocence, to execute pregnant women or children, to permit the advocacy of national, racial or religious hatred, to deny to persons of marriageable age the right to marry, or to deny to minorities the right to enjoy their own culture, profess their own religion, or use their own language. And while reservations to particular clauses of Article 14 may be acceptable, a general reservation to the right to a fair trial would not be.[70]

Again, human rights treaties, which are 'for the benefit of persons within their jurisdiction', are distinguished from those treaties which constitute 'mere exchanges of obligations between States.' That reservations that offend peremptory norms would not be compatible with the object and purpose of the Covenant seems to be uncontroversial.[71] However, the further assertion that provisions in the Covenant that represent customary international law may not be the subject of reservations has been criticised. The US stated that this was a sweeping premise that was wholly unsupported by and was in fact contrary to international

---

[68] GC 24 at para 7.
[69] See Part 4 G below.
[70] GC 24 at para 8.
[71] France reaffirmed its view that it does not accept the doctrine of *jus cogens*, n 63 above at para 2. In 2001 France announced that it had changed policy and did now accept the doctrine of *jus cogens*.

law.[72] The UK considered that it was 'doubtful' that the proposition represented existing customary international law and noted that states had not expressly objected to reservations on this ground. There was a clear distinction between choosing not to enter into treaty obligations and trying to opt out of customary international law.[73] France commented that it would be 'premature, to say the least, to claim that all of the examples cited in the report fit the definition of international custom. . . .'[74] Higgins has argued that these criticisms are not realistic. They assume that such reservations are not aimed at denying the norm, but merely denying the competence of the HRC to monitor the norm. However, 'the reality is that States don't make such a distinction—they seek rather to reserve the application of the right, with Committee non-competence in relation thereto being a necessary consequence.'[75] The assertion in the GC could only relate to customary international law that is universal or to that which is binding on the particular state. Some academic commentators have questioned the customary law status of the provisions referred to in this paragraph.[76] In particular, the customary law status of the prohibition on the advocacy of national, racial or religious hatred has been questioned in the light of reservations by a number of states. In reality those reservations have been directed to the most appropriate way of securing the prohibition or consistency with other ICCPR rights rather than denying its normative force.[77] The HRC itself has not suggested to states that such reservations were invalid, but rather that Article 19 on freedom of expression could be interpreted consistently with Article 20.[78] Similarly, the customary status of Article 27 (on minorities) has been questioned because the issue is still seen as controversial. However, it is strongly arguable that Article 27 does constitute a basic customary minimum. As noted, France has made a declaration to Article 27 which the HRC has treated as a valid reservation.[79]

9. Applying more generally the object and purpose test to the Covenant, the Committee notes that, for example, reservation to Article 1 denying peoples the right to determine their own political status and to pursue their economic, social and cultural development, would be incompatible with the object and purpose of the Covenant. Equally, a reservation to the obligation to respect and ensure the rights, and to do so on a non-discriminatory basis (Article 2 (1)) would not be acceptable. Nor may a State reserve an entitlement not to take the necessary steps at the domestic level to give effect to the rights of the Covenant (Article 2 (2)).[80]

---

[72] See n 61, above.
[73] See n 62, above.
[74] France, n 63 above at para 2.
[75] R Higgins, 'Introduction' to Gardner, *Human Rights as General Norms*, n 37 above, xv at xxviii.
[76] See M Nowak, 'The Activities of the UN HRC' (1995) 16 *HRLJ* 377.
[77] See, for example, the UK reservation to Art 20 ICCPR.
[78] See GC 10/19, A/38/40, 109.
[79] See 66 above. One possible reconciliation of the position in the GC with the HRC's treatment of the declaration as a valid reservation is that the reservation was concerned with the application of Art 27 rather than its substantive content.
[80] GC 24 at para 9. India made a reservation to Art 1 which attracted objections.

Self-determination is often considered to be a peremptory norm and would be contrary to the object and purpose of the ICCPR on that basis. Reservations to the basic implementation guarantees in Article 2 (1) and (2) would also seem to be fundamentally at odds with the object and purpose of the ICCPR.

10. The Committee has further examined whether categories of reservations may offend the "object and purpose" test. In particular, it falls for consideration as to whether reservations to the non-derogable provisions of the Covenant are compatible with its object and purpose. While there is no hierarchy of importance of rights under the Covenant, the operation of certain rights may not be suspended, even in times of national emergency. This underlines the great importance of non-derogable rights. But not all rights of profound importance, such as Articles 9 and 27 of the Covenant, have in fact been made non-derogable. One reason for certain rights being made non-derogable is because their suspension is irrelevant to the legitimate control of the state of national emergency (for example, no imprisonment for debt, in Article 11). Another reason is that derogation may indeed be impossible (as, for example, freedom of conscience). At the same time, some provisions are non-derogable exactly because without them there would be no rule of law. A reservation to the provisions of Article 4 itself, which precisely stipulates the balance to be struck between the interests of the State and the rights of the individual in times of emergency, would fall in this category. And some non-derogable rights, which in any event cannot be reserved because of their status as peremptory norms, are also of this character—the prohibition of torture and arbitrary deprivation of life are examples. [n 3: Reservations have been entered to both Article 6 and Article 7, but not in terms which reserve a right to torture or to engage in arbitrary deprivation of life.] While there is no automatic correlation between reservations to non-derogable provisions, and reservations which offend against the object and purpose of the Covenant, a State has a heavy onus to justify such a reservation.

The UK agreed that an automatic identification between non-derogability and compatibility with the object and purpose was too simplistic.[81]

11. The Covenant consists not just of the specified rights, but of important supportive guarantees. These guarantees provide the necessary framework for securing the rights in the Covenant and are thus essential to its object and purpose. Some operate at the national level and some at the international level. Reservations designed to remove these guarantees are thus not acceptable. Thus, a State could not make a reservation to Article 2, paragraph 3, of the Covenant, indicating that it intends to provide no remedies for human rights violations. Guarantees such as these are an integral part of the structure of the Covenant and underpin its efficacy. The Covenant also envisages, for the better attainment of its stated objectives, a monitoring role for the Committee. Reservations that purport to evade that essential element in the design of the Covenant, which is

---

[81] n 62 above at para 6. The Inter-American Court of Human Rights has accepted that reservations to a non-derogable right that did not deprive those rights of their basic purpose could be consistent with the object and purpose of the ACHR, *Restrictions on the Death Penalty* (1983) 4 *HRLJ* 345 at para 61.

also directed to securing the enjoyment of the rights, are also incompatible with its object and purpose. A State may not reserve the right not to present a report and have it considered by the Committee. The Committee's role under the Covenant, whether under Article 40 or under the Optional Protocols, necessarily entails interpreting the provisions of the Covenant and the development of a jurisprudence. Accordingly, a reservation that rejects the Committee's competence to interpret the requirements of any provisions of the Covenant would also be contrary to the object and purpose of that treaty.

This paragraph suggests that some limitations on remedies could be consistent with the object and purpose, but that would not be the case if no remedies at all are provided.

12. The intention of the Covenant is that the rights contained therein should be ensured to all those under a State party's jurisdiction. To this end certain attendant requirements are likely to be necessary. Domestic laws may need to be altered properly to reflect the requirements of the Covenant; and mechanisms at the domestic level will be needed to allow the Covenant rights to be enforceable at the local level. Reservations often reveal a tendency of States not to want to change a particular law. And sometimes that tendency is elevated to a general policy. Of particular concern are widely formulated reservations which essentially render ineffective all Covenant rights which would require any change in national law to ensure compliance with Covenant obligations. No real international rights or obligations have thus been accepted. And when there is an absence of provisions to ensure that Covenant rights may be sued on in domestic courts, and, further, a failure to allow individual complaints to be brought to the Committee under the first Optional Protocol, all the essential elements of the Covenant guarantees have been removed.

The UK did not 'wholly share' the HRC's concerns over reservations excluding the acceptance of obligations which would require changes in national law to ensure compliance. It argued that such states at least accepted the HRC's supervision under the reporting system of 'those Covenant rights guaranteed by their national law.'[82] However, as Higgins correctly observed, the purpose of the HRC is to supervise the Covenant rights, not to supervise compliance with national law.[83] The real issue is where a state systematically reserves all Covenant rights that are not already part of domestic law. In doing so, it is denying the autonomous status of the Covenant. The US reservations are open to criticism on this basis.

The GC then addressed the permissibility of reservations to OP1:

13. The issue arises as to whether reservations are permissible under the first Optional Protocol and, if so, whether any such reservation might be contrary to the object and purpose of the Covenant or of the first Optional Protocol itself. It is clear that the first Optional Protocol is itself an international treaty, distinct from the Covenant but closely related to it. Its object and purpose is to recog-

---

[82] n 62 above at para 8.
[83] Higgins, 'Introduction', n 75 above at xxix.

nize the competence of the Committee to receive and consider communications from individuals who claim to be victims of a violation by a State party of any of the rights in the Covenant. States accept the substantive rights of individuals by reference to the Covenant, and not the first Optional Protocol. The function of the first Optional Protocol is to allow claims in respect of those rights to be tested before the Committee. Accordingly, a reservation to an obligation of a State to respect and ensure a right contained in the Covenant, made under the first Optional Protocol when it has not previously been made in respect of the same rights under the Covenant, does not affect the State's duty to comply with its substantive obligation. A reservation cannot be made to the Covenant through the vehicle of the Optional Protocol but such a reservation would operate to ensure that the State's compliance with that obligation may not be tested by the Committee under the first Optional Protocol. And because the object and purpose of the first Optional Protocol is to allow the rights obligatory for a State under the Covenant to be tested before the Committee, a reservation that seeks to preclude this would be contrary to the object and purpose of the first Optional Protocol, even if not of the Covenant. A reservation to a substantive obligation made for the first time under the first Optional Protocol would seem to reflect an intention by the State concerned to prevent the Committee from expressing its views relating to a particular Article of the Covenant in an individual case.

The HRC referred back to this paragraph in its leading decision on reservations in *Kennedy* which is considered below.[84] France stated that, 'any maximalist interpretations would result in discouraging new states from acceding to the optional Protocol.'[85]

The GC continued:

14. The Committee considers that reservations relating to the required procedures under the first Optional Protocol would not be compatible with its object and purpose. The Committee must control its own procedures as specified by the Optional Protocol and its rules of procedure. Reservations have, however, purported to limit the competence of the Committee to acts and events occurring after entry into force for the State concerned of the first Optional Protocol. In the view of the Committee this is not a reservation but, most usually, a statement consistent with its normal competence *ratione temporis*. At the same time, the Committee has insisted upon its competence, even in the face of such statements or observations, when events or acts occurring before the date of entry into force of the first Optional Protocol have continued to have an effect on the rights of a victim subsequent to that date. Reservations have been entered which effectively add an additional ground of inadmissibility under Article 5, paragraph 2, by precluding examination of a communication when the same matter has already been examined by another comparable procedure. In so far as the most basic obligation has been to secure independent third party review of the human rights of individuals, the Committee has, where the legal right and the subject-matter are

---

[84] See Pt 4 G below.
[85] France, n 63 above at para 4.

identical under the Covenant and under another international instrument, viewed such a reservation as not violating the object and purpose of the first Optional Protocol.

The GC then addressed reservations to OP2:

15. The primary purpose of the Second Optional Protocol is to extend the scope of the substantive obligations undertaken under the Covenant, as they relate to the right to life, by prohibiting execution and abolishing the death penalty. [n 4: The competence of the Committee in respect of this extended obligation is provided for under Article 5—which itself is subject to a form of reservation in that the automatic granting of this competence may be reserved through the mechanism of a statement made to the contrary at the moment of ratification or accession.] It has its own provision concerning reservations, which is determinative of what is permitted. Article 2, paragraph 1, provides that only one category of reservation is permitted, namely one that reserves the right to apply the death penalty in time of war pursuant to a conviction for a most serious crime of a military nature committed during wartime. Two procedural obligations are incumbent upon States parties wishing to avail themselves of such a reservation. Article 2, paragraph 1, obliges such a State to inform the Secretary-General, at the time of ratification or accession, of the relevant provisions of its national legislation during warfare. This is clearly directed towards the objectives of specificity and transparency and in the view of the Committee a purported reservation unaccompanied by such information is without legal effect. Article 2, paragraph 3, requires a State making such a reservation to notify the Secretary-General of the beginning or ending of a state of war applicable to its territory. In the view of the Committee, no State may seek to avail itself of its reservation (that is, have execution in time of war regarded as lawful) unless it has complied with the procedural requirement of Article 2, paragraph 3.

The ICCPR does not expressly state the HRC's competence in respect of reservations, so it could only be a matter of implied or inherent jurisdiction. The GC addressed this question as follows:

16. The Committee finds it important to address which body has the legal authority to make determinations as to whether specific reservations are compatible with the object and purpose of the Covenant. As for international treaties in general, the International Court of Justice has indicated in the *Reservations to the Genocide Convention* Case (1951) that a State which objected to a reservation on the grounds of incompatibility with the object and purpose of a treaty could, through objecting, regard the treaty as not in effect as between itself and the reserving State. Article 20, paragraph 4, of the Vienna Convention on the Law of Treaties 1969 contains provisions most relevant to the present case on acceptance of and objection to reservations. This provides for the possibility of a State to object to a reservation made by another State. Article 21 deals with the legal effects of objections by States to reservations made by other States. Essentially, a reservation precludes the operation, as between the reserving and other States, of the provision reserved; and an objection thereto leads to the reservation being

in operation as between the reserving and objecting State only to the extent that it has not been objected to.

17. As indicated above, it is the Vienna Convention on the Law of Treaties that provides the definition of reservations and also the application of the object and purpose test in the absence of other specific provisions. But the Committee believes that its provisions on the role of State objections in relation to reservations are inappropriate to address the problem of reservations to human rights treaties. Such treaties, and the Covenant specifically, are not a web of inter-State exchanges of mutual obligations. They concern the endowment of individuals with rights. The principle of inter-State reciprocity has no place, save perhaps in the limited context of reservations to declarations on the Committee's competence under Article 41. And because the operation of the classic rules on reservations is so inadequate for the Covenant, States have often not seen any legal interest in or need to object to reservations. The absence of protest by States cannot imply that a reservation is either compatible or incompatible with the object and purpose of the Covenant. Objections have been occasional, made by some States but not other, and on grounds not always specified; when an objection is made, it often does not specify a legal consequence, or sometimes even indicates that the objecting party none the less does not regard the Covenant as not in effect as between the parties concerned. In short, the pattern is so unclear that it is not safe to assume that a non-objecting State thinks that a particular reservation is acceptable. In the view of the Committee, because of the special characteristics of the Covenant as a human rights treaty, it is open to question what effect objections have between States *inter se*. However, an objection to a reservation made by States may provide some guidance to the Committee in its interpretation as to its compatibility with the object and purpose of the Covenant.

France was unable to endorse the opinion that the provisions of VCLT on the role of state objections were inappropriate to address the problem of reservations to human rights treaties. It did not think different rules should apply and drew attention to the, 'unjustified assumption that State parties would not use their right to object to reservations with the appropriate discernment or care.'[86] The HRC continued by addressing its competence in relation to the validity and effect of reservations,

18. It necessarily falls to the Committee to determine whether a specific reservation is compatible with the object and purpose of the Covenant. This is in part because, as indicated above, it is an inappropriate task for States parties in relation to human rights treaties, and in part because it is a task that the Committee cannot avoid in the performance of its functions. In order to know the scope of its duty to examine a State's compliance under Article 40 or a communication under the first Optional Protocol, the Committee has necessarily to take a view on the compatibility of a reservation with the object and purpose of the Covenant and with general international law. Because of the special character of a human

---

[86] France, n 63 above at para 6.

> rights treaty, the compatibiliy of a reservation with the object and purpose of the Covenant must be established *objectively*, by reference to legal principles, and the Committee is particularly well placed to perform this task. The *normal consequence* of an unacceptable reservation is not that the Covenant will not be in effect at all for a reserving party. Rather, such a reservation will generally be severable, in the sense that the Covenant will be operative for the reserving party without benefit of the reservation. (*emphases added*)

The UK accepted that the HRC must necessarily be able to take a view as to the status and effect of a reservation where this is required in order to permit it to carry out its substantive functions under the ICCPR, namely, the reporting procedure, the individual petition procedure and the Article 41 inter-state procedure. It had a particular concern because of the use of the verb 'determine' in relation to the reservations. It commented that the HRC only had competence to the extent provided for by the ICCPR, that a conclusion on the status or consequences of a particular reservation could only be 'determinative' if it were binding on the reserving party and all other parties, and that there was a qualitative distinction between decisions judicially arrived at and determination without the benefit of full judicial process.[87] The US also stressed that the HRC had no power to render definitive or binding interpretations of the ICCPR. It is clear that the HRC does not make binding legal decisions and certainly its General Comments are not legally binding as such. Higgins has replied that too much should not be read into the verb 'determine'. Moreover, '[t]he answer cannot be that the Committee lacks authority to render binding interpretations or judgments. That is to confuse competence to do something with binding legal effect of that which is done.'[88] It is submitted that determining whether a specific reservation is compatible with the object and purpose of the ICCPR or an Optional Protocol is a necessary part of the HRC fulfilling its functions. A distinction in competence based on the distinction between whether bodies can issue binding decisions would lead to a view that the former European Commission on Human Rights would not have had the necessary competence but the European Court of Human rights would have. The European Commission did not follow this distinction.[89]

On the issue of severance there was also a strong reaction. For the US, the HRC's approach was completely at odds with established legal practice. For France it was incompatible with the law of treaties. In its view, the only course open is to 'declare that this consent is not valid and decide that these states cannot be considered parties to the instrument in question; it is for the states parties alone, unless the treaty says otherwise, to decide whether a reservation is incompatible with the object and purpose of the treaty.' The UK was more cautious, 'severability of a kind may offer a solution in appropriate cases, although its contours are only beginning to be explained in state practice'—however, severability would have to

---

[87] n 62 above at para 12. Presumably the ITLOS would satisfy the UK's criteria.
[88] n 75 above at xxii.
[89] See n 141 below.

be applied both to the reservation and the relevant provisions of the treaty. It considered this to be the solution adopted by the ICJ in the *Reservations Case*. Thus the only sound approach was that, 'a State which purports to ratify a human rights treaty subject to a reservation which is fundamentally incompatible with participation in the treaty regime cannot be regarded as having become a party at all.' However, it is not clear that the ICJ did consider this to be the only solution in the *Reservations Case*.[90] The language used by the UK sets a high test, namely 'fundamentally incompatible.' Moreover, 'participation in a treaty regime' is a rather ambiguous expression.[91] In any event, the HRC has followed [the] practice of the European Court of Human Rights (though there have only been a small number of Strasbourg cases). Moreover, what is referred to as the 'Strasbourg approach' has not elicited criticism from either the UK or France. It is notable that the wording of GC is very careful, viz., 'normal' and 'generally be severable.' For Higgins, 'the special character of human rights treaties militates in favour of severability without the setting aside of general acceptance, unless the latter course is absolutely unavoidable.'[92] Moreover, some state practice outside of the human rights treaties may also support the HRC's approach. Nelson has noted that, 'State practice to date with respect to "impermissible reservations" in the framework of the Convention on the Law of the Sea support the view that such reservations are null and void and that the reserving state remains a party to the Convention and is bound by the entire Convention—thus following the so-called integrity principle.'[93]

The GC continued by stating further general limitations on reservations and giving practical guidance:

19. Reservations must be specific and transparent, so that the Committee, those under the jurisdiction of the reserving State and other States parties may be clear as to what obligations of human rights compliance have or have not been undertaken. Reservations may thus not be general, but must refer to a particular provision of the Covenant and indicate in precise terms its scope in relation thereto. When considering the compatibility of possible reservations with the object and purpose of the Covenant, States should also take into consideration the overall effect of a group of reservations, as well as the effect of each reservation on the integrity of the Covenant, which remains an essential consideration. States should not enter so many reservations that they are in effect accepting a limited number of human rights obligations, and not the Covenant as such. So that reservations do not lead to a perpetual non-attainment of international human rights standards, reservations should not systematically reduce the obligations undertaken only to those presently existing in less demanding standards of domestic law. Nor should interpretative declarations or reservations seek to remove an

---

[90] n 32 above at 26.
[91] *Quare* whether it would cover general reservations by Islamic states by reference to consistency with Islamic law.
[92] n 75 above at xxvii.
[93] Nelson, '*Disguised Reservations*', n 42 above at 781–2. See also RW Edwards, 'Reservations to Treaties' (1989) 10 *Michigan J Int L* 362.

autonomous meaning to Covenant obligations, by pronouncing them to be identical, or to be accepted only in so far as they are identical, with existing provisions of domestic law. States should not seek through reservations or interpretative declarations to determine that the meaning of a provision of the Covenant is the same as that given by an organ of any other international treaty body.

20. States should institute procedures to ensure that each and every proposed reservation is compatible with the object and purpose of the Covenant. It is desirable for a State entering a reservation to indicate in precise terms the domestic legislation or practices which it believes to be incompatible with the Covenant obligation reserved; and to explain the time period it requires to render its own laws and practices compatible with the Covenant, or why it is unable to render its own laws and practices compatible with the Covenant. States should also ensure that the necessity for maintaining reservations is periodically reviewed, taking into account any observations and recommendations made by the Committee during examination of their reports. Reservations should be withdrawn at the earliest possible moment. Reports to the Committee should contain information on what action has been taken to review, reconsider or withdraw reservations.

The UK argued that the problems did not 'provide a justification for a different legal regime to regulate reservations to human rights treaties.' To create such a special regime by amendment of the Covenant would be a major task. To do so as part of the development of general international law would, all other considerations aside, be undesirable if the effect was to fragment this aspect of the law of treaties . . .'[94]. The HRC's response would presumably be that there was no intention to create a 'different regime' but to determine whether the VCLT regime provided answers to new issues. The VCLT remains the central focus but there were practical problems caused by doubts about the operation of the VCLT system in a human rights context. In particular, as Higgins notes, the HRC was trying to answer a question which was not at issue in the ICJ's *Reservations Case*, was not considered in the VCLT negotiations and was not answered in the text of the VCLT itself: 'in a human rights treaty, in respect of which a monitoring body has been given certain functions, is it implicit in its functions and in the operation of the principles of Article 19(3) of the VCLT, that the treaty body rather than the contracting parties should decide whether a reservation is or is not compatible with the objects and purpose of the treaty?'[95] The difference of view is one of degree. The UK also challenged the view that human rights treaties 'are not a web of inter-state exchanges of mutual obligations' and that 'the principle of reciprocity has no place.' Rather, it argued that bilateralism and reciprocity did operate in a real and practical sense. Therefore, the reaction of parties to reservations was of direct significance both in law and in practice. The limited application of bilateralism and reciprocity to human rights treaties has been supported

---

[94] N 62 above at para 3. Cf Craven, *Legal Differentiation*, n 170 below.
[95] See Higgins, 'Introduction', n 75 above at xvii–xxii.

by the European Court of Human Rights and the Inter-American Court of Human Rights.[96]

The GA has recommended to states parties that they continually review whether any reservation to the ICCPR should be upheld.[97] It has referred to the sovereign right of states to make reservations in accordance with the relevant rules of international law. Since 1993 its resolutions have encouraged states to consider limiting the extent of any reservations, to formulate reservations as precisely and narrowly as possible, and to ensure that no reservation was incompatible with the object and purpose of the Covenant or otherwise contrary to international law.[98]

E. The Work of the International Law Commission

The ILC has been considering the law and practice relating to reservations since 1993 with Alain Pellet as Special Rapporteur.[99] In turn, the Sixth Committee of the GA has considered the reports of the ILC. In accordance with its established practice, the Special Rapporteur prepared a detailed questionnaire on reservations.[100] Pellet considered the two extremes. First, that states parties alone were competent to decide on the admissibility of reservations. Secondly, that the human rights monitoring bodies were competent to decide the permissibility of reservations and to draw all the necessary consequences of that determination.[101] He considered that neither of these positions was satisfactory. He proposed a middle ground. He conceptualized the human rights treaty bodies as 'consultative in character' rather than 'jurisdictional' (having the power to make decisions which are binding on states) in character. The treaty bodies could and should assess whether reservations were permissible when that was necessary for the exercise of their functions. He accepted that the human rights bodies had been created to monitor the implementation of their respective treaties. Consistently with that purpose, they had to determine the specific obligations of parties under the treaty, including reservations. However, they could go no further than this. They could not draw any consequences from such an assessment in the absence of a decision by the state concerned. It was not acceptable for the bodies to consider that they had the competence to determine whether or not the state was bound by the treaty. Given the consensual basis of treaties, drawing their strength from the will of states, the state alone could know the exact extent of its reservation. It was

---

[96] See Part 4, K below; *The Effect of Reservations on Entry Into Force of the American Convention,* Advisory Opinion OC–282 (1982).

[97] GA Resolution 40/115 at paras 9–10.

[98] GA Resolution 48/119 at para 9.

[99] For the reports see A.CN.4/470 and Corr 1 (1st), A/CN.4/477 and Add 1 (2nd), A/CN.4/491, Add 1–6 (3rd); A/CN.4/499 (4th), A/CN.4/508/Add 1–4 (5th); A/CN.4/518 and Add 1–3 (6th); 526 and Add 1–3 (2002). For a review see ILC's Annual Report, A/57/10, ch IV (2002). The issues remain controversial.

[100] As of 27 July 2000, 33 states and 24 international organisations had answered.

[101] A/52/10 at paras 78–81.

neither possible nor desirable for experts, whose legitimacy drew on the treaty and thus on the will of states, to replace elected governments in deciding on the intentions of those governments.[102] The possibilities for a government whose reservation had been determined by a human rights body to be impermissible were: (a) to maintain the reservation after having examined the determination in good faith; (b) to withdraw the reservation; (c) to 'regularize' the situation by replacing the impermissible reservation with a permissible one or (d) to denounce (or renounce) the treaty (if that is legally possible).[103] Pellet objected to the assertion by the HRC that it was the sole judge of the permissibility of reservations. State objections also exerted control by exercising significant pressure and being a useful guide for the assessment of the permissibility of a reservation by the HRC. The objection carries little force as the HRC itself accepted that states had a role in objecting.[104] There were disagreements between members of the ILC and a wide range of views was expressed. Some were concerned that decisions on permissibility and effect could be made many years after the reservations were made and that this jeopardised the stability of treaty relations. States alone could determine the permissibility of reservations. Other ILC members accepted the thrust of the HRC's argument that the VCLT regime of objections had simply not worked satisfactorily and that the treaty bodies had a proper role as guardians of their respective treaties.

In 1997 the ILC adopted, with some hesitation, 'Preliminary Conclusions on Reservations to Normative Multilateral Treaties, Including Human Rights Treaties'.[105] Among these were that (i) the VCLT regime applied equally to normative, law-making treaties, such as the human rights treaties (paras 1–2); (ii) where a human rights treaty established a monitoring body, unless the treaty provided otherwise, the body was competent only to comment on and make recommendations as to the admissibility of reservations (para 5) (this appears to be an express disagreement with the HRC's view); (iii) the legal force of the findings made by monitoring bodies in the exercise of their power to deal with reservations could not exceed that resulting from the powers given to them for the performance of their general monitoring role (para 8); (iv) if a reservation was inadmissible it was the reserving state that had the responsibility to take action, for example, by withdrawing or modifying the reservation, or foregoing becoming a party (para 10); (v) the ILC's conclusions were without prejudice to the practices and rules developed by monitoring bodies within regional contexts (para 12). Even on these conclusions there were mixed views within the ILC and in the Sixth (Legal) Committee of the UN General Assembly.[106] There seems to be a consen-

---

[102] A/52/10 at para 83.
[103] See Pt 5 below for the HRC's view that the ICCPR is not open to denunciation.
[104] See GC 24 at para 17.
[105] A/52/10 at para 157.
[106] See A Aust, *Modern Treaty Law and Practice* (Cambridge University Press, Cambridge, 2000) at 124.

sus among states that the VCLT regime applies to all treaties, whatever their subject matter and character. The disagreements relate to how some of the key Articles of the VCLT are to be interpreted, the competence of the monitoring bodies to determine legal effect and whether these determinations are authoritative. The ILC does not intend to propose amendments to the VCLT. Rather it is preparing a 'Guide to Practice'.[107] The guidelines deal with the procedural aspects of the formulation of reservations and interpretative declarations, but not their permissibility.

F. The Evolving Debate

All of the human rights treaty bodies were asked to submit a reaction to the ILC's preliminary conclusions on reservations. The meeting of the Chairpersons of the treaty organs strongly supported the approach of the HRC. They considered that the Preliminary Conclusions were unduly restrictive and did not accord sufficient attention to the fact that human rights treaties, by virtue of their subject-matter and the role they recognised for individuals, could not be placed on precisely the same footing as other treaties with different characteristics. They submitted that the capacity of a monitoring body to perform its function of determining the scope of the provisions of the relevant convention could not be performed effectively if it was precluded from exercising a similar function in relation to reservations. They recalled two general recommendations adopted by the CEDAW and noted the proposal by that Committee to adopt a further recommendation on the subject in conjunction with the fiftieth anniversary of the Universal Declaration of Human Rights[108] and expressed their firm support for the approach reflected in the HRC's GC 24.[109] The HRC expressed, 'concern about the views expressed by the ILC in paragraph 12 of its Preliminary Conclusions', in which it 'emphasizes that the above conclusions are without prejudice to the practices and rules developed by monitoring bodies within regional contexts.' In this connection, the Committee considered that, 'regional monitoring bodies are not the only intergovernmental institutions which participate in and contribute to the development of practices and rules. Universal monitoring bodies, such as the Human Rights Committee, play no less important a role in the process by which such practices and rules develop; the Committee is therefore entitled to participate in and contribute to such development. In this context the Committee stressed that the proposition enunciated by the Commission in paragraph 10 of the Provisional

---

[107] See A/55/10, ch VII.

[108] See A/53/318 at paras 21–23. The CEDAW Committee has emphasized that states parties might be willing to encourage other states parties to withdraw reservations. See R Cook, 'Reservations to the Convention on the Elimination of All Forms of Discrimination Against Women' (1990) 30 *Virg.J.I.L.* 643; B Clarke, 'The Vienna Convention Reservations Regime and the Convention on Discrimination Against Women' (1991) 85 *AJIL* 281–321.

[109] A/53/125, Annex at para 18 (report of ninth meeting of Chairpersons).

Conclusions is subject to modification as practices and rules developed by universal and regional monitoring bodies gain general acceptance.'[110]

In 1997 the Chairman of the CERD proposed to the UN Sub-Commission on the Promotion and Protection of Human Rights that it undertake a study on reservations to human rights treaties. The Sub-Commission appointed Francoise Hampson as Rapporteur and she submitted a 'Working Paper' in 1998.[111] This highlighted the principal issues. It suggested that the major controversy was concerned with the question, 'What is the effect of the view of an enforcement or monitoring body that a reservation is invalid on the reserving State's ratification and on other parties?' The paper put the problem in terms of an evolving debate to which the Sub-Commission could contribute. An extended working paper is to be submitted in 2003.[112]

Some authoritative academic commentators have supported the HRC's views on its competence.[113] Aust has been more critical. He argues that:

> it would be wrong to see human rights treaties as a special case, and the International Law Commission seems disinclined to do so. The problem of the legal effect of objections is the same for all the multilateral treaties, it is just that the problem occurs more often, and more acutely, with human rights treaties because they have to reconcile not just different national policies, but different religious and social systems. Moreover, the phenomenon of constitutional and domestic law reservations does not seem to have existed when the Convention was adopted in 1969, due no doubt to the fact that the era of modern universal human rights treaties only really began in 1966 with the two International Covenants.
>
> ... The problem of determining whether a reservation is permissible, and in particular whether it passes the compatibility test, is further compounded by the absence in most cases of a standing tribunal or other organ with competence to decide such matters. Regional human rights treaties, such as the European Convention on Human Rights and the American Convention on Human Rights, each have a standing court. Most modern universal human rights treaties establish no more than a committee of (albeit distinguished) independent experts to monitor the way in which the parties carry out their obligations.[114]
>
> ... The (HRC) is not empowered to give decisions binding on the parties. Nevertheless, in 1994 in its General Comment No 24 the Committee, in the course of expressing views on the problems or reservations, said that it must necessarily take a view as to the status and effect of a reservation if this is needed in order to carry out its functions under the Covenant, in particular considering reports from parties. The Committee gave the impression that it could in such circumstances make an authoritative determination. This view of the Committee has been severely criticised since

---

[110] E/CN.4/Sub.2/1998/25, Report of the Secretary-General.

[111] E/CN.4/Sub.2/1999/28.

[112] E/CN.4/Sub.2/Res/2001/17.

[113] See Boerefijn, *Covenant on Civil and Political Rights*, n 14 above at 107–8; Ghandhi, *The Human Rights Committee*, n 3 above at 356–86; Nowak, n 76 above; A Cassese, *International Law* (Oxford Uiversity Press, Oxford, 2001) at 130–31.

[114] Aust, *Modern Treaty Law and Practice*, n 106 above at 122.

it was not given the power to pronounce on general questions of international law. Nor can it be equated to an international court or tribunal, which reaches decisions binding on the parties only after hearing full legal arguments.[115]

Although the HRC was only concerned with the Covenant, the issues it raises are also relevant to other multilateral treaties such as the UN Convention on the Law of the Sea, which expressly prohibit reservations. It is interesting to note that the Vice-President of the International Tribunal in the Law of the Sea has argued that the flexible system in the VCLT cannot be applied to 'disguised reservations'.[116]

G. The HRC's Subsequent Application of its Approach to Reservations: the Kennedy Case

The HRC has subsequently maintained its view that it has competence to decide on the validity and effect of reservations, although members have differed on what those effects should be. The leading decision is that in *Rawle Kennedy v Trinidad and Tobago*.[117] Trinidad and Tobago acceded to the (First) Optional Protocol (OP1) in 1980. In June 1998 it denounced OP1 in accordance with Article 12 thereof, and it immediately reacceded to it, but this time with a reservation which excluded the competence of the Human Rights Committee to receive and consider communications (petitions) relating to, 'any prisoner who is under sentence of death in respect of any matter relating to his prosecution, his detention, his trial, his conviction, his sentence or the carrying out of the death sentence on him and any matter connected therewith.'[118] Trinidad and Tobago explained its actions by reference to the decision of the Judicial Committee of the Privy Council in *Pratt and Morgan v The Attorney-General for Jamaica*.[119] That decision effectively set a five-year constitutional limit between sentence and execution of a death penalty. Exceeding the limit would violate a constitutional prohibition on inhuman or degrading punishment or treatment. Trinidad and Tobago had a similar constitutional provision. Its problem was that, even if it ensured that its domestic system operated expeditiously, the time taken by the HRC to consider an application under OP1 would often take the period beyond the five years. Mere submission of a communication to the HRC would prevent application of the death sentence even if the HRC found no violation. Therefore, Trinidad and Tobago consulted with the Chairperson and the Bureau of the HRC to see if it could obtain assurances that death penalty cases would be dealt with expeditiously

---

[115] *Ibid* at 123. See also Barrata, 'Invalid Reservations' n 39 above.

[116] Nelson, 'Disguised Reservations' n 42 above at 783–4.

[117] CCPR/C/67/D/845/1999, A/55/40, Apx; (2000) 21 *HRLJ* 18. See PR Ghandi, 'The HRC and Reservations to the Optional Protocol' (2001) 8 *Canterbury L.R.* 13.

[118] (1999) 20 *HRLJ* 280. Trinidad and Tobago also denounced the American Convention on Human Rights; *ibid* at 281.

[119] [1994] 2 AC 1.

and completed within 18 months of registration. It was informed that no such assurance could be given.[120] Trinidad and Tobago considered that this had led to an increasing abuse of the procedures under OP1 by persons sentenced to death after due process in the national system and recourse to the Judicial Committee. It commented that, 'This occasions increasing resentment by the population of Trinidad and Tobago and can have adverse effects on the national security interests of the country in respect of persons convicted of drug-related murders'.

The communication in *Kennedy* was submitted four months after Trinidad and Tobago's purported reservation to OP1 took effect. It submitted that the reservation significantly impaired the competence of the Committee under OP1 to hear communications as it purported to exclude from consideration a broad range of cases, including many which would contain allegations of violations of non-derogable rights. The details of Kennedy's arguments were that:

— the Preamble to OP1, as well as its Articles 1 and 2, all state that OP1 gives competence to the HRC to receive and consider communications from individuals subject to the jurisdiction of a State party who claim to be victims of a violation by the State party of *any of the rights* set forth in the Covenant. A State party to the OP1 therefore accepts a single obligation in relation to all of the rights enumerated in the Covenant and cannot by reservation exclude consideration of a violation of any particular right. The rights enumerated in the Covenant include non-derogable human rights having *jus cogens* status. A State party cannot limit the competence of the Committee to review cases which engage rights with such status, and thus a State party cannot, for example, limit communications from prisoners under sentence of death alleging torture. The Committee would be faced with real difficulties if it was to deal with communications only in relation to certain rights, as many complaints necessarily involved allegations of violations of several of the Covenant's Articles. Trinidad and Tobago's reservation was without precedent and, in any event, there was little or no support for the practice of making reservations *rationae personae* or *ratione materiae* in relation to the OP1.

— in determining whether the reservation was compatible with the object and purpose of OP1 it was appropriate to recall that a State may not withdraw from OP1 for the purpose of shielding itself from international scrutiny in respect of its substantive obligations under the Covenant. Trinidad and Tobago's reservation would in effect serve that purpose and accordingly allow such an abuse to occur.

— the breadth of the reservation was suspect because it precluded consideration of any communications concerned not just with the imposition of the death penalty as such, but with every possible claim directly or even indirectly connected with the case merely because the death penalty has been imposed.[121]

Therefore, it was argued that the reservation was incompatible with the object and purpose of OP1. An incompatible reservation was invalid and without effect.[122] It could be severed from Trinidad and Tobago's re-accession to OP1, leaving the

---

[120] The same response was received from the Inter-American Commission on Human Rights.
[121] *Kennedy* at paras 3.15–3.17.
[122] *Ibid* at para 3.14.

HRC with jurisdiction to determine the merits of the case. The general principle of international law was that it was for the body to whose jurisdiction a purported reservation was addressed to decide on the validity and effect of that reservation. Therefore, it was for the HRC to make those determinations rather than the state party. Reference was made to the HRC's General Comment 24 on reservations and the Order of the ICJ of 4 December 1998 in the *Fisheries Jurisdiction* (*Spain v Canada*) case.[123]

Trinidad and Tobago submitted that the HRC was not competent to consider the communication. The HRC had exceeded its jurisdiction both (i) in registering the communication and (ii) in purporting to impose interim measures under its rules of procedure (to ensure that Kennedy was not executed until the HRC had determined the case). It considered the actions of the HRC to be void and of no binding effect.

Significantly, all members of the HRC reaffirmed the assertion in GC 24 that it was for the HRC, as the treaty body of the ICCPR and OP1, to interpret and determine the validity of reservations made to these treaties.[124] It therefore rejected the view that it had exceeded its jurisdiction by registering the communication and requesting interim measures. It observed that it was axiomatic that it had to register a communication before it could determine admissibility in the light of a reservation. It was accepted that if the reservation was valid than the HRC would not have jurisdiction to consider the case on the merits. This represents the established jurisprudence of the HRC. The crux of the case was whether or not the reservation was compatible with the object and purpose of OP1 and, if not, what were the effects. The HRC then referred back it its own GC, in which it had expressed the view that a reservation aimed at excluding the competence of the Committee under the OP1 with regard to certain provisions of the Covenant could not be considered to meet this test:

> The function of the first Optional Protocol is to allow claims in respect of [the Covenant's] rights to be tested before the Committee. Accordingly, a reservation to an obligation of a State to respect and ensure a right contained in the Covenant, made under the first Optional Protocol when it has not previously been made in respect of the same rights under the Covenant, does not affect the State's duty to comply with its substantive obligation. A reservation cannot be made to the Covenant through the vehicle of the Optional Protocol but such a reservation would operate to ensure that the State's compliance with that obligation may not be tested by the Committee under the first Optional Protocol. And because the object and purpose of the first Optional Protocol is to allow the rights obligatory for a State under the Covenant to be tested before the Committee, a reservation that seeks to preclude this *would be contrary to the object and purpose of the first Optional Protocol*, even if not of the Covenant.

The HRC noted that the reservation under consideration had been entered after the publication of GC 24 and did not purport to exclude the competence of the

---

[123] (1998) ICJ Reps 453.
[124] *Kennedy* at para 6.4, and dissenting opinion at para 1.

Committee under OP1 with regard to any specific provision of the Covenant, but rather to the entire Covenant for one particular group of complainants, namely prisoners under sentence of death. However, in its view, this did not make it compatible with the object and purpose of OP1:

> on the contrary, the Committee cannot accept a reservation which singles out a certain group of individuals for lesser procedural protection than that which is enjoyed by the rest of the population. In the view of the Committee, this constitutes a discrimination which runs counter to some of the basic principles embodied in the Covenant and its Protocols, and for this reason the reservation cannot be deemed compatible with the object and purpose of the Optional Protocol. The consequence is that the Committee is not precluded from considering the present communication under the Optional Protocol.[125]

The HRC states the consequence without explaining it. However, the clear assumption is that it applied its reasoning in GC 24 that severance was the 'normal' response to an invalid reservation.[126] In a separate opinion, Henkin deigned to state that 'I concur in the result'.

H. The Dissent in Kennedy

The decision of the HRC was accompanied by a well-argued dissenting joint opinion of Ando, Bhagwati, Klein and Kretzmer. They explicitly agreed with the HRC having competence jurisdiction to register the communication, issue interim measures, and consider whether the communication was admissible both in terms of its validity, as determined by the object and purpose test, and its effect. The dissent was based on their view that the communication was not admissible because (i) the reservation was valid and (ii) even if not valid, it could not be severed from Trinidad and Tobago's consent to OP1. On validity the dissent argued:

> 5. The Optional Protocol itself does not govern the permissibility of reservations to its provisions. In accordance with rules of customary international law that are reflected in Article 19 of the Vienna Convention on the Law of Treaties, reservations can therefore be made, provided they are compatible with the object and propose of the Optional Protocol. Thus, a number of States parties have made reservations to the effect that the Committee shall not have competence to consider communications which have already been considered under another procedure of international investigation or settlement. These reservations have been respected by the Committee.
>
> 6. The object and purpose of the Optional Protocol is to further the purposes of the Covenant and the implementation of its provisions by allowing international

---

[125] Para 6.7. On the merits the HRC found a number of violations, see A/57/50, Vol. 2, 161.
[126] GC 24 at para 18.

consideration of claims that an individual's rights under the Covenant have been violated by a State party. The purposes and implementation of the Covenant would indeed best be served if the Committee had the competence to consider every claim by an individual that his or her rights under the Covenant had been violated by a State party to the Covenant. However, assumption by a state of the obligation to ensure and protect all the rights set out in the Covenant does not grant competence to the Committee to consider individual claims. Such competence is acquired only if the State party to the Covenant also accedes to the Optional Protocol. If a State party is free either to accept or not accept an international monitoring mechanism, it is difficult to see why it should not be free to accept this mechanism only with regard to some rights or situations, provided the treaty itself does not exclude this possibility. All or nothing is not a reasonable maxim in human rights law.

7. The Committee takes the view that the reservation of the State party in the present case is unacceptable because it singles out one group of persons, those under sentence of death, for lesser procedural protection than that enjoyed by the rest of the population. According to the Committee's line of thinking this constitutes discrimination which runs counter to some of the basic principles embodied in the Covenant and its Protocols. We find this argument unconvincing.

8. It goes without saying that a State party could not submit a reservation that offends peremptory rules of international law. Thus, for example, a reservation to the Optional Protocol that discriminated between persons on grounds of race, religion or sex, would be invalid. However, this certainly does not mean that every distinction between categories of potential victims of violations by the State party is unacceptable. All depends on the distinction itself and the objective reasons for that distinction.

9. When dealing with discrimination that is prohibited under Article 26 of the Covenant, the Committee has consistently held that not every differentiation between persons amounts to discrimination. There is no good reason why this approach should not be applied here. As we are talking about a reservation to the Optional Protocol, and not to the Covenant itself, this requires us to examine not whether there should be any difference in the substantive rights of persons under sentence of death and those of other persons, but whether there is any difference between *communications* submitted by people under sentence of death and communications submitted by all other persons. The Committee has chosen to ignore this aspect of the matter, which forms the very basis for the reservation submitted by the State party.

10. The grounds for the denunciation of the Optional Protocol by the State party are set out in paragraph 6.3 of the Committee's views and there is no need to rehearse them here. What is clear is that the difference between communications submitted by persons under sentence of death and others is that they have different results. Because of the constitutional constraints of the State party the mere submission of a communication by a person under sentence of death may prevent the State party from carrying out the sentence imposed, *even if it transpires that*

the State party has complied with its obligations under the Covenant. In other words, the result of the communication is not dependent on the Committee's views on whether there has been a violation and if so what the recommended remedy is, but on mere submission of the communication. This is not the case with any other category of persons who might submit communications.

11. It must be stressed that if the constitutional constraints faced by the State party had placed it in a situation in which it was violating substantive Covenant rights, denunciation of the Optional Protocol, and subsequent reaccession, would not have been a legitimate step, as its object would have been to allow the State party to continue violating the Covenant with impunity. Fortunately, that is not the situation here. While the Committee has taken a different view from that taken by the Privy Council (in the case mentioned in paragraph 6.3 of the Committee's views) on the question of whether the mere time on death row makes delay in implementation of a death sentence cruel and inhuman punishment, a State party which adheres to the Privy Council view does not violate its obligations under the Covenant.

12. In the light of the above, we see no reason to consider the State party's reservation incompatible with the object and purpose of the Optional Protocol. As the reservation clearly covers the present communication (a fact that is not contested by the author), we would hold the communication inadmissible.

The dissent also dealt with the correct approach to an invalid reservation because of the importance of the question and because the HRC had expressed a view on it. The dissent referred back to GC 24 and the critical reaction to it:

14. In paragraph 6.7 of its Views the Committee states that it considers that the reservation cannot be deemed compatible with the object and purpose of the Optional Protocol. Having reached this conclusion the Committee adds that '[t]he consequence is that the Committee is not precluded from considering the present communication under the Optional Protocol.' It gives no reason for this 'consequence', which is far from self-evident. In the absence of an explanation in the Committee's Views themselves, we must assume that the explanation lies in the approach adopted by the Committee in its General Comment no. 24, which deals with reservations to the Covenant.

15. In General Comment no. 24 the Committee discussed the factors that make a reservation incompatible with the object and purpose of the Covenant. In paragraph 18 the Committee considers the consequences of an incompatible reservation and states:

The normal consequence of an unacceptable reservation is not that the Covenant will not be in effect at all for a reserving party. Rather, such a reservation will generally be severable, in the sense that the Covenant will be operative for the reserving party without benefit of the reservation.

It is no secret that this approach of the Committee has met with serious criticism. Many experts in international law consider the approach to be inconsistent with the basic premises of any treaty regime, which are that the treaty obligations of a state are a function of its consent to assume those obligations. If a reservation is incompatible with the object and purpose of a treaty, the critics argue, the reserving state does not become a party to the treaty unless it withdraws that reservation. According to the critics' view there is no good reason to depart from general principles of treaty law when dealing with reservations to the Covenant.

16. It is not our intention within the framework of the present case to reopen the whole issue dealt with in General Comment no. 24.[127] Suffice it to say that even in dealing with reservations to the Covenant itself the Committee did not take the view that in every case an unacceptable reservation will fall aside, leaving the reserving state to become a party to the Covenant without benefit of the reservation. As can be seen from the section of General Comment no. 24 quoted above, the Committee merely stated that this would *normally* be the case. The normal assumption will be that the ratification or accession is not dependent on the acceptability of the reservation and that the unacceptability of the reservation will not vitiate the reserving state's agreement to be a party to the Covenant. However, this assumption cannot apply when it is abundantly clear that the reserving state's agreement to becoming a party to the Covenant is *dependent* on the acceptability of the reservation. The same applies with reservations to the Optional Protocol.

17. As explained in paragraph 6.2 of the Committee's Views, on 26 May, 1998 the State party denounced the Optional Protocol and immediately reacceded with the reservation. It also explained why it could not accept the Committee's competence to deal with communications from persons under sentence of death. In these particular circumstances it is quite clear that Trinidad and Tobago *was not prepared to be a party to the Optional Protocol without the particular reservation, and that its re-accession was dependent on acceptability of that reservation.* It follows that if we had accepted the Committee's view that the reservation is invalid we would have had to hold that Trinidad and Tobago is not a party to the Optional Protocol. This would, of course, also have made the communication inadmissible. [emphasis added]

This reasoning on the severance issue seems to come down to an appreciation of what the intention of Trinidad and Tobago was. It clearly knew what it was trying to do. The majority took the view that despite this there was not enough evidence to dispense with the 'normal' consequence, namely severance. It may only be possible to displace this normal consequence if there is an express statement of conditionality when the reservation is made.

Trinidad and Tobago accepted that it remained under the substantive obligations of the Covenant in relation to all individuals and all rights. So matters concerning the death penalty have subsequently been considered under the reporting procedure. In relation to the specific problem of the death penalty within a time period, there have been important developments in the jurisprudence of the Judi-

---

[127] *Quaere* whether this implied that they thought that it should be reopened.

cial Committee of the Privy Council. In *Thomas and Hilaire v Baptiste, Peterson and The Attorney-General*[128] it decided that (i) constitutional rights of due process would be infringed if individuals were executed while their petitions were being determined by the Inter-American Commission on Human Rights but that (ii) excessive delays before such tribunals (eg HRC) would not on their own prevent a State from executing a condemned person. In effect, where more than eighteen months elapsed while a case was pending before an international body the five-year limit would be extended by that amount of time. Given Trinidad and Tobago's stated reasons for denunciation of OP1, it seemed that this decision should have prompted reconsideration of its reservation.

However, after *Kennedy*, the response of Trinidad and Tobago was to denounce the first Optional Protocol as a whole.[129] In November 2000 the HRC in its Concluding Observations on Trinidad and Tobago stated that, 'The Committee places on record its profound regret at the denunciation of the Optional Protocol.' [130] Trinidad and Tobago formally responded in the following terms:

> In respect of the Committee's regret at the denunciation by Trinidad and Tobago of the first Optional Protocol to the International Covenant on Civil and Political Rights, Trinidad and Tobago was happy to be a party to the first Optional Protocol subject to its reservation that the Committee had no jurisdiction in respect of capital cases. It was the Committee itself, by its decision in the case of *Rawle Kennedy*, where by a majority of nine to four it declared the reservation of Trinidad and Tobago invalid, which left the Government of Trinidad and Tobago with no alternative but to withdraw completely from the Protocol.[131]

Trinidad and Tobago explained that subsequent Privy Council decisions had not removed the need for the original reservation:

> There was some misunderstanding about the Privy Council's *Thomas v Baptise* ruling to the effect that it allowed an indeterminate amount of time for human rights bodies to review petitions relating to capital cases, the interpretation being that if the human rights bodies took more than 18 months to review the petition, it no longer counted as part of the 18 months established by the *Pratt and Morgan* ruling. That resulted in a contradictory situation in the sense that where a prisoner was held on death row for up to two years in the domestic system it was considered cruel and unusual punishment, but the same did not hold true for delays of longer than 18 months before a human rights body. In a recent Jamaican case the Privy Council had given a new interpretation to the *Thomas v Baptise* case, effectively reapplying the *Pratt and Morgan* decision by stating that it had no intention of altering the overall five-year period for the review of petitions in domestic courts and before international human

---

[128] [1999] 3 WLR 249 distinguished in *Briggs v Baptiste* [2000] 2 AC 40.

[129] See SR 1840. By that stage it had also already denounced the Inter-American Convention on Human Rights.

[130] CCPR/CO/70/TTO.

[131] Comments by the Government of Trinidad and Tobago on the Concluding Observations of HRC on Trinidad and Tobago, CCPR/CO/70/TTO/Add lat para 20 (15/01/2001).

rights bodies. In the light of that interpretation, his Government still had a valid reason for its denunciation of the Optional Protocol.[132]

I. Can a Reservation be Made on Re-accession?

An unusual feature of Trinidad and Tobago's reservation was that it was made on re-accession. Aust has also cast doubt on whether this strategy was effective. Although not excluded by the Protocol, he raised the question of, 'whether a party can reaccede solely for the purpose of making a reservation which it did not make originally, and which it was then too late to make?'[133] In any event, even if the reservation is not prohibited, another party would be entitled to object to it and state 'definitely' that the objection precludes the entry into force of the Protocol as between that party and Trinidad and Tobago.

J. Reservations and the Reporting Procedure

The HRC applies its approach to reservations in its consideration of state reports. For example, it considered the initial report of the United States in March 1995[134] and adopted concluding observations on it.[135] It took note of the critical US response to GC 24 and drew attention to observations made by the Chairman of the Committee.[136] The HRC regretted the, 'extent of the State party's reservations, declarations and understandings to the Covenant. It believes that, taken together, they intended to ensure that the United States has accepted only what is already the law of the United States. The Committee is also particularly concerned at reservations to Article 6, paragraph 5, and Article 7 of the Covenant, which it believes to be incompatible with the object and purpose of the Covenant.'[137] It did not state the consequences of that incompatibility. It recommended that the US review its reservations, declarations and understandings with a view to withdrawing them, in particular reservations to Article 6, paragraph 5, and Article 7 of the Covenant.[138]

---

[132] SR 1840 at para 15. The case referred to is *Lewis (Neville) v Attorney General of Jamaica* [2001] 2 AC 50.

[133] See Aust, *Modern Treaty Law and Practice*, n 106 above at 130.

[134] CCPR/C/81/Add 4 and HRI/CORE/1/Add 49; See SR 1401–1402 and SR 1405–1406, 1413.

[135] CCPR/C/79/Add 50, A/50/40 at paras 266–304. The second periodic report of the US was due in 1998 but has not been submitted as of 1 March 2003.

[136] See SR 1406.

[137] *Ibid* at para 279.

[138] n 136 above at para 292. See also the Conclusions and Recommendations of the Committee Against Torture on the initial report of the US, 15 May 2000, A/55/44 at para 179, which expressed concern about the 'reservation lodged to Article 16, in violation of the Convention, the effect of which is to limit the application of the Convention.' The reservation states that: '[T]he United States con-

K. Comparative Practice

In *Belilos v Switzerland* an interpretative declaration by Switzerland was inter-preted by the European Court of Human Rights as a reservation which was invalid and severed, leaving Switzerland bound by the provision as if no reservation had been made.[139] After *Belilos* and *Weber*,[140] another case of severance, Switzerland threatened to withdraw from the ECHR but did not do so.

In *Loizidou v Turkey* the European Court of Human Rights held that the only permissible restrictions to declarations accepting the right of individual petition were temporal ones.[141] On this basis the limitations in the Turkish declaration of 1989 on competence *ratione loci, ratione materiae and ratione temporis* were ruled invalid. Among the arguments of the Court were that to have a system where parties were free to subscribe to separate regimes of enforcement of convention obligations would seriously weaken the role of the Commission and Court in the discharge of their functions, would diminish the effectiveness of the Convention as a constitutional instrument of European public order and was not consistent with the existence of express stipulations in the Convention regime that permit-ted states to limit their acceptance of the right of individual petition (eg Article 6(2) of the Fourth Protocol). Thus, having regard to the object and purpose of the ECHR, the consequences of the restrictions on its competence for the enforce-ment of the Convention for the achievement of its aims would be so far-reaching that a power to this effect should have been expressly provided for. However, no such provision exists in either Article 25 or Article 46[142] of the subsequent prac-tice of the contracting parties. Apart from Turkey, only Cyprus had made a dec-laration containing a restriction *ratione materiae* and this had been withdrawn after six years; that, even though the provisions on the right of individual petition had been modelled on Article 36 of the Statute of the ICJ, there was a fundamental difference between the ICJ and the European Court of Human Rights. The ICJ's jurisdiction was much more extensive and was not exclusively limited to direct supervisory functions in respect of a law-making treaty such as the ECHR; an analogy based on the provisions permitting restrictions on the right to petition from overseas territories was not accepted; for such declarations to be permissi-ble would create inequality between contracting state and run counter to the aim

---

siders itself bound by the obligation under Article 16 to prevent "cruel, inhuman or degrading treat-ment or punishment", only insofar as the term "cruel, inhuman or degrading treatment or punish-ment" means the cruel, unusual and inhumane treatment or punishment prohibited by the Fifth, Eighth and/or Fourteenth Amendments to the Constitution of the United States,' CAT/C/28/Add 5 at paras 3.1–3.53.

[139] Series A, No 132 (1989); I Cameron and F Horn, 'Reservations to the ECHR: the Belilos Case' (1990) 33 *GYIL* 69; S Marks, 'Reservations Unhinged: the Belilos Case before the European Court of Human Rights' (1990) 39 *ICLQ* 300.

[140] Series A, No 177 (1990).

[141] Even those restrictions have disappeared under Protocol 11 to the ECHR, which makes accep-tance of the right of individual petition mandatory (except for overseas territories).

[142] Series A, No 310 (1995) at 139. The judgement affirmed the approach of the European Com-mission on Human Rights in *Chrysostomos v Turkey*, 68 DR 216 (1991), (1991) 12 *HRLJ* 113.

expressed in the preamble of achieving greater unity in the maintenance and further realisation of human rights;[143] and that the special character of ECHR as a treaty for the collective enforcement of human rights. Some of the arguments employed by the European Court of Human Rights would also apply *mutatis mutandis* to the HRC and the ICCPR.

The implication of the reference to the ICJ's jurisdiction was to differentiate it from the ECHR system. Having found the restriction in the particular case (*ratione loci*) to be invalid the European Court of Human Rights further found that it could be severed from the declarations accepting the right to petition and so the merits could be considered. This was recognized as a bold judgement given clear statements from Turkish officials that the declarations had to be accepted in their entirety.[144] Given that the express intentions of Turkey seemed clear, the European Court of Human Rights effectively states that the ECHR system imposes substantial limits on a states parties possibilities for limiting the substance of its acceptance.[145] Harris, Boyle and Warbrick comment on *Loizidou* that, 'The judgement . . . contains a statement of principle which is crucial to the integrity of the system. . . .'[146] Its reasoning comes close to *caveat emptor*.[147]

The approach in *Loizidou* has been affirmed in its subsequent cases.[148] Turkey withdrew most of the objectionable features of its declarations under Articles 25 and 46 even before Protocol 11 came into force. However, it has not implemented the judgment on the merits of *Loizidou*.

L. Policy Guidance for States

The HRC has made it clear that as far as the ICCPR and its Protocols are concerned, severance will be the 'normal' approach to an incompatible reservation. The European Court of Human Rights has severed reservations in a small number of cases. States could have included express provisions on the legal effect of impermissible reservations in human rights treaties but they have not done so. The jurisprudence of the HRC was a creative attempt to insert a greater degree of certainty and predictability where the law of the VCLT was uncertain and the practice of states was varied and indeterminate. Existing states parties to the ICCPR and the OPs have a clearer idea of where they stand and what risks they are open to. The number of states parties is already large (149 as of 1 March 2003; with 104 being a party to OP1) and to that extent they are already caught within the HRC's approach. For example, France is a party to OP1 but when one of its interpretative declara-

---

[143] Cf, the preamble to OP1.

[144] Cf, *Kennedy* Pt G and H above.

[145] See the joint and separate opinions of Judges Golcuklu and Pettit.

[146] DJ Harris, M O'Boyle and C Warbrick, *Law of the European Court of Human Rights* (Butterworths, London, 1995) at 583–84.

[147] *Ibid* at 584.

[148] *Yagci et Sargin v Turkey*, Series A, No 319–A (1995); *Mansur v Turkey*, Series A, No 319–B (1995).

tions was challenged it was upheld.[149] States which are considering becoming parties (eg China) are forewarned of the dangers of making reservations of doubtful compatibility. A new state party could expressly state that its consent to the treaty is conditional on the validity of its reservations. There would seem to be no reason in principle why an existing state party could not do the same. Such a statement would have the status of an interpretative declaration.[150] The statement would be clear evidence of the consent or otherwise of the state concerned. The US comments on GC 24 are an example of a state providing evidence in a different form than an interpretative declaration but with the same intention. It stated that, 'The reservations contained in the United States instrument of ratification are an integral part of its consent to be bound by the Covenant and are not severable.'[151] It is submitted that, faced with such a statement the HRC could not, absent other evidence, apply its 'normal' approach of severance.[152]

Two of the States which have challenged the severance approach of the HRC, the US and the UK, are not parties to OP1 and face no current threat of a decision severing a reservation as a result of an individual petition.[153] For the US, the HRC stated in its concluding observations on its first report that:

> The Committee regrets the extent of the State party's reservations, declarations and understandings to the Covenant. It believes that, taken together, they intended to ensure that the United States has accepted only what is already the law of the United States. The Committee is also particularly concerned at reservations to Article 6, paragraph 5, and Article 7 of the Covenant, which it believes to be incompatible with the object and purpose of the Covenant.[154]

The example acutely demonstrates the policy dilemma for the HRC. There was no reference to the possible legal effect of such incompatibility. Assuming the normal response applies the HRC would regard them as severable. If they were regarded as so important to the US's consent to the ICCPR that the normal severance rule could not be applied, then the US would not be treated as a state party to the ICCPR.

It is difficult to draw any definitive conclusions. The HRC can simply be said to have taken no decision. Or it can be taken to have made clear to the US that

---

[149] See n 66 above.

[150] Such 'declarations' do not necessarily have to be made at the times specified in the VCLT for reservations to be made. A particular treaty may establish specific times, but states parties may not object to a later statement. There must be a good case for affording a later interpretive declaration the same weight as a contemporaneous one when it is concerned with a matter which only arises in the jurisprudence of an international organ subsequent to the ratification of the treaty by the state concerned.

[151] n 61 above.

[152] Cf WA Schabas, 'Invalid Reservations to the International Covenant on Civil and Political Rights: Is the United States Still a Party?' (1995) 21 *Brooklyn J.I.L.* 277, at 323, who puts the argument in a broader context of US practice and submits that, 'the general intent of the United States is to assume the norms embodied in the Covenant, even if its reservations concerning the death penalty are deemed inadmissible.'

[153] Both states could face the prospect under the inter-state complaint procedure in Art 41.

[154] CCPR/C/79/Add 50; A/50/40 at para 279.

the reservations referred to are invalid and would be regarded as severed, with the US continuing as a party. No member suggested that because of the reservation the US was not a party to the ICCPR.

5. SUCCESSION TO HUMAN RIGHTS TREATY OBLIGATIONS

In another challenging piece of jurisprudence, the HRC has strongly asserted that there is automatic succession to the human rights obligations in the ICCPR. The principle of automatic succession to human rights obligations was developed and applied in the context of the dissolution of the Former Yugoslavia and the USSR.[155] The HRC's practice was encapsulated in General Comment 26 on '*Issues relating to the continuity of obligations to the International Covenant on Civil and Political Rights*',[156] which was, in part, a response to the denunciation of the ICCPR by the Democratic People's Republic of Korea in July 1997. GC 26 provides:

1. The International Covenant on Civil and Political Rights does not contain any provision regarding its termination and does not provide for denunciation or withdrawal. Consequently, the possibility of termination, denunciation or withdrawal must be considered in the light of applicable rules of customary international law which are reflected in the Vienna Convention on the Law of Treaties. On this basis, the Covenant is not subject to denunciation or withdrawal unless it is established that the parties intended to admit the possibility of denunciation or withdrawal or a right to do so is implied from the nature of the treaty.

2. That the parties to the Covenant did not admit the possibility of denunciation and that it was not a mere oversight on their part to omit reference to denunciation is demonstrated by the fact that Article 41(2) of the Covenant does permit a State party to withdraw its acceptance of the competence of the Committee to examine inter-State communications by filing an appropriate notice to that effect while there is no such provision for denunciation of or withdrawal from the Covenant itself. Moreover, the Optional Protocol to the Covenant, negotiated and adopted contemporaneously with it, permits States parties to denounce it. Additionally, by way of comparison, the International Convention on the Elimination of All Forms of Racial Discrimination, which was adopted one year prior to the Covenant, expressly permits denunciation. It can therefore be concluded that the drafters of the Covenant deliberately intended to exclude the possibility of denunciation. The same conclusion applies to the Second Optional Protocol in the drafting of which a denunciation clause was deliberately omitted.

3. Furthermore, it is clear that the Covenant is not the type of treaty which, by its nature, implies a right of denunciation. Together with the simultaneously prepared and adopted International Covenant on Economic, Social and Cultural Rights, the Covenant codifies in treaty form the universal human rights enshrined in the Universal Declaration of Human Rights, the three instruments together often being referred to as the "International Bill of Human Rights." As such, the Covenant does

---

[155] See Boerefijn, n 14 above ch XIII; McGoldrick, n 7 above, 'Introduction' to paperback edition.
[156] A/53/40, annex VII, adopted on 8 Dec 1997.

not have a temporary character typical of treaties where a right of denunciation is deemed to be admitted, notwithstanding the absence of a specific provision to that effect.

4. *The rights enshrined in the Covenant belong to the people living in the territory of the State party.* The Human Rights Committee has consistently taken the view, as evidenced by its long-standing practice, that once the people are accorded the protection of the rights under the Covenant, *such protection devolves with territory and continues to belong to them, notwithstanding change in government of the State party, including dismemberment in more than one State or State succession or any subsequent action of the State party designed to divest them of the rights guaranteed by the Covenant.*

5. The Committee is therefore firmly of the view that international law does not permit a State which has ratified or acceded or succeeded to the Covenant to denounce it or withdraw from it. [emphases added]

The HRC applied this approach to Hong Kong so that China succeeded to the reporting obligation under Article 40 in relation to Hong Kong.[157] It is not clear if China agreed with this view. China was not a party to the Covenant and it was not included in the list from China to the UN Secretary-General regarding treaties which China had agreed would continue to apply to the Hong Kong Special Administrative Region (HKSAR). However, Annex I, Section XIII of the UK-China Joint Declaration on the Question of Hong Kong[158] provided that the 'provisions of (the Covenant) as applied to Hong Kong shall remain in force.' This was reiterated in separate notes by China and the UK. The matter was still not free from doubt. The UK took the view that the 'provisions' included the reporting obligation in Article 40. A narrower interpretation would have been that the provisions referred only to the rights but not to the reporting obligations. For a long period there was a studied ambiguity as to which interpretation China accepted. The Basic Law of Hong Kong provided that the provisions of the Covenant 'shall be implemented through the laws of the HKSAR.' China signed the Covenant in October 1998 and was expected to ratify in due course. However, it did not do so (and has not done so as of 1 March 2003). Nonetheless, it reported on Hong Kong in 1999 and this was considered by the HRC in 1999. For the HRC the legal obligation to do this was founded in the automatic succession of the obligations from the UK to China.[159] For China it was founded in the Joint Declaration with the UK. The end result is the same but the legal basis is different.

The GA simply 'took note' of GC 26. The UN Human Rights Commission was supportive of the HRC's approach as have been the chairs of the human rights

---

[157] See CCPR/C/SR 1803–SR 1805; A/C.3/51/SR 25; N Jayawickrama, 'Human Rights in Hong Kong—The Continued Applicability of the International Covenants' (1995) 25 *Hong Kong L.J.* 171; J Chan, 'State Succession to Human Rights Treaties: Hong Kong and the International Covenant on Civil and Political Rights' (1996) 45 *ICLQ* 928; A Byrnes, 'Hong Kong and the Continuation of International Obligations Relating to Human Rights After 1997', in B Leung and J Cheng (eds) *Hong Kong SAR: In Pursuit of Domestic and International Order,* 135 (Chinese University Press, Hong Kong, 1997).

[158] (1994) 33 *ILM* 1366.

[159] CCPR/C/79/Add 117, concluding Observations of HRC on China; Hong Kong at para 3.

treaty bodies. The other treaty organs have followed the same practice. The view of the HRC has been supported by some writers.[160] Aust considers that there is no authority for this view.[161] In contrast with the view of the HRC, he asserts that the 'sounder view is that in so far as a human rights treaty represents rules of customary international law a successor state will be bound by those rules, but only as a matter of customary international law.' In support of this he cites the judgment of the ICJ in the *Genocide Convention* (*Bosnia v FRY*) (*Preliminary Objections*) case in which it concluded that the Federal Republic of Yugoslavia was a party to the Genocide Convention because it had declared its intention to remain bound by the treaties to which the Socialist Federal Republic of Yugoslavia had been a party.[162] Thus it was the consent of the new state that was the basis of its obligations. If Aust's view is correct, then among the practical consequences would be that, where the new state's consent is not forthcoming, the state is not a 'state party'—it cannot attend the meetings of states parties, cannot nominate members of HRC because they have to be nationals of a state party, that a member of the HRC who was a national of a non state party would arguably no longer be entitled to retain their membership of the HRC, no further communications under OP1 could be considered by the HRC from that state as they would all be inadmissible, and no further State reports could be considered under Article 40. Aust's reliance on the ICJ decision alone is not convincing. An alternative argument is that the succession declaration by the FRY simply meant that the ICJ did not have to address the issue of automatic succession to human rights treaties. The issue may have to be directly addressed by the ICJ because on 24 April 2001 Yugoslavia requested a revision of the judgment of 1 July 1996 by which the ICJ declared that it had jurisdiction to adjudicate the case, based on Article IX of the Genocide Convention. Yugoslavia contended that a revision of the Judgment was necessary now that it has become clear that, before 1 November 2000 (the date on which it was admitted as a new Member of the United Nations), Yugoslavia did not continue the international legal and political personality of the Socialist Federal Republic of Yugoslavia, was not a Member of the United Nations, was not a State party to the Statute of the Court, and was not a State party to the Genocide Convention. Yugoslavia noted that, while on 8 March 2001 it submitted to the United Nations Secretary-General a notification seeking accession to the Genocide Convention, that instrument included a reservation to Article IX. Moreover, according to Yugoslavia, 'accession has no retroactive effect. Even

---

[160] See R Mullerson, 'The Continuity and Succession of States, by Reference to the Former USSR and Yugoslavia', (1993) 42 *ICLQ* 473. See the Report of the Secretary-General on 'Succession of States in Respect of Human Rights Treaties' (1995) 2 *International Human Rights Reports* 507.

[161] Aust, n 106 above, 305–31 at 308, citing M Shaw, 'State Succession Revisited', (1994) *Finnish Yearbook of International Law* 34; M Kamminga, 'State Succession in Respect of Human Rights Treaties' (1994) 5 *EJIL* 468.

[162] (1994) ICJ Reps 4 at paras 17, 23. He also refers to the separate opinion of Judge Weeramantry on automatic succession. Aust, *ibid* at 645 and M Wood, 'Participation by the Former Yugoslav States in the United Nations and in Multilateral Treaties' (1997) *Max Planck Yearbook of United Nations Law* 231.

if it had [retroactive effect] this cannot possibly encompass the compromissory clause in Article IX of the Genocide Convention, because the FRY never accepted Article IX and the FRY's accession [to the Convention] did not encompass Article IX.'[163] For all these reasons, Yugoslavia requested the Court to declare that 'there is a new fact of such a character as to lay the case open to revision under Article 61 of the Statute of the Court.' The ICJ rejected Yugoslavia's request in February 2003.

6. APPRAISAL

Given the state of human rights in the world the legalistic debate on reservations may seem rather arcane and 'academic' in the worst sense. It must be readily acknowledged that the debate may serve to mask other agendas related to the substance of universality and willingness of states to comply with treaty obligations. As Redgwell observed, 'while the language of discourse is treaty law the real issue is the incompatibility of different social and cultural traditions.'[164] That broader sociological and cultural context must not be forgotten. Similarly, the problem needs to be kept in perspective. As the UK noted, 'The question of compatibility with the object and purpose is confined to a small number of extreme cases',[165] and the HRC has to retain the confidence of States. If it does not maintain its credibility it will lose co-operation from States and the political will necessary to sustain it.

Nonetheless, there is a broader fascination with the debates on reservations and on succession. The assertions of jurisdiction by the HRC in relation to these issues have highlighted tensions between and within the 'legal order' of 'international human rights' and the classical legal order of 'public international law'. Human rights law has undoubtedly changed the nature and substance of public international law. It is, perhaps inevitably, subversive of the very legal order which created it. It constantly challenges its boundaries and exposes its lacunae.[166] While immensely technical and detailed, the debate on reservations has posed some fundamental questions of public international law and therefore have an application outside human rights law. For example, 'is there no objective reality to the concept of being contrary to the object and purpose of a treaty in the absence of objections by states.'[167] That is not a new legal question but it is being played out in a changing political and social context where the 'institutionalisation' of State relations through the creation of treaty organs operation implementation mechanisms (reporting, individual and inter-state complaints). The debate on reservations has also focused attention on how intention and consent interact and

---

[163] See www.icj-cij.org.
[164] Redgwell, n 37 above at 280.
[165] n 62 above at para 9.
[166] See Charlesworth and Chinkin, n 11 above.
[167] Higgins, n 75 above at xxiv.

whether consent to a treaty is singular or multilayered, whether the notion of 'consent' as the basis of legal obligation in human rights obligations is weakening even if the language remains the same,[168] and the growing acceptance of an international public interest element in human rights protection. The jurisdictional assertions by the HRC, particularly in the context of reservations, attracted criticism and concern on the basis that they might lead to the fragmentation of international law into a series of distinct regimes with different rules applying. The UK response to GC 24 was partly framed in this way.[169] The issue of reservations thus has to be placed in the broader context of the debates on the role and significance of reciprocity in the conceptual structure of human rights treaties, the competence of human rights organs and treaty bodies, and the place of the legal order or regime of human rights within (or even outside) the legal order or regime of international law.[170] However, similar arguments are also being advanced in areas of more traditional state-state interests such as the law of the sea.[171] The assertions of jurisdiction by the HRC have pushed those debates to a higher level. They will also encourage debate and challenge in other areas of international law practice where individual interests are a strong element. This would include international humanitarian law and international environmental law, and increasingly international economic law. Possibly the most challenging issue to come from the debate is whether the fundamentals of public international law can continue to evolve in response to the challenges of international human rights law or whether the latter will ultimately subvert the intellectual and philosophical basis of the former.[172]

---

[168] See C Tomuschat, 'Obligations Arising for States Without or Against their Will', (1993-IV) 241 *Hag Rec*, 195.

[169] See text to n 94 above.

[170] See M Craven, 'Legal Differentiation and the Concept of the Human Rights Treaty in International Law' (2000) 11 *EJIL* 489; B Simma, 'International Human Rights and General International Law' (1995) 4 *Collected Courses of the Academy of European Law* 153.

[171] See DZ Cass, 'The "Constitutionalisation" of International Trade Law: Judicial Norm-Generation as the Engine of Constitutional Development in International Trade' (2001) 12 *EJIL*, 39.

[172] See K KorKelia, 'New Challenges to the Regime of Reservations under the ICCPR', (2002) 13 *EJIL*, 437; R Goodman, 'Human Rights Treaties, Invalid Reservations and State Consent', (2002) 96 *AJIL*, 531.

12

Some Problems of Compulsory Jurisdiction before Specialised Tribunals

The Law of the Sea

ALAN BOYLE

1. INTRODUCTION TO THE JURISDICTIONAL PROVISIONS OF THE 1982 LAW OF THE SEA CONVENTION

This chapter will use law of the sea disputes to examine the problems faced by specialised international tribunals when deciding cases where some of the issues fall within their compulsory jurisdiction and others do not. Should a tribunal refuse to decide such a case on the ground that it lacks jurisdiction over all of the issues? Should it decide all the issues on the ground that it has jurisdiction over some of them? Should it try as far as possible to avoid the problem? Is there a coherent and principled solution? Firstly, however, a brief survey of compulsory dispute settlement under UNCLOS is a necessary prelude to discussion of these difficult issues of jurisdiction.

A. The Basic Framework

Fundamentally, the parties to the 1982 UN Convention on the Law of the Sea are free to settle their disputes by any peaceful means of their choice (Articles 279–280). Nothing compels them to use UNCLOS Part XV procedures or to go to any UNCLOS court or tribunal if they can agree on some other method or forum. Should the parties so desire, for example, they could take an UNCLOS dispute to the WTO Dispute Settlement Body, or anywhere else.[1] For this reason Article 283 requires all parties to a dispute to exchange views as a preliminary to any further steps. Article 284 also allows any party to invite the other to seek con-

---

[1] While it is important to remember that the 1982 UNCLOS is not covered by the 1994 WTO Understanding on Rules and Procedures Governing the Settlement of Disputes, the parties to such a dispute could by agreement confer jurisdiction on the WTO Dispute Settlement Body.

ciliation before invoking any other procedure. Informal resolution of any dispute is thus still possible if that is what the parties want.

Moreover, if the States concerned are parties to another agreement entailing compulsory binding settlement of the dispute, 'that procedure shall apply in lieu of the procedures provided for in [Part XV of UNCLOS], unless the parties to the dispute otherwise agree' (Article 282). Thus states which have made declarations under Article 36(2) of the ICJ Statute will remain subject to the compulsory jurisdiction of the ICJ even in UNCLOS cases. For these various reasons the 1982 Convention's provisions on compulsory dispute settlement are essentially residual: they apply only if the parties have not agreed to use some other forum or have not been able to settle the dispute by conciliation or any other means (Article 281). In this respect, UNCLOS disputes are fundamentally different from WTO disputes, which, if not resolved by diplomatic means, can only be brought to the WTO Dispute Settlement Body.[2]

No single forum has compulsory jurisdiction under the 1982 Convention. Instead, Article 287 allows the parties to choose the most appropriate or acceptable forum from four possibilities:

(i)   The International Court of Justice
(ii) The International Tribunal for the Law of the Sea
(iii) Arbitration
(iv) Special arbitration

The composition of these bodies reflects differences in their intended functions. The ICJ comprises independent judges who are either qualified for high judicial office or possess 'recognised competence in international law,' whereas ITLOS judges must be persons of 'recognised competence in the field of the Law of the Sea.'[3] In practice judges of both tribunals have expertise in law of the sea and in general international law, and there is little to choose between them in that respect. Arbitrators appointed under Annex VII need not be lawyers but must be 'experienced in maritime affairs', although in practice many of those nominated are international lawyers with no obvious nautical aptitudes. Special arbitrators appointed under Annex VIII similarly do not have to be lawyers, but will instead be persons selected for their expertise in the four areas for which special arbitration is available: fisheries, protection of the marine environment, scientific research, or navigation. What the Convention does not do is to allocate a specific functional jurisdiction to each of the four compulsory fora.[4] Rather, it leaves the choice of forum to the parties to the dispute, and gives them the freedom to select whichever they deem most suitable. There is thus no assumption that particular categories of UNCLOS dispute must be settled by any particular method; insofar

---

[2] 1994 WTO Understanding on Rules and Procedures Governing the Settlement of Disputes, Arts 1 and 3.
[3] Compare ICJ Statute, Art 2 and 1982 UNCLOS, Annex VI, Art 2.
[4] The exception to this proposition is the allocation of deep seabed disputes to the Seabed Disputes Chamber of ITLOS under Part XI of the Convention.

as the specific expertise of the tribunal is a relevant factor it is for the parties to decide what is needed.

Failing such agreement, however, arbitration under Annex VII becomes the residual forum for the exercise of compulsory jurisdiction in all cases.[5] Under Article 287 parties to the Convention may also make a declaration accepting in advance the compulsory jurisdiction of one or more of the four fora: this will of course operate only in relation to other States which have made the same choice. Where the parties to a dispute have accepted different fora, or have made no declaration, arbitration is again the residual forum. In practice very few of the parties have made such a declaration, so, by default, arbitration is at present the nominal preference of most states.[6]

UNCLOS dispute settlement is thus highly flexible and even when compulsory jurisdiction comes into play the 'cafeteria approach' to selection of forum preserves much of the parties' freedom of choice and their ability to take account of the context and needs of each dispute. In these respects it reflects the eclecticism of general international law, rather than the highly focused specialism of the WTO dispute settlement machinery.

B. What Is and What Is Not Subject to Compulsory Settlement under UNCLOS?

It is important to remember that under Part XV of UNCLOS compulsory procedures apply only to disputes concerning provisional measures, prompt release of vessels and interpretation or application of the 1982 UNCLOS or of any international agreement related to the purposes of the Convention (if it so provides).[7] The 1995 Agreement on Straddling and Highly Migratory Fish Stocks is the principal example of such a related agreement.[8] Disputes arising under customary international law, or under other treaties, are not subject to Part XV of the Convention unless the parties agree.

There are also significant exclusions from the obligation to submit disputes to compulsory settlement. Under Article 297 these include disputes over coastal State powers relating to the management of fish stocks and authorisation of scientific research within the exclusive economic zone. These exclusions reflect the reality

---

[5] Art 287(3): see eg the *Mox Plant Case (Provisional Measures)*, ITLOS No 10 (2001), between Ireland and the UK. The parties to such a dispute remain free to opt ad hoc for some other forum. Thus in both the *Saiga* and *Swordfish* cases, the parties chose not to arbitrate but referred the cases to the ITLOS or to a chamber of the ITLOS.

[6] Art 287(5). See L Sohn, 'Settlement of Law of the Sea Disputes' (1995) 10 *Int. J. of Marine and Coastal Law* 205.

[7] Arts 286, 288, 290, 292.

[8] Art 30 applies Part XV *mutatis mutandis* to disputes concerning interpretation and application of that Agreement or of any sub-regional, regional, or global fisheries agreement relating to straddling or highly migratory fish stocks. See AE Boyle 'Problems of Compulsory Jurisdiction and the Settlement of Disputes Relating to Straddling Fish Stocks' in S Stokke (ed), *Governing High Seas Fisheries* (Oxford University Press, Oxford, 2001).

that the management of resources within the EEZ is very much a matter for coastal State discretion.[9] Coastal states at the UNCLOS negotiations were not willing to subject their newly-found EEZ rights to international accountability, and the exclusions from compulsory jurisdiction were deliberate and necessary in the interests of consensus. Optional exclusions under Article 298 also cover maritime boundary delimitation and military activities. Lastly, Article 282 excludes from compulsory settlement any dispute concerning interpretation or application of UNCLOS which the parties have agreed to refer to some other procedure, provided this will result in *a binding decision*.[10]

Provision for compulsory binding settlement of disputes under UNCLOS is thus less comprehensive than it might at first sight appear. The practical effect of the exclusions contained in Articles 297 and 298 is that many of the most complex disputes—including those which have so far come before the ICJ or arbitration—will fall only partially within compulsory jurisdiction, if at all, because they relate to fisheries or equitable delimitation of boundaries. This fragmentation of issues may prove to be one of the most difficult features of Part XV.[11]

C. So What Problems Do the Cases Reveal?

The general lessons to be learned from the cases can be shortly stated: first, Part XV is excessively complicated and has proved very difficult to interpret and apply in practice, as can be seen especially in the *Southern Bluefin Tuna Arbitration*,[12] considered below.

Secondly, fisheries disputes may be better resolved by special arbitrators or by negotiation, rather than by judicial or arbitral tribunals composed of lawyers. Given that they turn essentially on scientific and technical issues assessments of stock levels and conservation needs, it is difficult to see how courts or non-specialist arbitrators could settle either the *Southern Bluefin Tuna Arbirtration* or the *Swordfish*[13] disputes. Moreover, in most fisheries cases the applicable rules are too imprecise and dependent on good faith negotiation between the parties. A judicial tribunal might clarify the issues and the meaning of the relevant articles of UNCLOS, but at best it can only encourage or facilitate a negotiated settlement between the parties.[14]

---

[9] See Arts 55–75, 238–62.

[10] See the *MOX Plant Case*, n 5 above, where Art 282 was found inapplicable because there was no such agreement. Art 282 reads: 'If the States Parties which are parties to a dispute concerning the inter-pretation or application of this Convention have agreed, through a general, regional or bilateral agree-ment or otherwise, that such dispute shall, at the request of any party to the dispute, be submitted to a procedure that entails *a binding decision, that procedure shall apply in lieu of the procedures provided for in this Part*, unless the parties to the dispute otherwise agree' (emphasis added).

[11] See AE Boyle, 'Dispute Settlement and the Law of the Sea Convention: Problems of Fragmenta-tion and Jurisdiction' (1997) 46 *ICLQ* 37.

[12] See AE Boyle, 'The Southern Bluefin Tuna Arbitration' (2001) 50 *ICLQ* 447.

[13] n 5 above.

[14] See *Icelandic Fisheries Case (UK v Iceland)* (1974) ICJ Rep 3; *Icelandic Fisheries Case (Germany v Iceland)* (1974) ICJ Rep 175.

Thirdly, the problems of overlap with other treaties/jurisdictions are not easy to resolve in principled and predictable ways. It is this last point that will be developed in this chapter, with specific reference to the *Southern Bluefin Tuna* and *Swordfish* disputes.

2. PROBLEMS OF OVERLAPPING/COMPETING JURISDICTION

A. Southern Bluefin Tuna Arbitration (2000)

This case started life in the International Tribunal for the Law of the Sea when Australia and New Zealand were granted provisional measures against Japanese high seas tuna fishing in the Pacific.[15] That Tribunal had held that the provisions of the 1982 UN Convention on the Law of the Sea (1982 UNCLOS) invoked by Australia and New Zealand appeared to afford a basis on which the jurisdiction of an arbitral tribunal might be founded; that the fact that the 1993 Convention on Conservation of Southern Bluefin Tuna applied between the parties did not preclude recourse to the compulsory dispute settlement procedures in Part XV of the 1982 UNCLOS; and that an arbitral tribunal would prima facie have jurisdiction over the merits of the dispute.[16] Notwithstanding this necessarily provisional view, when the parties then proceeded to arbitration, Japan maintained its initial preliminary objections, and the award handed down in August 2000 thus deals only with the jurisdiction of the arbitrators.[17]

This arbitration is the first to take place under Annex VII of the 1982 UNCLOS. Japan argued, however, that this dispute arose under and should be settled solely in accordance with the 1993 Convention on the Conservation of Southern Bluefin Tuna (1993 CCSBT). That agreement did not provide for compulsory dispute settlement, and according to Japan, by becoming parties to it Australia and New Zealand had precluded themselves from referring the same matters for arbitration under the 1982 UN Convention. Alternatively, Japan argued that the parties' declarations accepting the compulsory jurisdiction of the ICJ took precedence over arbitration under Article 282 and that in any event attempts to settle the dispute had not been exhausted. Japan also put forward a number of objections to admissibility, arguing that the dispute was essentially about science rather than law, and that the claimants had failed to identify a cause of action.

The arbitral tribunal held that there had been adequate efforts to negotiate a settlement, that there remained a legal dispute between the parties concerning the interpretation and application of both the 1982 UN Convention and the 1993

---

[15] R Churchill, 'The Southern Bluefin Tuna Cases' (2000) 49 *ICLQ* 979. See also articles by various authors in (1999) 10 *Ybk. Int. Env. L*, and B Kwiatkowska, 'The Southern Bluefin Tuna Cases' (2000) 15 *International Journal of Maritime and Commercial Law* 1.

[16] *Southern Bluefin Tuna Cases (Provisional Measures)*, ITLOS Nos 3 and 4 (1999), at paras 52–62.

[17] The arbitration was held at ICSID. For the full text of the award and the pleadings see the World Bank website at www.worldbank.org/icsid.

CCSBT, and it also rejected Japan's contention that the 1993 Convention should be treated as a *lex specialis*. Obligations under UNCLOS co-existed with and could determine the interpretation of the CCSBT, so that the dispute, 'while centred in the 1993 Convention, also arises under the UNCLOS.'[18] However, on the central issue of jurisdiction, the arbitral tribunal, from whose award only Sir Kenneth Keith dissented, found in favour of Japan on the ground that, by entering into the 1993 CCSBT, the parties had 'preclude[d] subjection of their disputes to section 2 procedures in accordance with Article 281(1) [of UNCLOS].'[19] Since it thus lacked jurisdiction to rule on the merits of the case, the arbitral tribunal also revoked the provisional measures imposed in the earlier proceedings. The reasons for this denial of jurisdiction, which is likely to remain controversial, are complex, and they have significant implications not only for law of the sea disputes but also for other treaty dispute settlement systems.

Two findings are central to the tribunal's conclusion. First, notwithstanding its acceptance of the applicants' argument that the dispute raised issues under both treaties, the tribunal saw it as 'artificial' to separate the UNCLOS elements from the broader dispute 'centred' on the 1993 Convention, although it did accept that there might be exceptional cases where such a separation is possible. Secondly, starting from the perspective that they were essentially faced with a dispute concerning the 1993 CCSBT rather than UNCLOS, the tribunal then considered whether Article 16 of the 1993 Convention met the terms of Article 281(1)(b) of UNCLOS. That provision excludes from compulsory jurisdiction any case where the parties have agreed to seek settlement of an UNCLOS dispute by other means unless 'no settlement has been reached by recourse to such means and the agreement . . . does not exclude any further procedure.' Article 16 does not in terms exclude any further procedure, but in one of the more unusual exercises in creative treaty interpretation by an international tribunal, the arbitrators noted that Article 16 was based on Article XI of the 1959 Antarctic Treaty, and found it 'obvious that these provisions are meant to exclude compulsory jurisdiction.'[20] They supported this interpretation by reference to the number of other post-UNCLOS treaties which also make no provision for compulsory dispute

---

[18] At para 52.

[19] At para 63. The relevant part of UNCLOS Art 281 (1) reads: 'If the States parties which are parties to a dispute concerning the interpretation or application of this Convention have agreed to seek settlement of the dispute by a peaceful means of their own choice, the procedures provided for in this Part apply only where no settlement has been reached by recourse to such means and *the agreement between the parties does not exclude any further procedure. . . .*' (emphasis added).

[20] At para 58. The relevant part of CCSBT Art 16 reads: '1. If any dispute arises between two or more of the Parties concerning the interpretation or implementation of this Convention, those Parties shall consult among themselves with a view to having the dispute resolved by negotiation, inquiry, mediation, conciliation, arbitration, judicial settlement or other peaceful means of their own choice. 2. Any dispute of this character not so resolved shall, with the consent in each case of all parties to the dispute, be referred for settlement to the International Court of Justice or to arbitration; but failure to reach agreement on reference to the International Court of Justice or to arbitration shall not absolve parties to the dispute from the responsibility of continuing to seek to resolve it by any of the various peaceful means referred to in paragraph 1 above.'

settlement, and by the assertion that Article 281 allows states to limit UNCLOS compulsory jurisdiction by agreement. There are two problems with this view of Article 281.

First, the fact that other agreements, even post-UNCLOS, make no provision for compulsory jurisdiction tells us nothing about the parties' intention with regard to the settlement of UNCLOS disputes. It is entirely obvious that Article 16 of the CCSBT is meant to exclude compulsory jurisdiction over disputes *under that convention*, but it is far from obvious that it is meant also to exclude compulsory disputes under UNCLOS. With all due respect to the learned arbitrators, this assertion simply lacks conviction.

Secondly, it is prima facie curious to use Article 281 to explain the relationship between the 1993 CCSBT and the 1982 UNCLOS Part XV. The more obvious article on which to rely for this purpose is Article 282, under which dispute settlement procedures of other agreements apply in lieu of UNCLOS Part XV, provided they entail *a binding decision*.[21] Of course Article 16 of the 1993 CCSBT does not entail such an outcome, so it could not have deprived the arbitrators of jurisdiction in this case, hence the implausible resort to Article 281.

But what is the effect of the tribunal's creative reading of Article 281, taken together with the unambiguous terms of Article 282? Under Article 281 a regional agreement which makes no provision for compulsory binding settlement of disputes will apparently exclude resort to UNCLOS Part XV on the assumption that is what the parties intended. Under Article 282 a regional agreement which makes provision for compulsory binding dispute settlement will also exclude resort to UNCLOS Part XV. These two articles could thus be reduced to a single simple proposition: regional agreements exclude UNCLOS dispute settlement. But if that is the law, why then does UNCLOS need two articles to achieve what could be expressed in one sentence? The obvious answer is that Article 281 was never intended to have the meaning attributed to it in this case. The context for which it seems more appropriately designed is one in which the parties to an UNCLOS dispute are seeking a negotiated settlement and agree to resort, for example, to conciliation. If this does not result in settlement, then the parties would remain free to use UNCLOS procedures unless they had agreed otherwise. Even if Article 281 were intended also to cover dispute settlement clauses in agreements such as the 1993 CCSBT, one comes back to the question: how is it possible to read into one agreement (the 1993 CCSBT) an intention to preclude resort to compulsory procedures in the event of disputes arising under another agreement (the 1982 UNCLOS)? Or, put another way, where is the justification for reading Article 16 of the 1993 CCSBT as applying both to disputes under that agreement and to disputes under UNCLOS? The arbitral tribunal offers none, save for its vague

---

[21] UNCLOS Art 282 reads: 'If the States Parties which are parties to a dispute concerning the interpretation or application of this Convention have agreed, through a general, regional or bilateral agreement or otherwise, that such dispute shall, at the request of any party to the dispute, be submitted to a procedure that entails *a binding decision, that procedure shall apply in lieu of the procedures provided for in this Part*, unless the parties to the dispute otherwise agree.' (emphasis added)

assertion that Article 281 so intends, and its reliance on those other treaties which also make no reference to UNCLOS, and which tell us only how the parties intend to handle disputes arising under those same agreements.

The core of the problem is the reluctance of the arbitrators to treat the case as raising UNCLOS issues separate from the CCSBT. There is no doubt that the case is about high seas fishing, and that there are relevant and applicable articles of UNCLOS,[22] as the ITLOS observed in the earlier proceedings. There is equally no doubt that, but for the CCSBT, a dispute concerning the interpretation or application of those articles would have fallen within UNCLOS Part XV compulsory jurisdiction. On the facts of this case, such a dispute, confined to the application of UNCLOS, might well have led to failure on the applicants' part to show a violation of the Convention, but that does not mean there is no UNCLOS dispute or that UNCLOS has no further relevance for parties to the CCSBT, as the arbitral tribunal itself admits. What the arbitrators may have believed is that they could not decide the UNCLOS issues without also deciding on interpretation and application of the CCSBT. Since it clearly had no jurisdiction over disputes concerning the latter, the tribunal may have felt unable to decide any other issues, including those concerning UNCLOS, which could not be separated. This would be a defensible position under a treaty which by no means makes binding settlement compulsory for all disputes and under which issues subject to compulsory jurisdiction may well be bound up with others which are not.[23] In effect an UNCLOS tribunal would then be required to deny jurisdiction over any of the issues unless it had jurisdiction over all of them. If the case can be understood in this way then its implications for dispute settlement would be important, but the tribunal makes no reference to any such principle of inseparability in justifying its dismissal of the case, apart from pointing to the 'artificiality' of treating it as an UNCLOS dispute.

On the other hand, if the inseparability of the UNCLOS issues is not the basis of this judgment, then the outcome is much more questionable. The arbitrators would then simply be reading Part XV of UNCLOS as impliedly subject to subsequent regional agreements, and as taking out of compulsory settlement any case which raises matters concerning both UNCLOS and another agreement on which the dispute is 'primarily centred'. Such an outcome should cause high seas fishing states to pause before entering regional fishery agreements which have no compulsory dispute settlement clause. If they do participate in such agreements they will stand in danger of losing the protection from coastal state 'creeping jurisdiction' which Part XV of UNCLOS at present provides in respect of high seas fishing. Moreover, it is far from certain when a dispute is 'primarily centred' on one treaty rather than another. Can there be disputes which have no primary centre in either treaty? Was the dispute considered below between Chile and the EC over sword-

---

[22] 1982 UNCLOS, Art 64 at 116–19.
[23] See AE Boyle, 'Dispute Settlement and the Law of the Sea Convention: Problems of Fragmentation and Jurisdiction' (1997) 46 *ICLQ* 37.

fish stocks primarily centred on UNCLOS, or on GATT, or was it really two separate disputes?[24] The arbitral tribunal's reasoning, rather than its actual conclusion, has opened up a minefield of uncertainty and confusion which it is probably going to take an authoritative judicial decision to unravel. Of course, the decision of the *Bluefin Tuna* arbitrators may simply be wrong, and it is far from certain, given its earlier views, that the International Tribunal for the Law of the Sea will follow the award's interpretation of Article 281.

B. Swordfish Case (ITLOS 2001)

This case involved a dispute between Chile and the European Community about conservation of swordfish stocks in the southeast Pacific. In order to put pressure on the EC to agree to abide by Chilean fisheries conservation regulations, Chile closed its ports to EC fishing vessels. The EC initiated proceedings in the WTO, alleging violation of the GATT agreement's provisions on transit of goods through ports and import restrictions. Chile responded by initiating proceedings under the 1982 UN Convention on the Law of the Sea, alleging violation of articles on conservation of migratory fish stocks on the high seas. The dispute was settled before either case could be heard by the WTO or the ITLOS.

Apart from demonstrating the value of compulsory dispute settlement provisions in both treaties, this dispute again raises the question how to handle disputes that fall partly within the compulsory jurisdiction of two different international tribunals. Could these two parallel cases have been kept separate from each other, and decided solely within the parameters of their respective governing treaties? Arguably, they could, in which case there is no problem. But it is not hard to envisage a different scenario. In proceedings before the WTO a coastal state might rely on an alleged violation of UNCLOS by a high seas fishing state in order to justify closure of its ports to their fishing vessels under Article XX of GATT.[25] Alternatively, the high seas fishing state may wish to contest the applicability of Article XX by pointing to coastal state failure to co-operate in violation of the high seas conservation articles of UNCLOS (Articles 116–9). Similarly, in UNCLOS proceedings, a high seas fishing state might point to violation of GATT's port transit article to justify an assertion that the coastal state had failed to co-operate as required by UNCLOS Articles 64 and 116–9. What these examples show is that the compatibility of the disputing parties' conduct with UNCLOS may be an issue which a WTO panel or the Appellate Body has to determine in order to decide whether a GATT violation is made out. The same may be true of WTO agreements in the context of UNCLOS proceedings.

---

[24] Chile–EC: *Case Concerning the Conservation and Sustainable Exploitation of Swordfish Stocks in the South-Eastern Pacific Ocean*, ITLOS No 7, Order No 2000/3 (2000).

[25] Eg Art XX(g): conservation of exhaustible natural resources, on which see the *Shrimp-Turtle* decision of the WTO Appellate Body, at n 28 below.

The problem, as this case illustrates, is that real-world disputes do not happen in the neat boxes envisaged by each treaty, and the answer to the question how we resolve such inter-related disputes is far from clear, nor is the correct approach. Seen simply in terms of compulsory jurisdiction, there is no doubt that ITLOS had compulsory jurisdiction over high seas fisheries disputes and that the WTO had compulsory jurisdiction over disputes concerning transit of goods through ports. It might be thought that there is also no doubt that a violation of UNCLOS is not within the compulsory jurisdiction of the WTO and similarly that a violation of the GATT is not within the compulsory jurisdiction of the ITLOS or of any other UNCLOS dispute settlement forum.[26] It is true that such claims cannot be initiated before the 'wrong' tribunal. It is not open to any state to resort unilaterally to the WTO to settle disputes arising under non-WTO agreements, any more than it is open to any WTO member to resort to the ITLOS or ICJ to adjudicate on a GATT complaint. To that extent there is no question of 'forum-shopping' in cases such as these.

It does not follow, however, that in deciding a dispute under a treaty over which it does have compulsory jurisdiction an international tribunal cannot incidentally determine questions arising under other treaties where it is necessary to do so in order to determine the dispute which is properly before it. The *Swordfish* case may well be a good example of just such a dispute. Here, unlike the *Bluefin Tuna* arbitration, the issue was not so much which tribunal had jurisdiction, but what law each should apply. Reference to other relevant agreements and rules of international law may arise as a question of priority of successive treaties in accordance with Article 30 of the Vienna Convention on Treaties and Article 311 of the 1982 UNCLOS, or in the context of interpreting and applying a treaty, in accordance with Article 31 of the Vienna Convention. Moreover, the express terms of Article 293 of UNCLOS require a tribunal with jurisdiction under the Convention to apply 'other rules of international law not incompatible with this Convention,' so it is clear that an UNCLOS tribunal is not exceeding its jurisdiction in doing so: indeed it would not be exercising its jurisdiction properly if it failed to apply such additional rules where relevant.

This is why other treaties, as well as customary international law, may be relevant and may have to be adjudicated even before a tribunal which would not otherwise have jurisdiction in a case confined to such matters.[27] Thus, in the *Shrimp-Turtle* decision,[28] the WTO Appellate Body referred, inter alia, to the 1992

---

[26] The 1982 UNCLOS is not a 'covered agreement' for the purposes of the WTO dispute settlement, nor would disputes under existing WTO agreements fall within the terms of UNCLOS Art 288(2) for the purposes of UNCLOS Part XV compulsory jurisdiction.

[27] The *Nuclear Tests* cases (1974) ICJ Reps. 252 and 457 illustrate the same point by showing how an alleged violation of high seas freedoms may require an UNCLOS tribunal to decide whether, for example, nuclear weapons tests are lawful in customary international law.

[28] *Import Prohibition of Certain Shrimp and Shrimp Products*, WTO Appellate Body (1998) WT/DS58/AB/R. For a much fuller treatment of the applicability of international law within the WTO Dispute Settlement Body, see J Pauwelyn, 'The Role of Public International Law in the WTO: How Far Can We Go?' (2001) 95 *AJIL* 535.

Rio Declaration on Environment and Development, the 1992 Convention on Biological Diversity, the 1982 UNCLOS, the 1979 Convention on Conservation of Migratory Species and the 1973 CITES Convention.[29] Rather than interpreting GATT Article XX (g) ('exhaustible natural resources') in accordance with whatever might have been the intention of the drafters in 1947, the Appellate Body took account of these much later and directly relevant instruments. In this respect it was following the approach adopted by the International Court of Justice in the *Gabčíkovo-Nagymaros Dam Case*,[30] when that court read the 1977 treaty between Hungary and Czechoslovakia in conjunction with subsequent developments in international environmental law.

3. CONCLUSIONS

While the *Southern Bluefin Tuna* arbitration may indicate that an international tribunal will refuse to exercise jurisdiction over a dispute not 'primarily centred' within its compulsory jurisdiction, both WTO and ICJ jurisprudence suggest a somewhat subtler approach which recognises that where a tribunal does have compulsory jurisdiction over a dispute concerning interpretation and application of a treaty, other rules of international law and other treaties may be part of the applicable law. For this purpose, it does not matter that the tribunal would have no jurisdiction to determine claims based on these other rules or treaties. Specialised tribunals with limited jurisdiction are thus not confined within the narrow parameters of their particular treaties when deciding disputes under those treaties.

Nevertheless, while this may ameliorate the jurisdictional constraints, it simply replaces them with the uncertainty of deciding what is the applicable law in any given dispute. Whether viewed in terms of jurisdiction or applicable law, the creation of specialised international tribunals has posed problems which remain to be more fully explored and which will continue to be a trap for the unwary.

---

[29] The extent to which Article 31(3) of the Vienna Convention on Treaties permits revision of a treaty by reference to other rules of international law is controversial however: compare Judge Bedjaoui in *Gabčíkovo* with Ireland's argument in the pending *Mox Plant* arbitration.

[30] (1997) ICJ Rep at 7.

13

Activism and Restraint in the European Court of Justice

STEPHEN WEATHERILL

1. INTRODUCTION

The title of this chapter immediately raises the question: activist or restrained *compared to what*? What is the fixed point against which the conduct of the European Court in the exercise of its jurisdiction should be measured? The purpose of the chapter is to dig deeper than the (admittedly not entirely inaccurate) caricature of the European Court as driven to act audaciously in a manner apt to expand its influence and with it that of the other institutions of the European Community. The case will be made that although this has some considerable force as a description of what has occurred, it is misleading to suppose that the European Court's rationale for acting in this way was and is simply maximising its jurisdiction. It will be shown that the de facto power of the European Court to give practical effect to its view of the nature of EC law was and remains heavily dependent on its capacity to induce national judges to accept its vision. Accordingly the key to understanding the Court's mission and, within it, its tendency to pursue activism or restraint lies in its desire to work constructively and harmoniously with courts in the Member States in order to develop a workable legal system for the EC underpinned by assumptions to which the judiciary at all levels feel able to subscribe. Extending the reach of Community law was possible and remains possible only in so far as the willing and active support of national courts is on loan to the European Court. This grants to national courts a far more significant control over the exercise of the European Court's jurisdiction than may be conveyed by the apparently hierarchical discourse that emphasized the supremacy of EC law. So the more recent caution that is visible in the Court's approach to the interpretation of some aspects of EC law, most conspicuously those relating to the limits of EC competence, may be provoked in part by the emerging debate about the perceived need for the nature and purpose of the European project to be re-assessed in the context of a broader anxiety to think creatively about the governance of an enlarged Union, but also, and more directly, it is shaped by the influence brought to bear by national judges. This, it will be argued, is an entirely desirable process, and, moreover, it illuminates the point that activism and restraint are part of a much richer process of constitutionalisation within the EC system than would be captured by an account that alleges only egregious ambition nurtured by the Luxembourg court.

2. THE CONSTITUTIONALISATION OF THE TREATIES

The early years of the European Community were marked by some audacious statements by its Court about the character of European Community law, and in particular about its relationship with national law.[1] The Treaty of Rome established the so-called preliminary reference procedure, which permits, and in some circumstances requires, a national court to ask the European Court to rule on a point of Community law raised in national proceedings. This was doubtless designed to reduce the risk that Community law would be subjected to different interpretations in different jurisdictions, which would in turn have damaged the likelihood of Community law serving as a common foundation for the achievement of the objectives of the Treaty. But the Treaty of Rome did not stipulate that Community law should be applied in national courts at all. And it said nothing about which legal order should prevail in the event of conflict between Community law and national law.

A. Direct Effect and Supremacy

Both these points were eagerly and vividly addressed by the Court at an early stage in the evolution of EC law. First, the application of Community law in national courts. In 1963 the Court decided that Community law may be directly effective, which means it may create legally enforceable rights before national courts and tribunals. This was the famous decision in *Van Gend en Loos*[2] in which the Court stated that:

> The objective of the EEC Treaty, which is to establish a common market, the functioning of which is of direct concern to interested parties in the Community, implies that this Treaty is more than an agreement which merely creates mutual obligations between the contracting states . . . the Community constitutes a new legal order of international law for the benefit of which the states have limited their sovereign rights, albeit within limited fields, and the subjects of which comprise not only Member States but also their nationals. Independently of the legislation of the Member States, Community law therefore not only imposes obligations on individuals but is also intended to confer on them rights which become part of their legal heritage.

---

[1] Little, if anything, in this chapter has to do directly with the current state of the non-EC EU, so it is of the Community rather than the Union that I write.
[2] Case 26/62, [1963] ECR 1.

One might question the Court's reasoning. For example, the existence of the preliminary reference procedure, which the Court claims in *Van Gend en Loos* indicates that the States had accepted that EC law had an authority capable of application before national courts, is not in fact decisive. It could perfectly well be concluded that the impact of Community law within the national legal order was a matter of national law and the question whether a particular judge could make use of the preliminary reference procedure consequently dependent on national constitutional traditions. I do not explore that issue further here. I insist only on the importance of appreciating the Court's style of reasoning—that the direct effect of Community law before national courts flows from the spirit and purpose of the Treaty, and that the Court is not confined to purely textual inquiry. Moreover it deliberately chooses to assert that this is a 'new legal order' (of international law) which operates 'independently of the legislation of the Member States.'

The second key constitutional principle asserted by the Court at an early stage is that of supremacy or primacy—that Community law overrides national law in the event of conflict between them. Again, this is not made explicit in the Treaty. But in 1964 the Court asserted that a hierarchy places Community law above national law. In *Costa v ENEL*[3] it explained:

> By contrast with ordinary international treaties, the EEC Treaty has created its own legal system which, on the entry into force of the Treaty, became an integral part of the legal systems of the Member States and which their courts are bound to apply. . . . The executive force of Community law cannot vary from one State to another in deference to subsequent domestic laws, without jeopardising the attainment of the objectives of the Treaty. . . . It follows from all these observations that the law stemming from the Treaty, an independent source of law, could not, because of its special and original nature, be overridden by domestic legal provisions, however framed, without being deprived of its character as Community law and without the legal basis of the Community itself being called into question.

Again, the principle that Community law is supreme and must prevail in the event of conflict with national law is drawn from the structure of the Treaty, as necessary to give effect to its ambitions. The Court is not deterred by the absence of explicit textual support in the Treaty; and the novel and independent character of Community law, explicitly contrasted with 'ordinary international treaties', is asserted by the Court even as it constructs that new legal order.

So in *Simmenthal* the Court added that '. . . every national court must, in a case within its jurisdiction, apply Community law in its entirety and protect rights which the latter confers on individuals and must accordingly set aside any provision of national law which may conflict with it, whether prior or subsequent to the Community rule.'[4] And in *Factortame* the Court declared that 'Community law must be interpreted as meaning that a national court which, in a case before

---

[3] Case 6/64, [1964] ECR 585.
[4] Case 106/77, [1978] ECR 629.

it concerning Community law, considers that the sole obstacle which precludes it from granting interim relief is a rule of national law must set aside that rule.'[5]

The Court has also added the doubtless logical but conspicuously bold confirmation that Community law overrides even national constitutionally protected rights. This was first clearly stated in *Internationale Handelsgesellschaft*.[6] Supremacy has a profound impact on national legal orders.

B. The Constitutional Courts of the EC

These are hugely sensitive issues. The Court is insisting, by combining direct effect and supremacy, that national courts should apply Community law and that, moreover, they should apply it in preference to any conflicting norm found within their domestic legal order. They should, if necessary, protect the Community law rights of an individual against preferences of that State expressed through legislation duly passed according to established democratic processes.

This sounds extraordinary. And it has been criticised, *inter alia* for the lack of textual support in the Treaty.[7] But actually it is not as extraordinary as it might appear. 'Supremacy' is not so new. It is orthodox that treaties and indeed international law generally constitute a higher form of law than national law and that incompatible national laws should be set aside. And the notion of 'direct effect'—that a legal provision of transnational pedigree may have effect within a national legal order—has a close counterpart in the international law notion of the self-executing treaty provision. Even the European Court's technique of legal reasoning is not quite as remarkable as one might think. Interpreting treaties on the basis of their spirit and purpose rather than simply their words is not only normal in public international law, it is in fact required under the Vienna Convention on Treaties. Article 31(1) provides that 'A treaty shall be interpreted in good faith in accordance with the ordinary meaning to be given to the terms of the treaty in their context and in the light of its object and purpose.' So the case can be made that EC law's supposed divergence from orthodox public international law is more a question of words than substance.[8]

---

[5] Case C–213/89, [1990] ECR I–2433.

[6] Case 11/70, [1970] ECR 1125.

[7] Cf H Rasmussen, *On Law and Policy in the European Court of Justice: a Comparative Study in Judicial Policymaking* (Martinus Nijhoff, Dordrecht, 1986); TC Hartley, *Constitutional Problems of the EU* (Hart Publishing, Oxford, 1999). The question of how to measure *due* restraint in interpretation is central yet elusive. Criticism of the Court in this vein demands that attention be paid to devising a theory of legal reasoning and interpretation; cf J Bengoetxea, N MacCormick and L Moral Soriano, 'Integration and Integrity in the Legal Reasoning of the European Court of Justice', in G de Búrca and JHH Weiler, *The European Court of Justice* (Oxford University Press, Oxford, 2001) ch 3. Such inquiry could be enriched by a comparative survey of interpretative practice among international tribunals and national constitutional courts (more visible in Rasmussen than Hartley's work).

[8] Cf O Spiermann, 'The other side of the story: an unpopular essay on the making of the EC legal order' (1999) 10 *EJIL* 763.

What is remarkable is not so much the European Court's pronouncements on the constitutional character of EC law, but rather the way in which national courts in the Member States have imported, accepted and faithfully applied those pronouncements. It is this that has come to make the EC legal order look different from that created by an 'ordinary' treaty and governed by public international law.

International treaties are mediated in different ways through the legal orders of States party to those treaties. Diverse national constitutional traditions affect the absorption of norms drawn from international treaties. At one level the same is true of the EC Treaty. Different national constitutional arrangements condition the way in which a bridge is built between the EC system and the national legal order.[9] Some Member States have constitutions which expressly provide for the application of international treaties by domestic courts. In other states, including the United Kingdom, a domestic act is required to provide the foundation for the application by national courts of legal rules deriving from an international source. In the UK, the European Communities Act 1972 did the trick as far as the Treaty of Rome was concerned. One might question whether these national approaches conform or are capable of conforming with the European Court's own perception of the status of EC law as of itself 'an integral part of the legal systems to the Member States . . . which their courts are bound to apply . . .', asserted in *Costa v ENEL*. This might take us into a potentially unrewarding argument about whether EC law is an independent source of law or whether it depends for its force within the national systems on the existence of some bridge recognised by the national system. I would be provisionally content with the suggestion that both approaches are right—within the terms laid down by their own systems—and that it is unhelpful to seek a single framework within which to resolve such collisions.[10] For the truly remarkable thing about the EC system is that the way in which it functions looks very much like the way which the European Court mapped out in the early 1960s. To be clear: that does not mean that substantive EC law is always interpreted and applied in full accordance with the more-or-less sophisticated instructions of the European Court, but it does mean that national courts do accept by and large that EC law is capable of direct effect in national proceedings and by and large they do not contest that within the scope of its application EC law prevails over national law. It may be that different national legal orders reach these conclusions through different routes,[11] and it may be that these routes do not coincide with the purity of the constitutional vision expressed by the Court in the 'heroic cases' of the 1960s. But, as an observable fact, EC law enjoys a depth of penetration into national legal and administrative culture which far transcends

---

[9] For a summary see S Weatherill and P Beaumont, *EU Law* (3rd edn, Penguin Books, London, 1999), ch 12; TC Hartley, *The Foundations of European Community Law* (4th edn Oxford University Press, Oxford, 1998), ch 8.

[10] Cf the evasive Art 53 of the EU Charter of Fundamental Rights.

[11] Cf A-M Slaughter, A Stone Sweet and JHH Weiler (eds), *The European Courts and National Courts: Doctrine and Jurisprudence* (Hart Publishing, Oxford, 1998); J Schwarze (ed), *The Birth of a European Constitutional Order: the Interaction of National and European Constitutional Law* (Nomos, Baden-Baden, 2000).

that of orthodox international treaties. This is the European Court's great genius and this is what makes good the assertion that EC law is truly *sui generis*, occupying a space somewhere between the law of a (federal) State and the law of an international organisation and performing functions that are similar to those performed by legal rules in both those types of system.

So the Court's early choice of terminology was inspired. It asserted the novelty of the EC legal order, while it described constitutional phenomena that were not materially distinct from orthodox international law principles. And, initially, it did it in cases with trivial facts that would not tend to grab attention. Its discourse of the 'new legal order' induced national courts to treat it as a new legal order, and thereby facilitated its absorption more deeply into national systems than would have applied to orthodox treaties. Thus, over time, the intriguing but highly contestable claim to novelty became reality.

In this way the EC legal order has been 'constitutionalised'.[12] The fundamental constitutional characteristics of EC law have much in common with those which one would expect to discover in the constitution of a federal-type State. In particular, supremacy appears to dictate a hierarchical relationship between the two levels of law-making, placing the (quasi-) federal rules on top. And of course there is much more to the claim of 'constitutionalisation'. The EC system has been developed under a model of teleological legal reasoning[13] that has led it, inter alia, to afford judicial protection to the individual who may be affected by the exercise of power by the Community institutions; general principles of Community law have been developed, in some instances without explicit textual support in the Treaty, which constrain the capacity to act of Community institutions and in some, albeit ill-defined, circumstances of national authorities too;[14] and the Treaty establishes institutionally relatively sophisticated forms of law-making which reflect forms of representative democracy at both national and European level, in the shape of the Council and the Parliament respectively. So this is a 'constitution' of sorts. It functions as a constitution in the 'thin' sense that it is constitutive of the system that is the EC legal order. But the Court is rhetorically bolder. In *Parti Ecologiste Les Verts v Parliament*[15] the Court described the Community as 'a Community based on the rule of law, inasmuch as neither its Member States nor its institutions can avoid a review of the question whether the measures adopted by them are in conformity with the basic constitutional charter, the Treaty. . . .' What seems to be at stake here is a constitution that is characterised by an assumption of the subjection of the exercise of public power to judicial control even in circumstances

---

[12] Eg JHH Weiler, *The Constitution of Europe: Do the new clothes have an emperor?* (Cambridge University Press, Cambridge, 1999), R Dehousse, *The European Court of Justice* (Macmillan, Basingstoke, 1998).

[13] Cf J Bengoetxea, *The Legal Reasoning of the European Court of Justice* (Oxford University Press, Oxford, 1993); A Arnull, *The European Union and its Court of Justice* (Oxford University Press, Oxford, 1999), ch 14.

[14] For a full survey see T Tridimas, *The General Principles of EC Law* (Oxford University Press, Oxford, 1999).

[15] Case 294/83, [1986] ECR 1339.

where this is not explicitly foreseen in the governing texts. The legal control of the institutions of the Community itself, which is what was in dispute in *Parti Ecologiste Les Verts*, was deepened by the Court's readiness to extend its powers of review beyond those explicitly conferred by the Treaty. This tends towards a stronger and thicker kind of constitution, of a type that might not be readily associated with an organisation existing beyond the State even if it is a 'new legal order of international law.' This rhetorical inflation has generated much debate about the nature and purpose of the current constitutionalised system, and about the feasibility and desirability of seeking to re-think the foundations of the system, which, on some but by no means all views, might involve devising a 'Constitution' for Europe.[16] My submission is that such an approach risks generating unproductive argument about choosing superior sources of legal and political authority in Europe, whereas the current position, in which the 'who is boss?' question does not need an answer, reflects the desirable core of the constitutional ambiguity created and nurtured by the European Court. *Both* sources of authority, national and European level, have complementary roles to play. The Court's approach permits this.[17]

What the European Court really did that was dramatic was not to coax the genie of the 'new legal order' out of the space that it found between the lines of the Treaty of Rome but rather to make national courts its willing allies in sustaining this vision, and thereby to transform the character of Community law into a transnational legal system that is also applied in the everyday life of the national legal order. EC law creates directly effective rights, and over time the Court has been gradually more assertive in specifying the nature of the remedies that must be made available within national legal orders in order to secure the vindication of those rights.[18] The trigger of 'direct effect' has been supplemented by rights to legal protection that are not dependent on the relatively limited circumstances in which direct effect is identified; the *Francovich* line of case law, concerning State liability to compensate individuals whose (not necessarily directly effective) rights have been infringed offers the boldest example.[19] In fact, direct effect is increasingly a catch-all phrase used to describe a broad range of circumstances in which EC law may exert effect in domestic legal proceedings,[20] to the point where, for

---

[16] Cf J-C Piris, 'Does the European Union have a Constitution? Does it need one?' (1999) 24 *ELRev* 557; P Craig, 'Constitutions, Constitutionalism, and the European Union' (2001) 7 *ELJ* 125; 'Special Issue: Can Europe have a Constitution?' (2001) 12/1 *Kings College Law Journal*.

[17] So its hint in Opinion 1/91 on the draft EEA Agreement [1991] ECR I–6084 that some parts of the EC system are of such importance that they could not be modified by the Member States (especially paras 71–2) has subsequently been wisely ignored. On what the Court might have meant see F Berman, 'Community Law and International law: How far does either belong to the other?' ch 12 in B Markesinis (ed), *Bridging the Channel: the Clifford Chance Lectures* (Oxford University Press, Oxford, 1996), especially at p 271; Tridimas, n 14 above at 37–8.

[18] For a recent survey see T Tridimas, 'Liability for Breach of Community Law: Growing Up and Mellowing Down?' (2001) 38 *CMLRev* 301.

[19] Cases C–6, C–9/90, *Francovich v Italian State,* [1991] ECR I–5357; see further Pt 3.4 below.

[20] Cf D Edward, 'Direct Effect, the Separation of Powers and the Judicial Enforcement of Obligations', in *Scritti in onore di Giuseppe Federico Mancini* (1998).

some commentators, it is time to abandon such gateways between EC and national law and to treat the system in a more overtly unified fashion.[21] But the core message is that EC law has permeated national law to an astonishingly deep extent. The Court's case law, absorbed at national level, has brought about and promoted the 'Europeanisation' of law in areas of remedies and procedure that might once have been thought largely, if not entirely, constitutionally off-limits the EC.[22] There are, of course, many reasons to wonder how helpful EC law's contribution really is.[23] But at this stage I content myself with description. EC law in many respects *is* national law; and national courts are European Community courts.[24]

C. The European Court's Working Environment

This invites a series of immediate and direct questions. How did the European Court get away with this feat of breathtaking constitutional acrobatics? How did it conjure up that magical legal transformation? Why did spellbound national courts accept this? Why did national political elites in the Member States not lash out at this audacious Court, which had (surely unexpectedly) converted EC law into a controlling device that could be enforced through the medium not only of transnational enforcement procedures but also the fierce grip of domestic courts? And why did legal academics not expose the Court's disingenuous hailing of a 'new' legal order as no more than new clothes for an old phenomenon, the international law of treaties?

There are answers of a sort to all these questions, although it took a long time for the task of piecing together persuasive accounts to be addressed. For the purposes of this chapter I focus first of all on the position of the political elites in the Member States. Why did they not seek to curb the Court's determination to cause a dramatic escalation in the constitutional vigour of EC law? Why, in short, were the principles of supremacy and direct effect allowed to survive, to flourish?

It would be admittedly foolish to offer an antiseptically clean account that seizes the level of explanatory generality in preference for examination of the role of individuals and particular institutional contexts. Moreover, accounts that speak glibly of the 'State' risk missing its disaggregation in practical politics into an array

---

[21] Cf S Prechal, 'Does Direct Effect Still Matter?' (2000) 37 *CMLRev* 1047.

[22] Eg R Caranta, 'Judicial protection against Member States: a new jus commune takes shape' (1995) 32 *CMLRev* 703; R Craufurd Smith, 'Remedies for Breach of EU Law in National Courts', in P Craig and G de Búrca (eds), *The Evolution of EU Law* (Oxford University Press, Oxford, 1999) ch 8; W Van Gerven, 'Of Rights, Remedies and Procedures' (2000) 37 *CMLRev* 501.

[23] Perhaps especially worthwhile amid the general welcome for *Francovich* (among EC lawyers) is the comment on its 'largely negative' aspects by C Harlow, 'Francovich and the Problem of the Disobedient State' (1996) 2 *ELJ* 199. See also for a critique of, *inter alia*, the judicial contribution F Snyder, 'The Effectiveness of European Community Law: Institutions, Processes, Tools and Techniques' (1993) 56 *MLR* 19; M Dougan, 'The *Francovich* Right to Reparation' (2000) 6 *Euro Public Law* 103; ET Swaine, 'Subsidiarity and Self-Interest: Federalism at the European Court of Justice' (2000) 41 *Harvard Intl LJ* 1.

[24] I Maher, 'National Courts as European Community Courts' (1994) 14 *Legal Studies* 226.

of competing public and private interest groups.[25] However, the most convincing set of accounts have at their heart the desire of the Member States to see their Treaty commitments credibly and reciprocally enforced. The bite of the European Court's constitutional pronouncements on the nature of Community law would be felt by defaulting States brought before their own national courts, not simply subjected to the Commission supervision envisaged by the Treaty. But this would be true of all States failing to comply with their Treaty commitments. Defection from the agreed *communautaire* bargain became vastly less feasible once the vigorous application of EC law by national courts became the norm. And a State gains more by seeing its partners denied the chance to cheat than it loses in relinquishing its own cheat card. So the Court is allowed autonomy to craft a stronger legal order than the Member States might originally have foreseen because it is acting as their agent in strengthening the credibility of the outcomes of inter-state bargaining. The Court, exercising a power delegated to its by the Member States, enjoys a degree of autonomy when acting in its distinctive institutional setting, and embrace of the principles of direct effect and supremacy did not at all carry the likelihood of a reaction designed to curtail it or its rulings.[26] In any event, Court rulings on the interpretation of the Treaty can be set aside only with the support of all the Member States acting at the inconveniently rare moment of Treaty revision. Court rulings therefore possess considerable insulation from State objections. Indeed, unanimity as the voting rule in Council is also crucial to the viability of this explanation of the readiness of the Member States to accept the constitutional path taken by the Court. A rule of unanimity prevails for Treaty revision, of course, but it is well known that unanimous voting was also the norm for the adoption of secondary legislation throughout the first thirty years of the Community's existence. It is normal to portray this as damaging, and of course, log rolling opportunities aside, the veto tends to suppress radical initiatives, either at Council level or even by stifling Commission readiness to propose ambitious initiatives. But the existence of unanimity in Council would typically suffice to see a measure adopted, even if the constitutional basis for the measure might have been distinctly hard to discover on a formal reading of the Treaty. In this way, consumer policy and environmental policy developed at EC level—lacking any explicit basis in the Treaty,[27] but backed by the unanimous support of the Member States.[28] The Court did not interfere. Quite the reverse. In *Procureur de la*

---

[25] Cf A-M Slaughter, 'International Law in a World of Liberal States' (1995) 6 *EJIL* 503; see generally in the EU context, S Hix, *The Political System of the EU* (Macmillan, Basingstoke, 1999).

[26] This nods (in alarmingly superficial manner!) towards a rich literature using and criticising a principal/agent model for understanding the relationship between Member States and EC institutions, particularly the Commission and the Court. See eg A Stone Sweet and J Caporaso, 'From Free Trade to Supranational Polity: the European Court and Integration' ch 4 in W Sandholtz and A Stone Sweet (eds), *European Integration and Supranational Governance* (Oxford University Press, Oxford, 1998); M Shapiro, 'The European Court of Justice', in P Craig and G de Búrca, n 22 above; D Wincott, 'A Community of Law? European Law and Judicial Politics: the Court of Justice and Beyond' (2000) 35 *Government and Opposition* 3.

[27] Until 1993 in the case of consumer policy, 1987 in the case of environmental policy.

[28] See S Weatherill and P Beaumont, n 9 above, ch 28.

Republique v Adbhu[29] it referred to environmental protection as 'one of the Community's essential objectives', although that could only be taken as a reference to legislative practice and political preferences for at the time the Community had no explicit competence at all in the field of environmental protection, never mind any pretension to its place as an 'essential objective'. Unanimity in Council was a high hurdle to cross; once crossed it allowed the EC legislature to fly into realms that it would have been difficult to argue were authorised by the Treaty. But typically there was no such argument. The legislature was responsible, alongside the Court, for deepening the practical scope of the EC legal order beyond that envisaged by the Treaty; all this 'ambitious' legislation was underpinned by the principles of direct effect and supremacy, cutting deep into State options for defection from the agreed bargain, but it was all legislation adopted by unanimity, so there was a commitment to its enforcement throughout the territory of all the Member States. So, in so far as they were aware of them, one can grasp why political elites in the Member States would be expected to regard the Court's great 'constitutionalising' judgments with, at least, equanimity and quite probably with approval.[30]

This would not fully explain why national *courts* would be content to swallow the European Court's view. There are a clutch of reasons which might help us to understand why supremacy and direct effect were largely absorbed by national courts. Karen Alter has recently published an important book which explores this matter.[31] She finds that the formal pull of legal reasoning plays a part; so too the attraction of empowerment promised to national judges by the chance to apply supreme Community rules. The picture is complex and needs to be broken down, *inter alia*, according to the substantive policy sectors involved and according to the incentives of different courts—for example, lower courts are much more obviously plainly 'empowered' than supreme constitutional courts within the Member States.[32] But it is significant that the point that 'their' States had agreed to the relevant rules at Community level under a requirement of unanimous voting in Council should not have been enough to calm judicial constitutional sensitivities about the validity of Community legal acts. Agreement at Community level is not at all the same thing as agreement achieved through the application of domestic constitutional processes. Agreement in Council may short-circuit democratic

---

[29]   Case 240/83, [1985] ECR 531.

[30]   Cf ground-breaking work by JHH Weiler in 'The Community System: the Dual Character of Supranationalism' (1981) 1 *YEL* 273; also K Alter, *Establishing the Supremacy of European Law* (Oxford University Press, Oxford, 2001), ch 5.

[31]   K Alter, *ibid.* See also B de Witte, 'Direct Effect, Supremacy and the Nature of the Legal Order', ch 5 in P Craig and G de Búrca, n 22 above; W Mattli and A-M Slaughter, 'The Role of National Court in the Process of European Integration: Accounting for Judicial Preferences and Constraints', ch 9 in A-M Slaughter, A Stone Sweet and JHH Weiler, n 11 above; D Chalmers, 'Judicial Preferences and the Community Legal Order' (1997) 60 *MLR* 164.

[32]   And so it is interesting and illuminating that the judicial anxieties of recent years about the direction taken by the Court (and the EU more widely) have been largely expressed by national constitutional courts; see below.

control at national level. For in so far as the agreed rules escaped the reach of the Treaty then, even if agreed unanimously, they are being agreed in a Community framework, and they may represent a shift of power from national to Community level which has not been foreseen by the Treaty as approved according to domestic constitutional arrangements. This will tend to subvert effective national-level control. The Community's 'functional creep', driven by the use of unanimous voting particularly under the harmonisation legal base, Article 100, and under Article 235,[33] attracted occasional criticism in the first 30 years of the Community's lifecycle[34] but never surfaced as a major anxiety before national courts. The issue which did, however, alert the legal and political community to the realisation that even a unanimity rule in Council would not be treated by (all) national courts as a sufficient reason for refusing to use national standards to check the validity of Community rules was human rights. German courts, in particular, made plain that in so far as Community rules infringed human rights standards constitutionally protected in Germany, then they would be challengeable on that basis and potentially invalid on German territory.[35] This was bark but never bite. But it directly challenges the logic of supremacy, for it envisages national standards overriding Community rules. And—though it is perilous to be too glib in identifying cause and effect—the European Court 'responded' by asserting the protection of human rights as a general principle of Community law.[36] In this way it may be taken to have hoped to have limited the likelihood of national invalidation of Community acts by itself asserting a readiness to perform a review function at Community level that would be no less rigorous than that prevailing under national law. One may deduce that it will have hoped to deter national courts from acting in a way that would destabilise the uniformity of application of Community law and to claim for itself the sole jurisdiction to rule on the validity of Community law. Whether or not the European Court is serious about the protection of fundamental rights or whether instead this was a device to sweeten national courts into accepting the full implications of the supremacy doctrine is a matter that has caused controversy.[37] But the German courts accepted that so long as protection of fundamental rights was sufficiently assured at Community level, they would not intervene to review Community acts against domestic standards.[38]

---

[33] Now Arts 94 and 308 respectively, both requiring unanimity in Council.

[34] Cf House of Lords Select Committee on the ECs, 1977–1978 (22nd Report); G Close, 'The Legal Basis for the Consumer Protection Programme of the EEC and Priorities for Action' (1983) 8 *ELRev* 221.

[35] Most prominently in the so-called 'Solange I' decision, available in English at [1974] 2 CMLR 549.

[36] Cf P Alston (ed), *The EU and Human Rights* (Oxford University Press, Oxford, 1999); T Tridimas, n 18 above, ch 6; K Lenaerts, 'Respect for Fundamental Rights as a Constitutional Principle of the European Union' (2000) 6 *Columbia Jnl Euro Law* 1.

[37] Cf JHH Weiler and N Lockhart's famously fiery 'Taking rights seriously: the European Court and its fundamental rights jurisprudence' (1995) 32 *CMLRev* 51.

[38] Compare 'Solange I' [1974] 2 CMLR 549 with 'Solange II' [1987] 2 CMLR 225. Cf J Kokott, 'Report on Germany', in A-M Slaughter, A Stone Sweet and JHH Weiler, n 31 above; R Dehousse, n 12 above at 62–66.

And—the key point—the system thereafter continued to operate much as the European Court envisaged in its judgments of the early 1960s. This has some claim to be treated as a paradox of supremacy. The European Court asserts that EC law comes first. But to make this a practical reality it was forced to listen to and respond to national courts, and to shape EC law with an eye to their anxieties. A brutal assertion that national courts may not and must not review EC rules would be sustainable only if their concerns about damage potentially caused by the shaping of EC rules are met and acknowledged. For otherwise the national courts might simply decline to comply with the European Court's instruction to allocate to Luxembourg the exclusive competence to rule on the validity of Community legislation. The European Court—the Union generally—has no coercive powers that it could bring to bear in such rebellious circumstances. Such a collision would be immensely serious for the viability of the EC legal order, as all judges would certainly appreciate. So, one may deduce, the European Court maintains the viability of its construction of the EC legal order by taking account of the messages sent from other judicial fora in Europe. This is indirect inter-court judicial dialogue; it is 'constitutional conversations'.[39] It is submitted that it is right that this should occur in Europe. And the result—in this instance, improved protection of fundamental rights—is not at all objectionable. Crucially, this does not at all put in question the Court's construction of a new and supreme legal order in the EC. Rather, it reminds us that what is really 'new' about that legal order is its willing digestion by national courts. Ensuring that co-operation continues, and ensuring that constitutional conversations conducted in good faith do not spill over into (irreconcilable) constitutional clashes, is the real mission pursued by the European Court. This explains and provides a basis for assessing its supposed activism or restraint. It also offers the appealing suggestion that the strongest reason for national courts to adhere to the European Court's approach does lie and should lie in the quality of the legal reasoning offered by the European Court in support for the full implications of its judgments.

3. THE IMPLICATIONS OF THE RISE OF QUALIFIED MAJORITY VOTING

As a general proposition the judgments of the European Court dealing with the constitutional character of EC law were absorbed into the legal orders of the Member States and in practical effect they were there applied. And the practice of unanimity in Council largely suppressed anxieties that the pool of law to which these principles of supremacy and direst effect attached had surpassed the limits allowed by the Treaty. Member States controlled the expansion of EC law, each holding a veto, and each had an incentive to embrace the Court's principles which decreased opportunities for defection by their partners from unanimously agreed

---

[39] Cf A Stone Sweet, 'Constitutional Dialogues in the European Community', ch 11 in A-M Slaughter, A Stone Sweet and JHH Weiler, n 12 above.

rules. A wickedly superficial summary, perhaps. But such was the 'benign neglect' enjoyed by the activist European Court for some 30 years.[40] The claim put forward in this section of the paper is that the constitutional and political environment has changed a great deal in recent years, with the result that the Court is under closer scrutiny, but that the Court's anxiety to practise the art of the possible in sustaining the virtues of the EC legal order remains consistent.

A. The Single European Act and After

The Single European Act was the first major formal revision of the original Treaties. It entered into force in 1987—that is, almost 30 years after the entry into force of the Treaty of Rome. And it fundamentally changed the nature of the environment in which the European Court (as well as the other institutions) operates, but it did so on several levels and the full implications may be difficult to appreciate under the weight of inevitable inter-linkages.

But there are two key connected impacts on which I would like to focus. First, the rise of Qualified Majority Voting in Council. Secondly, the 're-discovery' of sources for reinvigorating the Community legal order, which were not dependent on the activism of the Court, most prominently legislative energy and Treaty revision.

The Single European Act injected into the Community system a healthy dose of Qualified Majority Voting in the Council (hereafter QMV). Unanimity had been the norm, and remained the norm in some areas, but QMV was available for legislative activity in a number of areas, initially principally connected with the completion of the internal market but later extended by the Treaties of Maastricht, Amsterdam and Nice to cover ever wider fields, as embrace of an extended rule of QMV obtained a dynamism at times of EC Treaty revision. This was combined with an enhanced role for the Parliament under the co-decision procedure.[41] Although it is salutary to recall that most measures susceptible to adoption by QMV are in fact adopted unanimously, nonetheless QMV throws up the possibility of outvoted States, bound in law by legislation to which they object. This happens.

Of course, the logic of QMV insists on its necessity in a Community that is expanding, both geographically and functionally. A unanimity rule would, it is said, condemn the Community to legislative paralysis. The Member States, in so far as it is rational to ascribe a coherent view to such a disparate group of interests, must have judged that what they lose in being outvoted in some areas they more than make up for in outvoting in other areas. On the other hand, QMV risks damage to minority rights. It brings a tension to the Community system

---

[40] F Stein, 'Lawyers, Judges and the Making of a Transnational Constitution' (1981) 75 *AJIL* 1.
[41] These trends have occurred to a lesser extent, with a correspondingly less prominent emergent tension, in the non-EC EU.

relating to the proper definition of its reach which, at least seen from the standpoint of national governments, was suppressed under a regime allowing veto rights in the Council.

A prominent trend since the Single European Act has been a shift away front the brutal pre-SEA technique of vetoing measures requiring unanimity to more subtle methods for minorities to secure protection even where outvoting through the Community legislative process is a possibility or an actual fact.[42] In the constitutional architecture these take several guises, grouped under two principal headings. One variety involves minority acquiescence in the development of (potentially unwelcome) Community or Union initiatives induced by permission to stand aside from what is agreed. In different forms this covers derogations, 'opt-outs' and the Amsterdam innovation, 'enhanced co-operation.' This is the 'flexibility debate.'[43] The other variety involves express limits being placed on Community (and less prominently Union) activity, with the result that the minority is protected, without the need for a veto, simply because the Community is expressly forbidden from swallowing up a particular function. This sounds much like the principle that the Community possesses only the competence attributed to it by its Treaty which has always been the governing constitutional rule, and which is now found in Article 5(1) EC, but which was nevertheless of diminished practical importance in the days of unanimous voting in Council. But in the post-SEA regime of QMV new and more practical controls have been devised. So, for example, it is frequently and correctly observed that periodic Treaty revision has expanded Community competence, but one should also be aware how carefully defined the new competences have tended to be. For example, the Community has lately been allowed competence to act in the fields of public health, consumer protection and culture. But it is not a broad competence. It is a competence defined as supplementary to that of the Member States. The Community may, for example, adopt incentive measures, but harmonisation of public health laws is explicitly excluded by Article 152(4). The same is true of cultural policy under Article 151(5). Harmonisation in such areas is excluded under the new Treaty provisions. 'Subsidiarity' under Article 5(2) EC is fragile as an operationally useful device but as an expression of a general mood that an intensification of Community activity should be carefully justified it too fits the trend of thinking harder about how to define where the Community's intervention should end, in part reflecting how sensitive it is that Community competence should be seen to be readily expandable under a constitutional system which has robbed States of a braking veto. The growing interest in elaborating a 'hard list' of Community competences is similarly protective in motivation.

---

[42] Cf generally, identification of 'conservatory elements' vs 'constitutionalising elements', A Dashwood, 'States in the European Union' (1998) 23 *ELRev* 201.

[43] See G de Búrca and J Scott (eds), *Constitutional Change in the EU: from Uniformity to Flexibility?* (Hart Publishing, Oxford, 2000) for a collection of essays and copious bibliographic references.

B. 'QMV' and the European Court's Diet

It is on the Court I focus for the purposes of this paper. It cannot be divorced from its wider institutional environment. The tensions of 'QMV' have spilled over into the judicial arena. In the days of unanimity a State would simply veto a measure it did not wish to see adopted in Council. The ability to assemble unanimity in Council became the crucial determinant of the exercise of Community competence. No unanimity; no adopted measure. And vice versa, the existence of unanimity in Council would typically suffice to see a measure adopted even if the constitutional basis for the measure might have been distinctly hard to discover on a formal reading of the Treaty. So the constitutional principle that the Community has only the powers conferred on it by its Treaty became concealed and in a number of areas the Community underwent a functional expansion that owed little to a formal reading of the Treaty and rather a lot to, in particular, a very generous but unanimously approved reading of the permissible reach of the harmonisation programme envisaged by the Treaty and to use of what was Article 235 EC.

In a world of 'QMV' a State can be outvoted in Council. This ensures a sensitivity to the demarcation of Community competence which would have been of no practical relevance in a world of unanimity. The outvoted State may consider that the majority has interpreted the Treaty to confer a competence to act in the disputed field which is not authorised by the Treaty. This is a matter of legal interpretation. Having lost the political debate it may, therefore, transplant its objections to the legal forum, the Court, and seek to persuade the Court that the measure is legally invalid. The Court is thrust into majority *versus* minority disputes which simply did not arise in a world of unanimous voting.

The Court has been faced with submissions that legislation is invalid for violation of the principle of subsidiarity but thus far it has been content to confine its review to the margins. It allows the decision-maker, in this case the majority will expressed in Council plus the Parliament, a wide discretion in making choices about how to legislate. In both *United Kingdom v Council* and in *Germany v Parliament and Council*[44] applications for annulment by States that had not supported a challenged measure adopted by the Council failed. In the former case the UK was accused by Advocate-General Leger of having 'created some confusion by regularly invoking the principle of subsidiarity in the course of the proceedings —without, however, relying on it as a ground of annulment—and seemingly equating it with the principle of proportionality.' The Court grumpily insisted that 'the argument of non-compliance with the principle of subsidiarity can be rejected at the outset.' In *Germany v Parliament and Council* claimed non-compliance with the obligation to give reasons explaining just why the measure adhered to the principle of subsidiarity failed to impress the Court. It felt the

---

[44] Case C–84/94, [1996] ECR I–5755 and Case C–233/94, [1997] ECR 2405 respectively.

reasons could be sufficiently deduced from the challenged Directive's Preamble even though the actual word 'subsidiarity' did not appear therein. Invitation to review legislative acts for violation of the subsidiarity principle attracts (understandable) caution among the judges of the European Court.[45]

Complaints that the Community lacked the competence to adopt a particular act reach to the heart of the constitutional division of power between the EC and its Member States. From the perspective of the legal protection of disgruntled outvoted minorities, it is the ruling of the European Court of Justice in October 2000 in the so-called 'Tobacco Advertising' case, more properly *Germany v Parliament and Council*,[46] that demands examination. In this case, Germany, having been outvoted in Council under the rules governing qualified majority voting and so having lost the political battle, succeeded in winning the legal battle. The Court refused to accept that Directive 98/34 governing the regulation of tobacco advertising could be validly presented as a measure of harmonisation. The Court did not consider that the conditions required for reliance on the legal base in the Treaty permitting harmonisation of laws were present in the case and it in effect acted to protect the minority against encroachment by the majority of Member States into areas which had not been demonstrated to the Court's satisfaction to fall within the scope of the EC's attributed competence.

Fixing the precise nature of the firmer threshold limits on what may be validly achieved by the Community legislator in the name of harmonisation is important, but escapes the scope of this chapter.[47] What is of interest here is the alignment between the Court's ruling and a general mood that a Community able to act in wide fields of economic activity and to do so with the need only for a qualified majority of its Member States must, as part of a politically stable and durable bargain, also take seriously the limits of the competence that its Member States have been prepared to confer on it.

Germany voted against Directive 98/34 in Council, but it was passed by qualified majority vote and, with appropriate support from the Parliament, it was duly adopted in July 1998. Directive 98/34 established much stricter rules on the advertising and sponsorship of tobacco products than had been laid down by previous Community interventions in the field. It imposed a ban on all forms of advertising and sponsorship of tobacco products throughout the EC, subject to limited exceptions only which, inter alia, allowed advertising in retail outlets.[48] Before the Court, Germany argued that the Directive was not a measure of harmonisation within the scope permitted by the Treaty. Accordingly, argued Germany, (what are now) Articles 47(2), 55 and 95 were not available to the EC as a legal basis for the measure. The EC would therefore have to look elsewhere in its Treaty for the com-

---

[45] See D Wyatt, 'Subsidiarity and Judicial Review', ch 32 in D O'Keeffe (ed), *Judicial Review in European Union Law: Liber Amicorum Gordon Slynn* (Kluwer, The Hague, 2000).

[46] Case C–376/98, [2000] ECR I–8419.

[47] Cf S Weatherill, 'The European Commission's Green Paper on European Contract Law: Context, Content and Constitutionalism' (2001) 24 *JCP* 339.

[48] On the position before and after the judgment see T Hervey, 'Up in smoke? Community (anti-)tobacco law and policy?' (2001) 26 *ELRev* 101.

petence to adopt such a measure. The EC does have an explicit competence in the field of public health. This is (now) Article 152. But this provision is carefully and narrowly defined and, of particular pertinence, it explicitly places harmonisation of public health laws beyond the scope of the powers transferred to the Community. So if (what is now) Article 95 would not do, then (what is now) Article 152 would not do either. At the core of the case is objection to the EC's competence under its Treaty to intervene in the market in this way under the cover of the harmonisation programme. And it was this fundamental constitutional question tied to the relationship between the Community's powers and those reserved to its Member States on which the Court chose to focus when it delivered its judgment. The Court insisted that the express exclusion of harmonisation under the public health Title of the EC Treaty, now found in Article 152(4) EC, cannot be circumvented by recourse to other Articles of the Treaty. The key question therefore focused on whether the chosen 'other articles', those authorising harmonisation in pursuit of defined objectives, were in themselves constitutionally adequate to support a measure of the challenged type. The Court agreed with Germany that (what is now) Article 95 and its fellows governing harmonisation in the services sector had been wrongly used, for the measure was found to be insufficiently closely connected with the task of improving the conditions for the establishment and functioning of the internal market, as defined (post-Amsterdam) in Articles 3(1)(c) and 14 of the EC Treaty, to which (what is now) Article 95 is addressed.

This litigation would not have arisen under a regime of unanimous voting. Germany would have voted against the proposal and it would not have become law. A regime of majority voting forces attention to be paid to awkward questions surrounding the constitutional limits of EC action. The very fact that a Member State, having lost the political debate about the desirability of such intervention in Council, was willing to convert its opposition into a legal challenge to the validity of the measure demonstrates the current sensitivity to the question of demarcating the limits of Community competence. The Court, projected into this tense environment, showed itself duly scrupulous in expressing its fidelity to the constitutional rule found in Article 5(1) EC that the competence conferred on the Community is limited to that defined by the Treaty.[49] The striking flavour of this judgment is the explicit reference to the constitutional limits of the EC's competence, which are defined by the Treaty. This is out of line with the caricature of the Court as (manically) pro-integrative. Moreover, it is out of line with the lifecycle of the European Community which has thrived on dynamic growth, in many ways distinguishable from traditional international organisations precisely because it has been little restricted in practice by the limits on its activities imposed by its Treaty.

One might take the view that the Court has chosen to respond to the constitutional deficiencies of QMV by asserting a more rigorous review of the limits of the EC jurisdiction (although as a matter of principle this rigour cannot be con-

---

[49] In this vein, see especially paras 83, 106–107 of the judgment.

fined to cases where unanimity in Council is lacking, even though litigation may be so limited in practice). It is concerned now with minority protection, whereas pre-SEA there were no minorities (among the governments of the Member States). In that sense, the Court's mission to participate in the expansion of the impact of the Community legal order has come to be affected by the changed context in which Community law is today no longer grounded firmly in the consent of all the (governments of the) Member States. In fact, one reading of the judgment is that the Court has rather neatly looked beyond subsidiarity in searching for a workable tool to assert the Community's limited competence—not by trying to make something of the horrible imprecision of Article 5(2) but rather by focusing very precisely on the limits of Treaty-conferred competence under Article 5(1), and then taking this seriously in connection with the interpretation of (what are now) Articles 95 and 153 EC.

C. Competence Control Perceived and Practised by National Courts

I wish to insist in particular that it is also the views of national courts that have been crucial to the European Court's apparent increased readiness to take account of the constitutional principle that majority preferences expressed through the EC legislature should not be able to subvert the constitutional principle that the EC can do what its Treaty allows and no more, even though in the past there is evidence that unanimously approved legislation did tend to escape the strict limits of powers conferred on the Community by the Treaty. I submit that the Court's role in competence-review is now directly conditioned by its perception of the vital need to retain the active support of its national courts for the vision of EC law mapped out by the Court.

Germany is again the main source. In its *Maastricht* ruling[50] the Bundesverfassungsgericht issued what may readily be taken as a form of 'warning' to the European Court (and the other institutions) about the consequences of judicial (and legislative) activism in realms that lie beyond the reach of the mandate:

> [49] . . . subsequent important alterations to the integration programme set up in the Union Treaty and to the Union's powers of action are no longer covered by the [German] Act of Accession to the present Treaty [on European Union]. Thus, if European institutions or agencies were to treat or develop the Union Treaty in a way that was no longer covered by the Treaty in the form that is the basis for the Act of Accession, the resultant legislative instruments would not be legally binding within the sphere of German sovereignty. The German state organs would be prevented for constitutional reasons from applying them in Germany. Accordingly the Federal Constitutional Court will review legal instruments of European institutions and agencies to see whether they remain within the limits of the sovereign rights conferred on them or transgress them.

---

[50] [1994] 1 CMLR 57 (unofficial translation).

[99] . . . the Union Treaty as a matter of principle distinguishes between the exercise of a sovereign power conferred for limited purposes and the amending of the Treaty, so that its interpretation may not have effects that are equivalent to an extension of the Treaty. Such an interpretation of enabling rules would not produce any binding effects for Germany.

On a broad-brush interpretation, the message is that the European Court (especially, but not only, among the Union institutions) should stop pushing competence ever wider or else its rulings will lose binding effect—and that the national courts (or at least *this* national court) will rule on limits of Union competence for themselves. At one level there is nothing surprising about this. Distinguishing between the amendment of Treaties and their mere interpretation is an orthodox matter,[51] underpinned by the concern to ensure that anything so significant as amendment occurs only according to recognised constitutional arrangements at national level. An act lacking a basis in a Treaty should indeed be treated as invalid. More alarming is the Bundesverfassungsgericht's denial of the European Court's exclusive role in performing that review function. If national courts assume the power to review the validity of a Community act, there is a risk that the very validity of Community law will be treated in different ways in different States, thereby disturbing the uniform application of Community law and imperilling legal certainty.[52]

Furthermore, one may criticise the ruling for exhibiting a concern for 'democracy' but locating democracy's protection in a national context. Everling argues that with vigour and panache that

> The background of the *Maastricht* judgment seems to be an old-fashioned understanding of the State as a sovereign and independent body which is master of its fate. However, this conception, which is based on the self-sufficient nation State in the traditional meaning, does not correspond to the realities of the world at the end of the twentieth century. It is characterised by the interdependence of all public and private activities notwithstanding frontiers between States and by the incapacity of States to solve the problems existing in the modern world on their own. The *Maastricht* judgment is one of the events in the running dispute to find the right equilibrium between the Member States . . . and the Community. . . .[53]

The judgment contains an unsettling static, nationalistic representation of the social legitimacy of political entities and it is vulnerable to criticism across a wide spectrum.[54]

---

[51] Albeit that fixing the margin between the two is certainly difficult; cf n 7 above.

[52] This is the reasoning employed by the Court in asserting its exclusivity in this matter; Case 314/85, *Foto-Frost v HZA Lubeck-Ost*, [1987] ECR 4199.

[53] U Everling, 'The Maastricht Judgment of the German Federal Constitutional Court and its Significance for the Development of the European Union' (1994) 14 *YEL* 1 at 18–19.

[54] And has been pungently criticised and occasionally defended. For a flavour of the debate see eg M Herdegen, 'Maastricht and the German Constitutional Court' (1994) 31 *CMLRev* 235; H-P Ipsen, 'Zehn Glossen zum Maastricht-Urteil' (1994) 29 *Europarecht* 1; M Zuleeg, 'The European Constitution under Constitutional Constraints: the German Scenario' (1997) 22 *ELRev* 19; Papers by JHH Weiler, N MacCormisk, UK Preuss, D Grimm and J Habermas in *Special Issue on Sovereignty, Citizenship and the European Constitution* (1995) 1/3 *ELJ* at 219–307.

For all that, the *Bundesverfassungsgericht* is on to something. The European Court's grand claims to have 'constitutionalised' the Treaty are not fully matched by the reality, which sees *relatively* weak democratic control and poor transparency at the European legislative level. Moreover, the loyalty of the peoples of Europe to European-level governance is, as a general proposition, weaker than the bond linking them to State-level decision-making, not least because of the absence of true European political parties and a European media, which becomes ever more problematic for the perceived legitimacy of European rule-making as majority voting in Council increases in scope. This is not to embrace the embedded normative preference of the *Bundesverfassungsgericht* for the (apparently almost immutable) dominance of State institutions, but it is to accept that a problem of shaping viable, trusted multi-level governance for Europe has been exposed.

For the purposes of this chapter I focus on the claim that the Bundesverfassungsgericht in *Maastricht* delivered a message about the direction taken and to be taken by the EC legal order to the European Court, of the type that had also been delivered twenty years earlier by German judges in the human rights cases, but now arising in the context of the competence of the Union. And the core concern to sustain the loyalty of the national courts could scarcely be ignored by the European Court. The Court's authority is directly conditioned by its perception of the vital need to retain the active support of its national courts for the vision of EC law mapped out by the Court: and now here, in *Maastricht*, was a key national court expressing serious and profound anxieties about the spread of Community competence. So one might expect the European Court to pay greater heed to sensitivity about defining the outer limits of Community competence, in reaction to (admittedly belated) concerns of its national courts. Again—as with the human rights cases—this seems to be a paradox of supremacy. The European Court can only keep irreconcilable constitutional tensions between differently grounded legal orders at bay if it tempers its approach to the evolution of EC law by diluting it with concerns expressed at national level. The European Court cannot afford to have the German court invalidate an EC act, for the system would be in danger of fragmenting along national lines, so it should seek to allay the fears of the German court that might provoke it to threaten such a thing. Meanwhile, it is also arguable that the German court cannot itself afford to invalidate an EC act. It has not done so. And in *Maastricht* it did *not* find ratification of the Treaty by Germany to be unconstitutional. The chessplayer's maxim that the threat is worth more than the execution makes sense also from the perspective of the national court. This is a two-way judicial process of indirect dialogue which is, it is submitted, a good thing, both because it secures the accomplishment of the Court's mission (which is not to drive Community law forward and outward for the sake of it but rather to keep national courts harnessed to the task of making EC law a viable basis for the stabilisation of the European Union) and because there are genuine constitutional anxieties associated with 'competence drift', especially but not only in a world of QMV. Simply extending the competence of the

EC is not obviously a normatively acceptable stance—even if national courts were *not* resistant to its implications.

So the Community legal order is shaped by national anxieties. The 'Tobacco Advertising' case is the clearest example that this now involves a willingness in Luxembourg to identify what the Treaty does not allow the Community to do, and to protect minorities from over-ambitious majorities. As the Court stated in October 2000, there is no 'general power to regulate the internal market',[55] only a more limited power to harmonise, and this cannot be changed other than by unanimously agreed Treaty revision. And the 'two-way' process persists. The Bundesverfassungsgericht's ruling in *Bananas*, which in fact pre-dates *Tobacco Advertising* by a few months,[56] is not formally incompatible with *Maastricht* but is rather more evidently anxious to emphasise the unlikelihood of the threat of invalidation being carried out at national level, in contrast to the darker, more threatening tone of *Maastricht*. This is not to claim naively that all is for the best in the best of all possible judicial worlds, but it is to draw attention to the constructive reality of inter-court, inter-jurisdiction constitutional balancing and rebalancing.

D. The Wider Environment of Judging

'Tobacco Advertising' is the latest and most high-profile example of the Court's ability to signal its fidelity to the principle of attributed powers. It has on other occasions also retreated to the language of the Treaty as a reason for refusing to accept new constitutional advances pressed on it, even where such textual scrupulousness has not characterised the development of the relevant area of law in the past. The climate has changed. At this stage of an already lengthy Chapter I will do more than briefly sketch these cases. They are not here presented as part of some crude argument that the Court is on the retreat because it fears being routed by hostile national judges or because it identifies its powers as vulnerable to a scythe wielded by the Member States at time of Treaty revision. The process is more subtle, and in my submission a more positive reading is appropriate. The Court is aware of the changing institutional and constitutional environment and it is responding to it. The legal order which it has nurtured is developing, perhaps in unforeseen ways, but certainly in ways that implicate a greater number of actors with which the Court must develop a *modus vivendi*; national courts, but also, strikingly and much more prominent since the Single European Act in 1987, a more active Community legislature released from the bonds of Council unanimity and a regular process of periodic Treaty revision.

So, for example, in *Grant v South West Trains*[57] the Court, declining to interpret the existing law of discrimination to catch discrimination based on sexual orien-

---

[55] Case C–376/98, n 46 above at para 83.
[56] 2 BvL 1/97, 7 June 2000. See G Nicolaysen and C Nowak, 'Teilrueckzug des BVerfG aus der Kontrolle der Rechtmaessigkeit gemeinschaftlicher Rechtsakte' (17/2001) 54 *NJW* 1233.
[57] Case C–29/96, [1998] ECR I–621.

tation, referred explicitly to the potential for legislative action in the field adopted under a provision in the Amsterdam Treaty which was, at the time of the ruling, not yet in force. It is now Article 13 EC. This was judicial deference to other sources of law-making. In its Opinion in Accession by the EC to the ECHR[58] the Court observed that 'as Community law now stands, the Community has no competence to accede to the Convention.' Despite the Court's active role over the years in extending the reach of human rights within the Community legal order,[59] it would not take this extra step because of the perceived confines of the principle that the Community has only the powers conferred on it by its Treaty—the constitutional point being that the taking of such a step rested with the Member States acting unanimously at a time of Treaty revision. The Court in that Opinion explicitly ruled out using legislative powers found in the Treaty 'in substance . . . to amend the Treaty.' The echo of the Bundesverfassungsgericht's *Maastricht* ruling would be hard to miss. Then in *Paola Faccini Dori v Recreb Srl*[60] the Court refused to accept that a Directive may be applied directly in national proceedings to impose an obligation on a private party. Directives have no horizontal direct effect. The Court's reasoning was based explicitly on the limited competence conferred by the Treaty. It stated that 'The effect of extending that case-law [on vertical direct effect] to the sphere of relations between individuals would be to recognize a power in the Community to enact obligations for individuals with immediate effect, whereas it has competence to do so only where it is empowered to adopt Regulations.'

If one considered the Court's 'mission' to be to extend the reach of Community law, then these decisions would shock. But that is not the Court's mission, at least not directly. The Court has always been aware of the importance of the art of the possible, and it is very much not in its interests to extend the reach of Community law, if that extension is likely to be spat out by the national courts. Then, there really would not be a 'European' legal order for there would be no 'European courts' within the national legal orders any more. In part, then, these decisions may be taken as reactions to perceived reluctance on the part of national courts to follow the Court's lead. To this extent they form part of the Court's mission to build a viable Community legal order, and to do so in full awareness that national courts are readier to examine more closely the Court's choices than they used to be. But this is closely linked to the point that the possibility of revision of the Treaty to achieve what the Court now considers to lie beyond its reach is perfectly viable. Treaty revision can and does occur. So here too the Single European Act provided the crucial break with the past. Not only did it induce caution about over-ready expansion of the Community legal order because of the risk that minority rights might be undermined under a QMV regime, it also pointed to the now realistic possibility that law reform could be carried through via Treaty revision. So the

---

[58] Opinion 2/94 [1994] ECR I-1759.

[59] Cf nn 36-39 above and relevant text.

[60] Case C-91/92, [1994] ECR I-3325. Confirmed in eg Case C-192/94, *El Corte Inglés SA v Cristina Blázquez Rivero* [1996] ECR I-1281.

pre-1987 argument that 'if the Court does not develop the law, who will?' loses much of whatever force it might be thought previously to have possessed. In the 'amendment vs. interpretation debate', amendment had suddenly become a genuine prospect. Ambitious interpretation at the margins of Community competence was correspondingly less vital, and arguably less constitutionally appropriate. Part of the context may be that the Court fears that if it is not cautious the Member States may take the opportunity at a time of Treaty revision not simply to adjust its jurisprudence but to curb its powers. That the Court has lost some autonomy from the Member States as Masters of the Treaty as a result of the rise of Treaty revision may be part of the story. But this could be over-stated. It takes *all* the Member States to sign up to this venture. Court-curbing is thus far (implied) threat not execution. Even the overturning of Court rulings interpreting the Treaty by revising the Treaty is very rare.[61] A more subtle reading of the Court's attitude to the possibility of Treaty revision, genuine now where it was not 15 years ago, is that the Court, composed of lawyers conditioned by notions of proper judicial restraint, is aware that its constitutional environment has changed and it may quite willingly defer to Treaty revision as a more legitimate way to proceed. Not least because the constitutional pillars of the system are already erect.

It is not just the live possibility of Treaty revision that affects the environment in which the Court carries out its function of providing an authoritative interpretation of Community law. The Single European Act is once again the watershed. Legislative activity was made more vigorous, because of the injection of QMV. Here too the argument that if the Court does not develop the law, who will—so powerful in explaining *Cassis de Dijon* as a basis for breaking the legislative log-jam in the shaping of the internal market[62]—is undermined. This suggests that the Court might curtail its willingness to extend the reach of Community law by adopting a broad interpretation, but in this instance not because of perceived limitations to the scope of competence attributed by the Treaty but rather because it is willing to concede that although the matter may fall within the scope of Community law, it, the Court, is not the appropriate institution to achieve the development pressed on it. These are, in short, instances of the Court exhibiting deference to legislative methods for changing the law.[63] And in the very interpretation of the law underpinning the widening fabric of Community regulatory activity, there is scope for inquiry into how forthright is the Court's modern contribution. The EC today is a great deal more than a market-maker and the deeper that Community law carries the potential to curtail

---

[61] Cf R Dehousse, n 12 above ch 6.

[62] Cf R Dehousse, n 12 above ch 3 and 143–5; K Armstrong and S Bulmer, *The Governance of the Single European Market* (Manchester University Press, Manchester, 1998), especially ch 6.

[63] Eg Case C–9/93 *IHT Internationale Heiztechnik Gmbh v Ideal Standard GmbH*, [1994] ECR I–2789 in which the Court observed that the result pressed on it (rendering void under national law assignments made for part only of the Community) could be achieved only by a Directive adopted under Art 100a (now 95) and not by the application of Art 30 (now 28). See also Cases C–122/99P and C–125/99P *D v Council* [2001] ECR I–4319 at paras 37–38.

the autonomy of national choices in the field of social policy, broadly understood, the more delicacy with which its institutions are likely to tread. I here compress a vast area of inquiry into a wholly inadequate summary, but this mood can be detected in the Court's approach to the interpretation of the scope and meaning of primary law[64] and of secondary legislation.[65]

This is not to portray a timid Court. The picture demands (but cannot within the scope of this chapter receive) a rich, sectorally nuanced examination. It also demands a degree of scepticism about the accuracy of even speaking of 'the Court', given the improbability that a single vision can be sustained under such a vicious workload ranging across ever wider areas and when cases are dealt with only infrequently by all or even most of the judges sitting together. But (to fall headlong but wittingly into that trap) I contend that 'the Court' is more constitutionally cautious today, but that it remains capable of remarkable dynamism. The *Francovich* ruling demonstrates that the discourse of a new legal order still has some vitality and that the Court may still play a law-making role.[66] In that decision it held, without any explicit support in the Treaty, that a State's failure to implement a Directive may have the consequence that an individual suffering loss as a result can recover damages from the State as a matter of Community law before a national court. In the post-*Francovich* ruling in *Brasserie du Pêcheur SA* and *Factortame* the Court confirmed that a right to reparation in cases of loss caused to individuals as a result of breaches of Community law was 'inherent in the system of the Treaty', and it reached this decision in the face of the constitutional objections by the German government to alleged judicial usurpation of the function of the legislature.[67] The quest to strengthen the enforcement of rules underpinning the internal market provoked the Court to its remarkable ruling in *CIA Security Internatioal SA v Signalson SA and Securitel SPRL*.[68] It decided that where a

---

[64] See eg T Hervey, 'Social Solidarity: a Buttress against International Market Law?' in J Shaw (ed), *Social Law and Policy in an Evolving EU*, (Hart Publishing, Oxford, 2001); E Szyszczak, 'Free Trade as a Fundamental Value of the EU', in K Economides (ed), *Fundamental Values* (Hart Publishing, Oxford, 2000); K Mortelmans, 'Towards Convergence in the application of the rules on free movement and on competition?' (2001) 38 *CML Rev* 613; M Poiares Maduro, 'Striking the elusive balance between economic freedom and social rights in the EU', ch 13 in P Alston (ed), n 36 above; S Weatherill, 'Recent case law concerning the free movement of goods: mapping the frontiers of market deregulation' (1999) 36 *CMLRev* 51; R van den Bergh and P Camesasca, 'Irreconcilable Principles? The Court of Justice exempts collective labour agreements from the wrath of antitrust' (2000) 25 *ELRev* 492.

[65] See eg P Eekhout, 'The European Court of Justice and the Legislature' (1998) 18 *YEL* 1; J Hunt, 'Success at Last? The amendment of the Acquired Rights Directive' (1999) 24 *ELRev* 215; C Kilpatrick, 'Community or Communities of Courts in European Integration? Sex Equality Dialogues between UK Courts and the ECJ' (1998) 4 *ELJ* 121; cf discussion in this vein of Case C–29/96 *Grant*, n 57 above by I Canor, 'Equality for Lesbians and gay men in the EC Legal Order' (2000) 7 *Maastricht Journal of European and Comparative Law* 273.

[66] N 19 above and relevant text.

[67] Joined Cases C–46/93 and C–48/93 [1996] ECR I–1029 at para 24 of the judgment.

[68] Case C–194/94, [1996] ECR I–2201.

Member State neglects to notify draft national technical regulations to the Commission in breach of the obligations set out in Directive 83/189, it may not rely on those regulations in subsequent proceedings before national courts.[69] The Court's ruling attaches a meaningful penalty to State failure to abide by the obligations of notification stipulated by the Directive, even though the Directive stipulated no such penalty. It thereby induces compliance with requirements of transparency on which the Commission pins great faith in its 'post-1992' strategy for the management of the internal market.[70]

A hypothesis would be that the Court is likely to be particularly cautious in dealing with cases that lie at the margins of Community competence. That is where national court sensitivity to the constitutional implications of European Court activism seems strongest, especially now that QMV is the norm, and where, therefore, the threat of national court defection is most significant. Also, it is where Treaty revision is the more evidently appropriate way forward and where perceived over-ambition by the Court might therefore lead to significant disquiet at the political level. This might help to explain the boldness of decisions such as *Francovich*—concerned not with extending the substantive areas in which the Community is competent but rather dealing only with the implications before national courts of defection from rules that have already been duly agreed. National court and Member State governmental hostility might be reckoned less probable. The Court's coalitions with the Commission are also worth exploring as another potentially relevant factor in explaining judicial interpretative ambition or its absence. In relation to *Francovich* itself one might recognise that the Court's ruling did much to underpin the Commission's desire to see more effective policing of the rules of the internal market game at national level. Similarly the Court's ruling in *CIA Security* was seized upon with delight by the Commission, which had in fact long held the view that this should be the legal consequence of non-notification.[71] This community of interest between Court and Commission in strengthening market-building echoes that plain at the time of *Cassis de Dijon* itself.[72]

---

[69] Cf subsequently Case C–226/97, *Johannes Martinus Lemmens* [1998] ECR I–3711; Case C–443/98, *Unilever Italia SpA v Central Food SpA* [2000] ECR I–7535, criticised by S Weatherill (2000) 26 *ELRev* 177.

[70] Cf J Jans, 'National Legislative Autonomy? The Procedural Constrains of European Law', (1998/1) *LIEI* 25; S Weatherill, 'A Case Study in Judicial Activism in the 1990s: the Status before national courts of measures wrongfully un-notified to the Commission', in D O'Keeffe (ed), n 45 above ch 31. More generally see S Weatherill, 'New Strategies for Managing the EC's Internal Market', in M Freeman (ed), *Current Legal Problems* (Oxford University Press, Oxford, 2000), vol 53; K Armstrong, 'Governance and the Single European Market', in P Craig and G de Búrca, n 22 above.

[71] Cf S Weatherill, 'Compulsory Notification of Draft Technical Regulations: the Contribution of Directive 83/189 to the management of the internal market' (1996) 16 *YEL* 129.

[72] Eg Commission Communication, OJ 1980 C256/2. Cf D Wincott, 'Political Theory, Law and European Union', in J Shaw and G More (eds), *New Legal Dynamics of the European Union* (Oxford University Press, Oxford, 1995).

4. CONCLUSION

The thesis of this chapter holds that the Court has the same mission as it had 40 years ago—to make a viable legal order for Europe—but that the environment within which it today seeks to fulfil that mission is constitutionally and institutionally much more complex. This is the context in which to assess its activism and restraint. I have conspicuously omitted an overtly normative dimension from this account. To an extent the purpose of the chapter has been the profoundly unambitious one of insisting that activism and restraint make little sense as labels in the abstract, and must instead be tied into an account of the rationales for a particular stream of judicial decision-making and the context in which such decisions are taken. I have argued that activism and restraint practised by the European Court are best *understood* against a background rhythm that emphasises the mutual interdependence of the Luxembourg court and its national judicial allies and the extent to which the doctrine of supremacy in EC law is in practical terms a basis for constructive inter-court dialogue. This seems to me to be a more satisfying explanation than one which favours a portrayal of the European Court's approach as explicable with reference to an intent to maximise its own jurisdiction and that of the other EC institutions. Although, of course, over the early years of the Community's development, that was very much what in fact happened, more recent trends—including national judicial scepticism— have changed the environment in which the Court works and its outputs bear the mark of a new caution. But is any of this desirable? Was the Court justified, is the Court justified, in its distinctive approach to legal reasoning? I would confine myself to the observation that here too a simple activism versus restraint model is inadequate to assess the implications of the Court's case law. The Court needs to be placed in a wider context which insists that the function of the European Union is to 'tame' the nationalistic urges of its States.[73] The Court has been responsible for the elaboration of a constitutionalised order in which the exercise of State power in Europe is subject to vigorous control. Politically and economically, States are capable of damaging other States; this hardly requires any illustration drawn from European history. This is why the Treaty was drafted; this is the context, object and purpose that should govern its interpretation.[74] By subjecting States to agreed transnational legal rules, these rough edges may be taken off, leaving States in existence but stripped of their capacity for harmful excess; by making real the

[73] Eg N MacCormick, *Questioning Sovereignty* (Oxford University Press, Oxford, 1999); JHH Weiler, *The Constitution of Europe*, n 12 above; D Curtin, 'Postnational Democracy: the European Union in search of a Political Philosophy' (Inaugural Lecture, Universiteit Utrecht, 1997). Cf also in a more specifically legal context I Pernice, 'Multi-level constitutionalism and the Treaty of Amsterdam: European Constitution-Making Revisited' (1999) 36 *CMLRev* 703, also a rich source of bibliographic references; cf also J Shaw, 'Postnational constitutionalism in the European Union' (1999) 6 *JEPP* 579; C Joerges and J Neyer, 'From Intergovernmental Bargaining to Deliberative Political Processes: the Constitutionalisation of Comitology' (1997) 3 *ELJ* 273.

[74] Art 31(1) of the Vienna Convention on Treaties, s 2.2 above.

enforcement of these rules the European Court can be taken to have made a major contribution to the successful prosecution of the European integrative project. To achieve this end it has brilliantly secured the support of the national courts, and, with their active participation, it has gradually shaped and continues to shape the EC legal order. It is a mission that has been in many respects successful, and, I submit, it is a mission that is of great value in underpinning 'constitutionalisation' in Europe as a multi-level phenomenon in which, at the level of both legal and political power, there is a complementary not antagonistic relationship between Member States and European institutions.

14

The Assertion of Jurisdiction by the European Court of Justice

JOHN USHER

1. INTRODUCTION

While the title of this chapter refers to the 'assertion' of jurisdiction by the European Court of Justice, it will commence by examining a number of situations where the European Court of Justice has recognised, or indeed imposed, limits on its jurisdiction, before moving to consideration of the extent to which the European Court of Justice may be regarded as having adopted an extensive approach to aspects of its jurisdiction, and whether it has purported to develop new jurisdiction.

The chapter will conclude by looking at the European Court of Justice's approach to the possibility that other tribunals may have jurisdiction over the same matters, and by analysing a few situations where there has apparently been a conflict between the European Court of Justice and other tribunals with regard to the same subject matter.

2. WHAT LIMITS HAS THE EUROPEAN COURT OF JUSTICE RECOGNISED OR IMPOSED ON ITS JURISDICTION?

A. Actions for Annulment

In direct actions for annulment the European Court of Justice has taken a strict approach to *locus standi* in particular with regard to the possibility for private litigants to seek the annulment of general legislation. This began in the context of the old ECSC Treaty, under Article 33 of which, private rights of action were conferred only on coal and steel undertakings and associations of such undertakings within the meaning of that Treaty, so that Case 66/76 *CFDT v Council*,[1] an action

---

[1] [1977] ECR 305.

brought by a trade union, was doomed to failure,[2] Article 33 being held to confer no *locus standi* on other associations or individuals. With regard to the acts which could be challenged, under Article 33 of the ECSC Treaty coal and steel undertakings could challenge individual decision or recommendations emanating from the Commission[3] which concerned them without further restriction, but could only challenge general decisions or recommendations of the Commission (roughly equivalent to regulations and directives under the EC Treaty) which they considered to involve a misuse of powers affecting them. It was then held in Case 13/57 *Eisen-und Stahlindustrie v HA*,[4] that misuse of powers was the only ground for annulment which could be relied upon in such an action—and until the judgment in Cases 140, 146, 221 and 226/82 *Walzstahl v Commission*,[5] given more than thirty years after the Treaty entered into force, it would appear that no applicant under Article 33 of the ECSC Treaty had succeeded in substantiating such an allegation.

Under Article 230 of the EC Treaty, so far as individuals are concerned, a number of different situations have to be distinguished. First of all there is the situation of a decision addressed to the individual who wishes to challenge it and there, in principle, there is no problem, other than remembering to do so within the basic time limit of two months plus extensions on account of distance, which in the UK's case amounts to two months and 25 days assuming the act in question was published in the Official Journal. This may seem a tight time limit, but it was worse under the Coal and Steel Treaty where the time limit for an action for annulment was only one month and 25 days.

However, there are some decisions which appear to be individual in nature, but which are not treated as individual decisions. For example, if the Commission is requested to do something which, in effect, would require it to amend general legislation or introduce new general legislation and it writes back to say that it is not going to do it, then it cannot be claimed that it is an individual decision because in reality it is refusing to change general legislation, and the same criteria must be met as would be required to challenge the general legislation as such.[6]

As far as decisions addressed to other individuals are concerned, it is necessary in the terms of Article 230 to show direct and individual concern. Since decisions are by definition only binding on their addressee(s), this might in some ways be

---

[2] See also Case 222/83 *Differdange v Commission* [1984] ECR 2889, where a local authority tried unsuccessfully to bring an action.

[3] Art 38 provides for acts of the Council or the European Parliament to be challenged only by the Commission and the Member States. It may be wondered whether this would be treated as a special rule excluding any action by a coal or steel undertaking, or whether the rule laid down in *Les Verts* with regard to acts of the Parliament under the EC Treaty (see n 51 below and relevant text) would be followed if an act of the Council or Parliament under the ECSC Treaty did affect the legal position of a coal or steel undertaking. Similarly, as mentioned above, Art 35(6) of the TEU gives the Court jurisdiction to review the legality of framework decisions and decisions only in actions brought by a Member State or the Commission. It therefore confers no right of action on private litigants.

[4] [1957 and 1958] ECR 265, 277.

[5] [1984] ECR 951.

[6] See eg Case T–22/98, *Scottish Soft Fruit Growers v Commission*, [1998] ECR II–4219.

thought to be rather difficult because an individual decision does not in principle affect anybody else. However, in particular areas, it is now well recognised by the European Court that individual decisions do in fact affect other people, particularly in the area of competition law where now, for more than 20 years, since the first *Metro* case,[7] there has been an acceptance that, for example, complainants in a competition procedure before the Commission can challenge the outcome. It is more or less treated as a dispute between the undertakings involved in the procedure before the Commission and whoever is unsuccessful can challenge the outcome. A similar theory has been applied in the areas of dumping[8] and state aids,[9] even though the acts at issue in dumping cases are usually regulations rather than individual decisions.

However, the simple fact of complaining to the Commission does not automatically give the complainant standing to challenge the outcome of that procedure. It is only where a complaint is made in the context of a defined Community procedure like in competition law, or state aids or dumping that the complainant is likely to be recognized as having an interest. Thus, in the famous *Greenpeace* case,[10] challenging the way environmental assessments were or were not made in relation to certain developments in the Canary Islands, the fact that it Greenpeace had complained was treated as not giving it direct and individual concern, and it has to be concluded that if there is no specific procedure laid down, the fact of complaining does not automatically give the right to seek the annulment of the outcome of the procedure. More generally, this decision illustrates the fact that it is very difficult to mount public interest litigation as a non-privileged litigant before the European Courts. The fact that there may be a general interest is not enough; it is still necessary to show that you are directly and individually concerned, which remains extremely difficult.

Moving on to decisions addressed to Member States, here very often a decision addressed to a Member State in reality will deal with the situation of a particular undertaking. So, a decision addressed to a Member State ordering it not to pay state aid to a particular undertaking will very clearly affect the situation of that undertaking and there is a lot of case law indicating that such undertakings could then challenge the Commission's decision.[11] In other areas it is not so clear cut, but there is a rule of thumb developed over 30 years ago[12] and recently reaffirmed,[13] that if the Member State to which the decision is addressed has no real discretion in how to apply that decision in relation to the applicant, it may well be regarded as *directly* concerning the applicant. Whether it *individually* concerns the applicant depends on whether it can be regarded as affecting him or her by

---

[7] Case 26/76, *Metro SB Grossmärkte v Commission* [1977] ECR 1875.
[8] Case 264/82, *Timex* [1985] ECR 849.
[9] Case 169/84, *Cofaz* [1986] ECR 391.
[10] Case T–585/93, *Greenpeace v Commission* [1995] ECR II–2205; affirmed in Case C–321/95P, *Greenpeace v Commission* [1998] ECR I–1651.
[11] Case 730/79, *Philip Morris Holland v Commission* [1980] ECR 2671.
[12] Case 62/70, *Bock v Commission* [1971] ECR 908.
[13] Case C–391/96P, *Compagnie Continentale v Commission* [1998] ECR I–2377.

virtue of his or her specific situation or by virtue of an attribute specific to him or her—does the factual situation differentiate the applicant from all other person and distinguish him or her individually just as in the case of the person addressed?[14]

The real problem, however, arises in the context of challenging general legislation, more particularly Regulations, although there appears no reason in principle why the same rules should not apply to Directives.[15] Under the terms of Article 230 of the EC Treaty, 'natural or legal persons may institute proceedings against a decision addressed to that person or against a decision which, although in the form of a regulation or a decision addressed to another person is of direct and individual concern to the former'. In other words, if the wording is taken literally it appears that a challenge can only be mounted to a decision and in order to challenge a regulation it has to be shown that it is, in reality, an individual decision and not general legislation.

Without going through the detail of 20 or 30 years of conflicting case law, it may be submitted that it is not easy to reconcile some of the things that have been said by the Court. There is one line of case law that says if the act at issue is genuinely general legislation it cannot be challenged.[16] There is another line which, effectively, says if it is of direct and individual concern it can be challenged even if it is a real regulation.[17] There were more of the former than of the latter until the famous *Codorniu* case,[18] which involved the question of the validity of a regulation limiting the use of the word of *crémant* to describe sparkling wine. The regulation limited the use of the term to sparkling wine produced in France and Luxembourg. Now, unfortunately Codorniu was a Spanish wine producer who not only produced *crémant* but actually had the word *crémant* as part of his trademark. The result of the regulation therefore was that he could not use his trademark—a dramatic effect in anybody's terms as far as this producer was concerned, and it was perhaps hardly surprising that he sought its annulment. The Court clearly found it a matter of some difficulty—the action was brought in 1989 and judgment was finally given in 1994. It therefore took five years before agreement was reached on a judgment. But *Codorniu* says plainly and clearly that if an act which is genuinely a regulation nevertheless directly and individually concerns a particular litigant, that litigant is entitled to challenge it. It does not have to be shown that in law it is a decision; it is enough to show that it is of direct and individual concern to the person who brought the action.[19]

---

[14] Reaffirmed in Case C–50/00P, *Unión de Pequeños Agricultores v Council* (25 July, 2002).

[15] See eg Case C–298/89, *Gibraltar v Council* [1993] ECR I–3605.

[16] See eg Case 64/69, *Cie française commerciale et financière v Commission* [1970] ECR 221 and Case 162/78, *Wagner, Schlüter & Maack v Commission* [1979] ECR 3467.

[17] See eg Case 100/74, *CAM v Commission* [1975] ECR 1393 and Cases 239/82 and 275/82, *Allied Corporation v Commission* [1984] ECR 1005.

[18] Case C–309/89, *Codorniu v Council* [1994] ECR I–1853.

[19] After some hesitation, the current approach of the Court of First Instance is to ask first whether the act is of general application, and secondly to consider, even if it is of general application, whether the applicant is nevertheless directly and individually concerned—see eg Cases T–32/98 and T–41/98, *Netherlands Antilles v Commission* [2000] CFI II–201.

Not only was his action held to be admissible but Codorniu won on the substance: his trademark dated back to the 1920s but it was only in the 1970s that, for example, Luxembourg had started using the word *crémant*. The Court, therefore, held that it was a breach of the principle of equality of treatment to allow the name to be used by Luxembourg producers but not by Spanish producers. Few applicants are, however, likely to find themselves in the situation of Codorniu.

Otherwise, as far as regulations are concerned, there is not usually too much difficulty in proving direct concern, because regulations by definition are law for everybody, including individual subjects of the law. The great problem is usually proving individual concern, ie that the regulation picks the applicant out rather differently from anybody else. Here again questions arise as to whether or not there is discretion given to a Member State in applying the regulation,[20] and as to whether the applicant has been picked out because of what they themselves have individually done or because of their individual situation.[21]

It must, however, be emphasised that the simple fact that an act called a regulation only applies to a small number of economic operators is not enough to make it of direct and individual concern to them. In the view of the Court, if it is a small economic sector and a regulation applies to it, it is no different in concept from it being a large economic sector and the regulation applying to it.[22] There must be something which picks the applicant out differently from everybody else. This, of course, happens most frequently in the context of anti-dumping regulations where very often the producer will be named: if applicants are named and their products have an anti-dumping duty imposed on them there is no difficulty in showing that they are individually concerned.[23] This was the earliest area in which regulations were regularly held to be of direct and individual concern to individual litigants.

Leaving on one side the particular problems faced by individual litigants under Article 230 of the EC Treaty, there is the broader issue that in principle, the remedy under the EC Treaty cannot be used to challenge an act of the European Council, which is an institution of the European Union, not of the European Community. There are several examples where that has failed, in particular attempts to annul the declaration that the Maastricht Treaty had come into force. The actions were simply rejected on the basis that there was no jurisdiction to annul acts of the European Council under the EC Treaty.[24]

B. References for Preliminary Rulings

In the context of references for preliminary rulings, while the European Court has through most of the history of this procedure held that it is not for it to take

[20] Case 123/77,*UNICME v Council* [1978] ECR 845.
[21] See eg Case 41–44/70, *International Fruit Co. v Commission* [1971] ECR 411 and Case C–354/87, *Weddel* [1990] ECR I–3847.
[22] Case 101/76, *Koninklijke Scholten Honig v Council and Commission* [1977] ECR 797.
[23] Cases 239/82 and 275/82, *Allied Corporation v Commission* [1984] ECR 1005.
[24] Case T–584/93, *Roujansky v Council* [1994] ECR II–585.

cognisance of the facts or criticise the reasons for the reference,[25] it has also stated that it may look behind the reference to ascertain whether the question of Community law is necessary to the settlement of a genuine dispute before the national court, as in Case 104/79, *Foglia v Novello*.[26] It would appear that the dispute in that case was not thought to be genuine because it was an action before an Italian court between Italian parties designed to obtain a ruling that a provision of French legislation was incompatible with EC law, a matter on which the Italian parties were both agreed. However, in Case 26/81, *Rau v De Smedt*,[27] the Court accepted a reference from a German court designed to obtain a ruling that a provision of Belgian legislation was incompatible with EC law, and it has subsequently repeated that on a reference it should not consider the facts or the motive for the reference,[28] and that it should not refuse to reply to a reference simply because the national court had not explained the relevance of the questions to the dispute.[29]

However, more recently there have again been examples of the Court 'filtering' references, albeit using slightly different language. In Case C–83/91, *Meilicke*,[30] the Court stated that it would not answer hypothetical questions, finding that one of the parties to the national proceedings was trying to test out a personal hypothesis of company law theory (the question related to the interpretation of one of the Directives on the harmonisation of company law), which was not relevant to the dispute. It may be suggested that this is not very different from the test of the genuineness of the dispute set out in *Foglia v Novello* and that it involves the Court in considering the facts and the motive for the reference.[31] Furthermore, in Case C–428/93, *Monin Automobiles*,[32] which was a reference from a juge-commissaire conducting winding-up proceedings, it was found that the answers to the questions referred were not needed for the purposes of the winding-up and therefore were not objectively required for his decision, an approach which seems to involve the European Court in reviewing the order made by the national judge. On the other hand, a question arising out of a hypothetical situation was treated as admissible in Case C–200/98, *X AB and Y AB v Riksskatteverket*.[33] These two Swedish companies had asked the relevant tax authorities to indicate the tax treatment which would be given to three alternative forms of a proposed transaction, and the reference was made by the body hearing appeals against such a preliminary decision (Regeringsrätten). It would appear that under Swedish law, the preliminary decision would, once it became definitive, bind the tax authorities and serve as the basis of assessment, if the applicant continued with the action envisaged. In those circumstances, the Court found that the Regeringsrätten must be held to

---

[25] See eg Case 5/77, *Tedeschi v Denkavit* [1977] ECR 1555.
[26] [1980] ECR 745.
[27] [1982] ECR 3961.
[28] Cases 2–4/82, *Delhaize* [1983] ECR 2973.
[29] Cases 98, 162 and 288/85, *Bertini* [1986] ECR 1885.
[30] [1992] ECR I–4871.
[31] Contrary to the view it stated in *Delhaize*, n 28 above.
[32] [1994] ECR I–1707.
[33] [1999] ECR I–8261.

be carrying out a judicial function, and it was therefore for the Regeringsrätten to decide whether a preliminary ruling was necessary and to determine the relevance of the questions to be referred.

Nevertheless, in Cases C–320–322/90 *Telemarsicabruzzo*,[34] the Court held that it would not answer questions where the relevant factual and legal situation was not stated.[35] It may be suggested that this similarly reflects the fact that it is not the role of the Court to answer questions outside the context of a specific dispute.

Furthermore, and correlative to the availability of the action for annulment, the Court has held that a reference may not be made where an action for annulment was clearly available, a view which it did not appear initially to hold. In Case 156/77, *Commission v Belgium*,[36] albeit in the context of a discussion as to whether a Member State can invoke the 'plea of illegality' under Article 241 to contest the validity of a decision it could have challenged under Article 230, the Court expressly recognised that the validity of a Community act can always be queried under Article 234 even if the time-limit for challenging it under Article 230 has expired, the justification being that Article 234 is available in relation to any Community act, and was intended for the sole benefit of national courts (presumably: rather than individual parties).

The question whether a party who could have challenged the Community act at issue could nevertheless raise the question of its validity before the national court was, however, expressly raised in the terms of the order for reference in Case 216/82, *Hamburg University v HZA Hamburg Kehrwieder*,[37] where the national court asked both whether the applicant could have brought a direct action for annulment and whether a question of validity could be raised before a national court after the time limit for a direct action for annulment had expired. In his Opinion, AG Slynn suggested, on the basis of a direct precedent,[38] that the Commission Decision at issue (which determined whether goods of the type imported by the application qualified for duty-free entry as scientific equipment) was of direct and individual concern to the applicant even though addressed to all the Member States since it was triggered by the applicant's importation. However, he distinguished the case law holding that actions for damages cannot be used to circumvent the time limits on actions for annulment on the basis that it involved two types of action brought before the same court, whereas the challenge to validity is brought before a national court, which may then refer the matter to the European Court.

However, the Court responded on a somewhat different basis. It observed that the decision had to be notified to the Member States, that it did not have to be

---

[34] [1993] ECR I–393.
[35] A view followed also in Case C–386/92, *Monin Automobiles* [1992] ECR I–2049, where it was held that the reference was inadmissible since there was no indication of the context in which the questions arose.
[36] [1978] ECR 1881.
[37] [1983] ECR 2771.
[38] Case 294/81, *Control Data Belgium v Commission* [1983] ECR 911.

published in the Official Journal, that it was for the national authorities to reject the applicant's request for duty-free admission following the Commission's decision, and that the national authorities' decision might be adopted some time after the notification of the Commission's decision. It therefore concluded that the rejection of the application by the national authorities was the only measure of which the applicant had necessarily been informed in good time and which it could challenge in the courts 'without encountering any difficulty in demonstrating its interest in bringing proceedings', and that by virtue of the general principle underlying Article 241 of the EC Treaty on the plea of illegality,[39] the applicant should be able, in proceedings brought under national law against the rejection of its application by the national authorities, to plead the illegality of the Commission decision on which the national decision adopted in its regard was based. In so deciding, the Court expressly stated that there was no need to consider the wider issue of the general relationship between Articles 230 and 234. The point was, however, raised again in Case C–188/92 *TWD Textilwerke Deggendorf v Bundesminister für Wirtschaft*.[40] There, the Commission had addressed a decision to Germany under the state aids rules of the EC Treaty finding subsidies paid to the applicant to be both procedurally and substantively in breach of the Treaty, and requiring those subsidies to be recovered. A few months later, the German authorities notified the decision to the applicant, and informed it of the possibility of bringing an action for annulment under Article 230, but the applicant did not bring such an action. A further few months after that, the relevant German Minister issued a decision effectively requiring the subsidies to be repaid, and the applicant challenged this decision before the German courts, invoking the invalidity of the underlying Commission decision. The question referred to the European Court, therefore, asked specifically if the validity of the Commission decision could be raised before the national courts.

AG Jacobs suggested that to allow a party, who could clearly have brought an action for annulment, to plead the illegality of such a decision before a national court would enable it to circumvent the fact that the decision had become definitive with regard to that party once the limitation period for an action for annulment had ended. Therefore, for reasons of legal certainty and to preserve the coherence of the Community system of judicial remedies, he suggested that when an individual's standing under Article 230 was beyond doubt and he had been informed of the decision in good time but had not brought a direct action, no plea of illegality under Article 234 should be allowed either. The Court followed this approach, distinguishing the *Hamburg University* case on the grounds that there the party concerned would have had 'difficulties' in showing locus standi to

---

[39] However, the Court made no mention of its leading decision in relation to Article 241 in Case 92/78, *Simmenthal v Commission* [1979] ECR 777 holding that the plea of illegality is only available in relation to acts which could not be challenged directly by anyone other than a Community institution or a Member State. The point was however expressly adverted to in the Court's later judgment in *TWD Textilwerke Deggendorf* (below).

[40] [1994] ECR I–833.

bring an action for annulment, whereas in *TWD Textilwerke Deggendorf* there was no doubt that an action for annulment could have been brought. AG Jacobs suggested that by limiting this approach to situations where there was no doubt that an action for annulment could be brought, the Court (or the national court) would avoid having to decide whether there was 'direct and individual concern' under Article 230[41] before allowing a question of invalidity to be raised before it, as feared by some commentators.[42] It may nevertheless be suggested that even to distinguish between cases where there is no doubt and cases where there may be difficulties will require a preliminary investigation of the same sort, particularly since the relevant case-law has not been marked by total consistency. This introduces some of the problems of admissibility which have beset direct actions before the Court and which had previously been remarkably lacking in references for preliminary rulings, and necessarily requires the European Court to go behind the national court's reference to investigate the situation of the parties and the factual background.

It would nevertheless appear that where a private party has brought a direct action for annulment in due time, that party may also plead the invalidity of the relevant Community act when challenging national measures giving effect to the Community act in proceedings before the national courts,[43] thus leaving open the possibility that the same point may be taken by the same party in an action for annulment before the Court of First Instance and in a reference for a preliminary ruling before the European Court itself. Conversely, it may be doubted whether a question of the validity of a Community act may ever be taken before a national court by a governmental agency after the time limit for an action for annulment has expired, since there is no doubt that a Member State may seek the annulment of any binding Community act.

It may also be suggested that the approach taken in *TWD Textilwerke Deggendorf*, that a question of invalidity cannot be raised before a national court by a party who could have brought an action for annulment but failed to do so in time, would cause particular problems if applied to references under Article 41 of the ECSC Treaty. As has been seen, coal and steel undertakings had relatively little difficulty in establishing *locus standi* to bring an action for annulment under Article 33 of that Treaty; their problem was rather the substantive one of proving that a Commission decision which was general in nature constituted a misuse of powers. Indeed, the leading case under the ECSC Treaty involved a situation where it might have been expected that an action for annulment would have been brought: in Case 168/82 *ECSC v Ferriere S. Anna*,[44] an Italian steel undertaking had gone into

---

[41] The situation would, however, be the antithesis of that under Art 230: the question of invalidity would only be admissible if the act at issue was *not* of direct and individual concern to the private party raising the point.

[41] See G Bebr, 'Direct and Indirect Control of Community Acts in Practice', in *The Art of Governance, Festschrift in Honour of Eric Stein* (Nomos Verlagsgesellschaft, Baden-Baden, 1987), 91.

[43] Cases 133–136/85, *Walter Rau Lebensmittelwerke* [1987] ECR 2289, which was distinguished on the basis that the action for annulment had been brought in time in *TWD Textilwerke Deggendorf.*

[44] [1983] ECR 1681.

insolvent liquidation owing 27 million lire of unpaid ECSC levy, and the Commission sought to prove in the liquidation for this sum. During the course of proceedings before an Italian court, the Commission issued a decision addressed to the steel undertaking declaring that the debt owed to the Commission was to be treated as a preferred debt in the same way as a similar debt owed to the Italian state. It was then the Commission itself which suggested[45] that the Italian court should refer the validity of the decision to the European Court if it was not prepared to give effect to it, and no point of admissibility was taken or raised. This case shows a welcome degree of flexibility between the available remedies. However, the lack of references on questions of validity under the ECSC Treaty would appear both to indicate that where an action for annulment is relatively easily available, there is no real history of litigants abusing its time limits by later raising questions of validity before national courts, and that it may be difficult to find an appropriate national form of action.

3. HAS THE EUROPEAN COURT OF JUSTICE INTERPRETED ITS JURISDICTION EXTENSIVELY?

A. Actions for Annulment

There are undoubtedly situations where the European Court of Justice has gone beyond the letter of its jurisdiction. In the context of direct actions for annulment under the EC Treaty, while it has been seen that the Court had held that it had no jurisdiction to annul acts of the European Council under the EC Treaty,[46] it will check to see whether the other pillars are being used to circumvent Community powers. In reality there is not as clear cut a division as there might be between what can be done under the second and third pillars of the European Union on a common foreign and security policy and on police and judicial cooperation in criminal matters, and what can be done under the European Community Treaty. It is now clear that the European Court takes the view that if it is alleged that something was done, for example, under the third pillar, which, arguably, should have been done under the Community Treaty the Court will, in fact, investigate that situation because clearly there would be a breach of the Community Treaty if the institutions could avoid its procedures by using the European Union pillar. That happened in an action brought by the Commission against the Council with regard to rules enacted under the third pillar about airport transit visas[47] (when there was a provision on visas in the European Community Treaty),[48] and the

---

[45] The rationale would appear to have been that to have brought an action for annulment would have risked the undertaking's assets in costs, whereas on a reference there was no obligation for the undertaking to appear or be represented.

[46] Case T–584/93, *Roujansky v Council*, n 24 above.

[47] Case C–170/96, *Commission v Council* [1998] ECR I–2763.

[48] Then Art 100c of the EC Treaty.

Court held it could check whether they were trying to circumvent the European Community provisions or whether this was genuinely something which fell under the then scope of the third pillar. In fact, they held it did fall under that scope but nonetheless took the view that they had jurisdiction to check the matter.

It is also the case that there may be Union Acts which are covered by Community legislation, in particular the current rules on transparency and availability of documents. Thus in the *Svenska Journalistförbundet* case,[49] the Court took the view that it could deal with access to certain documents relating to activities of the Union because they fell within the access provisions laid down by a Community decision.

It should be added, for the sake of completeness, that following the entry into force of the Amsterdam Treaty, there is for the first time a limited direct action for annulment in relation to certain acts under the third pillar. Article 35(6) of the Treaty on European Union gives a right of action to the Member States or the Commission, but only to Member States or the Commission, to challenge decisions, or framework decisions, adopted by the Council under the new third pillar. Judicial review may therefore be seen to be creeping into that area, although there are still no express remedies for individuals.

Perhaps one of the clearest examples of the Court's extensive interpretation of its jurisdiction may be found in the way it asserted jurisdiction over the acts of the European Parliament before the Treaty so provided, and also allowed the Parliament to litigate to protect its prerogatives before the Treaty so provided. The Council and Commission have always enjoyed the same rights to bring an action for annulment as the Member States, but the Parliament, on the other hand, originally appeared to enjoy a right of action only under the EC and Euratom Treaties and only with regard to failures to act on the part of the Council and Commission, and to be liable to have an action brought against itself only with regard to its acts under the ECSC Treaty and then only by the Commission. It did, however, have the same right to intervene in other proceedings as any other Community institution, as was held in Case 138/79, *Roquette v Council.*[50]

With regard to the Parliament's liability, in 1986, the European Court went beyond holding that the Coal and Steel remedy could be used against acts which also produced effects under the EC and Euratom Treaties to allow an action to be brought under Article 173 (now Article 230) of the EC Treaty against an act of the European Parliament. The point arose in Case 294/83, *Les Verts v European Parliament*,[51] which involved a challenge by the French Greens to decisions of, and rules adopted by, the European Parliament concerning appropriations granted as a contribution to the information campaign for the second direct elections to the Parliament.

The Court held that the general scheme of the Treaty was to make a direct action available against all measures adopted by the institutions which are

---

[49] Case T–174/95, *Svenska Journalistförbundet v Council* [1998] ECR II–2289.
[50] [1980] ECR 3333, 3357.
[51] [1986] ECR 1339.

intended to have legal effects. Since, unlike the Coal and Steel Treaty, the EC Treaty contained only one provision relating to an action for annulment, Article [173], the Court held that this provision must be regarded as being of general application. It further held that an interpretation of it which excluded measures adopted by the European Parliament from those which could be contested would lead to a result contrary both to the spirit of the Treaty and to its system. If Article [173] were not so extended, measures adopted by the European Parliament in the context of the EC Treaty could trespass into the powers of the Member States or of the other institutions or exceed the limits set for the Parliament's powers, without it being possible to refer them for review by the Court. A formal rewriting followed in the Treaty amendments agreed at Maastricht in 1991, so that under the revised version the Court may review the legality of 'acts of the European Parliament intended to produce legal effects vis-a-vis third parties.'

With regard to the Parliament's rights of action, it did attempt to bring a direct action for annulment in Case 302/87, *European Parliament v Council*.[52] It there sought to challenge the Council decision laying down general rules, pursuant to the Single European Act, for delegating powers to the Commission, otherwise rejoicing in the name of comitology. The Court there suggested that there was no necessary correlation between the ability to be the defendant in an action for annulment and the ability to bring such an action. It further indicated that the remedies available to the European Parliament were essentially political, in particular censure of the Commission, and that if the European Parliament wished action to be taken before the Court against another institution it should, in principle, ask the Commission to act on its behalf.

However, the European Court was subsequently persuaded to change its mind in Case C–70/88, *European Parliament v Council*,[53] with regard to legislation laying down maximum levels of radioactive contamination for foodstuffs following the Chernobyl nuclear accident. Although this action was brought against the Council of Ministers, in reality the Parliament was challenging the action of the Commission, which had put forward the proposal for this legislation on the legal base of Article 31 of the Atomic Energy Treaty, which merely required the Parliament to be consulted, whereas the Parliament argued that it should have been based on Article 100a (now Article 95) of the EC Treaty, which would have required the use of the cooperation procedure with the Parliament. The Parliament, therefore, argued that the second case showed that the Commission could not be relied upon to act on its behalf to challenge a measure where the Commission itself had drafted that measure on a legal basis other than that considered appropriate by Parliament. The Parliament, therefore, suggested that there was a lacuna which the Court should fill by allowing the European Parliament to bring an action for annulment at least in so far as that was necessary to protect its own prerogatives. Interestingly, the Commission, whilst intervening to support the Council on the

---

[52] [1988] ECR 5615.
[53] [1990] ECR I–2041.

substance, nevertheless supported the Parliament's arguments with regard to admissibility.

After having noted that the Parliament was not expressly mentioned either in Article [173] of the EC Treaty or Article 146 of the Euratom Treaty, the Court also pointed out that the Parliament could not bring an action as a legal person under the second paragraph of those provisions, because it did not itself enjoy legal personality. After having referred to the 1988 judgment, the Court accepted that the second case did indeed show that there may be circumstances where the remedies available to the European Parliament were either ineffective or uncertain, in particular noting that although the Commission may in principle be obliged to ensure that the prerogatives of the Parliament are respected, this could not go to the extent of requiring the Commission to bring an action for annulment which it itself believed to be ill conceived. The Court, therefore, concluded that the remedies available under the Treaties were not adequate to ensure the proper control of an act of the Council or Commission which breached the prerogatives of the Parliament. The Court further suggested that the institutional balance established by the Treaties required each of the institutions to exercise its powers in such a manner as to respect the powers of the other institutions, which in particular implied that a breach of that principle should be subject to judicial control. The Court, therefore, held that a judicial remedy must be available to ensure respect for the Parliament's prerogatives.

However, the Court was not willing simply to add the Parliament to the Council and Commission as privileged litigants under Article [173] of the EC Treaty or Article 146 of the Euratom Treaty; rather, it suggested that the Parliament would be required to show that it had an interest in bringing the action. Nonetheless, the Parliament's prerogatives could not be breached without a judicial remedy being available and the failure to make such a provision in the Treaties must give way to the fundamental interest in maintaining respect for the institutional balance established by the Treaties. The Court, therefore, in effect created a new version of the action for annulment for the Parliament; it held that the Parliament could bring an action for annulment before the Court directed against an action of the Council or the Commission on condition that this action was intended to safeguard the Parliament's prerogatives, and that it was based on the grounds relating to the violation of those prerogatives. Amongst those prerogatives was the Parliament's role in the legislative process, in particular its right to participate in the cooperation procedure. Therefore, in claiming that a Treaty base had been used which deprived it of the opportunity to participate in the cooperation procedure, the Parliament was indeed invoking an alleged breach of its prerogatives.

The Court's judgment was followed in the Treaty amendments agreed at Maastricht, which added a new sentence to the first paragraph of what is now Article 230, giving the Court jurisdiction 'in actions brought by the European Parliament and by the European Central Bank for the purpose of protecting their prerogatives', and the Nice Treaty has further amended Article 230 to give the Parliament the same rights of action as the Council and Commission. The extensive interpretation of its jurisdiction by the European Court would, therefore, appear in this case to have met with the approval of the politicians.

B. References for Preliminary Rulings

In the context of references for preliminary rulings, a striking example of the Court's extensive interpretation of its jurisdiction may be seen in the way it has claimed exclusive jurisdiction over questions relating to the validity of EC legislation, even though such jurisdiction was expressly conferred only by the ECSC Treaty.

Article 41 of the ECSC Treaty gave the Court an exclusive power to pronounce on questions of validity, but no jurisdiction on questions of interpretation. However, the ECSC rule on validity has been extended to the EC Treaty in Case 314/85, *Foto-Frost*,[54] and the EC rule on interpretation has been extended to the ECSC Treaty in Case C–221/88, *ECSC v Busseni*.[55] In the latter case, the Court held that although Article 41 of the Coal and Steel Treaty gave it power only to consider the validity of Community legislation on a reference from a national court, nonetheless it would be inconsistent with the logic of the Treaties for it to have power to interpret Community law under the corresponding provision of the EC and Euratom Treaties, but have no power to do so in the context of the Coal and Steel Treaty.[56] The European Court, therefore, arrogated to itself also jurisdiction to interpret provisions of legislation made under the Coal and Steel Treaty on a reference from a national court.

Conversely, in the *Foto-Frost* judgment, although only Article 41 of the ECSC Treaty gives the Court *exclusive* jurisdiction to consider the validity of Community legislation at issue before national courts, Article 234 of the EC Treaty being silent on the point, it was held that under the EC Treaty also only the European Court may declare Community legislation invalid, since it must be valid or invalid for the Community as a whole, not just within one national jurisdiction.[57] In this context it may be observed that difficulties arise from the drafting of Article 68, introduced by the Treaty of Amsterdam, applying the system of references for preliminary rulings to the new Title IV on Visas, Asylum and Immigration. Under Article 68, there is only provision for references from 'a court or a tribunal of a Member State against whose decisions there is no judicial remedy under national law', but that court or tribunal 'shall', if it considers that a decision on the question is necessary to enable it to give judgment, request the Court of Justice to give a ruling. If the European Court alone may pronounce on the validity of Community legislation, this both leaves the lower courts with some awkward

---

[54] [1987] ECR 4199.
[55] [1990] ECR I–495.
[56] *Ibid.*
[57] n 54 above.

questions and seems to indicate that all such cases will have to be appealed to the highest level.[58] A solution was suggested in the negotiations leading to the Nice Treaty: a proposal was put forward by the 'Friends of the Presidency'[59] to the effect that the normal rules of Article 234 should apply in the context of Title IV, subject to the Court continuing, as under the current Article 68(2), not to have any jurisdiction to rule on any measure or decision taken pursuant to Article 62(1) relating to the maintenance of law and order and the safeguarding of internal security. These suggestions were not, however, taken up in the texts adopted at Nice.

A different example of an extensive approach to the jurisdiction to give preliminary rulings may be seen in the way the Court also claimed competence to interpret GATT as a (deemed) Community act, in Cases 267–269/81, *SPI, SAMI.*[60] The original version of GATT was negotiated before any of the Communities existed, but it was there held to constitute an act of the Community institutions to the extent that at least since the Community became a Customs Union in July 1968 it must be regarded as having replaced its Member States with regard to the rights and duties arising under such multilateral trade agreements. The same view has been taken also of decisions of bodies created under agreements entered into by the Community, such as a decision of the EC/Turkey Association Council in Case C–192/89, *Sevince.*[61]

4. HAS THE EUROPEAN COURT OF JUSTICE PURPORTED TO DEVELOP NEW JURISDICTION?

It may be suggested that the European Court of Justice has exercised a jurisdiction not laid down in the Treaty texts (albeit with the encouragement of those Member States which submitted observations) in Case C–2/88, Imm. *Zwartveld,*[62] where it acceded to a request from a Dutch judge to order the Commission to allow its officials to give evidence in criminal proceedings before that judge.

The Dutch judge was investigating an alleged fraud involving breaches of the Community fish quota system, and the fish marketing system. The Dutch judge claimed that in order to proceed with his investigation he needed access to certain reports prepared by Commission officials, and also required those officials to give evidence before him. The Commission refused to transmit the reports to the Dutch judge, so he then sent a request to the European Court asking it to order the Commission to produce the documents and to order the inspectors to give evidence before him. The Dutch judge was obviously aware of the difficulty of

---

[58] Though it has been suggested that the *Foto-Frost* doctrine should not apply in the context of Art 68, see A Arnull, *The European Union and its Court of Justice* (Oxford University Press, Oxford, 1999) at 70–71.

[59] Presidency n of 31 May 2000 (CONFER 4747/00).

[60] [1983] ECR 801.

[61] [1990] ECR I–3461.

[62] [1990] ECR I–3365.

finding a legal base on which the European Court could act, but he himself invoked Articles 1 and 12 of the Protocol on the Privileges and Immunities of the European Communities; Article 1 provides that the property and assets of the Communities shall not be subject to legal measures of constraint without the authorization of the Court of Justice, and Article 12 provides, amongst other things, that the immunity of Community officials with regard to acts performed by them in their official capacity is subject to the jurisdiction of the Court in disputes between the Communities and their officials and other servants. He also invoked the Council of Europe conventions on assistance in criminal matters, on the basis that, although the Community itself was not a party to them, nonetheless they should be considered as forming an integral part of the Community legal order, which itself indicates an interesting development of the Court's well-known case law holding that the principles underlying the European Convention on Human Rights are general principles which must be recognized within the Community context, even though the Community itself is not a party to the Human Rights Convention.[63]

The reaction of the Commission was to claim that the Dutch judge's application was inadmissible. It argued that the Treaty must be regarded as exhaustive with regard to the remedies available before the European Court, and it emphasised that the only way a national court could bring a matter before the European Court was by a reference under what is now Article 234 of the EC Treaty, and in the Commission's view that was not relevant because the Dutch judge was not seeking the interpretation of a provision of Community law. The Commission also suggested that Articles 1 and 12 of the Protocol on the Privileges and Immunities of the European Communities were not relevant in this context. Asked by the Court as to its substantive reasons for refusing to produce the reports or to allow its inspectors to give evidence, the Commission took the line that its inspectors' reports were internal documents which did not necessarily reflect the Commission's position, and their communication could harm relations between the Commission and Member States in the delicate area of supervision of the fisheries market. The Commission also invoked Article 2 of the Protocol on Privileges and Immunities, which provides that the archives of the Communities shall be inviolable; the Commission claimed that Article 2 contained no exemptions, so that the Court had no power to lift that immunity.

With regard to the appearance of its inspectors as witnesses, the Commission indicated that it was not willing to indicate the identity of its inspectors or to authorise them to give evidence, because if they did so, it would affect their work and the degree to which they were able to exercise effective supervision on behalf of the Community. On the other hand, the Commission did declare its willingness to prepare a report for the Dutch judge to the extent that this would not compromise the Commission's supervisory functions, and indicated that it might

---

[63] See eg Case 36/75, *Rutili* [1975] ECR 1219 at 1232.

designate specific officials to give evidence before the Dutch judge, but he, in turn, refused to accept this offer.

Following a procedure analogous to that which would have been used if this had been a reference for a preliminary ruling under Article 234 of the EC Treaty, the Court invited the Community institutions and the Member States to submit observations, and such observations were received from the Council, the Parliament, Germany, France, Greece, Ireland, Italy, The Netherlands, Portugal, and the United Kingdom. Obviously, the case aroused a great deal of interest.

The Court's own reasoning began with a reference back to the famous case of *Costa v ENEL*,[64] emphasising the passage in that judgment which held that the EC Treaty had created its own legal system which became an integral part of the legal systems of the Member States. The Court then referred to its judgment in the *les Verts* case, which has been discussed in the context of actions for annulment, pointing out that the EC is a Community based on law, to the extent that neither the Member States nor the institutions may escape from judicial control over the conformity of their actions to the Treaty, which the Court described as a constitutional charter. It went on to say that in this Community based on law the relationship between the Member States and the Community institutions is governed, by virtue of Article 10 of the Treaty, by the principle of loyal cooperation, which not only requires that Member States take all necessary measures to guarantee the effective implementation of Community law, including the use of criminal penalties if necessary, but this principle also required the Community institutions to observe reciprocal duties of loyal cooperation with the Member States. This duty to cooperate was of particular importance in the relationship with national judicial authorities responsible for ensuring respect for Community law within the national legal order. In the light of this, the Court held that the privileges and immunities of the Communities were not absolute, and that the specific privileges and immunities accorded to Community officials were for their own personal protection. The Protocol could not, therefore, be used to avoid the duty of loyal cooperation owed to national judicial authorities. The Court suggested that where a request for information or evidence came from a national judge who was investigating alleged breaches of Community law, it was the duty of any Community institution, and in particular of the Commission entrusted with ensuring that the provisions of the Treaty are applied, to give active support to the national judge by handing over the documents and authorizing the officials to give evidence.

In seeking to establish its own authority to order the Commission to comply with this basic duty of loyal cooperation, the Court invoked Article 220 of the Treaty, under which the Court is required to ensure that in the interpretation and application of the Treaty the law is observed. The Court held that by virtue of this provision it must ensure that an appropriate remedy must be available to enable it to exercise judicial control over the Commission's performance of its duty of loyal cooperation towards a national judicial authority. The Court, therefore, held

---

[64] Case 6/64, [1964] ECR 585.

it had jurisdiction to examine in this particular instance whether the refusal to cooperate was justified in the light of a need to avoid interference with the operation and independence of the Communities. The Commission was therefore ordered to deliver the documents requested by the Dutch judge to him, and to authorise its officials to give evidence before him, unless it could show that there were imperative reasons relating to the operation or independence of the Communities which would justify the refusal to deliver those documents or to authorize thatevidence to be given.

In fact, therefore, the Court would appear to have granted a new remedy not expressly foreseen in the Treaties, by virtue of two general provisions of the Treaty, Articles 10 and 220. Reference to Article 220 as a basis for the Court's action was not, however, totally new; in Case 17/74, *Transocean Marine Paint Association v Commission*,[65] Advocate-General Warner suggested that Article 220 was a legal basis under which the European Court could take account of general principles of law derived from the laws of the Member States, on the basis that they formed part of 'the law', of which it was the Court's duty to ensure the observance. With hindsight, however, the use of Article 10 can be seen to be of increasing importance in the legal relationship between Community institutions and Member States and in the legal duties of Member States. Thus when, in the *Hurd* case,[66] the question of the national taxation of a teacher at a European School arose, the Court held that while it had no jurisdiction to interpret the agreement between the Member States establishing the European Schools, nevertheless by virtue of Article 10 a Member State could not use its tax system in such a way as to harm the Community budget, and in the early days of the Community the parallel Article 86 of the Coal and Steel Treaty had been used in Case 6/60, *Humblet*,[67] where it was held that no account could be taken of an official's Community income in calculating the rate of tax on his national income, to require higher rate tax to be repaid. Furthermore, the principle that a Member State may be liable in damages for a breach of Community law established in Cases C–6/90 and 9/90, *Francovich v Italy*,[68] is based in part on the idea that among the obligations laid down by Article 10 is that of eliminating the illegal consequences of a breach of Community law.

Whatever may be thought of its legal basis, it may be suggested that in practical terms the remedy invented in *Zwartveld* is useful. It would be a serious lacuna in the Community legal system if no court had power to order a Community institution to cooperate with a national judicial authority seeking to enforce rules of Community law. However, the door would appear to have been opened to the exercise of new sorts of judicial control in the complex relationship between Community institutions and Member States, going beyond the broad interpretation which the Court had already given to the express powers under the Treaties. Nevertheless, so far this decision does not appear to have opened the floodgates to the

---

[65] [1974] ECR 1063.
[66] Case 44/84, [1986] ECR 298.
[67] [1960] ECR 1125.
[68] [1991] ECR I–5357.

exercise of a general jurisdiction. It may also be wondered whether it was in fact necessary for the Court to take the approach it did in *Zwartveld*. In Case C–54/90, *Weddel v Commission*,[69] traders who had unsuccessfully bid in a Community tendering procedure requested the Commission to allow the officials concerned to give evidence in proceedings against the Dutch authorities who had conducted the tendering procedure at the national level. The Commission again refused, and the traders simply brought an action for the annulment of the Commission's decision of refusal. It may, however, be suggested that it would not be appropriate for a national judge to have to become a party to litigation before the Court in order to be able to require Community officials to give evidence before him.

5. WHAT IS THE EUROPEAN COURT OF JUSTICE'S APPROACH TO OTHER TRIBUNALS EXERCISING OVERLAPPING JURISDICTION?

The issue of the creation of international tribunals which might deal with matters also falling within the jurisdiction of the European Court has arisen in a number of requests under Article 300 for an Opinion as to the compatibility of a proposed international agreement with the EC Treaty, and the European Court of Justice has always rejected provisions which create or would recognise tribunals with overlapping jurisdiction. Thus, the EC may not become a party to the European Convention on Human Rights without a formal Treaty amendment, as was held in *Opinion 2/94*.[70] The Court there declared that, without a Treaty amendment, it would go beyond the scope of what is now Article 308 for the Community as such to become a party to the European Convention on Human Rights. It suggested that Article 308 is designed to fill gaps in the Treaty, and that it cannot serve as a basis for widening the scope of Community powers beyond the general framework created by the provisions of the Treaty as a whole, and in particular it cannot be used as the basis for the adoption of provisions whose real effect would be to amend the Treaty without following the correct procedure.

With regard to the specific question of accession to the European Convention on Human Rights, the Court noted that the Community had no express or implied powers for this purpose. On the other hand, it accepted that fundamental rights were an integral part of the general principles of law whose observance that Court ensures;[71] however, it took the view that accession to the Convention would involve a substantial change in the Community system for the protection of human rights, because it would require the Community to enter into a distinct international institutional system, and to integrate all the provisions of the Convention into the Community legal order. It concluded that this would be of constitutional significance, going beyond the scope of Article 308, and would,

---

[69] [1992] I–871.
[70] [1996] ECR I–1759.
[71] See JA Usher, *General Principles of EC Law* (Longman, London, 1998).

therefore, require Treaty amendment. While couched in diplomatic language, it may be suggested that one of the fundamental issues was that both the European Court and the European Court of Human Rights could find themselves considering the validity of Community acts in the light of the Human Rights Convention, and that the question would have to be faced of the possible primacy of the views of the Court of Human Rights in this context.

Similar issues were faced more overtly in two earlier Opinions in which the creation of international tribunals in which European Court of Justice members would have participated were rejected. *Opinion 1/76*[72] concerned a proposed agreement with Switzerland on the setting-up of a fund to encourage the laying-up of surplus barge in the Rhine area. This agreement would have created, inter alia, a tribunal composed in part of judges of the European Court. The Court pointed out that in so far as the proposed agreement would constitute a Community act, it could be in receipt of references from national courts as to its interpretation, yet similar questions could also have arisen directly before the tribunal. The possibility might, therefore, arise that on a reference, the Court would be unable to find a quorum of judges who had not already considered the point as members of the tribunal. It suggested that if there was to be a tribunal, it should not include members of the Court, and for this and other reasons held the proposed agreement to be incompatible with Community law.

This point was repeated in *Opinion 1/91*[73] with regard to the first draft of the European Economic Area Agreement, which would have set up an EEA Court five of the eight judges of which would be from the European Court. However, the Court added a further consideration, noting that the EEA Court would have to rule on the respective competences of the Community and the Member States as regards the matters governed by the provisions of the agreement; it held that this jurisdiction was likely adversely to affect the allocation of responsibilities defined in the Treaties and therefore the autonomy of the Community legal order, respect for which had to be assured by the European Court under what is now Article 220 of the EC Treaty. It therefore concluded that to confer that jurisdiction on the EEA Court was incompatible with Community law.

However, the Court's views were not requested with regard to the WTO dispute settlement procedure in *Opinion 1/94*[74] on aspects of the Community's competence with regard to the Uruguay Round agreements, but it is here that the real conflicts of approach have arisen.

6. HAVE CONFLICTS OF INTERPRETATION OCCURRED?

A number of examples can be found of differences of approach to the same material as between the European Court of Justice and GATT/WTO Panels. The

---

[72] [1977] ECR 741.
[73] [1991] ECR I–6079.
[74] [1994] ECR I–5267.

clearest example with regard to the interpretation of a specific provision of Community legislation came before the European Court in Cases 67–85/75, *Lesieur Cotelle v EC Commission.*[75] The Court there held that a subsidy granted to processors for oil seeds, harvested and processed within the Community, under EC Council Regulation 136/66,[76] was intended as a guarantee for growers of the seeds. The plaintiffs were in fact oil millers and not seed growers. The Court said that in so far as the regulation was intended to give guarantees, the latter related to colza seed farmers and not processors, as appeared from Article 24 of the regulation, according to which the derived intervention price guaranteed that producers would be able to sell their produce at a price which, allowing for market fluctuations, was as close as possible to the target price. The subsidies granted to seed processors were not intended to guarantee the processors fixed payment for their processing but to enable them to buy Community seed at prices close to the target price. The Court concluded that the oil millers could not claim any guarantee under the regulation.

However, in the oilseeds dispute with the United States,[77] a GATT panel took a different view from the European Court as to the legal nature of the subsidies. The GATT panel took the view that a payment not made directly to the producers is not paid 'exclusively' to them within the terms of Article III: 8(b) of GATT, and found that the EC Regulations did not in fact ensure that payments to producers were based on the prices processors actually had to pay when purchasing Community oilseeds.

In the context of protection of health, there is effectively a culture clash between the approach of the European Court of Justice to the EC hormones in beef legislation in Case 160/88, *Fedesa v Council,*[78] and the approach of the WTO panels and Appellate Body to that legislation. From the 1980's, until the entry into force of the current text of Article 152 of the EC Treaty on the protection of human health, Community health legislation relating to agricultural products, such as Council Directive 85/649[79] prohibiting the use in livestock farming of certain substances having a hormonal action, was adopted under Article 37 of the Treaty alone, rather than in conjunction with Article 94, as had been the previous practice. This practice was tested in two actions brought by the United Kingdom against the Council with regard to the legal base for the Directive on the use of hormones in beef, and a Directive on the minimum standards for keeping battery hens, in Cases 68/86 and 131/86, *United Kingdom v Council.*[80] The European Court held that agricultural legislation could not ignore requirements of general interest such as consumer protection or the protection of the health and life of both humans and animals, so the fact that it pursued those requirements did not take

[75] [1976] ECR 391.
[76] OJ 1966 at 3025.
[77] 25 January 1990, see P Pescatore, W Davey and A Lowenfeld, *Handbook of GATT Dispute Settlement* (Kluwer, The Hague, 1991) 525.
[78] [1988] ECR 6399.
[79] OJ 1985 L382/228.
[80] [1988] ECR 855 and 905.

it outside the scope of Article 37 if it regulated the production and marketing of agricultural products. This approach was continued more recently in Case C–269/97, *Commission and European Parliament v Council*,[81] where the Commission and Parliament argued that Council Regulation 820/97[82] on the identification and registration of bovine animals and the labelling of beef and beef products, introduced as a reaction to the BSE crisis, should have been adopted as an internal market measure under Article 95 (which involves co-decision with the Parliament) rather than under Article 37 (which only involves consultation of the Parliament). The Court held that it was entirely appropriate to take account of public health considerations in the context of Article 37, particularly in the light of the introduction of the then Article 129, the predecessor of the current Article 152, which required that health protection measures should form a constituent part the Community's other policies.

In its series of judgments with regard to the prohibition of hormones in beef, the European Court stated that 'in view of the divergent appraisals which had been made, traders were not entitled to expect that a prohibition on administering the substances in question to animals could be based on scientific data alone.'[83] It was further held that the requirement of what was then Council Directive 81/602 on the prohibition of certain substances having a hormonal action[84] that the Commission should take account of scientific developments did not preempt 'the conclusions which may be drawn therefrom by the Council in the exercise of its discretion.'[85] This may be contrasted with the insistence by the WTO Appellate Body[86] on the production of scientific evidence when these measures were challenged as being in breach of the Uruguay Round Agreement on the Application of Sanitary and Phytosanitary Measures.[87]

Another area of EU activity which has fallen foul of WTO rules is the market in bananas introduced by Council Regulation 404/93.[88] This used a complex system of tariff quotas and import licensing, designed in particular to help producers in the ACP countries party to the Lomé Convention, and those who traded in ACP bananas. It was the allocation of 30% of the quota licences to operators who marketed Community and/or traditional ACP bananas which was one of the factors which led the WTO Appellate Body[89] to hold that there was a breach of Article II of the General Agreement on Trade on Services, requiring 'no less

[81]   [2000] ECR–I-6069.
[82]   OJ 1997 L117/1.
[83]   Case C–331/88, *R v SoS for Health ex p Fedesa* [1990] ECR I-4023 at para 10.
[84]   OJ 1981 L222/32.
[85]   N 83 above at para 10.
[86]   WT/DS26/AB/R and WT/DS48/AB/R.
[87]   A highly perceptive analysis of this difference of approach may be found in J. Scott, 'On Kith and Kine (and Crustaceans): Trade and the Environment in the EU and WTO', in JHH Weiler (ed), *The EU, the WTO and the NAFTA—Towards a Common Law of International Trade* (Oxford University Press, Oxford, 2000), 125.
[88]   OJ 1993, L47/1.
[89]   WT/DS27/AB/R.

favourable treatment' for service providers from other participating states. Fairly clearly, the differential import system itself was difficult to reconcile with the most-favoured nation principle laid down in Article I of GATT[90] or the non-discriminatory administration of quotas required by Article XIII, and the EC therefore negotiated a waiver at the time of the Uruguay Round, which was extended in 1996. However, it was held that this waiver was so drafted as to be appropriate only for the most-favoured-nation clause, and that it did not extend to Article XIII, so that the EC was in breach of the requirement for non-discriminatory administration of quotas.

While the European Court of Justice refused to allow GATT to be invoked to contest the EC banana regime eg Case C–280/93 *Germany v Council*,[91] thus avoiding a direct confrontation, the rationale for this approach is worthy of further consideration. It has already been mentioned that before the Uruguay Round Agreement, to which the Community as such is a party, the Court had declared that the Community had replaced member states in the GATT,[92] that the provisions of the GATT were binding on the Community, and that from the entry into force of the Common Customs Tariff on 1 July 1968 GATT was to be treated as a Community act for the purposes of interpretation. Nevertheless, the Court has consistently held that the general scheme of the GATT, being characterised by flexibility and possibilities of derogation, was such that its provisions could not give rise to rights enforceable before national courts. Thus, as a matter of Community law, the provisions of the GATT may not be invoked to challenge the validity of national legislation.[93] More intriguingly, the earliest judgment in the matter[94] held that provisions of the GATT could not be invoked before a national court to challenge the validity of Community legislation unless they could be shown to be directly effective. While the concept of direct effect may hardly seem to be relevant in a direct action for the annulment of a Community act brought by a Member State which is itself party to GATT, it has been held in the context of such an action[95] that it is only if the Community intended to implement a particular obligation entered into within the framework of GATT, or if the Community act expressly refers to specific provisions of GATT,[96] that the Court can review the lawfulness of the Community act in question from the point of view of the GATT rules.

---

[90] Indeed, Art 168(2)(a)(ii) of the Fourth Lomé Convention required the Community to take the necessary measures to ensure more favourable treatment than that granted to third countries benefiting from the most-favoured-nation clause for the same products.

[91] [1994] ECR I–4973.

[92] Cases 21–24/72, *International Fruit Co NV v Produktschap voor Groenten en Fruit* [1972] ECR 1219, Case 38/75, *Douaneagent der NV Nederlandse Spoorwegen v Inspecteur der Invoerrechten en Accijnzen* [1975] ECR 1439, Cases 267–269/81, *Amministrazione delle Finanze dello Stato v SPI* [1983] ECR 801.

[93] Cases 267–269/81, *ibid.*

[94] Case 21–24/72, n 92 above.

[95] Case C–280/93, *Germany v Council* [1994] ECR I–4973.

[96] Cases C–70/87, *Fediol* [1989] ECR 1781; Case C–69/89, *Nakajima v Council* [1991] ECR I–2069.

This approach has been maintained in the aftermath of the Uruguay Round Agreements.[97] Thus in Case C–307/99, *OGT Fruchthandelgesellschaft v HZA Hamburg-ST Annen*,[98] it was held that the validity of the common organisation of the market in bananas under an amended version of Council Regulation 404/93[99] could not be challenged by traders invoking Articles I and XIII of GATT 1994, even though a WTO Panel in a Report dated 12 April 1999 had found that this amended version was in breach of those provisions. The Court repeated that the WTO Agreement and the agreements and understandings annexed to it 'are not in principle among the rules in the light of which the Court is to review the legality of measures adopted by the Community institutions', adding that Regulation 404/93, as amended, was not designed to ensure the implementation in the Community legal order of a particular obligation assumed in the context of the GATT, and that it did not expressly refer to specific provisions of the GATT. A transitional regime has in fact been introduced by Council Regulation 216/2001,[100] the recitals to which refer expressly to the recommendations of the dispute settlement body. So far as the services question is concerned, a new Article 19 provides that the tariff quotas may be managed in accordance with 'the method based on taking account of traditional trade flows . . . and/or other methods.' Under an agreement with the United States in 2001,[101] a small tariff quota is to be reserved exclusively for bananas of ACP origin—which will require a waiver from Article XIII of GATT, which the US and Ecuador[102] have agreed to help to achieve. It may, however, be suggested that the use of such waivers tends to support the European Court's view that the WTO provisions do not lay down absolute directly enforceable rules.

7. CONCLUSION

While the European Court of Justice itself would probably take the view that it has interpreted rather than asserted its jurisdiction, its jurisprudence gives some fairly clear delineations. This jurisprudence dose not necessarily take the form of empire-building: examples may be found of restrictive interpretation, in relation to private actions for annulment, and the use of references for preliminary rulings by those who could have brought actions for annulment in order to try to circumvent the procedural limitations on such actions. There have also, however, been examples of extensive interpretation, in particular to ensure that bodies which issue legally binding acts in the Community context are subject to judicial review, to ensure the uniform control of the validity of Community acts, and to

---

[97] Case C–149/96, *Portugal v Council* [1999] ECR.
[98] 2 May 2001.
[99] OJ 1993 L47/1.
[100] OJ 2001 L31/2.
[101] Commission MEMO/01/135 (11 April 2001).
[102] Commission IP/01/628 (2 May 2001).

ensure the uniform interpretation within the Community of international agreements entered into by the Community. The only example of what might arguably be called the assertion of general jurisdiction is again in reality concerned with ensuring judicial control over the activities of EC bodies in the context of the legal process. On the other hand, the Court clearly regards itself as bound to safeguard the jurisdiction conferred upon it by the Treaties, as is evidenced by its hostility to the creation of, or accession to, other international tribunals with overlapping jurisdiction or membership—though conflicts of approach have already manifested themselves in the WTO context.

Index